The McGraw-Hill Guide to

ENGLISH
LITERATURE

The McGraw-Hill Guide to

ENGLISH LITERATURE

Volume One
Beowulf to Jane Austen

KAREN LAWRENCE
BETSY SEIFTER
LOIS RATNER

McGRAW-HILL BOOK COMPANY

New York   St. Louis   San Francisco   Auckland   Bogotá
Guatemala   Hamburg   Johannesburg   Lisbon   London   Madrid
Mexico   Montreal   New Delhi   Panama   Paris   San Juan
São Paulo   Singapore   Sydney   Tokyo   Toronto

THE MCGRAW-HILL GUIDE TO ENGLISH LITERATURE

1 2 3 4 5 6 7 8 9 DOC DOC 8 7 6 5

ISBN 0-07-036704-3

LIBRARY OF CONGRESS CATALOGING IN PUBLICATION DATA

Lawrence, Karen
  The McGraw-Hill guide to English literature.

  Bibliography: p.
  Includes index.
  Contents: v. 1. Beowulf to Jane Austen.
  1. English literature—History and criticism.
I. Seifter, Betsy. II. Ratner, Lois. III. Title.
PR85.L4   1985   820'.9   84-12626
ISBN 0-07-036704-3 (v. 1)

The editor for this book was Karl Weber; the editing supervisor was Marthe Grice.

BOOK DESIGN BY PATRICE FODERO.

*This book is dedicated to our three supportive husbands,
Peter Lawrence, Julian Seifter, and Stephen Ratner, and
to the children who came into being during the seven years
of its composition: Andrew and Jeffrey, Andrew and Charles,
and Philip and Peter.*

PREFACE

Like a guide who leads his companions through unfamiliar terrain, making sense
of the territory, this book attempts to illuminate some of the vast expanse of
English literature. The uniqueness of *The McGraw-Hill Guide to English Literature*
lies in its format and completeness. It provides questions and answers on works
by almost all the major authors of English literature, from medieval to modern.
By example rather than prescription, the guide attempts to teach students fruitful
ways to think and write about different kinds of literature, including fiction,
poetry, drama, and the essay. The dual purpose of the guide is to demonstrate
general approaches to literature and to give useful analyses of specific texts that
college students are likely to encounter in their classes. This book certainly is
not meant to replace the study of the texts themselves, but is intended instead
as a useful supplement to them. Without sacrificing the richness, complexity,
or variety of English literature, we attempt to cover the most significant aspects
of these texts.

The guide appears in two volumes, corresponding to the division in most
year-long survey courses and anthologies. Volume One includes Old English
through eighteenth-century literature and is divided into seven parts: Old English Literature, Middle English Literature, the Renaissance, the Seventeenth
Century, the Restoration, the Neoclassical Age, and the Emergence of the
Novel. Volume Two includes nineteenth- and twentieth-century literature, and
has five parts: the Romantic Age, Victorian Poetry and Prose, the Victorian
Novel, Modern Poetry, and the Modern Novel and Drama. To provide a context
for the discussions of individual texts, each part is introduced with a timeline
which charts important political and literary events of the period. Chapters
correspond to individual authors (except, of course, in the case of anonymous
texts), and for each author there is a short chronology, which lists important
dates and events in his or her life. In addition, each chapter includes a list of

suggested readings for further study. The initials at the end of each chapter indicate the writer responsible for the material in that chapter.

This book is envisioned as primarily for the college student who desires help in the study of English literature. Although some students may want to read through the guide, most will dip into it for help on particular writers being studied. It may prove particularly useful in preparing the student for the type of essay exams likely to be encountered in literature courses. The guide should also be a valuable resource for the teacher as well as the student of literature, who will find it a repository of significant questions on, as well as helpful analyses of, individual texts. As teachers of literature, we have tried to provide material that is very beneficial to class preparation.

No other guide of this kind and comprehensiveness exists today. We hope that students and teachers will find *The McGraw-Hill Guide* a helpful and stimulating companion in their study of literature.

K. L.

B. S.

L. R.

ACKNOWLEDGMENTS

In the seven years from the conception of this project to its fruition, a few people have been indispensable to our efforts. Chief among them is Barry Weller at the University of Utah, who read the manuscript in draft form and offered us the benefit of his considerable critical intelligence. He made insightful changes, both editorial and substantive, throughout the work, but particularly in Part Four, The Seventeenth Century.

Karl Weber has been the other significant participant in this enterprise, and for Karl's editorial expertise we are extremely grateful. In addition, he is responsible for the Chronologies in Volume One.

Finally, we would like to thank Karl Weber and Teresa Carriero for their joint efforts in producing the Timelines.

K. L.
B. S.
L. R.

CONTENTS

Part One

OLD ENGLISH
LITERATURE

T I M E L I N E

The Age

449: Invasion of England by Jutes, led by Hengist. Angles and Saxons soon follow

476: Fall of Roman Empire

484: First schism between western and eastern churches

550: Conversion of Wales to Christianity by St. David

563: St. Columba founds monastery on Isle of Iona

597: St. Augustine sent by Pope Gregory I to convert Anglo-Saxon England to Christianity

671: Birth of Caedmon, first English poet

700: Translation of the Psalms into Old English

735: Death of Bede, monk and first English historian

771: Charlemagne becomes ruler of the Franks

800: By this date, Danish raids on England have begun; wars with Danes continue through 9th century. Charlemagne crowned Holy Roman Emperor

849: Birth of King Alfred the Great

871: Alfred becomes king of West Saxony. By his death in 899 has united England

878: Alfred recaptures London from Danes

994: Successful Danish invasion of England; King Sweyn founds a short-lived English-Danish dynasty

1066: Death of King Edward the Confessor; accession of Saxon king Harold. Norman king William conquers England; Norman French becomes the literary, governmental language of England until about 1300

The Authors

400

450

500

550

600

650

700   Probable date of composition of *Beowulf* (700–750)

750

800

850

900

950

1000   Probable date of *Beowulf* manuscript (1000)

1050

1100

BEOWULF

C H R O N O L O G Y

A.D.43   Roman Emperor Claudius sends an army of 40,000 to conquer Britain, which is inhabited by a number of Celtic tribes. Within about three years, most of the island has been subjugated. For the next three centuries, romanization of Britain advances slowly.

314   Christianity, by this time both tolerated and widespread within the Roman Empire, has made some progress in Britain, as indicated by the presence of bishops from London and York at a church council in Gaul (modern-day France).

410   Now in decline, the Roman Empire withdraws from Britain. Both the Latin language and Christianity decline in influence in Britain as a result.

449   Beginning of the invasion of Britain by a group of Teutonic tribes: the Jutes and the Angles from what is now Denmark, and the Saxons and Frisians from what are now Germany and the Low Countries. These invaders, over the next century, will push the native British Celts west and north, virtually eradicating their language and culture and replacing them with their own Teutonic dialects and Germanic warrior culture. From the Teutonic speech of these so-called Anglo-Saxons the English language will develop.

520   Known date of a raid by Hygelac, king of the Geats (a tribe in what is now Sweden), on the Frisians. Hygelac is mentioned in *Beowulf* as the Geatish king during the youth of Beowulf, himself a Geat. Therefore, to the extent that the events recounted in *Beowulf* are historically based, they may be dated in the early years of the sixth century.

525   Death of Hrothgar, king of the Danes and a prominent character in *Beowulf*.

597   Pope Gregory I appoints St. Augustine (not the bishop of Hippo but a Roman Benedictine monk) head of a mission charged with converting the Anglo-Saxon inhabitants of Britain to Christianity. Within about a century, almost all of Britain will have been converted to Christianity. The Germanic warrior code of heroism will not die overnight, however; rather, it will mingle with and influence the now-dominant Christian ethical system, so that literary works such as *Beowulf* will represent a combination of pagan and Christian elements.

669   Theodore of Tarsus, a Greek bishop, is named archbishop of Canterbury. He establishes a school at which the Greek and Latin languages are taught, thus facilitating the spread throughout Britain of classical culture. By the end of the eighth century, Britain will boast an appreciable number of scholars able to read Virgil's *Aeneid* and other classical epics, which may thus have exercised a direct or indirect influence on Old English heroic poems such as *Beowulf*.

700–750   The most probable period of composition of *Beowulf*, though some scholars claim that the poem dates from the late seventh century, while others put it as late as the early ninth century. Around this time a *scop*, that is, a professional court poet, either wrote *Beowulf* or, more likely, transcribed his own version of an orally transmitted folk epic dealing with the Beowulf story. It is not known where *Beowulf* was written, although West Mercia (now known as the West Midlands) is the most likely location.

1000   Approximate date at which the so-called *Beowulf* manuscript, containing the only extant text of the poem, was produced. It is likely that two or three transcriptions of the poem intervened between its original composition and the writing of the manuscript we have. One of four surviving manuscripts which contain almost all known Old English poetry, the *Beowulf* manuscript also includes other texts, such as a fabulous life of St. Christopher, a collection of travelers' tales called *Wonders of the East*, and a *Letter of Alexander the Great to Aristotle*. Nothing is known of the history of this manuscript until the seventeenth century.

1066   Date of the Norman conquest of England, which will place the country under French rule and virtually eliminate the use of Old English as a literary language. When English reemerges in the thirteenth century, it will have been transformed by the Norman influence, making the purely Teutonic language of *Beowulf* into a foreign tongue for all later English-speaking generations.

1571   Birth of Sir Robert Cotton, renowned antiquarian and book collector, who obtained the *Beowulf* manuscript for his library at Ashburnham House. From its presence in the famous Cotton Collection comes the manuscript's technical designation as Cotton Vitellius A.xv.

1731   The *Beowulf* manuscript is damaged in a fire at Ashburnham House; some lines and words are lost, though not enough to render the text unintelligible. The manuscript is removed to the British Museum in London, where it remains to this day.

ESSAY QUESTIONS WITH ANSWERS

1.1 At one point in the epic, Beowulf is called "the protector of seafarers" (XXIII, meaning Section XXIII), and the sea itself represents a significant force in the lives of the Germanic tribes depicted in the poem. What is the function of the sea in *Beowulf*? Which incidents indicate its importance?

Answer The sea carries a major thematic significance in *Beowulf*. It represents an ever-present danger to the Danes, an elemental force which must be guarded and continually watched. At the same time, it symbolizes a trial to all those who try to traverse it: the man who successfully does battle with the sea becomes a hero to his people and, in the case of Beowulf, their king.

Beowulf may be seen as divided into two sections, both of which are directly concerned with the sea. In the first section, Beowulf must cross the sea in order to meet and destroy the monster Grendel. And after Grendel has been killed, Beowulf must travel to the undersea lair of Grendel's mother to battle with and destroy her. The blood spilled in this battle, which Hrothgar and his retainers see staining the water during the fight, effectively symbolizes the danger lurking in the sea in *Beowulf*. Furthermore, the first half of the poem contains other important references to the power and danger of the sea. The account of the swimming match is an example: in the mead hall, Beowulf is challenged by Unferth, who accuses him of having exercised a lack of judgment in his youth by entering into a foolhardy swimming match with Breca and, in fact, losing the competition. But Beowulf defends himself: "I maintain that truth that I had more strength in the sea, hardship on the waves, than any other man" (VIII). He tells Unferth that he killed nine sea monsters and that he remained in the water for so long merely to protect Breca.

In the poem's second section, the *Beowulf*-poet recounts another swimming feat of the hero. After the slaying of Hygelac by the Frisians, Beowulf returns to his people by swimming the entire expanse of water with thirty sets of armor on his back. At last, of course, Beowulf dies of the wounds suffered in his battle with the dragon; he is carried home to the land of the Geats so that they may honor their king. But even after death Beowulf seems to remain for the Geats as the warden of the seas: "Then the people of the Weather-Geats built a mound on the promontory, one that was high and broad, wide-seen by seafarers, and in ten days completed a monument for the bold in battle . . ." (XLIII).

1.2   What happens in the Finnsburg episode? What is the relationship of this interpolated tale to the rest of the poem?

Answer   In this interpolated tale, a battle between the Danes and the Jutes (or Frisians) is described. Hildeburh, a Danish princess, is married to Finn, the king of the Jutes. Both parties hope that this marriage will help to heal the feud between them; thus, Hildeburh is described as the "peace-weaver." However, when the Danes come to visit Hildeburh and Finn, a quarrel erupts (no specific reason is given). After a bloody battle in which the son of Hildeburh and Finn is slain, a temporary peace is achieved when the Danes consent to respect Finn's authority. But the following spring, the fighting is again renewed. This time, Finn himself is killed and Hildeburh is carried back to her Danish homeland.

Though the Finnsburg episode seems, on first reading, to have little connection with the rest of *Beowulf*, it can, on closer examination, be seen to have a thematic relationship with the poem. The story turns on the idea of vengeance and the necessity of exacting *wergild* ("man-price" or "man-worth") from the slayer. The familial relationship was of enormous traditional and emotional significance in Old English poetry, as in life. Relatives of a dead man had a legal and moral duty to exact *wergild*. This need to avenge one's king or one's family is certainly central to Beowulf's own history. Then, too, the themes of this episode can be seen to reverberate in other portions of the poem, for example, Beowulf's story of King Hrethel, whose inability to avenge his son's death when one brother has accidentally killed the other causes him to take his own life.

The *Beowulf*-poet also evokes many of the traditional values and political concerns common to all of the Germanic tribes. The story of King Finn, which also exists independently in another fragment called *The Fight at Finnsburg*, broadens the world of the poem, enlarging and enriching its traditional foundations. An epic is generally thought to represent the history of a people or the development of an entire race, and the inclusion of the Finnsburg lay adds considerably to *Beowulf's* stature as an epic poem.

1.3   Before he dies, Beowulf takes off his armor and his ring to give them to Wiglaf, saying, "You are the last of our race, of the Waemundings" (XXXVIII).

What does the *Beowulf*-poet imply about the future of the tribe following the passing of Beowulf?

Answer   Beowulf is the complete Germanic hero: a warrior of great prowess, a king generous with his treasure, and a ruler who defends and protects his people at the expense of his own life. From the opening episode of the poem, the reader sees Beowulf's extreme courage and wisdom. When challenged by Unferth, he defends the deeds of his youth with a strong and moderate speech and then goes on to prove his prowess by destroying both of the monsters who are ravaging Hrothgar's kingdom. The respect given to Beowulf by all who meet him emphasizes his heroic stature. When the Geats arrive in the land of the Danes, the watchman on duty is struck by the sight of Beowulf: "I have never seen a mightier warrior on earth than is one of you, a man in battle-dress" (III). Even the monster Grendel senses that he has made a mistake in choosing Beowulf for one of his victims: "Straightway the fosterer of crimes knew that he had not encountered on Middle-Earth, anywhere in this world, a harder hand-grip from another man" (XI). Throughout the poem, the *Beowulf*-poet reinforces the hero's stature with additional examples of his brave deeds and excellent rule.

Beowulf's successor Wiglaf, however, serves as a contrast, representing a diminution of the heroic ideal. For example, Wiglaf is first introduced to the reader when he, like all the lesser men of the tribe, flees in fear from Beowulf's final battle. Though he feels remorse for deserting his king and returns to finish the fight, his stature as a hero is diminished.

Further the *Beowulf*-poet predicts a disastrous end for the Geats. Wiglaf himself speaks of the future of the nation. He is "a man sad at heart" (XXXIX) when he strips the warriors who deserted Beowulf of their armor, and he tells them that they must expect a period of war once Beowulf's death becomes known to the Franks, Frisians, and Swedes. The poem ends on an elegiac note as the warriors mourn the passing of their great king. It appears that Beowulf's death signals the end of the Geatish people and certainly of the glory they won during Beowulf's reign. As J. R. R. Tolkien remarked in his famous essay on Beowulf, ("*Beowulf: The Monsters and the Critics*," 1936), "It is an heroic-elegiac poem; and in a sense all its first 3136 lines are the prelude to a dirge . . . one of the most moving ever written."

                                                                L.R.

SUGGESTED READINGS

Brodeur, A. G., *The Art of Beowulf* (1959).

Chambers, R. W., *Beowulf: An Introduction to the Study of the Poem*, 3d ed. (1959).

Irving, E. B., *Introduction to Beowulf* (1969).

Sisam, K., *The Structure of Beowulf* (1965).

Part Two

MIDDLE ENGLISH
LITERATURE

T I M E L I N E

The Age

1346:   English defeat French at Crécy

1347:   Black Death devastates Europe

1366:   Petrarch writes *Canzoniere*
Treaty of Brétigny gives England control of much of France

1367:   King addresses Parliament in English rather than French

1377:   Death of Edward III; accession of Richard II

1378:   Great Schism begins; papacy disunited until 1417

1381:   Peasants' Revolt in England under Wat Tyler crushed

1396:   Birth of Johann Gutenberg, inventor of printing by movable type

1399:   Richard II deposed; Henry IV succeeds

1413:   Death of Henry IV; accession of Henry V

1422:   Death of Henry V; accession of 6-month-old Henry VI

1428:   Joan of Arc leads French armies against England

1453:   End of Hundred Years' War (England and France)

1474:   William Caxton prints the first book in English

1483:   Death of Edward IV; his sons, Edward V and Prince Richard, disappear. Their disappearances are blamed on their uncle, who claims the throne as Richard III

1485:   Defeat of Richard III by Henry Tudor, who ascends the throne as Henry VII

1507:   Ordination of Protestant reformer Martin Luther

The Authors

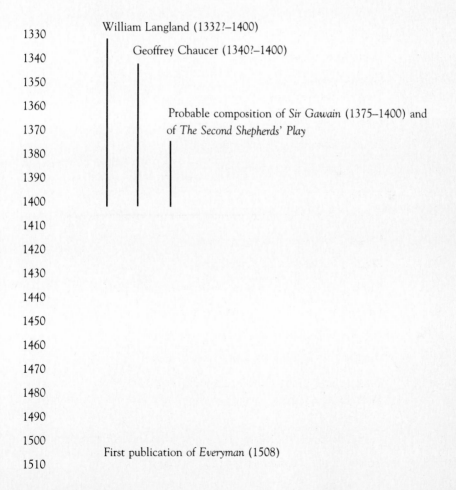

1330	William Langland (1332?–1400)
1340	Geoffrey Chaucer (1340?–1400)
1350	
1360	Probable composition of *Sir Gawain* (1375–1400) and
1370	of *The Second Shepherds' Play*
1380	
1390	
1400	
1410	
1420	
1430	
1440	
1450	
1460	
1470	
1480	
1490	
1500	First publication of *Everyman* (1508)
1510	

SIR GAWAIN AND THE GREEN KNIGHT

CHRONOLOGY

1100   By this date, several legends are extant from which *Sir Gawain and the Green Knight* will later derive its main themes and motifs. Many of these sources are Celtic (as is the bulk of the source material from which the Arthurian legends are derived). The two most important for *Sir Gawain*: (1) The Welsh prose narrative *The Mabinogion*, especially its tale of Pwyll and Arawn, which is probably the ultimate source of the motif of the temptation of a knight by a lady, later used in *Sir Gawain*; (2) *Bricriu's Feast*, an Irish prose narrative about the legendary hero Cuchulain, in which the idea of a beheading match, central to the plot of *Sir Gawain*, first appears. It is likely that these sources derive in turn from even older, unknown Celtic legends.

1300   By this date, numerous French and Anglo-Norman (that is, French and English) romances based on Arthurian themes have been composed. Several make use of the motif of the beheading match; many, including the romances of *Lanzelet*, *Yder*, and *Lancelot del Lac*, center on the temptation of a knight by a lady. Gawain appears prominently in many of the romances of this period. Written for performance, perhaps with musical accompaniment, before a courtly audience, these romances were undoubtedly familiar to the unknown English author of *Sir Gawain*.

1375–   Probable date of composition of *Sir Gawain*. It was written by some unknown
1400   author, probably in Lancashire, in the northwest Midlands of England. The poem may have been written to be part of a Christmas celebration at some court. It is distinctly medieval and provincial in its use of native English

themes and traditions and of the ancient alliterative verse form (rather than the more "modern" Italian or French forms favored by the contemporary poet Chaucer, for instance). The Middle English dialect in which *Sir Gawain* is written is also distinctly northern and provincial. Many attempts have been made to find a name for the unknown author, but all are sheerly speculative.

1400   By this date, the single manuscript in which *Sir Gawain* survives has evidently been written. The manuscript, housed in the British Museum and known as Cotton Nero A.x, also includes three other alliterative poems: *Pearl*, *Purity* (or *Cleanness*), and *Patience*. All three emphasize the teaching of Christian doctrine; *Pearl* is considered one of the most moving religious poems in English. Similarities in themes, vocabulary, and style have led most scholars to conclude that all four poems are the work of a single poet, called either the *Pearl*-poet or the *Gawain*-poet. A fifth poem, *St. Erkenwald*, found in a separate manuscript, may be by the same poet; its style is similar. It is quite inferior to the poems in the *Gawain* manuscript, however.

1835   Around this time, the manuscript of *Sir Gawain* is discovered by the scholar William Madden in the British Museum, where it had remained virtually unnoticed for centuries.

1839   Sir Frederick Madden publishes the poem as *Syr Gawayne*; beginning of modern study and appreciation of the work.

1864   The Early English Text Society publishes *Sir Gawain*, along with the other poems from the Cotton Nero manuscript.

1925   Publication of the edition of *Sir Gawain* edited by J. R. R. Tolkien and E. V. Gordon; generally considered the definitive edition. Over the next several decades, many adaptations and translations of the poem into modern English appear; these help find the poem a wider audience, especially since the West Midlands dialect in which it was written is much further from modern English than, say, the language of Chaucer.

ESSAY QUESTIONS WITH ANSWERS

2.1 *Beowulf* and *Sir Gawain and the Green Knight* are two of the most famous works of English medieval literature. Although the two poems have certain elements in common (supernatural phenomena, a hero who undergoes a series of trials, a feudal court), they also differ from one another significantly. (In fact, as many centuries separate the two medieval works as separate *Sir Gawain* from our own time.) What are the most important differences between the two poems?

Answer The thematic and stylistic differences between *Beowulf* and *Sir Gawain* are in part due to the generic differences between an Old English epic and a Middle English romance. In *Beowulf*, the primary virtues of the hero are bravery and military prowess. Grendel and the other monsters in the poem represent evil threats to the very survival of the warrior society. The challenge that the Green Knight presents, on the other hand, is more a challenge to the reputation and integrity of Arthur's court than to its survival. It is the code of courtesy and civility at the court which is disrupted by the sudden and rude intrusion of the Green Knight.

By the time *Sir Gawain* was written, the literary tradition of courtly love, which placed erotic relations within a feudal chivalric code of honor, had developed. In keeping with this tradition, the theme of love and sexual temptation is central to the romance, whereas it is absent from the Old English epic. Gawain must prove himself not only when challenged by the Green Knight, but also when tempted by the lady.

The importance of love and courtesy in the chivalric tradition is apparent in the diction of *Sir Gawain* as well as its plot and theme. Whereas *Beowulf* abounds in stock phrases suggestive of life's struggle (such as "battle brave," "grim and greedy," "fierce spirit"), the diction of the romance concerns mores and appearances as well as morals (for example, "noble knights," "loveliest ladies," "comeliest kings," and "fair folk").

The tone of the two poems also differs markedly. *Beowulf* is solemn and portentous: beginning and ending with a funeral, it is much gloomier than *Sir*

Gawain, which treats of games and flirtations and begins and ends in celebration. Although a note of sobriety does enter *Sir Gawain* through the chastening of its hero, the tone of the romance is still much lighter than that of the epic. The world of *Sir Gawain* seems magical and, at times, whimsical, whereas the world of *Beowulf* is mythical and austere.

2.2   Discuss the relationship between the significance of the pentangle on Gawain's shield and the events of the poem.

Answer   As the poet pauses to tell us, the pentangle's "endless knot" forming five interconnected points is an icon for Gawain's perfection and the interdependence of his virtues. Yet the events of the poem suggest an unraveling of the knot, a failure of the system of values that proceeds from what seems like a small mistake: the knight's acceptance of the lady's magic girdle.

The pentangle is a symbol of natural perfection. Gawain is said to be "faultless in his five senses" and unfailing in his "five fingers" (that is, possessing the virtues of generosity or magnanimity, fellowship, chastity, courtesy, and pity). His faith in the five wounds of Christ and five joys of Mary suggests that he is the ideal *Christian* knight; loyalty to his lord, the cornerstone of feudal culture, is combined with devotion to Christ. Yet in accepting the magic girdle, Gawain fails a crucial test of virtue and reveals how difficult it is for a man to be the ideal Christian knight. Gawain's motives are complex. His act of courtesy to the lady can be viewed as revealing cowardice and lack of piety as well. For in avoiding an insult to the lady, Gawain demonstrates his fear of death and momentary lapse of faith in God's (and Mary's) protection. Hence, courtesy conflicts with purity and loyalty; the system of values represented by the pentangle sometimes includes internal contradictions. The picture of Gawain as the perfect Christian knight presented at the beginning of the poem is shown to be at least partly false; a darker moral confusion is revealed beneath the festive and decorous atmosphere of the court, and a more somber tone surfaces in the poem.

2.3   To what extent can the author of *Sir Gawain and the Green Knight* be credited with originality?

Answer   Many a modern reader, approaching *Sir Gawain* with the kind of expectations created by an acquaintance with modern literature, might respond to this question as follows: *Sir Gawain* displays no originality at all. The diction is hackneyed, the characters are caricatures, the plot is a series of predictable tests. The poem is full of conventional superlative phrases like "loveliest ladies," "comeliest king," and so on; the poet uses language in anything but an original way. When characters are described in these terms, complex characterization becomes impossible, and stereotypes reign. Gawain, the best knight in Arthur's court, is destined to perform tests which justify his reputation. There is no surprise in the workings of the plot; we know that by the end of the poem, Gawain will prove himself to be both cunning and courageous.

Such an answer, however, erroneously applies modern standards of originality to a fourteenth-century poem. It ignores the differences between the medieval romance and the modern novel, and so overlooks the special kind of originality that infuses the composition of the poem.

The formulaic diction of "fair ladies" and "noble knights" is a commonplace of the oral narrative poetry from which Sir Gawain traces its descent. And even though the Gawain-poet uses these stock phrases, he subtly questions their validity. In the course of the poem, the moral tests to which Gawain and the other members of Arthur's court submit demonstrate how the reputations encapsulated in these descriptive tags must be earned. By the end of the poem, we see Gawain earn the reputation he has been accorded at the beginning. We see what it means to be the best of knights, and we see that even the best of knights has human frailties and foibles.

The originality of the poem resides primarily in its ingenious variations on traditional themes and motifs rather than in any representation of complex psychology, although the poem's presentation of the process by which Gawain's pride is humbled is by no means psychologically naive. The Gawain-poet's sophisticated aesthetic shaping of the story accounts for much of the poem's special interest. The three scenes of temptation in the bedroom, for example, are juxtaposed against the three scenes of the hunt in such a way that they ironically comment upon one another. Also, as a number of critics have observed, the Gawain-poet takes certain common plot elements from existing folklore, for instance, the "beheading game," the "temptation story," and the "exchange of winnings," and combines them in a unique way. The Gawain-poet's originality, then, consists of his witty manipulation and complex shaping of traditional elements and the ingenious use he makes of the resources available to him.

2.4   Sir Gawain is artfully constructed by means of counterpoint and repetition. The poem begins and ends with a festive scene in Arthur's court; there are two episodes of Gawain's wandering in the wood, three temptations of Gawain, three confessions he makes, and two courts (Arthur's and Bertilak's). Discuss the functions of these uses of repetition in the poem.

Answer The repetitions in the poem impart a sense of ritual, historically at the heart of medieval culture and aesthetically at the heart of the medieval genre of romance. The scenes of feasting and celebration described throughout the poem show medieval culture to be ritualistic and ceremonious, a culture in which the repetition of ritual forms is the visible sign of medieval people's civilizing attempt to create order and meaning.

In the construction of the poem, the repetition is an important element of the romance genre, in which a major theme is the necessity of discriminating between two similar appearances. In the world of romance, two courts may appear similarly decorous and two women similarly beautiful, but the knight on his quest and the reader in his journey through the poem must learn to distinguish the true from the false, the good from the bad. For example, in Spenser's *Faerie Queen*, a sixteenth-century romance, the Red Cross Knight encounters the evil lady (Duessa) in the disguise of the ideal lady (Una). In *Sir Gawain*, too, both the knight and the reader must distinguish between the true and the false, what seems and what is.

The use of repetition in *Gawain* thus establishes a set of contrasts: Bertilak's court versus Arthur's; Guinevere versus Bertilak's lady. Elsewhere the repetition involves triads; for example, Gawain undergoes three temptations. (Critics have interpreted this variously. John Gardner, for example, using medieval theories of psychology as a basis, sees the first as a purely sexual temptation, the second as a test of Gawain's ability to control his "irascible soul," the third as a test of his "rational soul.") Similarly, Gawain makes three confessions: to the priest, to the Green Knight, and to Arthur and his court. Again, repetition functions to establish contrast. When Gawain confesses to the priest after accepting the magic girdle, his confession smacks of complacency and glibness. The narrator's description, however, alerts the reader to the fact that true penance does not come so easily: "And he absolved him of his sins as safe and as clean/ As if the dread Day of Judgment should dawn on the morrow/ And then he made merry amid the fine ladies/ With deft-footed dances and dalliance light" (lines 1183–1186, Borroff's translation). In contrast, Gawain's second confession to the Green Knight is a truer act of contrition. Gawain has learned to see his own frailties, his own shortcomings.

The final confession before Arthur and his court completes the process through Gawain's acceptance of public shame. The final court scene thus contrasts with the earlier one: Gawain has learned what it means to be a knight; he has both been humbled and earned his reputation as the best possible knight. Through the symmetry in the poem, the reader is meant to see the difference between its beginning and end, that is, the difference between the court's complacency at the beginning and its greater wisdom at the end.

K.L.

SUGGESTED READINGS

Benson, Larry D., *Art and Tradition in Sir Gawain and the Green Knight* (1965).
Burrow, John A., *A Reading of Sir Gawain and the Green Knight* (1966).

WILLIAM LANGLAND

C H R O N O L O G Y

1332   Probable birth date of Langland; born at Cleobury Mortimer in Shropshire, son of Stacy (that is, Eustace) de Rokayle, a small landowner. Virtually nothing is known with certainty about the life of the author of *Piers Plowman*; even his name may have been different. So this fact and every other assertion about Langland are largely conjecture, derived mainly from the author's apparently autobiographical comments in *Piers Plowman* itself.

1340–
1352   Langland is probably educated at the monastery of Great Malvern in preparation for the priesthood. Some scholars contend that he may have studied at Oxford University as well. However, it appears that his patron, whose identity is unknown, died before Langland's education could be completed, so that he took only minor orders and never advanced very far in an ecclesiastical career.

1362   Evidently living in Cornhill with his wife Kit ("Kitte") and daughter Colette ("Kalote"). Earns a meager living saying holy offices for well-to-do families.

1370   Composition of the so-called A text, one of the three differing versions in which *Piers Plowman* survives. The A text consists of a prologue, eight books of *The Vision of Piers Plowman*, and four books of *The Life of Do-Well*. Like the other versions of the poem, it is an allegorical dream-vision setting forth Christian doctrine and ethical teachings, along with satire on the sins and follies of the time, particularly the oppression of the poor by the rich and the corruptions of the late medieval church. (This corruption would lead, in time, to various reform movements both within and without the church;

the Reformation, the Counter-Reformation, and the split between Protestants and Catholics would ultimately result. Most nineteenth-century scholars and critics, when they mentioned *Piers Plowman* at all, considered it interesting mainly as a precursor of these religious movements.)

1376   Outbreak of pestilence in England, producing great suffering and death among the poor, with whom Langland lived and sympathized.

1377–1379   Composition of the B text, the second version of *Piers Plowman*. This is a greatly enlarged version, including the prologue and twenty books. Most critics regard the B text as the best, and most modern editions and translations are based primarily on the B text.

1381   The Peasants' Revolt (also known as Wat Tyler's Rebellion), an unsuccessful and cruelly suppressed uprising by the poor against a series of harsh taxes and unfair price increases imposed by the nobility. Langland would probably have sympathized with the grievances of the rebels.

1392   Composition of the C text of *Piers Plowman*, consisting of a prologue and twenty-three books.

1400   Death of Langland. For the next century and a half, *Piers Plowman* will be a popular work; numerous manuscripts exist containing one or another of the three versions of the poem, and printed copies of the work appear to have been well received.

1561   Last publication of *Piers Plowman* until the nineteenth century. During the sixteenth, seventeenth, and early eighteenth centuries, the Middle English in which Langland wrote was considered increasingly obscure and difficult. Readers and critics during the neoclassical period, in particular, regarded the English of Langland and Chaucer's day as crude and indecipherable. Ironically, readers of today probably find Middle English easier to read than did readers of two and three centuries ago; greatly increased knowledge of linguistics provides today's readers with scholarly support that makes Langland (and Chaucer) quite approachable.

1813   *Piers Plowman* reprinted for the first time since 1561.

1886   Publication of the definitive edition of *Piers Plowman*, a two-volume edition containing all three texts, edited by W. W. Skeat.

ESSAY QUESTIONS WITH ANSWERS

3.1 Discuss the character and function of the dreamer in "The Fair Field Full of Folk" (Passus I).

Answer In the first lines of the poem, the narrator puts on the rough garb of a secular hermit, signifying his roles as a wanderer and an outsider. Thus, in the opening sequence, he is a spectator whose distance from the affairs of the world allows him to adopt the satirical perspective which colors his description of the field of folk. He also serves as an intermediary with whom the reader can identify. The intimacy of the first-person narration invites us to participate in the dream-vision and in the dreamer's sense of wonder, scorn, and puzzlement.

The dream-vision, it should be noted, is one of the commonest medieval literary devices. Derived from classical models, it had passed into English literature as early as the eighth-century *Dream of the Rood*, by the Old English poet Cynewulf. At about the same time as *Piers Plowman* was being written, the *Gawain*-poet used the form in his elegiac dream-vision *Pearl*, and Chaucer's *Book of the Duchess* is another contemporary example. Because it was commonly assumed that dreams were either morally or prophetically significant, the dream-vision provided a useful method for an author to present a religious or satiric vision in symbolic form. Since the dream-vision was presented not as a fiction concocted by the author but as a revelation inspired by some outside power, the authority of the vision's contents was enhanced by the device.

In addition to the dream format itself, the style of the narration further contributes to the persuasiveness of the vision in *Piers Plowman*. The narrator's blunt, homely language suggests that he is an ordinary, honest fellow who is to be trusted. For example, his comment on lawyers ("You might better measure mist on Malvern Hills/ Than get a 'mum' from their mouths till money is showed" [B.I.88–89, meaning B text, Passus I, lines 88–89]) has the slightly cynical but genial tone of proverbial wisdom, as well as a vivid specificity drawn from its reference to a real place which was in fact Langland's home district. In remarks such as this, the narrator sounds like the *eiron* of satire—an acute observer who speaks with the authority of ironic understatement.

Thus not only through the immediacy of the first-person "I" but through a distinctively colloquial style, the narrator mediates between the reader and the dream-vision, his reliable and familiar voice providing an avenue into the strange allegorical world of the poem.

3.2   In the opening vision of the field of folk, the dreamer describes a crowded landscape inhabited by people of many different classes and trades. This vision constitutes a satiric portrait of fourteenth-century English society: the poet vividly details items of dress, rural and urban customs, and religious and secular abuses, even quoting actual London street cries as the vision fades. However, the dream has a further allegorical significance. Discuss the dream's symbolic level of meaning, and explain how the poet communicates it to the reader.

Answer   The dreamer's first glimpse is of the "fair field full of folk" (B.I. 17) set between a high tower and a deep dale. A timeless vision is suggested, with the world of mortals poised between the tower of truth, God, and heaven on the one hand, and the dark valley of death, Satan, and hell on the other. It is true that the trimly built tower and the "deep dark ditches, dreadful to see" (B.I.16) are only suggestive metaphors, but what they suggest is a symbolic arena. Langland's medieval audience would have expected the dream-vision to contain symbolic details, and it seems likely that they would have recognized the allegory here. (In the C text, a later version of the poem, these features are identified explicitly as the Tower of Truth in the east and the Dale of Death in the west.)

The first description of the folk themselves ("all manner of men, the mean and the rich,/ Working and wandering, as the world asks" [B.I.18–19]) indicates that the spectacle is one not just of chaotic detail, but of humanity's general condition and pilgrimage on earth. The theme of "wandering" is later developed into the quest for salvation of the soul, and "working" becomes an important motif in two senses: simple labor, such as Piers's rural toil, is seen as a basis of the virtuous life, and "good works," such as the Samaritan's charity, are seen as a key to salvation.

The closing lines of the dream report the cries of street hawkers vending food and drink. The invitation to eat and imbibe conveys the idea of gluttony and of fleshly pleasures generally. In medieval allegory, worldly pastimes and mild social abuses were frequent emblems of the whole array of human sins. Thus, just below the clutter of realistic detail in the vision is the delicate suggestion of the abstract themes of the poem as a whole: human nature and eternal life, sin and salvation.

3.3 In the dream-vision of the harrowing of hell (Passus XXI), the narrator sees a figure "resembling the Samaritan and somewhat Piers Plowman" (B.XXI.8), entering Jerusalem on an ass like a knight going to a joust. When the dreamer inquires of Faith who the jouster is, Faith replies that he is Jesus, who "shall joust in Piers's arms,/ In his helmet and in his hauberk, *humana natura*" (B.XXI.22–23). Thus, the figure is identified simultaneously with the Good Samaritan, Piers Plowman, a medieval knight, and the Savior. Discuss the significance of this multiple layering of identities.

Answer   The primary example in Christian theology of the fusion of identities is the Incarnation, when "the Word was made flesh" as the Son of God appeared in the guise of human nature. The mingling of human and divine in the figure of the jouster may therefore be explained by religious doctrine. In the traditional Christian view, Christ was both man and God, both the second Adam and the creator of the world, both the sacrificial victim and the God to whom the sacrifice was offered. Thus the multiple identities of the jouster are a natural outgrowth of a viewpoint central to Christianity.

From this viewpoint grew a literary technique which also explains the fusion of different characters into a single emblem. Medieval allegory, with its habit of identifying concrete contemporary realities with transcendent abstractions, often subordinates "horizontal" chronology to a "vertical" scheme of types. According to this religious typology, all past events are seen as types, models, or figures of future events, and the future is interpreted as the fruition of the past. Spiritual meaning is continuous and permanent, manifested again and again in every period of Christian history, past, present, and future.

Langland's description of Piers thus suggests something beyond simple allegorical parallels or the four levels of significance (literal, allegorical, moral, and anagogic or mystical) involved in much medieval scriptural exegesis. Spiritual implication does not stand outside the text on a separate conceptual plane, but exists within passages of realistic description, imbuing ordinary reality with metaphysical suggestion. The simultaneity of the actual and the spiritual derives precisely from the figural or typological approach, which recognizes the truth of temporal history but sees it as foreshadowing all coming events, up to and including the Last Judgment, or as fulfilling the providential design which originated with the Creation. Langland is thus continually able to place any given moment in the perspective of eternity and to represent all living things as incarnations of spiritual significance.

Typological interpretation, along with the fourfold method of exegesis, was commonly applied to scripture. Thus, the Old Testament story of Abraham prefigures God's willingness to sacrifice his only begotten son for the sake of humanity; and the Good Samaritan's act of charity parallels Christ's intercession on behalf of suffering humanity. In *Piers Plowman* these figures are important not only as conceptual types or symbols but as real persons, for their spiritual significance becomes manifest only in their temporal, earthly existence. Thus both figures are initially described as actual living men. Abraham is a white-headed old man "as hor as an hawethorn" (C.XIX.184), and his vision of God has a homely, realistic quality: " 'In a somer ich seyh him,' quath he, 'as ich sat in my porche' " (C.XIX.242). The Samaritan is also presented in realistic terms: examining the wounded man, he "perseyvde by his pous he was in perel to dye" (C.XX.21). The "porche" and the "pous [pus]" are telling details which ground these men firmly on the earth. At the same time, both utter prophetic statements that make clear their typological roles as precursors or analogues. Abraham speaks of a "sacrifice" to God with wine and bread and wishes for "a newe lawe" (C.XIX.265–266); the Samaritan maintains that "the blod of a barn [bairn]" (C.XX.84) is necessary to save the wounded man. These statements, alluding to future events outside the men's literal knowledge, link them to the new faith and to the fulfillment which Christ's coming represents. The two men do not symbolize truth; rather, truth is revealed through them and is incarnate in them.

In the case of Piers, Langland creates his own figure, revealing spiritual meaning in yet another incarnation. Piers is simultaneously a particular fourteenth-century peasant, a Christian pilgrim, and a type of Christ. The rich fusion of Piers Plowman (the good common man), the Samaritan (the charitable man), the knight (the brave man jousting against a satanic foe), and Christ (the Redeemer in the form of man) is possible only given the medieval concept of a divine plan which reveals itself everywhere in types and figures, thus uniting the spiritual realm with the natural world and encompassing past, present, and future.

3.4   The story of the harrowing of hell (Christ's victorious descent into hell, after the Crucifixion and before the Resurrection, to release the souls held captive there) is interrupted at the point of Christ's death on the cross by a long debate among the four daughters of God: Mercy, Truth, Peace, and Right-eousness. Only after much quasi-legal discussion of Christ's right to release the souls in hell does Christ himself appear at hell's gate as a shining light to complete the dramatic action. Analyze this interruption of the story, evaluating its logic and its effect.

Answer   The interruption of the dramatic story of the Passion by a lengthy debate suggests Langland's interest in underscoring the lesson or moral of that story. Following the form of a sermon, he presents his narration as an example— a biblical text—which requires interpretation in the form of didactic commentary. The debate of the four daughters indicates the main significance of the Harrowing of Hell: the replacement of the Old Law (represented by Truth and Righteousness) by the New Law of love (represented by Peace and Mercy). The expulsion of man from paradise turns out to be a "fortunate fall"; by sinning and experiencing woe, man evoked God's mercy and Christ's love and, paradoxically, initiated a new era of grace and hope.

After the set speeches of the daughters, outlining this doctrine, the fiends of hell legalistically argue whether Satan has a right to the sinners' souls. Christ then speaks, answering the legal question in the riddles of Christian paradox: the sinners have died that they might live; Christ's life has paid for their lives; grace wins out over guile. Only after this rather thorny discussion of theological meanings can the story proper continue with the release of the souls and the ringing of Easter bells to signal Christ's Resurrection.

The effect of the interruption is complex. In part, the set speeches clarify the subject, diagraming the ideas and illustrating their interrelationships. In part, the declamatory outbursts generate an air of suspense as the reader waits for Christ's triumphant descent and rise. After the Harrowing of Hell, the joyous exclamations of the daughters of God and the singing, music making, and bell ringing are climactic, not only because of the quickened tempo of the lines but because they represent a release from suspense, as debate and argument dissolve in a scene of glad reconciliation.

3.5   Using one of the seven deadly sins (Passus VII, "The Confession of the Folk") as an example, discuss Langland's techniques for personifying abstract vice.

Answer   The poet begins his description of Covetous with a sketch of his physical attributes. All of these features—his lean and hungry look, his beetling brow and thick lips, his bleary eyes, his jowls hanging down like a leather purse, his hacked beard, and his old rags—manifest the idea of grasping avarice. The portrait is like a cartoon, all the visual details selected according to the controlling concept of greediness. Ironically, Covetous's obsession with gain leads to material impoverishment, which is a sign of spiritual poverty as well: his poverty is a metaphor for the punishment that inevitably accompanies sin.

After presenting the physical caricature, Langland expands his description, developing it into a full character sketch of a social type. Covetousness has a name—Sire Hervy; a trade—he is a draper with tricks for falsely measuring the cloth he sells; and a wife—Rose the retailer, who owns false scales and sells diluted ale. The tangible reality of the greedy couple brings the concept of sin down to the concrete level of petty crime. The passage constitutes a piece of specific social history, for Covetous represents the failings of the mercantile class of the fourteenth century.

Thus, by means of selective visual detail and comic stereotyping, Langland presents an idea in homely, familiar terms, making abstract covetousness into a vivid character type whom the reader can readily recognize. The fourteenth-century reader would have recognized him even more readily, for he might well have been victimized by just such a double-dealing merchant. But although the sketch is partly comic in effect, its purpose is moral and didactic. The humor is meant to evoke not only laughter but scorn, and the commentary of Repentance which runs through Passus VII places each humorous sketch in a serious context.

3.6 Discuss Langland's use of prosodic devices in the following passage in which Christ addresses Satan:

> And now bygynneth thy gyle agayne on the to turne
> And my grace to growe ay wyddere and wyddere.
> The bitternesse that thou hast browe, now brouk hit thysulve;
> That art doctour of deth, drynke that thou madest!
>   For I that am lord of lyf, love is my drynke
>   (C. XXI. 398–402) ◆

> (And now begins your guile against you to turn
> And my grace to grow ever wider and wider.
> The bitterness that you have brewed, imbibe it yourself
> Who are doctor of Death—drink that you made.
>   For I that am lord of Life, love is my drink)

Answer Although Langland is not a courtly poet like Chaucer, aware of and interested in the continental poetry of the day, he is capable of certain sophisticated poetic effects within the predominantly conversational rhythms of his four-stress line. Often attacked for his rude meter, his naive alliteration, and his lack of rhyme, he is nonetheless an eloquent representative of the older, native English tradition. The basis of Langland's versification is a four-stress line consisting of two hemistichs (half-lines), an *a* verse and a *b* verse, the two verses separated by a heavy caesura or pause. The *a* verse has two alliterated stresses and the *b* verse has one stressed word which alliterates with the *a* verse and one which doesn't. Much variation is possible within this system, and Langland at times departs from the expected pattern of alliterations. What remains constant is a rhythmic repetition of sounds regularly interrupted by rests or pauses. This pattern, although it lacks both meter and rhyme, is nonetheless musical and coherent.

In the lines cited above, the repeated consonantal sounds correspond to the verbal stress called for by the meaning of the lines, thus producing a swinging rhythm which links the alliterated words. The resulting rhythmic drive, with its varying numbers of unstressed syllables following each stressed syllable, reproduces the inflections of idiomatic spoken English. Within this steady conversational rhythm, the caesura—midline rest or break—at times provides a dramatic pause before a major assertion. For example, the pause at the center of "The bitternesse that thou hast browe, now brouk hit thysulve" and "For I that am lord of lyf, love is my drynke" creates the effect of an emotional outburst in the second half of the line. In the first instance, the effect is of flinging Satan's drink back in his face ("brouk hit thysulve"), and in the second, the effect is of triumphant explanation, for Christ is "lord of lyf" precisely because "love is my drynke."

Working against the familiar conversational rhythms of the lines is the artificial patterning of the alliterative sounds themselves. In the lines cited above, some of the alliterations fall into antithetical pairs: "gyle" versus "grace," "doctour of deth" versus "lord of lyf." By means of such sound patterns, thematic contrasts are introduced into the texture of the verse without violating its colloquial rhythms.

B.S.

SUGGESTED READINGS

Salter, E., and D. Pearsall, eds., *York Medieval Texts: Piers Plowman* (1969).

Traversi, Derek, "Langland's Piers Plowman," in *The Age of Chaucer* (ed. B. Ford) (1954).

GEOFFREY CHAUCER

C H R O N O L O G Y

1340	Probable date of birth. Son of John Chaucer, a wealthy wine merchant, and Agnes de Copton, whose family had minor connections at court.
1348	Black Death causes widespread suffering in England. Chaucer is probably a student at St. Paul's Almonry in London.
1357	By this date is known to be serving as a page in the houshold of Lionel, earl of Ulster, later duke of Clarence and a son of King Edward III.
1359–1360	Fights with the king's forces in France; is taken prisoner and ransomed. Is later entrusted with messages from Prince Lionel to England.
1361–1365	Chaucer's activities doubtful; may be a law student at the Inner Temple in London, or may be in Ireland attending Lionel (by this time the duke of Clarence). Also may be at work on his translation of the classic French poem on courtly love, the *Roman de la Rose*. (Only a part of Chaucer's translation survives.)
1366	By this date is married to Philippa, a lady in attendance on the queen.
1367	Serving as yeoman in the king's household. Date of the first address to Parliament by the king in the English language, marking the reascendancy of English after three centuries of the dominance of French following the Norman conquest.

1368	Chaucer is named squire. Sent abroad on a diplomatic mission for the king.
1370	Again sent abroad as a diplomat. Writes the *Book of the Duchess*, an elegy in the form of a dream-vision, in commemoration of Blanche, wife of John of Gaunt, the duke of Lancaster. John of Gaunt will be Chaucer's primary noble patron from this point on.
1372–1373	Traveling in Italy on a diplomatic mission. May first encounter the writings of Dante, Petrarch, and Boccaccio at this time. They will have a major impact on Chaucer's own writings.
1374	Chaucer receives a pension from John of Gaunt and is named controller of customs and subsidy in the Port of London; also granted a daily pitcher of wine by the king. During the next years will live in London; probably writes many of his finest poems at this time, including the *House of Fame*, the *Parliament of Fowls*, *Troilus and Criseyde*, and the *Legend of Good Women*. Probably also translates Boethius's *Consolation of Philosophy* (classic of late Latin stoicism) at this time.
1376–1377	Travels to France to negotiate a peace treaty and a royal marriage.
1378	Granted a royal pension. Visits Italy as a diplomat for the second time.
1385	Named justice of the peace for Kent; also elected to Parliament. Probably plans and begins writing his masterpiece, *The Canterbury Tales*, at this time.
1387	Death of Chaucer's wife.
1391	Named deputy forester of the royal forest in Somersetshire; lives there, probably working on *The Canterbury Tales*. Is evidently involved in astrological studies, probably with a group of colleagues; writes a *Treatise on the Astrolabe*, an early scientific treatise.
1395	At Christmas is noted as in attendance on Henry, earl of Derby, son of John of Gaunt.
1399	Accession of the earl of Derby to the English throne as Henry IV. Chaucer writes the witty "Complaint of Chaucer to His Purse," asking for royal favor; his royal pension is increased as a result. Takes an apartment in the garden of the Lady Chapel of Westminster Abbey.
1400	Death of Chaucer. He is buried in the east aisle of the south transept of Westminster Abbey. Later, other poets will be buried nearby, creating the famous Poets' Corner.
1478	First publication of *The Canterbury Tales* (by William Caxton, the first English printer). A second edition follows in 1481. Throughout the fifteenth

and sixteenth centuries, Chaucer is greatly esteemed; most references to his work acknowledge him as the greatest English poet.

1602   Last reprinting of Chaucer's work until 1687; beginning of a period of neglect. During the seventeenth and eighteenth centuries, Chaucer's language was considered too archaic and uncouth for easy or pleasurable reading. Also, understanding of the proper pronunciation of his lines disappeared, so that Chaucer's poetry no longer seemed to scan. As a result, his work was little read, though his name was still known as that of the father of English poetry.

ESSAY QUESTIONS WITH ANSWERS

"General Prologue" of The Canterbury Tales

4.1 Who is the narrator of the "General Prologue"? Discuss his character and his purpose in the prologue.

Answer The narrator of the "General Prologue" is Chaucer himself in the fictional guise of a pilgrim who is on his way to Canterbury and has met the other pilgrims purely by chance. This fictitious Chaucer joins in the landlord's story-telling competition; indeed, "Chaucer" is the only pilgrim from whom we have two tales.

The persona which Chaucer adopts as this fictitious pilgrim is not that of an intelligent, astute interpreter of events, well-read, articulate, and courtly—like the actual Chaucer—but rather a simple pilgrim, whose only function is to give a description of the other pilgrims and to report the tales they have told without offering any personal judgment. The landlord refers to this pilgrim as a quiet, unassuming sort of man who stands apart from the others. This naive pose is enunciated as the narrator tells the reader, "Al have I nat set folk in his degree/Here in this tale as that they sholde stonde:/ My wit is short, ye may wel understonde" (lines 746–748). The reader is intended to see through this ironic understatement to Chaucer's satiric purpose—the characters' inadvertent revelations of their own obsessions, follies, and weaknesses. By adopting the simple pose of the naive observer, Chaucer allows the pilgrims to reveal themselves more effectively than a more intrusive narrator could.

4.2 How do the portraits of the Knight, the Parson, and the Plowman differ from the other characterizations in the "General Prologue" to The Canterbury Tales?

Answer These three portraits are idealized descriptions of representative members of England's three "estates": the nobility, the clergy, and the laborers.

Unlike the more realistic likenesses Chaucer provides of the other pilgrims, with their foibles and obsessions vividly and sometimes satirically presented, these characterizations are intended to impress the reader with the worthiness and innate nobility of each of these ideal pilgrims. The portrait of the Knight stresses his heroic character, his bravery in battle, and his gracious manner: "He was a verray, parfit, gentil knight" (line 72). The Parson, for all his lack of worldly riches, possesses two far more valuable assets—his love of Christ and his love of his fellow man. Furthermore, he is wise enough to understand the transitory nature of mere earthly pleasures: "That if gold ruste, what shal iren do?" (line 502). Chaucer stresses, too, the diligence and integrity with which the Parson carries out his priestly duties. His brother, the Plowman, is a manual laborer who digs ditches and carries dung; yet he, too, is "living in pees and parfit charitee" (line 534), working willingly to help the poor, even without pay.

Taken together, these representative portraits reveal part of the social structure of late medieval England as well as one of Chaucer's aims in *The Canterbury Tales*—to present a portrait of a rounded society. The society Chaucer portrays has room for both bad and good characters, for corruption and abuses, as well as for an ideal standard of behavior upheld by a conception of social order and a Christian ethical system.

4.3 Discuss the characterizations of and the relationships between these pairs of pilgrims: the Parson and the Plowman; the Physician and the Pardoner; the Wife of Bath and the Prioress.

Answer   Chaucer links the descriptions of two of his idealized characters, the Parson and the Plowman, through their family relationship—that is, the fact that they are brothers. This linking of two social classes, clergy and laborers, in drawing upon and interrelating the best example of each group reinforces Chaucer's presentation of man's better nature and offers the reader two totally sympathetic portraits of these seemingly lower-class members of Chaucer's party. Furthermore, it suggests the Christian idea that all men are brothers, a notion best exemplified by these two pilgrims.

The Physician and the Pardoner, on the other hand, share a metaphoric brotherhood: the Physician is supposed to heal the sick body, while the Pardoner should give solace for sicknesses of the soul. Each of these pilgrims, however, performs his chosen duty only for the material wealth it will bring him. In his description of the Physician, Chaucer ingeniously plays upon the medieval belief in the medicinal value of gold ("For gold in physik is a cordial" [line 445]), and he describes in detail the Physician's elegant apparel. The portrait of the Pardoner is still more scathing; his repulsive appearance, his false relics, and his almost obscene flattery are described in detail. No doubt Chaucer is making the point that, before they can claim the ability to help humanity, these two false physicians must first learn to cure their own greed.

In contrast, the Wife of Bath and the Prioress are linked neither by blood nor by occupation but rather by their common gender. They differ from the male pairs, too, in that they are apparently opposites rather than "twins." The Wife of Bath is an earthy woman, driven by a combination of economic necessity, pride, impulse, and animal instinct. She is outspoken on the tricks of love and marriage, and the reader may suspect that her purpose in this pilgrimage is not religious but matrimonial: to seek a suitable partner for yet another marriage.

The Prioress might seem at first to be a perfect contrast to this woman of the flesh, for she seems in some ways to represent an ideal of virginity devoted to a life of piety. She sings the service beautifully, and she wears those attributes of the religious life, the rosary and brooch. However, the description is made ambiguous by various allusions to her secularly female qualities. Her worldliness and vanity are implied by references to her clothing, table manners, and courtly behavior. Her feminine charms receive more emphasis than does her celibacy. Even her motto, *Amor vincit omnia* ("Love conquers all"), is at least ambiguous; it could serve equally well as an encomium to earthly or to heavenly loves.

In setting up pairs of this kind, Chaucer suggests some of the patterns of class and character which underlie the variety of medieval society. Furthermore, the similarities and differences among the characters throw into sharper relief the particular qualities of each.

4.4   Analyze the characterization of the Monk.

Answer   The portrait of the Monk is dominated by images of his ruling passion—hunting. The first line of the description (line 165) speaks of the pilgrim as a very fine monk ("a fair for the maistrie"), but once his fondness for the outdoor life is revealed in the second line, the narrator bypasses any conventional description of a cleric in favor of a hilarious account of this particular cleric's obsession. Animal references abound in the next forty lines: "daintee hors," "fissh," "grehoundes," "fowl," "hare," and many more. But the most effective device Chaucer uses is to alternate almost line by line between the two disparate poles of the Monk's life. For example, "And when he rood, men mighte his bridel heere/Ginglen in a whistling wind as clere/And eek as loude as dooth the chapel belle" (lines 169–171). This technique, repeated several times, is extremely effective and reaches its natural climax in the couplet "His bootes souple, his hors in greet estate—/Now certainly he was a fair prelat" (lines 203–204). The satiric intent is clear.

L.R.

"The Miller's Tale"

4.5 In *The Canterbury Tales*, the physical description of a character often reveals the kind of person he is. How does the description of the Miller in the "General Prologue" function to establish his character?

Answer The crudity and energy of the Miller, reflected in the tale he tells, are first revealed in his description in the "General Prologue" (lines 547–568). The animal imagery used to describe him conveys his brute strength and his coarseness: like a ram or a bull, the Miller butts a door with his head; his beard "as any sowe or fox was reed"; and the tufts of his wart are "Rede as the bristles of a sowes eres." The Miller's lasciviousness and brutishness are suggested by the red of his hair (the traditional color of lust and anger) and by his habitually flared nostrils ("His nosethirles blake were and wide"). The hairy wart on his nose is a physical blemish which symbolizes the moral marks on the character of this bully and cheat. But it is the Miller's mouth which most seems to impress the narrator; it is, he says, "as greet . . . as a greet furneys." This oversized feature suggests the fiery energy and gluttonous appetite of the Miller, as well as his loquaciousness and love of tall tales. His musical instrument, the bagpipe, further contributes to his portrait as a blowhard and helps to prepare us for the farcical, energetic, and exaggerated tale he tells.

The congruence between physical attributes and inner character is a commonplace of the genre of comedy, related to the medieval theory of the "humors." The Miller is a "type" or stereotyped version of a lecherous and wrathful man in whom the choleric humor was thought to predominate.

4.6 What is the relationship between the Miller and his tale and between the Miller's prologue and his tale?

Answer The obscene story of adultery, lechery, and deception told by the Miller fits its teller. The sympathy which the Miller extends to the crafty scholar Nicholas is appropriate for a man who himself deceives his customers. Chaucer calls the Miller's tale "a cherles tale," and this is true in two senses: it is both a story told by a churl and a story about a churl.

The circumstance of the introduction of the tale also creates a dramatic coherence between the telling of the tale and the tale itself. After the completion of the Knight's tale, the Host next directs the Monk to tell his story, to repay or "quite" the Knight's noble tale, but the Miller, drunk and obstreperous, defies the laws of courtesy and rudely interrupts the Host. The Miller refuses to be silenced; he will "quite" the Knight's tale with a "noble tale" of his own about the humiliation of a carpenter by a clerk. Both the Host and the Reeve object to this rude interruption, though for different reasons: the Host realizes that the Miller's drunken tale will be anything but "noble," while the Reeve fears that the story of the cuckolded carpenter is intended as an insult to himself.

The narrator—the fictional Chaucer—apologizes for repeating the Miller's story and cautions the reader that, if he chooses to read the "cherles tale," he must take responsibility: "Blameth nought me if that ye chese amis" (line 72). The staging of this comic struggle for control of the narration and Chaucer's own disclaimer of responsibility is one of the many sophisticated devices used in the tales to involve the reader in the action of the drama as well as to allow Chaucer to explore a range of narrative possibilities. Thus, although "The Miller's Tale" may appear to be purely a bawdy story, it is told by a very skillful and sophisticated poet who places it in a dramatic network in which teller, tale, and narrative event play off one another in a complex way.

4.7 "The Miller's Tale" is a kind of love story, involving a cuckolded husband, two lovesick suitors, and a beautiful young woman. Discuss the use of romance conventions within the tale and the differences between "The Miller's Tale" and a conventional romance.

Answer Both Absolon and Nicholas are described as prepared to die for their love for Alisoun, a description which is a medieval romance convention. Throughout "The Miller's Tale," much ceremonial wooing occurs; Absolon serenades his would-be lover under her window, and Nicholas is described as a fine singer and a good lover, two virtues often extolled in the genre of the romance.

But the Miller includes the trappings of romance for the purpose of deflating the idealization of love at the center of romance. He thus "quites" the Knight's chivalric tale not with a true romance but with a *fabliau*, a short, comic tale that involves middle- and lower-class characters in an outrageous, often obscene plot. Nicholas's abbreviated courtship of Alisoun ends with his seizing her "queinte," and Absolon's idealization of his lady ends with a kiss on the "ers." The suitor who wins the lady employs cleverness and deception rather than courtesy and honesty; his aim is clearly sexual gratification rather than a chaste chivalric love from afar. Finally, the fair lady herself is a country wench rather than a courtly maiden. In his *fabliau*, Chaucer stands the romance on its head, showing the fleshly desires masked by the ceremonious wooing of romantic lovers.

4.8 Although the French word *fabliau* derives from the same root as the English "fable," the concepts of justice and morality are quite different in the two genres. Discuss justice and morality in "The Miller's Tale."

Answer As in the traditional fable, punishment is meted out to the "sinners" at the end of "The Miller's Tale." The avaricious carpenter loses the possession he greedily guards: the chastity and fidelity of his wife. Absolon's idealization of romance, fatuous regard for niceties, and general over-fastidiousness are all punished in his humiliation by Alisoun. "Hende" Nicholas is punished for overreaching; he's so self-congratulatory about his own wit that he can't resist trying to improve on Alisoun's trick and thus gets scalded in the "toute." In each case the punishment comically fits the crime, and the tricksters receive their comeuppance.

From this fitting distribution of justice, however, Alisoun is exempt. The language which introduces her suggests that she is different from the male characters. She is compared to nature: her body is small like a weasel's; she is more pleasurable to see than a pear tree and softer than the wool of a ram. Chaucer seems to exempt Alisoun from punishment in his tale, as if her natural passions somehow transcend the world of the suitors' comic social maneuvers.

K.L.

"The Nun's Priest's Tale"

4.9 "The Nun's Priest's Tale" has a "frame" consisting of the opening description of the poor widow and the concluding description of a rural fox hunt. What is the effect of this frame?

Answer The opening description of the widow's "simple lif" contrasts sharply with the luxurious splendor in which Chauntecleer lives with his harem of hens. This contrast is developed on several levels. The poor woman has a plain but healthful and contented existence: her "bowr" and her "hall" are a single-room cottage; her simple diet saves her from repletion, gout, and apoplexy; and her daily fare, its simplicity suggested by the plainness of its hues ("Milk and brown bread"), contents her. At the same time, the description hints at social satire, for the "ideal" poverty presented here is clearly not far above starvation and want.

The satire is sharpened by the contrast between the widow's impoverished, if noble, existence and the riot of indulgence prevailing in the barnyard. Chauntecleer is described as a kingly swaggerer ruling his roost with royal splendor. His cockscomb, battlemented like "a castel wal," and his plumage, a blaze of bright colors including jet, azure, lily white, and gold, symbolize his pride, the castle image contrasting with the widow's humble cottage, the rainbow colors with her simple life of "whit and blak." Later on, Pertelote's long speech on Chauntecleer's "rede colera," an overabundance of the choleric humor caused by "replexiouns . . . fume . . . and complexiouns," completes the contrast between a healthy, balanced life and a diseased self-indulgence. Again the contrast is not simple, for Chaucer's ironic implication is that the widow is not only admirably self-restrained but regrettably "pinched," while Chauntecleer, for all his excesses, is somehow heroic in his vitality.

The widow is absent throughout the main narrative, chiefly because the presence of a real human being would interfere with the comic symbolism of the beast tale, in which rooster, hen, and fox take on human traits. When she reenters the tale in the boisterous fox hunt toward the end, the intrusion of the human world into the animal world again provides a significant contrast. The reader is pulled back from the mock-epic drama of Chauntecleer into the real world, where a cock is no sublime hero but simply a barnyard creature with a certain economic value. The turning point of the story, in which Chauntecleer outfoxes the fox, occurs after the realistic fox hunt scene and concludes the beast allegory of pride and flattery. In his narrow escape from the fox, Chauntecleer learns the folly of believing in his own inflated boasts. But the earlier explosion of human activity onto the scene has already helped to deflate Chauntecleer's self-aggrandizing pretensions by emphasizing his strictly animal nature.

4.10   Chauntecleer concludes his speech on dreams with a compliment to his lady, Madame Pertelote:

> *Mulier est hominis confusio,*
> Madame, the sentence of this Latin is,
> "Womman is mannes ioye and al his blis."

The Latin actually means, "Woman is man's ruination." Discuss the thematic significance of Chauntecleer's mistranslation.

Answer   In this scene, the cock is trying to placate his wife after arguing with her about the validity of dreams. It is possible that Chauntecleer's mistranslation is unintentional: he simply doesn't know Latin. In this case, the passage would be yet another illustration of the cock's comic pretensions to knowledge and authority, and the joke would be on him. Taken another way, however, as a conscious falsification, the mistranslation attests to Chauntecleer's cleverness in rhetorical persuasion. His quotation is designed to mollify his wife and end the argument and is thus the first instance of flattery in the tale.

That the error is intentional is perhaps the more likely possibility, for flattery is both a major theme of "The Nun's Priest's Tale" and an essential feature of the plot. Verbal trickery occurs at two crucial points later in the story: when Chauntecleer, succumbing to flattery, is captured by the colfox; and when the colfox, succumbing to flattery, allows him to escape. In part, the effect of these episodes is comic, for a trickster's transparent manipulation of a dupe makes an amusing spectacle. At the same time, Chaucer hints that only an exaggerated self-love can make one vulnerable to such obvious stratagems.

The tale further demonstrates that the ability to use flattery does not imply superior moral insight; in fact, the plot consists of a series of comic reversals in which the characters blithely outwit each other. Chauntecleer plays on his wife's vanity to end their domestic spat, but he immediately falls victim to his own pride when the fox asks for a demonstration of his crowing. The fox exploits Chauntecleer's self-infatuation, but immediately succumbs to his own vanity when Chauntecleer suggests that he defy his pursuers. Chauntecleer is actually his own worst flatterer, for his self-delight in having won the argument with Pertelote on the infallibility of dreams makes him forget his own point. Having flattered himself into complacency, he disregards the ominous import of his own dream and thus is open to the fox's advances.

Such reversals are the stuff of farce, and the characters of "The Nun's Priest's Tale" are caricatures of human folly, enacting a boisterous comedy of errors.

4.11   The brief story of Chauntecleer's capture by and escape from the colfox is interrupted by several apparent digressions. These include Pertelote's praise of laxatives, Chauntecleer's proof of the validity of dreams, and the narrator's discussion of predestination versus free will. Discuss the significance of these speeches, and explain what they contribute to the story.

Answer   Each of these speeches is based on a specific type of oration outlined in medieval rhetorical theory. Pertelote's speech is an encomium, a speech in praise of some object; Chauntecleer's argument is a confirmation of a commonplace; and the narrator's commentary is a thesis argument analyzing pro and con. These grandiloquent digressions are rhetorical devices which, like the tale's allusions to epic, extend the story beyong its barnyard setting. By bringing in medical lore, cosmological speculations, and rhetorical decoration, Chaucer emphasizes the discrepancy between the world of his animal fable and the world at large.

The resulting irony cuts two ways. The elevated speeches and intellectual arguments undercut the pomposities of the speakers: the figures of the nagging housewife, the argumentative braggart, and the moralizing narrator seem ridiculous posed against the great systems of human knowledge. At the same time, the lowly speakers make the knowledge itself seem suspect. The methods of proof and logical speculation as employed by barnyard orators and simple-minded priests suddenly seem comical, doubtful, and pretentious.

The digressions, then, contribute to an underlying theme of "The Nun's Priest's Tale": the pervasiveness, and indeed the inevitability, of vanity. The stylistically inflated speeches are themselves illustrations of vanity, punctured repeatedly by the deadpan reminders that the tale is really about a cock and hen. It is the ironic counterpoint between the lofty set pieces and low-life activity (for example, Chauntecleer's "treading" Pertelote) that makes all the grandiose pretensions seem foolhardy and ridiculous.

Finally, the rhetorical exhibitions contribute to the comic tone of the tale. There is a playful quality to the showy orations in which the speakers pompously offer their scientific explanations, pagan and scriptural examples, and citations of authority. Pertelote's elaborate encomium of purges is absurd because the subject matter is so indecorous, especially in light of her "romantic" role as beautiful damsel. Chauntecleer's catalogue of "ensamples" becomes a game of ingenious elaboration as he comes up with proof after proof confirming that dreams are infallibly true. And the narrator's comments on destiny and womankind, coming in the midst of Chauntecleer's confrontation with the fox, comically interrupt the story with an academic discussion, leaving the reader in suspense about the outcome of the crisis. Thus, each of these exercises in logic and eloquence is both an entertaining set piece and an illustration of the comic irrelevancy of self-display. They keep the satire light and amusing without sacrificing the satiric point.

4.12 What stylistic devices contribute to the mock-heroic tone of "The Nun's Priest's Tale"? Discuss their cumulative effect.

Answer   Many features of "The Nun's Priest's Tale" are borrowed from the elevated literary modes of the epic and the chivalric romance. Among these features are:

1. The description of Chauntecleer as hero (lines 29–44; 359–363)
2. The description of Pertelote as a court lady (lines 49–55)
3. The fateful dream (lines 72–87) which ironically comes true
4. The interpolated tales about dreams that have come true (lines 154–329)
5. The use of elaborate circumlocution to establish time (lines 367–370)
6. The narrator's moralistic commentary on the story (on the transience of joy [lines 385–389]; on necessity versus free will [lines 414–430]; on women [lines 430–439]; on flattery [lines 505–510 and 616–617]; on fortune [lines 582–584])
7. The apostrophe to a god ("O Venus," lines 522–526)
8. The elevated comparisons to figures from legends of Troy, Carthage, and Rome (lines 535–545 and 549–553)

Human pretensions of all kinds are satirized by the use of these inflated descriptions in a story about barnyard fowls. When aired in a chicken coop, the heroic ideal, the aristocratic code of courtly love, fashionable opinions about medicine, dreams, and fate, and proverbial wisdom all become ridiculous.

The success of the satire depends not only on the discrepancy between the elaborate language and the trivial subject but also on the narrator's deadpan style of reporting. It is significant that, apart from Chauntecleer's interpolated tales about dreams, the mock-heroic rhetoric belongs not to the characters but to the narrator. With tongue in cheek he steadfastly maintains that his story is true (lines 391–392); laments his rhetorical inadequacy (lines 527–534); passionately cries out against murder ("O false mordrour, lurking in thy den!" [lines 406–409]); and bewails Chauntecleer's betrayal by his patron saint Venus ("Why woldestou suffre him on thy day to die?" [line 526]). As a writer the narrator is both self-conscious and highly emotional; ostensibly concerned about matters of authenticity and style, he is at the same time caught up in the drama he is describing. He thus exhibits some of the same comic inconsistencies as Chauntecleer himself. Both seem to talk for the sheer pleasure of talking and have trouble bringing an argument to a conclusion. Both also have an eye on their effect on their audience. Thus Chauntecleer adduces a number of authorities to prove his point about dreams (St. Kenelm, line 290; Macrobeus, lines 302–306; Daniel, lines 307–309; Joseph, lines 310–312; Pharaoh, lines 313–315; Cresus, lines 318–320; Andromache, lines 321–327), but ends by placating his wife and entirely forgetting the dream about the fox which motivated his lengthy oration in the first place. The narrator goes on at length considering the question of necessity versus free will (lines 414–430), making some fine distinctions along the way (for example, defining "simple necessitee" in contrast to "necessitee condicionel"), but ending with "I wol nat han to do of swich matere:/ My tale is of a cok" (lines 431–432). He goes on to attack "Wommenes conseils" (line 436) but then, for fear of offending women, retracts his argument, comically attempting to put the speech into Chauntecleer's mouth ("Thise been the cokkes wordes and nat mine:/ I can noon harm of no womman divine" [lines 445–446]). In a sense Chauntecleer and the narrator seem to be in competition for the limelight. Both are persuasive and charming verbal show-offs, bent on impressing their audiences.

The linguistic inflation exhibited by both the narrator and the hero of the tale has thematic significance. The narrator's straight-faced advice to the reader to discern the moral implications of the story ("Taketh the fruit, and lat the chaf be stille" [line 623]) ignores the fact that "The Nun's Priest's Tale" is practically all chaff. The tendency of the language to overextend itself and become pure fluff makes it an unreliable medium for statements about human nature, moral values, or philosophical truths. The failings of the language are exactly the failings of the human beings, and beasts, who speak it. Thus a story about vanity and self-love is told in an exhibitionistic style which is the equivalent of Chauntecleer's crowing.

B.S.

SUGGESTED READINGS

Donaldson, E. T., *Chaucer's Poetry: An Anthology for the Modern Reader* (1958).

Howard, Donald R., *The Idea of the Canterbury Tales* (1976).

Robertson, D. W., Jr., *A Preface to Chaucer: Studies in Medieval Perspectives* (1962).

Schoeck, Richard, and Jerome Taylor, eds., *Chaucer Criticism: The Canterbury Tales*, Vol. I (1960).

THE SECOND SHEPHERDS' PLAY

C H R O N O L O G Y

Fifth Century — The remnants of classical theater, as performed in Rome, are suppressed on moral grounds by the late Roman emperors, who have been converted to Christianity. As a result, there will be virtually no regular theatrical activity in Europe throughout the early Middle Ages.

Tenth and Eleventh Centuries — The first glimmerings of a rebirth of the theater occur, within the context of the church itself. Dramatic elements of the Christian liturgy, such as the sections of the Mass narrating Christ's Last Supper, begin to be elaborated by the use of dialoguelike antiphonal chanting and dramatic gestures. These brief dramatic scenes slowly grow into devotional playlets, though they remain part of the liturgy.

Twelfth Century — By this time, some religious drama has moved outside the confines of the liturgy. Christmas and Passion plays, for example, are now performed outside the church building and are no longer part of the Mass. The play *Adam*, depicting the Creation and Fall of Man, is one of the best examples of this early drama; written in Anglo-Norman French, it may have been performed in England and probably represents a forerunner of the cycle plays of later centuries.

1311 — Pope Clement V sets aside the Thursday after Trinity Sunday as a holy day celebrating Christ's institution of the Mass at the Last Supper. Known as Corpus Christi Day, it is to include a procession, out of which will later grow the processional productions of the cycle plays. Corpus Christi Day usually falls in June, when the weather is generally conducive to outdoor performances.

1318   Date of the earliest recorded Corpus Christi processions in England.

1378   By this date, the Corpus Christi cycle plays are being performed in York and probably elsewhere in England. The plays, produced by the various craft and merchant guilds of a town under the auspices of the church, depict events of Old and New Testament history from the Creation through the life of Christ and down to the Second Coming and the Last Judgment. In some towns, the plays are performed on wagons that move in procession from place to place; members of the audience could sit in one location and see all the plays in turn. In other towns, the pageant wagons seem to be stationary, with the audience moving from one location to the next.

Texts of four English pageant cycles still exist: the York cycle, containing forty-eight pageants; the Wakefield cycle, thirty-two pageants; the so-called N Town cycle (sometimes called the *Ludus Coventriae*), forty-three pageants; and the Chester pageants from other cycles. However, the best known of all the extant pageants are the highly sophisticated plays from the Wakefield cycle attributed to the anonymous author, probably a cleric, known as the Wakefield Master. *The Second Shepherds' Play* is one of these.

1457   Recorded visit of Queen Margaret to Coventry, where she sees the cycle plays performed in procession. Within a few decades, however, local productions by guilds appear to be on the decline in most English towns. It is possible that professional or semiprofessional acting troupes may have begun taking the plays on tour from town to town instead.

1565   Date of a manuscript containing the inventory of possessions of the Grocers Guild of Norwich, featuring the fullest extant description of a pageant wagon (a "howse of waynskott painted and builded on a carte with fowre whelys").

1567   Queen Elizabeth I sees four pageant plays at Coventry; however, they are apparently performed at fixed locations by this time, with the audience moving from stage to stage for the different plays.

1576   The cycle plays have been in decline for about a century. They are now dealt a deathblow by the passage of laws forbidding the representation of Christ or God on stage as idolatrous. (The reformed English church is behind this repression.) As of this date, the Wakefield productions are halted. Throughout England, the master copies of the pageants, mostly in the possession of parish churches, are destroyed—hence the small number of manuscripts of the plays surviving into the twentieth century.

ESSAY QUESTIONS WITH ANSWERS

5.1 *The Second Shepherds' Play* has two parts: the first climaxes in the discovery of the stolen sheep in the cradle; the second, in the adoration of the Christ child in the manger. Discuss the relationship between these two scenes.

Answer The scene in which Mak's theft of the sheep comes to light has the qualities of farce. Set in the rural hut of Mak and Gill, the episode is filled with comedy based on the efforts of the husband and wife to assert that the stolen sheep is indeed their child. Knowing the truth, the audience recognizes the comic double meanings behind such remarks as Mak and Gill's declaration that they would rather eat their own child than deceive the shepherds. However, this farcical scene is not merely irrelevant to the serious sacred scene it precedes. The scene of the sheep in the cradle parodies the Nativity of Christ, the Lamb of God. Both nativities are set in humble surroundings and are attended by three adoring shepherds who bring gifts to the newborn baby. Furthermore, both center on an infant "disguised"—the sheep dressed in child's clothing, Christ incarnate in human form.

It may be argued that the mock-nativity staged by the scoundrel Mak is incongruous, perhaps even sacrilegious. However, the farcical incident prepares for the religious climax in several ways. The parallels between the two nativities reinforce the significance of Christ's birth for the ordinary Christian laborer. In addition, the comic version illuminates the central mystery of the Nativity; the strangeness of the divine birth is prefigured by the comic "miracle" of the sheep born to Mak and Gill. The shepherds' generosity toward the "child" in each episode symbolizes the significance of Christ's birth as the triumph of love and charity.

For the Christian, the birth of Christ represents God's decisive intervention in human history, by which the merely human was redeemed. Watching the henpecked, grumbling, deceitful Mak, for whom the birth of a child is only an economic hardship rather than a miracle, the audience would have recognized the contrast to the state of grace made possible for human beings by Christ's birth.

5.2 Which of the following interpretations of Mak's character are best supported by the play? Why?

1. Mak is the devil, an agent of evil who appears in disguise and uses the arts of magic to deceive the good shepherds.
2. Mak is a Falstaff, a merry rogue who plays tricks on his unsuspecting fellows.
3. Mak represents unredeemed man, a sinner, who promises to reform and, by the grace of the shepherds, escapes serious punishment.
4. Mak represents Joseph, husband of Mary and foster parent of a miraculous child.
5. Mak is a criminal who represents a threat to society and must be expelled.

Answer Interpretations 2 and 3 are the best, as they capture both the realistic and symbolic aspects of Mak's character. Part of his dramatic function is to provide an element of farce, which would have appealed to the townsfolk gathered to watch the cycle of mystery plays. His mimicry of a southern English accent, his lively bickering with his wife, and his ingenious answers to the shepherds' questions establish him as a trickster figure who lends humor and life to the drama. In this sense, he dimly prefigures a character like Falstaff, Shakespeare's roguish yet lovable buffoon.

On the symbolic level, Mak represents the nature of "everyman" since the Fall of Adam. Although he is the obvious sinner among good shepherds, his sin symbolizes original sin, whereby man is fallen and must be redeemed by the grace of God.

Interpretation 4 is correct in seeing Mak as part of the "Holy Family" in a mock-nativity, but the parodic aspect of the parallel should be emphasized. Mak is no Joseph but a burlesque Joseph who lacks the dignity and submission to God's will that characterize the true Joseph. Interpretation 1, in its simple equation of Mak and the devil, works against the comic tone of the play. It also contradicts the plot: the devil as the embodiment of evil is eternally damned, while Mak seems capable of redemption. Interpretation 5 likewise ignores Mak's comic qualities and the happy resolution of the episode through the intervention of the shepherds. He is not hanged, but only "tossed in a blanket," a playful form of punishment, and he promises to reform. Notions of expulsion and execution are foreign to the world of the play, where divine grace operates to save all humanity.

5.3   *The Second Shepherds' Play* contains many anachronistic references to events that had not occurred by the historical time of Christ's nativity. Among these anachronisms are the numerous oaths using the names of Christ and Mary, the allusions to England (which did not exist as a nation at the time of Christ), and the references to the feudal system, which did not come into being until the Middle Ages. Discuss the effect of these anachronisms in the play.

Answer   At first glance, these references might appear confusing to the audience, because they destroy the sense of historical time and place. We might assume that the playwright forgot the historical facts and naively transposed the action to his own era and country, fourteenth-century England.

However, this view neglects the medieval playwright's religious conception of time and place. By including anachronistic references, he reflected the theological view of the timelessness of divine history: past, present, and future exist simultaneously in the eye of God, and the events of Christ's life transcend historical time. Furthermore, the familiar oaths and contemporary place names give the biblical story of the Nativity an immediacy for the audience.

5.4   *The Second Shepherds' Play* opens with a series of three complaints delivered by the shepherds and closes with the shepherds singing together in celebration of Christ's birth. Contrast these two scenes.

Answer   The opening complaints show each of the shepherds in isolation, lamenting his wretched condition. Coll complains of the bitter weather and his mistreatment by rich landholders, Gib bemoans his shrewish wife, and Daw complains of the cold and his physical discomfort. Together these speeches suggest the hard lot of the impoverished laborer in fourteenth-century England and establish a social theme in the play. There is a strong bias against the powerful throughout the drama, a rough satirizing of institutions and authorities.

At the end of the play, we see the three shepherds joyously adoring the Savior. Instead of laments, Coll, Gib, and Daw offer gifts and hymns of praise. Instead of isolation, the scene portrays unity and harmony. So, more broadly, does the shepherds' forgiving Mak for his crimes at the play's end.

Thus, the play moves from the realm of social and secular discontent to that of divine fulfillment, representing the redemption of humanity through God's grace. The emphasis on poverty in the opening episodes of the play is repeated but transformed in the scene in the manger. Not only is Christ himself poor ("In a crib was he laid,/ He was poorly arrayed" [lines 688–689]), but he is also redeemer of the poor and oppressed. The Christian doctrine "The meek shall inherit the earth" is given dramatic form in the play.

K.L.

SUGGESTED READINGS

Kolve, V. A., *The Play Called Corpus Christi* (1966).
Woolf, Rosemary, *The English Mystery Plays* (1972).

EVERYMAN

C H R O N O L O G Y

1350–
1400

Popularity of the so-called *Pater Noster* plays in several English towns, including York, Lincoln, and Beverley. These plays, apparently performed from pageant wagons in much the same manner as the Corpus Christi plays, are designed to instruct the laypeople of the church in the meaning of the Lord's Prayer; they involve dramatization of the seven deadly sins, against which the seven petitions of the Lord's Prayer are thought to be directed. In their allegorical quality, the *Pater Noster* plays foreshadow the later morality plays, such as *Everyman*.

1405–
1425

Approximate date of *The Castle of Perseverance*, the first complete morality play we have. Like *Everyman*, it dramatizes the moral struggles of an individual Christian by the use of allegorical characters representing virtues and vices. It is also a good deal longer than *Everyman*, and not as interesting. The manuscript of *The Castle of Perseverance* is unique in containing a detailed diagram with instructions for stage production, calling for a large circular arena with a castle in the center and surrounded by four scaffolds from which actors would speak. It can be inferred that the fifteenth- and sixteenth-century productions of morality plays were often elaborate and colorful affairs.

1465

Approximate date of *Mankind*, another important morality play.

1480

Approximate date of *Wisdom*, yet another.

1495

Publication of the Dutch morality play *Elckerlijc*, by Peter Dorland of Diest. Because of its strong similarities to *Everyman*, many have speculated that one of the two plays may be a version of the other, or perhaps that both derive from some source no longer extant. In any case, a comparison of the two plays shows *Everyman*'s closeness to continental religious thought in the emphasis on the role of the institution of the church in the salvation of the individual. *Everyman* is probably written at around this same time.

1508   First publication of *Everyman*; it will be reprinted three times during the next three decades. Throughout the first half of the sixteenth century, the morality play is the dominant dramatic form in England. Numerous morality plays are written, most of them apparently for performance by itinerant acting troupes. Some moralities are also written for noble or courtly audiences, often by well-known authors and scholars.

1516   *Magnificence*, by the poet laureate John Skelton; an example of the morality play by a learned professional author for a noble audience.

1550–
1600   Morality plays continue to be popular, alongside the humanist dramas of Medwall and Heywood and the early Elizabethan dramas of Greene, Peele, Kyd, and Marlowe. Examples of late morality plays: *Enough Is As Good As a Feast*, by William Wager, and *The Conflict of Conscience*, by Nathaniel Woodes.

1901   After centuries of neglect by readers and critics, interest in *Everyman* is revived by the London production of William Poel.

1911   Hugo von Hofmannsthal's German translation, *Jedermann*, is produced at Salzburg. The best-known modern stage presentation of *Everyman*, it becomes an annual event at Salzburg after 1920, except for the period 1937–1945, when the Nazi regime forbids its presentation.

ESSAY QUESTIONS WITH ANSWERS

6.1   Discuss the message of the play *Everyman* and the technical means by which it is dramatized.

Answer   *Everyman* is an allegory of human preparation for death; the characters are abstractions which represent forces in the world affecting the human soul. By using the allegorical method the playwright is able to convey his didactic message to the audience. The central message of the play is that only good deeds can redeem a person from eternal damnation. Worldly goods, friends and relations, physical attributes, and even knowledge cannot win God's favor. Furthermore, the drama emphasizes the solitude of "everyman"; each human being must go alone to meet his maker, stripped not only of the props of society but even of those personal qualities that make a person valuable in life. Everyman himself represents the figure of Adam as the archetypal man; as a result of the Fall, man is fated to die and may be saved only by the grace of God.

This doctrine of salvation is conveyed by the interaction of a series of personified forces with Everyman. The false friends all desert him, and the good attributes rally around him, but only Good Deeds descends with him into the grave. The characters in the play do not represent personal characteristics of a particular man but rather the general features of human behavior. The speeches of the characters are not personally expressive or idiosyncratic; rather, they serve as vehicles for the didactic themes of the play.

By means of the allegorical presentation, the conflict takes place among the characters rather than within the soul of Everyman himself. The allegory makes visible what would otherwise be a purely internal struggle. Consequently, the resulting drama is not psychological in the modern sense. Instead it is a kind of sermon made more vivid, concrete, and meaningful by theatrical presentation.

6.2   The modern reader might consider the plot of *Everyman* a miserable failure: it is thin, boring, repetitive, simplistic, and predictable. Furthermore, it has neither a turning point nor a climax, and it ends in bleak despair with

Everyman descending into the grave. To what extent can *Everyman* be defended against these charges?

Answer   *Everyman* may be simple in design, yet it is neither simplistic nor static. The interactions between Everyman and his false friends provide the dramatic moments of the play. For example, Fellowship first offers his unconditional aid and then almost comically reverses himself as soon as he learns of Everyman's destination. This act of abandonment is repeated by Kindred and Cousin, the repetition heightening the viewer's sense of Everyman's isolation. The final rejection of Everyman by his "allies"—Knowledge, Beauty, Five Wits, Discretion, Strength—is another painful twist of the plot which occurs at the end of the play.

The generally repetitive and predictable quality of the action is significant in two ways. First, the repeated desertions of Everyman dramatize the slow and painful act of separation from the world, as the individual is gradually stripped of all his human entanglements and attachments in order to confront God as a naked soul. Second, the repetitions of the play serve to remind the audience of a home truth it would prefer to forget:

> The story saith: Man, in the beginning
> Look well, and take good heed to the ending,
> Be you never so gay.
>
> (lines 10–13)

From the moment when Everyman is suddenly, in the midst of life, surprised by Death, the effect is of something at once familiar and profound. It is by presenting again and again exactly what the audience anticipates that the play acts as a vivid reminder of the story every man knows. Instead of moral ambiguity and tragic choice, the play dramatizes inevitability, illustrating the familiar truths of human experience: *memento mori* ("remember death") and *sic transit gloria mundi* ("thus passes the glory of the earth").

Despite the familiarity and inevitability of the action, the play does offer a final crisis and resolution. The major turning point of the plot is the moment at which Good Deeds, who is lying on the floor weak and prostrate through most of the action, finds the strength to arise and join Everyman in his pilgrimage. In religious terms, this is the act which reverses the inevitability of man's fate. Death is not the ultimate destination, for Good Deeds is man's salvation, providing the means to achieve a further life beyond the grave.

The final action of the play, the descent of Everyman and Good Deeds into the grave, is the resolution of the plot, the ultimate climax of the soul's pilgrimage. Since, according to Christian belief, man dies in order to gain eternal life, the image of descent bears the symbolic resonance of the soul's ascent. The play is thus not solely a reminder of human mortality and a dramatization of tragic inevitability; it implies a kind of choice and holds forth the promise of spiritual immortality.

6.3 Discuss the characterization of Fellowship and compare him with the other personifications in the play.

Answer Although Fellowship represents an abstract idea, he does suggest a type of human personality. He is a hail-fellow-well-met who turns out to be a fair-weather friend. The dramatist gives Fellowship many speeches protesting his devotion and fidelity and then just as many forswearing his promise and emphatically refusing aid. Thus the lines "For, in faith, and thou go to hell,/ I will not forsake thee by the way" (lines 232–233) are directly negated by "In faith, then will not I come there!" (line 262). The effect is of absurd self-contradiction as the character performs an abrupt about-face. In the figure of Fellowship, which presents a recognizable, though comically simplified, portrait of a real social type, allegory overlaps with caricature.

Other characters in *Everyman*, while lacking the solidity and presence of Fellowship, have moments when they exhibit an arrestingly individual quality. Thus Cousin suffers a comical discomfiture similar to Fellowship's; he is driven to retract his former vow ("we will live and die togither" [line 324]) with a "lame" excuse: "No, by Our Lady! I have the cramp in my toe:/ Trust not to me" (lines 356–357). There is a hint of grief and fear in Beauty's response to Everyman's fate ("What, into this grave, alas?" [line 794]), which contrasts with Strength's tough indifference ("Thy game liketh me not at all" [line 809]).

Nonetheless, most of the other abstractions in the play lack the rounded human dimensions of Fellowship. For example, Goods does not behave like any recognizable human figure; he exists mainly to deliver a speech on the vanity of worldly possession. Five Wits, Beauty, and Discretion are almost indistinguishable. The distinctive treatment of Fellowship may derive from the fact that "fellowship" refers to a feeling among human beings, rather than to our relation to material objects or physical qualities.

6.4 Though understanding the central message of *Everyman* requires no special knowledge of theology, two characters in the play represent specific aspects of Christian doctrine. Explain the significance assigned to Good Deeds and Confession for the salvation of the individual Christian soul.

Answer   According to fifteenth-century Catholic dogma, good deeds (or "works") were a necessary step toward redemption. Furthermore, the priest as intercessor and the seven sacraments, including penance, as ritual acts of purification were intended to help the individual sinner toward a state of grace.

Everyman, written in the fifteenth century, is a pre-Reformation play. In contrast to the Protestant emphasis on salvation by faith, the drama places much emphasis on salvation by works and on the sacramental acts administered by a priest. This emphasis sets the individual's struggle for grace firmly in a social context. Instead of a solitary, internal quest for justification by faith alone, Everyman's search for salvation is implicitly supported by his actions in the world and by the church as well. The very existence and performance of *Everyman* reinforces the sense of a social setting, since the play dramatizes for the community the plight of each member of the community. The drama brings theological doctrine to an audience which is in some sense a congregation as well. Though Everyman goes to his grave ostensibly stripped of all "companions," he paradoxically has the company and support of his deeds, his church, and his fellow human beings.

B.S.

SUGGESTED   READINGS

Cormican, L. A., "Morality Tradition and the Interludes," in *The Age of Chaucer*
    (ed. B. Ford) (1954).
Craig, H., *English Religious Drama of the Middle Ages* (1955).
de Vocht, H., *Everyman: A Comparative Study of Texts and Sources* (1947).
Nicoll, A., *The Development of the Theatre* (1937).
Young, Karl, *The Drama of the Medieval Church* (1933).

Part Three

THE RENAISSANCE

T I M E L I N E

The Age

1474: William Caxton prints the first book in English

1483: Death of Edward IV; his sons, Edward V and Prince Richard, disappear. Their disappearances are blamed on their uncle, who claims the throne as Richard III

1485: Defeat of Richard III by Henry Tudor, who ascends the throne as Henry VII

1507: Ordination of Protestant reformer Martin Luther

1508: Michelangelo begins painting the ceiling of the Sistine Chapel

1509: Death of Henry VII; accession of Henry VIII

1517: Luther posts his ninety-five Theses, begins the Protestant Reformation

1528: Severe outbreak of plague in England

1531: Henry VIII named supreme head of the church in England

1542: Inquisition established by Pope Paul III

1547: Death of Henry VIII; accession of Edward VI

1553: Death of Edward VI; accession of Mary, a Roman Catholic

1558: Death of Mary; accession of Elizabeth I, a Protestant

1574: Richard Burbage receives license to open a theater in London

1588: Defeat of the Spanish Armada; apex of England's power under Elizabeth

1592: Plague kills 15,000 in London

1595: Irish revolt suppressed

1603: Death of Elizabeth I; accession of James I

1618: Thirty Years' War begins

1620: Pilgrims sail to America on the *Mayflower*

1625: Death of James I; accession of Charles I

The Authors

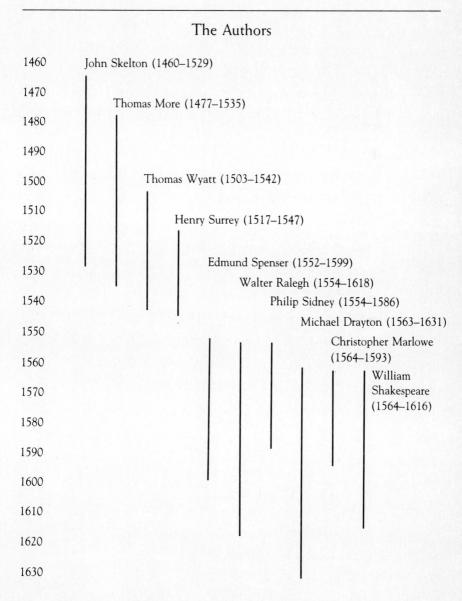

1460	John Skelton (1460–1529)
1470	
	Thomas More (1477–1535)
1480	
1490	
1500	Thomas Wyatt (1503–1542)
1510	
	Henry Surrey (1517–1547)
1520	
1530	Edmund Spenser (1552–1599)
	Walter Ralegh (1554–1618)
1540	Philip Sidney (1554–1586)
	Michael Drayton (1563–1631)
1550	
	Christopher Marlowe (1564–1593)
1560	
	William Shakespeare (1564–1616)
1570	
1580	
1590	
1600	
1610	
1620	
1630	

JOHN SKELTON

C H R O N O L O G Y

1460	Born, probably in Yorkshire. Virtually nothing is known of his background or early education, but he evidently receives some musical training.
1479	Probably receives a degree from Peterhouse College, Cambridge University, around this date.
1483	Writes his *Elegy on Edward IV*, first notable poem. Around this time is also translating works from Latin, including the letters of Cicero (these translations are now lost).
1488	Skelton probably receives title of poet laureate from Oxford University around this time; this event may be the reason Skelton set up his own calendar system, numbering years beginning with this year. Skelton also enters the service of King Henry VII as a poet and a writer of dramatic entertainments for presentation at court; he is one of many poets and scholars in the king's employ at this time, but one of the few native English ones.
1489	Writes poems commemorating events at court, including a lost poem on Prince Arthur's creation as Prince of Wales and an elegy on the earl of Northumberland. At the king's request, writes a poem responding to an attack by the French diplomat Robert Gaguin upon King Henry.
1492	Visits France as part of the king's entourage; is laureated at the University of Louvain, perhaps as a political compliment to King Henry.
1493	Laureated by Cambridge University; only poet ever so honored.

1494   Becomes tutor to Prince Henry (later King Henry VIII); lives with him at Eltham, near Greenwich. Writes Latin poem dedicated to him.

1497   Translates into English a moral allegory by Guillaume de Guilleville, *La Pélerinage de la vie humaine*, perhaps partly for the instruction of his royal pupil. This work is now lost.

1498   Is ordained as deacon and priest; spends a year in religious study, and may have written his religious lyrics at this time. Also writes *The Bowge of Court*, a dream allegory satirizing the evils of life at court (*bowge* means free room and board, to which Skelton himself was entitled).

1499   Publication of *The Bowge of Court*. Skelton meets the famous humanist scholar Desiderius Erasmus during the latter's visit to the English court.

1501   Writes *Speculum principis* (Mirror for a prince), a manual of moral instruction for Prince Henry, who is now in his teens.

1502   Skelton loses his position as royal tutor in a reorganization at court.

1504   Skelton is given the living of the parish of Diss in Norfolk, probably as a reward for his years of royal service; will retain the nominal position of rector of the parish until his death, although he lives at Diss only a small part of the time.

1505   Receives honorary M.A. degree from Cambridge. Is at work on his most characteristic poems, such as the mock-elegy *Philip Sparrow*; it is thought that most of his poems in the so-called skeltonic meter date from his years at Diss. Skelton also develops a reputation as a bawdy-tongued, wild-living man at this time; many legends about his misadventures grow up, to be collected and published many years after his death as the *Merie Tales of Skelton*.

1509   Is probably in London for the coronation of his former pupil King Henry VIII; presents him with a commemorative peom beginning, "The Rose both White and Rede/ In one Rose now dothe grow," one of the earliest literary representations of the union of the houses of Lancaster and York in the symbol of the two roses.

1511   Hoping for a place at court, Skelton presents the king with a volume containing a revised version of his *Speculum principis* together with a *Complaint to the King* (a humorous poem lamenting his lack of royal favor).

1512   Is evidently living at court again by this time. Writes Latin verses praising Henry, and presents the king with a personally annotated copy of the *Chronique de rains*, a book about King Richard the Lion-Hearted. Is named *orator regius* (court poet and rhetorician).

1513   Accompanies King Henry on a trip to France. Commemorates Battle of Flodden Field in the *Ballade of the Scottyshe King*.

1514   On the invitation of the king, takes part in the first recorded English flyting (a duel of insult and invective); result is the *Poems against Garnesche*.

1516   Writes *Magnificence*, his only surviving play; it is an allegory satirizing follies at court. Also *Against Venomous Tongues*, the first in a series of poems attacking Cardinal Wolsey, Henry's powerful adviser.

1521   Writes *Speak, Parrot*, another satire against Wolsey; it makes its point so discreetly and with such heavily veiled symbolism that it is exceedingly hard to interpret today.

1522   Writes *Colin Clout*, another anti-Wolsey satire. Also writes *The Tunning of Elinor Rumming*, a comical poem caricaturing an alewife and her eccentric customers; one of Skelton's most popular poems.

1523   Writes *Why Come Ye Not to Court?*, his last anti-Wolsey satire. Hereafter, when Skelton mentions Wolsey, it is to compliment him; the cardinal's enmity may have grown too dangerous. Publication of the *Garland of Laurel*, an account of and defense of his own life in allegorical verse.

1526   Several lyrics published in *Dyvers Balettys*, an anthology.

1528   Publishes *A Replication against Certain Young Scholars*, an attack on the heresy of two Cambridge students; Skelton had a lifelong reputation as hating heresy, especially in the form of Lutheranism.

1529   Death of Skelton. He is buried in the parish church at Westminster.

1568   First collected edition of Skelton's works is published.

ESSAY QUESTIONS WITH ANSWERS

Colin Clout

7.1 Near the beginning of the poem, the narrator announces his name and his intentions:

> I purpose to shake out
> All my conning bag,
> Like a clerkly hag.
> (lines 4–6)

Skelton thus establishes the genre of the poem: a satiric commentary on the world by a learned old man ("a clerkly hag"). How does this passage contribute to the satiric persona of Colin Clout?

Answer Colin Clout characterizes his own poetic style in terms suggesting a buffeted, unkempt, beggarly scarecrow. Numerous adjectives—"ragged," "tattered," "jagged," "rain-beaten," "rusty," "moth-eaten" (lines 7–10)—evoke the idea of shabby clothing or armor, seemingly inappropriate garb for a scholarly observer of society. But Clout's stylistic "dress" *is* appropriate in the sense that it accords with the decorum of satire. The sixteenth-century notion of satire, derived from the classical conception of the genre, called for the use of rough meter and harsh language to chastise social and moral abuses. (Renaissance writers believed, mistakenly, that the word "satire" was etymologically linked to the name of the ancient Greek goat-man, the satyr; accordingly, they assumed that satire should be rude and rough in style, as befitting the unmannerly satyr.) The satirist, then, was an indignant man, who vented his moral disapproval in the plain speech of invective. Thus Colin Clout is referring to an established stylistic convention when he rejects beautiful, seductive language and gilded rhetoric for the blunt honesty of the satiric voice.

The idea that a poem contains a kernel of truth (a "pith," line 12) hidden beneath the language but visible to the discerning reader ("If ye take well therewith," line 11) is another conventional literary notion to which the narrator appeals. Renaissance literary theory generally stressed the ethical significance of poetry, the pill of instruction beneath the sugar-coated surface of words. Here, although the surface is rude, not polished, the same notion of delving beneath the appearances applies. The satirist, as truthteller and oracle, engages in riddling diatribes which must be properly interpreted to be understood.

The meter, like the imagery, contributes to our understanding of Colin Clout's satiric role. Skelton's distinctive meter, known as skeltonic, conveys by its jagged and irregular but emphatic rhythms a quality of impetuous, breathless speech. Short lines containing two or three beats and rhyming in units of two, three, four, or more lines create the effect of a spontaneous, urgent utterance. This metrical pattern probably derives from Old English prosody, in which alliterated accents were loosely distributed over a four-beat line consisting of two hemistichs, or half-lines. Thus Old English verse fell naturally into two-beat units, with the accents at irregular intervals. Skelton retains the colloquial energy of the older alliterative verse, but adds a driving impulse through the element of rhyme and the emphasis on brief bursts of speech. The satirist appears as a man stung into speech, driven by his outrage and scorn to harsh, plain-spoken, "artless" outbursts.

Skelton uses both imagery and meter to establish a certain kind of narrator for his poem—a speaker who is to be trusted precisely because of his homely diction, his rude versifying, and his urgent tone. By drawing on the conventions of satire as they were understood at the time, he creates a persuasive persona to articulate his moral criticisms of a corrupt society.

7.2   Skelton's critique of society begins with the sweeping statement

> For, as far as I can see,
> It is wrong with each degree.
> (lines 13–14)

He elaborates on this thesis by focusing on the conflict between laymen and churchmen. Discuss the perspective from which Colin Clout offers his satiric comments.

Answer   Colin Clout, standing apart from society as an acute spectator, seems to view its follies from afar. From this satiric vantage point, the whole world appears to be topsy-turvy. Invoking the medieval concept of "degree," Clout points to the disorder which has disrupted the normal and proper hierarchical relationships in society. Instead of harmonious interaction among the various stations or levels on the social ladder, ". . . each of other blother [babble],/ The one against the other" (lines 20–21). The strife between laity and ecclesiastics is of particular gravity, for the clerical abuses that occasion that strife represent a perversion of the spiritual role of God's ministers. Rather than shepherding the souls of those under their protection, the prelates

> . . . been so haut,
> They say, and look so high
> As though they woulde fly
> Above the starry sky.
> (lines 25–28)

Skelton thus locates the ills of the world in vices which pervert and disorder the God-ordained design of human relationships. Envy, wrath, and "babbling" against one's neighbor destroy Christian amity and good fellowship. Pride, the first of the seven deadly sins, causes churchmen to strive ambitiously upward in a search for temporal wealth and power, abandoning their responsibility for the spiritual well-being of their brethren.

Colin Clout's railing against the world primarily takes the form of antiecclesiastical satire. Concentrating on the vices of the clergy, he uses the sinning churchman as the type of fallen Adam and an example of errant mankind. The traditional satiric perspective—that is, the penetrating, disinterested view which unerringly diagnoses disease and disorder—and the late-medieval theme of clerical abuses, prominent in works ranging from Langland's *Piers Plowman* to Chaucer's *Canterbury Tales*, together condition the nature of Skelton's poem.

"Mannerly Margery Milk and Ale"

7.3 Discuss the tone of the poem.

Answer The tone of the poem is to some degree ambiguous, as is the dramatic situation, because the whole ballad consists of a somewhat enigmatic and fragmentary dialogue. The punctuation and line assignments of any given version of the poem are the result of editorial emendations rather than firm textual evidence. Nonetheless, it is possible to discern a general modulation in the poem's tone from comic bawdry at the beginning to a note of poignancy in the final stanza. The lively, colloquial dialogue between the seductive clerk and "Mannerly Margery," with its many idiomatic expressions and exclamations, has the quality of a comic sketch or farcical contention played out by familiar types. The animal imagery (popinjay, pode [toad], hackney, bull) gives the poem a bawdy air: it implies the reduction of the human activity to "barnyard doings," which we are invited to watch with amused detachment. Finally, the refrain ("With Mannerly Margery milk and ale") is wittily ironic. Although the "milk and ale" refer literally to Margery's chief domains, the dairy and alehouse, the phrase has a further implication: Margery's manners are so impeccable that, whatever the request, she will serve up *only* milk and ale.

The seduction occurs "offstage," between stanzas 3 and 4; this ironic omission of the main event of the little domestic drama contributes to a marked shift in tone. What has been a rather farcical physical tussle becomes a small but revealing exposure of human nature: the male deceiver is revealed as a callous dealer in flesh ("The best cheap flesh that ever I bought" [line 24]), and the saucy servingmaid is shown as suddenly vulnerable ("Wed me, or else I die for thought" [line 26]).

Skelton thus takes a traditional theme of the romantic ballad, the maid betrayed, and combines its bawdy and tragic elements in a subtle mixture of tones.

B.S.

SUGGESTED READINGS

Carpenter, Nan C., *John Skelton* (1967).
Fish, Stanley E., *John Skelton's Poetry* (1965).
Nelson, William, *John Skelton, Laureate* (1939; reprinted, 1969).

THOMAS MORE

C H R O N O L O G Y

1477	Born in London. Son of John More, a prosperous lawyer. Little is known of More's mother, who died during his infancy. He attended St. Anthony's School in London (dates unknown).
1490	Becomes a page in the home of John Morton, archbishop of Canterbury and lord chancellor of England. Service in the home of a prominent man was a common part of the education of a promising young man.
1492	Enters Oxford University, probably with the intention of pursuing a career in the church.
1494	Leaves Oxford and takes up the study of law at the New Inn in London, probably at his father's insistence.
1499	While continuing his study of law, meets the great Dutch humanist scholar and author Desiderius Erasmus, who is then visiting England; this begins a lifelong friendship.
1501	Is admitted to the bar. Gives a series of public lectures on St. Augustine's theological work *The City of God*; his lectures are widely admired by the learned men who attend them. Around this time is living in a Carthusian monastery and pursuing a life of prayer and devotion while also practicing law; the combination of worldly and spiritual pursuits will characterize More throughout his life.
1504	Elected to the House of Commons. Soon gains notoriety for opposing King Henry VII in Parliament; despite his youth, engineers a defeat for the king

over a financial bill. As a result, receives threats against his life, and is forced to leave politics until the king's death in 1509.

1505   Marries Jane Colt. Meets with Erasmus for the second time. Translates from Latin *The Life of John Picus*, the biography of a contemplative Italian scholar, after whom some say More wished to model his own life.

1506   With Erasmus, writes a series of translations from the Latin author Lucian.

1510   By this time has established a highly successful London law practice. Is elected to Parliament again, and also named under-sheriff of London (legal counselor to the city government). *The Life of John Picus* published.

1511   Death of More's wife; he later marries widow Alice Middleton.

1515   Is sent by the king to Flanders to negotiate a commercial contract with Prince Charles of Castile. Meets with European humanists; probably begins writing of *Utopia* in Latin.

1516   *Utopia* completed and published in France. More refuses offer of a royal pension, wishing to owe his loyalty to the city of London, still his primary employers.

1517   More defends the rioters after the Evil May Day demonstrations (involving attacks by Englishmen on foreign workers). Represents the pope in a quarrel with King Henry VIII. Is sent on another diplomatic mission to France; becomes a member of the king's council.

1518   Resigns his position with the city of London in order to resolve the conflict between his service to the king and to the city. Third edition of *Utopia* printed, including More's *Epigrammata*, a collection of almost 300 poems in Latin, some original, some translations from the Greek Anthology. Publication of More's *Letter to Germanus Brixius*, setting forth his humanist theory of education. Around this time, More is educating his own children and those of some of his relatives at home; he is among the first to educate daughters along the same lines as sons, and More's daughters will later be distinguished scholars and writers in their own right.

1521   More named under-treasurer and chancellor of the exchequer. Is knighted. Visits Bruges and Calais on diplomatic mission.

1522   Writes with his daughter Margaret *The Four Last Things*, a treatise on mortality.

1523   Elected Speaker of the House of Commons. Publishes, under a pseudonym, the *Responsio ad Lutherum*, defending the Roman Catholic church against the criticisms of Martin Luther.

1524	Named high steward of Oxford University.

1525   Named high steward of Cambridge University. Resigns position as under-treasurer; is named chancellor of the duchy of Lancaster. Known as one of the king's closest advisers.

1526   Is a leader in the seizing and burning of Lutheran books in England.

1529   Publishes the *Dialogue concerning Tyndale*, an anti-Lutheran tract. Sent to France as a diplomat, where he succeeds in heading off a possible alliance of France and Spain against England. After the fall of Cardinal Wolsey, More's chief rival among the advisers of Henry VIII, is named lord chancellor.

1531   King Henry, unable to obtain permission from the pope to divorce his wife Catherine, forces the English clergy to acknowledge him supreme head of the church in England. Growing conflict between Henry and More, who is a firm supporter of the papacy.

1532   More resigns the chancellorship, claiming ill health; his real motives probably include his unhappiness over Henry's seizure of control over the church and his desire to devote more time to study and writing.

1533   Publication of the *Apology of Sir Thomas More*. Henry has the English church grant an annulment of his marriage to Catherine, freeing him to marry Anne Boleyn. More refuses to attend Anne's coronation.

1534   The Act of Succession is passed, acknowledging the validity of Henry's marriage to Anne Boleyn. More refuses to swear an oath confirming the act, saying that it would violate his conscience. Is imprisoned in the Tower of London. Writes A *Dialogue of Comfort against Tribulation*, a devotional masterpiece setting forth Christian consolation for human suffering. Also writes a "Treatise on the Passion" and other devotional works.

1535   Is tried and condemned for treason and beheaded.

1551   Publication of Ralphe Robinson's English translation of *Utopia*.

1557   Publication by More's nephew William Rastell of More's collected English works.

ESSAY QUESTIONS WITH ANSWERS

Utopia

8.1 Raphael Hythlodaeus, the wayfarer who reports on the customs and practices of the Utopians, is the chief character in *Utopia*. However, More creates a conflict of viewpoints by introducing a fictional version of himself to question and at times oppose Hythlodaeus. Compare the beliefs of these two characters and analyze the significance of their contrasting opinions.

Answer The two men are diametrically opposed in their views: Hythlodaeus is a moral absolutist and idealist, "More" (the character) a moral relativist and realist. The contrast runs throughout *Utopia* as a whole.

Hythlodaeus is primarily a philosopher, opposing the viciousness and duplicity of practical politics with rational, ethical, and religious principles. For example, he protests against the inhumane practice of capital punishment by citing divine law: " 'God has said, "Thou shalt not kill," and shall we so lightly kill a man for taking a bit of small change?' " (Book I). He refuses to participate in government on the grounds that the advice of a truly learned man would be rejected by royal councils, which are devoted only to self-interest.

"More" responds by urging pragmatic, flexible policies. He mentions "another philosophy, more practical for statesmen, which knows its stage, adapts itself to the play in hand, and performs its role neatly and appropriately. . . . Whatever play is being performed, perform it as best you can" (Book I). "More" suggests that, although the world is imperfect, it is the only "stage" available to man, and the realistic choice is to act in that world. In general, More is skeptical of perfect worlds—utopias—since man himself is an imperfect creature with irrational passions and vices: "For it is impossible that all should be well unless all men were good, a situation which I do not expect for a great many years to come!" (Book I).

At the end of Book II, the two views first stated in Book I are sharply contrasted. Hythlodaeus delivers an impassioned speech against the injustice of wealth and the evils which greed and pride produce in a commonwealth. Following this outburst, "More" reflects that the Utopians are especially absurd in trying to maintain a state which abolishes money, but he refrains from saying this to Hythlodaeus, who, he thinks, is too dogmatic to tolerate any criticism. Once again, idealism clashes with pragmatism.

Despite the fact that he names one of these two characters "More," More the author does not use either man simply as a mouthpiece for his own views. In fact, both characterizations are partly playful: Hythlodaeus's Greek name means "expert in trifles" or "well learned in nonsense," and the "Thomas More" in the book is deliberately caricatured as a somewhat gloomy pessimist, a "doubting Thomas." Thus More uses the contrast between the two men partly to expose the limitations of each position. Visionary idealism appears foolish next to hardheaded practicality, while skepticism appears shabby next to moral commitment. At the same time, the strong points of each position are revealed: Hythlodaeus's absolutism is attractively pure, and "More's" pragmatism attractively clear-eyed.

It is probable that More's ambiguity about his personal views is not solely a literary strategy but a practical response to the repressiveness of the contemporary political climate. He lived in an age in which a man could be imprisoned or executed not merely for espousing "incorrect" beliefs but even for failing to clearly affirm "correct" ones. More's humor and irony are thus a means of implying subtle criticism and, at the same time, protecting himself.

8.2 On what underlying principles do Utopians base their society?

Answer The foundation of the Utopian state is human reason, which is applied to all questions of domestic and public management. Rational and logical considerations, as defined by More, determine the ethics, amusements, laws, and religious practices of the inhabitants. More in this way presents a perfect opposite to the irrationality and vicious impulse which he sees as dominating sixteenth-century European society.

Pleasure, in the broad sense of that term accepted by Epicurean philosophy, is a central value of Utopian culture. Though today we normally use the word to denote the merely superficial or frivolous, pleasure as defined rationally is not antithetical to but equivalent to virtue. Any action or activity must be judged by the amount, quality, and duration of the pleasure which it produces. Given these premises, bodily pleasures and physical indulgences like eating and sex fall low on the scale, with virtuous conduct and intellectual activity at the apex. Reason dictates that the virtuous life, which promises both a lifetime of spiritual and mental fulfillment and the ultimate enjoyment of an eternal heavenly abode, is the most enduring and sublime of pleasures.

Likewise, rational analysis leads the Utopians to disdain gold and silver. The

Utopians infer from the fact that these metals are found buried in the earth that God's intention was for man to ignore or scorn them. The proverbial wisdom of the adage "The love of money is the root of all evil" informs Utopia's attitude. If riches are an invitation to the sinful passions of avarice and pride, they have no place in a rational society which substitutes reason for base instinct. Necessities and useful commodities are seen as a natural, practical medium of exchange, while gold and silver are mere "tinsel," useful only for making chamberpots or children's baubles.

Utopian religious principles, too, are founded on rational considerations. The Utopians infer the existence of a Creator from the evidence of the natural world. Similarly, they deduce the immortality of the soul as a logical consequence of humanity's God-ordained nature, further espousing belief in salvation as the necessary foundation of all morality.

Reason, then, affects every aspect of Utopian society, from the individual's choice of a marriage partner to the commonwealth's conduct of international affairs. The rationality of the Utopians is not only ethical but natural and pleasurable, for people, according to both Utopian and humanist philosophy, are by definition rational beings who derive pleasure from being true to their essential nature. In the exercise of their reason, More suggests, human beings are capable of striving toward the perfection of a utopia.

8.3 How seriously are the political, philosophical, and religious views expressed in *Utopia* meant to be taken?

Answer Critics vary widely in their views concerning this aspect of *Utopia*. One group of critics, including Michelet, Knox, and Campbell, regard the work as a learned Renaissance joke, or *jeu d'esprit*, which is ironic in intention: in this view, More presents a "perfect" society which is deliberately, and comically, imperfect. Other critics, like Kautsky, Oncken, and Ames, view *Utopia* as a serious argument for such social philosophies as communism, democracy, or colonialism. R. W. Chambers treats it as a religious sermon addressed to sinning Christians, and Edward Surtz as a subtle philosophical tract grounded in Christian humanism. This divergence of views makes it clear that the tone of *Utopia* is highly ambiguous, perhaps intentionally so.

The very title of the work creates a tonal ambiguity, the Greek compound *u-topia* meaning either "good place" (*u* = *eu*) or "no place" (*u* = *ou*). More suggests two ideas simultaneously: Utopia is a paradise on earth, a perfect model or blueprint for society; and it is also a whimsical fiction, an impossible ideal that exists "no place."

Indeed, More's use of Greek coinages to name people and places is one of the major techniques by which he introduces a joking and playful tone. Hythlodaeus, the spokesman for Utopia, is a man "well-learned in nonsense"; the Polylerites of Book I, whose ideal laws and practices anticipate those of the Utopians in Book II, are "the people of much nonsense"; the name of the chief city of Utopia, Amaurotum ("darkling city"), is a playful allusion to foggy London; and the name of Utopia's chief river, Anydrus ("waterless"), is a play on opposites. Finally, the chief governors of Utopia, the syphogrants, derive their name from the Greek for "silly old men." Thus, the seriousness of More's philosophical criticisms is compromised by the very names he assigns his people and places.

In addition, the Utopian travelogue is punctuated by comic episodes which undercut the seriousness of the social and ethical principles Hythlodaeus so earnestly outlines. For example, the moralistic denunciation of precious metals and gems as useless temptations encouraging vanity and greed modulates into a humorous description of the Utopians' golden chamber pots and pearl and ruby baubles for children. The section climaxes in an emperor's-new-clothes fable, with a Utopian child loudly remarking that a gorgeously appareled Anemolian ambassador is a "big booby . . .still wearing pearls and jewels as if he were yet a little boy!" (Book II). Similarly, in the requirement of a premarital physical inspection of a prospective marriage partner, the sober rationalism of the Utopians acquires an absurd air. The Utopians' argument is that choosing a mate demands the same careful evaluation as buying a horse; but, of course, treating human sexuality and love as identical with horse dealing is absurdly reductive, an equation made comic by its obvious discrepancy and incongruity. Generally, More's depiction of the rationalism of the Utopians produces a slightly ironic effect. Their incessant recourse to the logical processes of analogy and deduction ignores a vast realm of human experience, especially that of personal belief, which rests on faith and emotion rather than on evidence and proof.

On the other hand, many passages in Utopia have the authentic ring of serious criticism and argument. Book I introduces the themes of injustice (in the discussions of hanging for thievery and of land enclosures), political immorality (in the discussion of foreign policy and financial management), and reform (in the discussions of the role of a learned man in government and the possibility of communism), and so grounds the entire fiction in the real world of sixteenth-century Europe. The humanists of the period, men like More and his friend Desiderius Erasmus, intended to play an active role, as advisers to kings and other rulers, in bettering this world. Thus More's fiction, which raises real contemporary problems and hypothesizes solutions, cannot be regarded as merely an entertaining joke.

In Book II the emphasis on ethics and reason, if at times too insistent, nevertheless contributes gravity and sobriety to the work. Hythlodaeus's indignant diatribes against the self-interest, greed, and pride of Europeans, his triumphant descriptions of the just and amicable legal and social relations among the Utopians, and his moving defense of communism as a moral and natural means of distributing resources are both eloquent and persuasive. It would appear, then, that Hythlodaeus is the truthteller and that Utopia is indeed the perfect society. But More complicates this scheme—for example, by making "More" the character a pragmatist who rejects communism because it robs men of incentive, or by making the Utopian methods of warfare a perfect parallel, rather than a perfect opposite, to regrettable European practices. Thus More refuses simply to label any social theory right or wrong, making readers sift and analyze for themselves. And, as we have seen, he lightens the tone of the whole with punning allusions and comic anecdotes which poke fun at the rational idealism and perfectionism of the Utopians.

Thus the tone of the work is double; it veers between the earnest and the playful, communicating ideas indirectly rather than presenting them straightforwardly in the manner of a tract. According to the Renaissance theory of *serio ludere* ("to play seriously"), truth was best conveyed by paradox. More enlivens his moral discourse by means of amusing anecdotes and linguistic play and at the same time effects his serious purpose of illuminating the political, social, economic, and religious problems of his day.

8.4   Discuss the structures of Books I and II of *Utopia* and the relationship between them.

Answer   Book I of *Utopia* is set up as a philosophical debate on government, with legal, social, political, economic, and military issues brought forward for discussion. Using real historical personages, such as Peter Giles, Cardinal Morton, and Thomas More himself, as well as the fictional traveler Raphael Hythlodaeus, More the author plays with the boundaries between fiction and fact, offering a range of viewpoints on the social ills of contemporary Europe in an open-ended debate.

Book II, largely narrated by Hythlodaeus, presents the solution to the problems posed in Book I. Book II has the format of a travelogue, wittily imitating contemporary travel literature in its precise detailing of the strange habits and customs of foreign peoples. More playfully hints that Utopia is in some sense a perfect opposite to England. In contrast to Great Britain, a roughly triangular island above the equator, Utopia is a perfectly circular subequatorial isle, whose chief city and river are analogues to London and the Thames. In a more far-reaching sense, Utopia is the opposite of England and of all modern Europe in its substitution of natural reason for base impulse and animal will and in its moral code of benevolence, justice, virtuous pleasure, and religious tolerance. However, the fictional world of Utopia is not merely an abstract blueprint for a society. It has the coherence and fullness of a microcosm, a "little world," with houses, gardens, games, meals, and garments described in fascinating detail.

The interplay between fact and fiction, between political thesis and imaginative hypothesis, continues throughout the work. If Book I is mainly factual in its references to actual events and practices, and Book II mainly fictional in its descriptions of a never-never land, the threads of satire and narrative are nonetheless closely interwoven. At the very end of *Utopia*, More remarks to the reader on his own mixed and skeptical response to what he has heard from the visionary traveler Hythlodaeus. In this last paragraph, the relaxation of tension and the return to a natural-sounding kind of speech return the reader to the "real world"; but, in a sense, reality has been present throughout, in the web of allusions and analogues to contemporary society from which the fictional Utopia is constructed.

B.S.

SUGGESTED READINGS

Chambers, R. W., *Thomas More* (1957).

Surtz, Edward L., *The Praise of Pleasure: Philosophy, Education and Communism in More's Utopia* (1957).

Sylvester, Richard S., ed., *The Complete Works of Sir Thomas More* (1963–   ).

THOMAS WYATT

C H R O N O L O G Y

1503   Born at Allington Castle in Kent. Son of Sir Henry Wyatt, an important member of the king's court, and Anne Skinner Wyatt. Wyatt appears to have been involved in the life of the royal household from an early age.

1516   Page at court. May have entered St. John's College, Cambridge University.

1520   May have received M.A. from Cambridge. Marries Elizabeth Brooke, daughter of Thomas, Lord Cobham.

1523   Acts as a royal emissary, beginning a long career as diplomat and ambassador.

1524   Fights in a royal tournament at Christmastime.

1526   Repudiates his marriage, apparently on the ground of his wife's adultery. Serves on a diplomatic mission to France under Sir Thomas Cheney.

1527   Sent on a mission with Sr. John Russell to Rome and Venice. Is captured by Spanish soldiers, then engages in an invasion of Roman territory; escapes, perhaps with the help of the messenger sent to ransom him. The episode helps to enhance his reputation as a resourceful young courtier.
Translates Plutarch's *De Tranquillitate Animi* as *The Quyete of Mynde*; it is presented in compliment to the queen and published the following year (the only work of Wyatt's to be printed during his lifetime).

1528   Sent to France as marshal of Calais; remains there until 1530.

1532   Travels to France with King Henry VIII; is reputed to be a close personal friend of the king.

| 1533 | Serves as chief ewerer at the wedding feast of Henry VIII and Anne Boleyn. |

1534   Briefly imprisoned for a scuffle with some soldiers in London, in which a sergeant is killed; soon returns to favor.

1535   Named high steward of the Abbey of Malling.

1536   Again imprisoned, for reasons unclear; may have been implicated in the scandal surrounding Anne Boleyn, who falls at this time. Released after six weeks, and is soon named sheriff of Kent, indicating his return to royal grace.

1537   Sent to Spain as ambassador to the court of Emperor Charles V; remains abroad for the next two years. His mission, to improve relations between England and Spain and to prevent too close a tie between the Catholic powers of Spain and France, is never fully achieved.

1538   In England briefly, bearing messages from the emperor. Probably conceives a son by his mistress, Elizabeth Darrell.

1540   Wyatt's patron Thomas Cromwell, formerly lord privy seal, falls from favor, is arrested and executed. In consequence, Wyatt is charged with treason and again imprisoned. However, the charges are flimsy, and Wyatt is released after two months.

1541   Commissioned as an officer and sent to Calais in command of 300 soldiers.

1542   Named chief steward of the manor of Maidstone and a vice admiral of the navy. Sent as ambassador to escort the Spanish envoy from Falmouth to London. On the way is exposed to rain and cold, falls ill, and dies at a friend's home in Dorset.

1549   *Certayne Psalmes*, containing Wyatt's translations from the Book of Psalms, is published.

1557   Publication of *Songs and Sonnettes* (usually known as *Tottel's Miscellany* after its publisher, Richard Tottel). This volume contains most of the poetry of Wyatt as well as that of Henry Surrey; it was extremely popular and enormously influential throughout the Elizabethan period, introducing a host of continental themes, forms, and styles to English lyric poetry. The Egerton and Devonshire manuscripts, which modern scholars consider the best textual basis for Wyatt's poetry, circulated throughout the sixteenth century. Unlike *Tottel's Miscellany*, in which words were changed and meters regularized, these manuscripts preserve the harsh diction and difficult metrics for which Wyatt is now admired.

ESSAY QUESTIONS WITH ANSWERS

"The long love that in my thought doth harbor"

9.1 Wyatt's "The long love that in my thought doth harbor" and Surrey's "Love, that doth reign and live within my heart" are both translations of the same fourteenth-century sonnet by the Italian poet Francis (Francesco) Petrarch from his *Canzoniere*, a cycle of love songs. Compare the two English sonnets.

Answer   Because both poems are based on the same original, the symbolic "action" of the sonnets is similar: a personified love shows himself in the lover's face, thus displeasing the beloved. Fearful, love retreats to the heart, the lover following. The poem ends with the lover's vow of continued faithfulness. Both Wyatt and Surrey capture Petrarch's witty separation of love, personified as a knight, from the lover himself, who is an innocent valet or squire faithfully attending on his master. Thus, the poet-lover cannot be blamed by the mistress for his actions, as he is only following orders issued by his captain, love.

Despite this basic similarity in the development of the main conceit, however, the two poems are quite different in tone. Surrey more fully exploits the image of love as a chivalric "lord," who has "captured" the poet's heart like a fort, is "clad in arms," and shows cowardice in fleeing from the beloved. The poet explicitly distinguishes between the "guilt" of "my lord" and his own "faultlessness." Furthermore, the poem is metrically smooth and uses simple, conventional lyric rhymes (pain, refrain, plain; desire, ire; apace, face). With elegant musical fluency, Surrey creates a polished lyric which indirectly compliments the mistress as victor in the symbolic battle, using a style that suggests emotional resignation.

By contrast, Wyatt's version of Petrarch's sonnet is rougher, harsher, and more intense. Wyatt treats love as an unruly individual who actively rushes to and fro. Love does not merely "rest" his banner in the poet's face, as in Surrey's poem, but "presseth" into the lover's countenance, "spreading his banner" like a blush across the poet's features. Wyatt implicitly lays blame on love, referring to the mistress's displeasure at "his hardiness," but he does not emphasize his own innocence or separateness from love. Wyatt further increases the emotional intensity of the poem by his use of vivid metaphor and complex rhythms. Love flees not simply to the "heart," but to the "heart's forest"; the word "forest," with its connotations of thickets and undergrowth, suggests a psychological landscape bristling with feelings and dark enough to hide in. The diction, rhythms, and rhymes of the poem also contribute to the harsh, "bristling" tone of the piece. Three-syllable Latinate words—"residence," "negligence," "reverence," "hardiness," "enterprise"—stud the lines, acting like stumbling blocks to the flow of the meter. Drawn from the language of the worlds of business and politics rather than of love, these words suggest that the poet is a plain man, speaking his mind with rough earnestness.

Both Wyatt and Surrey conclude their sonnets with couplets which vow, with witty irony, the lover's faithfulness not to the mistress but to love. But what is most remarkable about the two translations is not their expected similarities but their surprising differences. Surrey's version is the smooth, sweet, polished working-out of a conceit; Wyatt's, a dramatic and vigorous poem of complaint.

"They flee from me"

9.2 "They flee from me" consists largely of plain statement, the only developed metaphor a mainly implied one occurring in the first stanza. Analyze this metaphor, discussing its function in the poem as a whole.

Answer The opening line of the poem sounds literal, but the second line ("With naked foot stalking in my chamber") introduces an implied metaphor. The language suggests the timid approach of half-wild creatures, who have been "tamed" and made "gentle" to the point where they will "take bread at my hand." Wyatt's complaint is that this domesticated breed has reverted to its original wild state, thus deserting him.

Part of the power of this initial figure derives from its restraint and its ambiguity. Because Wyatt characterizes the pronoun "They" solely by figurative language, the word has a wide range of potential reference. The theme of fickleness is established, but the fickle ones could be the poet's fellow courtiers or his mistresses, and the betrayal either political or erotic. The "bread" offered and received is, in either case, a conferring of favors or advantage.

The refusal to define the subject precisely or state the context literally lends the first stanza a universal dimension: the poet's solitary self is posed against unspecified others, the "They" of the first line. Part of the effect is to create a general portrait of the "others" as a breed or "kind": their wildness, expressed by their flight and "ranging," is essential to their nature, despite the short-lived meekness or apparent tameness they have exhibited.

It is only in stanzas 2 and 3 that Wyatt specifies a sexual context and narrows the theme to the fickleness of women. These stanzas sketch a brief narrative in which happiness yields to erotic disappointment. The intimate love scene which constitutes the center of the poem is a vivid memory of a gentle moment, quickly followed by the final stanza of complaint: "But all is turned . . . ." The poet has been forsaken because of his mistress's "newfangleness," her wild restlessness.

The metaphoric resonance of the initial description runs through the poem, coloring the image of a specific unhappy love affair with a general view of human nature. The opening metaphor linking "They" with a domesticated breed of wild animal makes the woman in the poem representative of her "breed," which is both womankind and, in a broader sense, all humanity. Thus the last line of the poem circles back to the original figure of a breed or kind with its pun on "kindly." The phrase "But since that I so kindely am served" has a double reference to the idea of compassion ("kindness") and to the idea of the nature (or "kind") of woman. Ironically it is the nature of woman, as of man, to be unkind, to flee from faithfulness in the pursuit of novelty and distraction.

9.3 Show how Wyatt uses the following words and phrases to suggest the ground of his complaint in the poem: "gentle," "gentleness," "a strange fashion of forsaking," "goodness," and "newfangleness."

Answer Generally, all these words refer to a code of conduct or behavior. The way in which Wyatt develops this strand of language invokes a standard of breeding and courtesy against which errant womankind is measured.

The word "gentle," in its root sense, refers to breeding, good birth, and proper upbringing. (This sense of the root *gen* is present in the words "gentry," referring to persons of property, and "gentility," with its connotations of politeness and delicacy.) Thus, in the opening image the gentleness of the women connotes not only their softness and humility but their good breeding. In the third stanza, the poet implies that his own courtesy has been taken advantage of, his own humane and civilized conduct flouted: "But all is turned thorough my gentleness/Into a strange fashion of forsaking."

"Strange," in the line just quoted, means both "eccentric" and "alien" or "foreign." The poet's mistress, in rejecting him, is violating both natural decorum and the amorous code of courtesy; consequently, she is both unnatural and barbarous (literally, "strange" or "foreign"). Wyatt's ironic reference to her "goodness" in politely "permitting" him to depart ("And I have leave to go, of her goodness") only underscores the true incivility beneath her surface breeding.

The notion of woman's eccentric or errant behavior is further elaborated by the word "newfangleness." In the Renaissance, as now, this word signified a love of trivial innovation, a fickle dalliance with fads and fashions; thus, the idea it conveys is associated with the closing line of the first stanza, "Busily seeking with a continual change." The charges of restlessness, insatiable appetite, and "strangeness" are summarized in the ironic phrase "kindely served": the mistress violates "kind" (that is, nature) in her disregard for breeding (gentleness, goodness) and in her attraction to superficial diversions (newfangleness).

By these indirect references to the Renaissance concept of a decorum governing the relationship between the sexes, Wyatt skillfully blends complaint into argument: he shifts the ground from personal bitterness to public judgment, accusing the mistress not merely of offending him personally but of a misdemeanor against the code of love.

9.4 How does the rhyme scheme of the poem relate to its imagery and meaning?

Answer Within the fixed rhyme scheme of the lyric (*ababbcc*), Wyatt displays a range of musical effects, thus varying the tonal qualities of each stanza. In the first stanza, he uses slant rhymes: instead of chiming perfectly, the rhyme words delicately echo each other by means of assonance (similar vowel sounds) and consonance (similar consonants). In the words "chamber" and "remember," the major vowel sound subtly shifts. (In Wyatt's time, the same slight shift would have existed.) This rhyming pair modulates into "danger," which again alters the vowel and introduces the soft *g* picked up in the couplet ("range"/ "change"). The musical properties of the end words—the soft consonants *m*, *b*, and *g* and the fluid vowel sounds—create a sound pattern analogous to the poem's theme of modulation and change. The rhymes themselves suggest the action of wild creatures, approaching, hesitating, and taking flight.

The second stanza uses exact rhymes, but it contributes musical variety to the poem through its colloquial rhythms. "Thanked be fortune it hath been otherwise,/ Twenty times better . . ." explodes the smooth iambic pentameter rhythm with three emphatic stresses in the first four syllables of the second line, creating the illusion of a spontaneous oral outburst.

In the last stanza of the poem, the rhymes become difficult. "Gentleness," "goodness," and "newfangleness" are polysyllabic words which do not produce perfect chimes but are bound together only by the suffix -*ness*. They lend the lines a choppy, stumbling quality, their dissonance reinforcing the mood of discontent and disruption expressed in the poet's accusations.

The closing couplet does rhyme perfectly, and pointedly, for the words "served" and "deserved" both derive from the same root. Once again, the poem's musical properties underscore its significance. By using "mirror" words, the poet suggests a tit-for-tat relationship: he will dish up to the mistress—serve back to her—what has been served up to him. Thus the rhyme wittily reinforces the idea of vengeance implied in the lines.

"My lute awake"

9.5 What is the function of the refrain?

Answer The main function of the refrain is to provide a form for the poet's feeling. The refrain articulates the stanzaic structure of the poem, with the repeated, slightly varied reference to the silenced lute concluding each dramatic pronouncement: "my song is futile," "my lady has rejected me," "I will be revenged," and "you will be sorry." In a sense, the phrase "My lute be still, for I have done," with its variations throughout the poem, is an attempt to exorcise the bitter emotion expressed in each verse by emphasizing the poet's desire for resignation and renunciation, as he repeatedly tries to place his painful attachment to his mistress in the past.

The refrain is also an elegant method of emphasizing the dramatic occasion, that is, the performance of a singer entertaining an audience with lute in hand. (It is not certain whether or not the poem was ever actually performed as a song in this way; but, since many sixteenth-century lyrics were set to music and performed at court, it is quite possible that Wyatt had such a purpose in mind.) In using the lute simultaneously as a symbol of the lover's emotion and as his instrument of self-expression, Wyatt dramatizes the act of renunciation. It is in the course of the song and, in fact, by means of the song, that the lover arrives at the resolution of his inner conflict. The "mirror" relationship between the first and last stanzas reinforces the sense of a completed circle, a journey ended. Announcing at the outset the beginning of a performance, Wyatt concludes with a reference to the ending of that performance: "And ended is that we begun,/ Now is this song both sung and past;/ My lute be still, for I have done." Thus the effect is of dramatic simultaneity and ironic doubleness: the absolute "end" of private feeling coincides with the end of the performance, as intimate and bitter sentiments are transformed into a song of renunciation, a work of art shaped out of personal experience.

9.6 Wyatt's stanzas describing his mistress's bleak future ("Perchance thee lie, withered and old") may be compared to Donne's poem "The Apparition" and Drayton's sonnet "There's nothing grieves me but that age should haste." These latter, composed almost a century later, likewise express a feeling of vengeful bitterness toward the rejecting lady. Comment on this theme of revenge, as it appears in Wyatt's "ballet" and in the later love poetry of the Renaissance.

Answer These poets would seem to be violating the conventional pose of the Petrarchan lover, whose undying fidelity to the chaste mistress finds expression in elaborate compliment. But the "anti-Petrarchan" posture of bitterness, accusation, and revulsion was itself a convention, appearing in love poetry throughout the sixteenth century. This stance was in part a rhetorical convenience, providing new "matter" for sonnets and ballads and psychological variation for the poetic persona. The new matter derives from the old, for behind it is the traditional Renaissance preoccupation with the transience of beauty. The realization that beauty inevitably fades could become a ploy in a *carpe diem* argument of seduction: beauty does not last; therefore, the mistress should enjoy her youth while she can. But the destructive effects of time could also be held over the disobliging lady as a threatened punishment for her disdain.

The revenge theme in love lyrics sometimes appears as a specifically satiric reaction against the sweetness of amorous lyrics. Drayton's vivid portrait of his decayed mistress represented a display of invention at a time when "sugared sonnets" had become a stale poetic commodity. It is likely, too, that the anti-Petrarchan stance is a reflection of poetic temperament. Wyatt and Donne are often compared on the basis of their similarly "masculine" and vigorous styles: both are metrically irregular and both employ colloquial diction. But they are also related in tone, often striking a note of defiance or sexual dissatisfaction. Wyatt's description of his lady lying abed and moaning in futility for an imaginary lover is close in mood to Donne's portrait of his supine mistress spurned by her lover, who is present but shrinks from her in pretended sleep. Thus, the two poets share a candor of tone and an immediacy of effect in postulating a specifically sexual revenge.

The anticonventional bitter pose, then, constituted its own convention. Specific historical factors such as satiric reaction to prevailing modes and individual poetic temperament led some poets to transform the sweet Petrarchan complaint into a strident imprecation.

"Farewell, Love"

9.7 Discuss the attitudes toward love expressed in the sonnet.

Answer The poem begins with a rather conventional treatment of love, which gradually deepens into bitter irony. In the opening quatrain the poet bids farewell to the "laws" and "lore" (wisdom) of love; he thus suggests the traditional idea of love as an elaborate ritual or game with its own rules and technical wisdom. Against this amorous "learning" he poses the philosophy of Seneca and Plato, the goal of which is "perfect wealth" or well-being. The tone thus far is witty and rather playful, as Wyatt sets up one system of thought against another.

However, in the second quatrain love is revealed as *false* learning ("blind error"), a form of knowledge which is harmful, trivial, and confining. Thus, in the third quatrain the references to love's "authority" (rightful claim to respect) and "property" (special power or elemental virtue) are frankly ironic; love is, in fact, a worthless pursuit fit only for "idle youth" who, out of ignorance, obey its precepts.

The bitter conclusion of the poem grows gradually out of another strand of imagery which associates love not with law and logic, but with deceit, entrapment, and "unsoundness." The "baited hooks" of the first quatrain clearly connote a seductive danger. In contrast to this alluring aspect of love is the reference, in the second quatrain, to the "sharp repulse, which pricketh aye so sore." Paradoxically, love both attracts and repels, but in either case it injures the unwary victim. In the third quatrain, Cupid's "brittle darts" are paradoxically both injurious and futile. Weapons of war designed to pierce, the arrows are nonetheless fragile and breakable. The "rotten boughs" in the last line of the poem suggest some kind of tree or ladder, which beckons the climber on to his own destruction. The underlying sexual connotation is that the mistress's limbs are "rotten," that is, diseased, presumably because of her unfaithfulness.

Thus Wyatt develops a complicated, ambivalent picture of love by means of paradox and irony. Love appears as wisdom, but is in fact false knowledge; love seduces only to destroy; love is both powerful and fragile, apparently sound but structurally rotten. The brittle darts and rotten boughs of the close are vivid images suggesting bitter disgust, as Wyatt climaxes his poem of renunciation with direct denunciation. Whatever its appearances and powers, love is finally rejected as a negative and destructive emotion.

B.S.

SUGGESTED   READINGS

Muir, Kenneth, *Life and Letters of Sir Thomas Wyatt* (1963).

Smith, Hallett, "The Art of Sir Thomas Wyatt," *Huntington Library Quarterly*, 9 (1946).

Southall, Raymond, *The Courtly Maker: An Essay on the Poetry of Wyatt and His Contemporaries* (1964).

Thomson, Patricia, *Sir Thomas Wyatt and His Background* (1964).

Tillyard, E. M. W., *The Poetry of Sir Thomas Wyatt: A Selection and a Study* (1949).

HENRY HOWARD
EARL OF SURREY

C H R O N O L O G Y

1517   Henry Howard born at Kennighall, estate of the Howard family, one of the noblest in England. Son of Thomas Howard, earl of Surrey, and his second wife, Elizabeth. In 1524, Thomas is named duke of Norfolk, whereupon Henry is given the title of earl of Surrey. He is educated at home; one of his tutors may have been John Clerk, a distinguished Roman Catholic scholar and writer.

1530   At the request of King Henry VIII, Surrey becomes a companion to the duke of Richmond, the king's illegitimate son and a royal favorite; they live together at Windsor, establishing an intimate friendship.

1532   Surrey accompanies Henry VIII and Richmond on a visit to the French court, where it is likely that Surrey is introduced to Italian poetry; he probably begins writing his early love lyrics and his English adaptations of Italian poems at this time. Also in 1532, Surrey marries Lady Frances Vere, daughter of the earl of Oxford. The marriage is mainly a political alliance between the families; husband and wife will not live together until three years later because of their tender years.

1533   Surrey's parents separate. The marriage has been an unhappy one; fourteen years later, Surrey's mother will testify against his father at the latter's trial on treason charges.

1536   Surrey serves as a minor court officer in the trial of Anne Boleyn, wife of Henry VIII. Later in the year he serves as a soldier under his father in the campaign against the northern rebellion known as the Pilgrimage of Grace.

Both father and son, however, are widely suspected of secret sympathies with the rebels.

1537 Surrey is imprisoned for striking Sir Edward Seymour, who had accused him of sympathizing with the northern rebels; is soon freed.

1539 Amid fears of a possible war against the Roman Catholic powers of Europe, Surrey is put in charge of the defense of Norfolk against an anticipated invasion. None takes place.

1540 Surrey is recorded as having performed with distinction at a tournament in honor of the new queen, Anne of Cleves.

1541 Named Knight of the Garter. Catherine Howard, Surrey's cousin, becomes Henry VIII's wife and the new queen; apex of the Howard family fortunes at court.

1542 Catherine Howard falls from grace, is tried and executed; Surrey attends the execution. He is again briefly imprisoned for challenging another courtier, John Leigh. Poet Sir Thomas Wyatt dies; Surrey writes the memorial poem beginning, "Wyatt resteth here, that quick could never rest," published in a commemorative volume; it is Surrey's first printed poem and one of his finest.

1543 Surrey again imprisoned, this time for riotous behavior on the streets of London; his reputation as a reckless and headstrong young courtier firmly established. Also takes part in the siege of Landrecy in France.

1544 Undertakes construction of a large house in classical style at Mount Surrey near Norwich; supposed to be the earliest English classical building. This project will seriously deplete his wealth over the next three years.

1545 Further military service; is named marshal of the field and then lieutenant general; is wounded and also reprimanded for exposing himself to unnecessary danger.

1546 Loses a battle at St. Etienne. The king, evidently feeling that he has erred in giving a responsible military post to one so young and willful, recalls Surrey to England. Surrey returns home embittered by this setback; becomes part of one of several factions jockeying for power in anticipation of the death of Henry VIII, who has grown ill; his enemies at court become more numerous than ever in consequence.

1547 Surrey and his father are arrested on charges of treason. Thomas Howard is imprisoned for five years, but his son the poet is executed.

1553 Publication of Gavin Douglas's English translation of the *Aeneid*. This work, which had circulated in manuscript form for several years before its printing, had evidently influenced Surrey during the later 1540s, when he worked on his own version of the *Aeneid*.

1554   Publication of Book IV of Surrey's translation of the *Aeneid*; one of the earliest major English works written in blank verse (i.e., unrhymed iambic pentameter). Intended as a suitable English equivalent for Virgil's Latin hexameters, blank verse on Surrey's model will be used by the great Elizabethan dramatists and become the dominant meter in English for narrative and dramatic poetry.

1557   Publication by Richard Tottel of Books II and IV of Surrey's *Aeneid* (evidently all that he produced). Also of *Songes and Sonnettes*, usually known as *Tottel's Miscellany*, containing most of Surrey's lyric poetry as well as that of Wyatt and other minor poets. This enormously popular anthology was the means by which Surrey's experiments with many Italian lyric forms became common currency among the still greater Elizabethan poets who were to follow.

ESSAY QUESTIONS WITH ANSWERS

"The soote season"

10.1 "Surrey's poem is both simple and simple-minded, consisting of a boring list of clichés describing spring." How valid is this criticism of "The soote season"?

Answer The poem does indeed consist of a catalogue of images of spring, but it creates a vivid, particularized, and effective "definition" of the abstraction "spring." (It should be pointed out that the word "summer" [line 5] was used in the sixteenth century to refer to the season we call spring.) Each line presents a picture of bird, beast, fish, insect, or greenery as part of a composite portrait of the season. The effect is simple but beautifully achieved.

Many of the images, like those of the "swift swallow" and "busy bee," are clichés we automatically associate with spring. It is probable, of course, that these phrases were considered somewhat less hackneyed at the time they were composed; in fact, it could be contended that it was the very flood of poems produced by Surrey and others in the sixteenth century that made such images seem overworked and trite. However, even assuming that some of the language is conventional, part of the poem's disarming directness derives from its unembarrassed use of familiar images shared by all people contemplating the round of the year. In many ways the lyric is a showcase for the charm and appeal of literary conventions. As critical comments by contemporary writers suggest, sixteenth-century readers of love lyrics would probably have found these conventions delightful in themselves, the inherent loveliness of the familiar subject matter only adding to their pleasure. That the matter was conventional would make it easy for both poet and audience to concentrate on and enjoy small variations in its treatment.

Finally, pleasure could be derived from seeing a convention successfully embodied in its traditional form, with every expectation met. The "game" of the sonnet, with the anticipated reversal in the concluding couplet, is played out by Surrey in a highly satisfactory fashion.

Surrey shows his skill in the way he integrates the familiar sights of spring by means of a unifying conceit or metaphor which associates vernal regeneration with the idea of new clothing or finery. The hill and vale are "clad" in green (line 2); the nightingale wears new feathers (line 3), the hart new horns (line 6), the buck a new hide (line 7), the fishes new scales (line 8), the adder a new skin (line 9). The prevalence of active verbs ("springs," "flings," "slings," "mings") creates an impression of vitality and movement. Even the repetitive syntax has a functional significance. Almost every line in the poem has the same grammatical form, but the monotony of the assertions adds to the impression of the near universality of springtime joy, from which only the poet is excluded.

The final couplet extends the description beyond the physical into the psychological, as the poet compares his inner state to the joyous burgeoning around him. The last word of the poem is a pun on the verb and noun "spring"; what springs up in the poet in springtime is sorrow, not gladness.

Thus Surrey, heaping up conventional images in a simple accumulation, evokes the experience of seasonal change and relates it to the unhappy lover's isolation from the natural world. The elaboration of a central conceit, the use of lively verbs, and the structural twist supplied by the couplet revive the familiar theme of the sonnet, making it newly evocative.

10.2 "Surrey's rhyme scheme, which uses only two rhymes, is dull and predictable." How valid is this criticism?

Answer In a sense, the restriction of the rhymes to only two constitutes a tour de force, an exhibition of the poet's ingenuity in coming up with yet another pair of like sounds for the same rhyme. Surrey uses the relative predictability of the rhyme words to his own advantage: capitalizing on the stock vocabulary of simple ballads and songs, he creates a fresh statement through subtle variation. The simple *abab* rhyme scheme, with the familiar chime of brings/sings/springs and vale/tale/pale, suggests an artless ease, an unsophisticated burst of expression. But in fact the rhymes are not artless: the recurrence of the word "springs," once with reference to a spray of flowers and a second time to describe the poet's sorrow, is a clever pun; and the emphasis on the verbs created by their use as rhyme words suggests a feeling of gay abandon and vitality.

Alliterative effects also add to the music of the poem, from the "soote season" and "bud and bloom" of the opening line, through the "buck in brake" and the adder's slinging away of her slough, to the closing phrase, "my sorrow springs." Like Shakespeare's seasonal songs in *Love's Labour's Lost* and *As You Like It*, Surrey's sonnet creates an air of simple, fresh, spontaneous expression through a sophisticated and subtle interweaving of familiar materials. The "artless" rhymes contribute to this genuinely artful effect.

B.S.

SUGGESTED READINGS

Casady, E. R., *Henry Howard, Earl of Surrey* (1938).

Mumford, I. L., "Italian Aspects of Surrey's Lyrics," *English Miscellany*, 16 (1965).

EDMUND SPENSER

C H R O N O L O G Y

1552 Probable birth date of Spenser. Son of John and Elizabeth Spenser, middle-class London tradespeople.

1561– Attends the Merchant Taylors School, headed by Richard Mulcaster, a
1569 well-known progressive educator who stresses the importance of English language and culture alongside the classics.

1569 Enters Pembroke Hall, Cambridge, as "sizar" (poor student). Begins long-lasting friendship with scholar Gabriel Harvey. Spenser's versions of poems by Du Bellay and Petrarch are published in anthology *The Theatre of Voluptuous Worldlings*.

1573 Receives B.A. from Cambridge.

1576 Receives M.A. from Cambridge; within a year, makes his first visit to Ireland.

1578 Serves as secretary to Bishop John Young of Rochester; then is employed by Robert Dudley, the earl of Leicester, and makes acquaintance of Philip Sidney, Leicester's nephew. With Sidney and Edward Dyer, begins to explore possible adaptation of classical meters to English verse.

1579 Publishes *The Shepheardes Calender*, with a dedication to Sidney and a critical commentary by "E.K." (probably Edward Kirke, a Cambridge colleague of Spenser's). The *Calender* is a critical and financial success. Probable date of Spenser's marriage to Machabyas Chylde, but little is known for certain about this marriage. Spenser also writes *Mother Hubberds Tale*, a political satire not published until 1591.

1580   Spenser is appointed secretary to Lord Grey de Wilton, lord deputy of Ireland; settles with him in Ireland. *The Faerie Queene* is under way; Gabriel Harvey is given portions of it to read.

1581   Named clerk in chancery for faculties, government post Spenser will hold until 1588.

1582   Rents New Abbey, outside Dublin. Meets Lodowick Bryskett, who will tell in his *Discourse of Civill Life* (1606) of hearing Spenser explain his plan for *The Faerie Queene* at this time.

1588   Acquires castle of Kilcolman in county Cork, along with a 3000-acre estate.

1589   Is visited by Sir Walter Ralegh, who approves of *The Faerie Queene* and persuades Spenser to return with him to London, where Queen Elizabeth expresses her favor toward Spenser's work.

1590   Books I–III of *The Faerie Queene* published, with a dedication to the queen and the letter to Ralegh explaining the allegorical plan of the poem. Spenser returns to Ireland.

1591   Publication of *Complaints*, including nine poems by Spenser, most notably *Mother Hubberds Tale*, *The Ruines of Time*, and *Daphnaida*, an elegy on Lady Douglas Howard. Granted a pension of £50 for life by Queen Elizabeth.

1592   Meets Elizabeth Boyle.

1594   Marries Elizabeth Boyle, probably in Cork, Ireland; she is the subject of most of the love sonnets in *Amoretti* and of the *Epithalamion*.

1595   Publication of *Amoretti* and *Epithalamion*, and of *Colin Clouts Come Home Again*, a poem concerning life at the court in London, along with *Astrophel*, an elegy for Philip Sidney. Spenser visits London with Books IV–VI of *The Faerie Queene*, hoping that they will win him the queen's favor and advancement at court.

1596   Books IV–VI of *The Faerie Queene* published; so are the *Fowre Hymns* and the *Prothalamion*, celebrating the betrothal of the daughters of the earl of Worcester. Disappointed in his hopes for advancement at court, Spenser returns to Ireland.

1598   Appointed sheriff of Cork. Tyrone's rebellion in Ireland results in the sack of Spenser's castle at Kilcolman and probably his impoverishment. Spenser returns to London, bearing dispatches to the Privy Council there from Sir Thomas Norris, lord president of Munster.

1599   Death of Spenser, apparently in poverty, leaving two sons and a daughter. Buried in Westminster Abbey.

1609   Publication of *The Faerie Queene*, including the *Two Cantos of Mutabilitie*.

1633   Publication of Spenser's prose tract *A Veue of the Present State of Irelande* (probably written in 1596); it defends the repression of Ireland by the English.

ESSAY QUESTIONS WITH ANSWERS

Amoretti
Sonnet 54: "Of this worlds theater in which we stay"

11.1 What is the major conceit which shapes the poem? What are its thematic implications?

Answer Spenser uses the familiar Renaissance metaphor of the world as a stage and human beings as actors to portray the relationship between lover and mistress. The theatrical imagery suggests that the sonneteer addressing his lady is, in a sense, an actor, playing to a demanding audience of one. In elaborating this central conceit, Spenser introduces a subtle complexity into the stock Petrarchan situation of the aggrieved lover confronting his disdainful mistress.

The typical poet-lover, as he appears in sonnets from the time of Petrarch up to Elizabethan times, suffers from unrequited love, which turns pleasure to pain and produces intense, paradoxical emotional states: the lover freezes and burns, rejoices and despairs, and laughs and weeps as his fortunes in love wax and wane. Here Spenser uses theatrical imagery to suggest the conscious artistry, even the exhibitionism, of the sonneteer who so flamboyantly displays his feelings to the public. Spenser's persona (the "I" of the poem) acts out his passions in a highly self-conscious way, designing his "pageants" to appeal to the "spectator" (the beloved). He is not above self-disguise and masquerade ("And mask in myrth lyke to a comedy") or exaggeration ("I waile and make my woes a tragedy") in order to move the lady to compassion. The explicit references to theatrical genres (pageant, masque, comedy, tragedy) reinforce the idea of impersonation and performance.

The couplet constitutes a traditional complaint against the unfeeling, aloof, distant mistress. However, the conceit of the theater partly undercuts the wounded lover's accusation: perhaps the lady is not a "senceless stone" but rather a more discerning playgoer. The reference to her "constant eye" (line 9) suggests that she is unwavering, unmoved; but it also indicates a scrutinizing and discerning attitude. Her laughter in lines 11 and 12 reveals that she is unconvinced by the lover's histrionic portrayal of the heights and depths of his passion; she remains detached and amused.

Thus, by means of the theatrical metaphor, the poem acquires a double resonance. On the one hand, it presents a thoroughly conventional argument, with the sonneteer lodging his complaint against the mistress through a vivid portrayal of his own futile labors and torments. On the other hand, it is a witty exposé of an underlying playfulness in the sonnet form, itself a minipageant designed to delight, and of the foolishness of the lover's excessively dramatic posturings.

Sonnet 64: "Coming to kiss her lips, (such grace I found)"

11.2 Spenser uses an "emblem" to catalogue the lady's physical beauties: the central metaphor of the mistress as a garden, a kind of walking flower bed. What is the effect of this highly conceited description?

Answer Taken literally, as a pastiche of visual images, the description suggests the ludicrous portrait of a woman constructed piecemeal out of various blossoms. But the use of the emblem is comic only if taken literally. The intended effect of invoking the beauties of the natural world is to endow the mistress with their value: she is as fragile, beautiful, sweet, and natural as those other products of God's handiwork, the rose, the gillyflower, and the columbine.

The catalogue of the lady's physical attributes is not only complimentary but erotic. Naming the "parts" and seeking an apt floral simile for each becomes a sensuous journey from face to breasts, as the poet lingers over the mistress's roselike cheeks, her stemlike neck, and her budlike nipples. The sonnet becomes a celebration of feminine beauty, not as a realistic portrait but as an evocation of the sensual idea of that beauty.

11.3 Discuss the evocation of the sense of smell in the sonnet.

Answer Although the allusions to flowers are partly visual (for example, the red of the rose and the white of the bellamours), the poet's emphasis throughout the poem is on the aroma of the blossoms he names. On drawing near to his mistress, his first impression is of smelling "a garden of sweet flowers," and he begins his list of her physical beauties with the odor of her lips, "like unto Gillyflowers." The imagery of smell reinforces the erotic effect of the anatomical catalogue: the poet seems to be burying his face in the fragrant "bouquet" of his mistress's body.

The emphasis on aroma has a further, metaphysical connotation, alluding to a kind of "spiritual fragrance." The phrase "such grace I found" alludes not only to the lady's gracious reception of the poet as he kisses her, but to the grace of soul and being which emanates from her. In the Renaissance, the word "odor" frequently had reference to the soul, a sweet aroma signifying a state of spiritual grace ("Let the swete odour of devocyon and prayer spyre out and ascende up to thy lorde" [*The Pilgrimage of Perfection*, 1526]). Thus the couplet contains a near pun, combining sensual ardor with a religious sense of the mistress's worth:

> Such fragrant flowers do give most odourous smell,
> But her sweet odor did them all excell.

The Shepheardes Calender, *"The November Eclogue"*

11.4 How do the features drawn from the conventions of the classical pastoral elegy contribute to "The November Eclogue"?

Answer Aspects of Spenser's poem which may be traced to the genre of pastoral elegy include the mourning for an allegorical shepherd or shepherdess, here known as Dido; the reflections on regeneration in nature, in contrast with human mortality; and the motif of the sympathetic lamentation of the entire living world over the death of the heroine ("all nature mourns"). The chief Christian elements superimposed on this classical framework are the idea of resurrection and the immortality of the soul and the idea of Dido's new heavenly abode, which together constitute the major philosophical consolations offered in the elegy.

As the first English rendering of the classical pastoral elegy, Spenser's "November Eclogue" reveals the strength convention may have as a means of conveying significance and sentiment. Through such consciously artificial and "unreal" devices as a quaintly rustic setting and a "rough" shepherd who is yet a polished poet, Spenser establishes an allegorical framework for a lyric meditation on human mortality. The dead shepherdess is a symbolic figure in a symbolic landscape. The pastoral "green world," distant from the realms of city and court, suggests a golden age or prelapsarian Eden, where man is close to nature and to God's cosmic design as expressed in the cycles of seasonal growth and decay.

In his reflections on death and his evocation of a responsive nature, Spenser exploits the symbolic code of the classical elegy, which went beyond simple commemoration of an individual to a deeper consideration of the universal human condition since man's Fall.

Spenser skillfully combines the pagan conventions he employs in his expression of sorrow with a religious consolation, moving from a poignant depiction of universal desolation and loss to a joyous recognition of Dido's continued life in another world. He thus superimposes on the gravely dolorous elegiac structure a pattern of descent and ascent, the rising movement of the close specifically associated with the drama of resurrection.

The pastoral conventions, then, give the poem allegorical and symbolic resonance as well as providing a basic pattern on which Spenser can embroider his Christian variations.

11.5 Analyze the structure of "The November Eclogue."

Answer The narrative framework, consisting of a dialogue between Colin and Thenot on the proper matter for a song befitting the winter season, places the eclogue in the scheme of *The Shepheardes Calender* as a whole. It establishes the sense of a specific rhetorical occasion and prepares the reader for a specific poetic genre, the elegy; the poem itself thus becomes an artistic performance or set piece demonstrating Colin's (and Spenser's) skill in a particular form of composition.

Despite Colin's disclaimer that his "rhymes been rugged and unkempt" (line 51) and despite the consciously rustic diction, the elegy itself is elaborately patterned, its structure skillfully framed to suggest a dramatic progression. Two-thirds of the poem is devoted to a downward movement: Colin invokes the Muse of tragedy, Melpomene, and calls on his shepherd companions to join in his lament; he compares human mortality with the regenerative cycles of nature; he itemizes Dido's virtues; and he describes all nature in mourning. The repeated refrain "O heavy hearse . . . O careful verse" creates an air of ritual commemoration; this is plainly a *ceremony* of mourning, not a spontaneous outburst of emotion. The nadir of the poem is the stanza on mutability, in which the lament expands into a recognition of universal desolation and loss.

A sudden shift occurs toward the end of the elegy as the poet turns from evocation and commemoration of loss to joyful recognition and celebration: "But maugre death, and dreaded sisters' deadly spite,/ . . . She hath the bonds broke of eternal night." The change in the refrain at this point ("O happy hearse . . . O joyful verse") draws attention to the central paradox of Christian belief: people die to live, fall to rise. As Spenser develops his vision of Dido at play in the Elysian fields of paradise, he treats her as an intercessor for the mortal throng below, gone before to join the ranks of the saints. Thus the occasion for mourning passes and the sorrowful question "Why live we any longer then?" changes to "Why wail we then?"

The inner structure of the elegy, then, constitutes a dramatic progression from sorrow to joy and an enactment of the pattern of resurrection, the descent into death followed by the ascent to eternal life. The epilogue between Thenot and Colin serves to complete the poetic act, distancing the lament as a finished artifact and drawing the reader back into the homely, rustic world of the shepherds.

11.6   Analyze the nature imagery in "The November Eclogue."

Answer   Spenser uses the pastoral setting to express two opposing attitudes toward nature. On the one hand, he depicts a poignant contrast between humanity and nature: mortals, though the chief "branch" and "bud" of virtue, cannot return from death, while the perennial "floweret of the field" blooms afresh after its wintry interment. The contrast between natural rebirth and human evanescence derives from Greek idylls and from Old Testament sources such as the books of Job and Ecclesiastes. Only toward the end of the poem does Spenser introduce the New Testament notion of the immortal soul received into a Christian heaven, a rebirth parallel to the regeneration of the flowers of the field, but transcending the natural order.

The second attitude toward nature involves a sympathetic identification between human beings and all other living forms. Spenser depicts the autumnal landscape of his "November Eclogue" as a grieving being, with the fading leaves, dried streams, and melting rains suggesting a mournful withering, gasping, and weeping. Not only vegetative life but birds and beasts join with the human mourners in lamenting the passing of Dido. Thus Spenser exploits the natural setting of the poem to suggest a sense of universal depletion and desolation.

Both the difference and the likeness between nature and humanity become means of expressing sorrow and loss. The contemplation of humanity's lonely fate and of nature's emblematic decline constitutes the downward movement of the poem, which reaches its nadir in the stanza on mutability: "O trustless state of earthly things, . . ." (line 153). The last four stanzas then create a rising movement, reaching a supernatural apotheosis. The transient and imperfect realm of earthly nature is left behind in the ecstatic vision of Dido in paradise, where the beauty of nature is eternal and perfect: "The fields aye fresh, the grass aye green."

Epithalamion

11.7 In the *Epithalamion*, written to celebrate his own marriage to Elizabeth Boyle of Kilcolman, Ireland, Spenser drew on the classical convention of the "marriage song" (Greek *epithalamion*, "song over the marriage bed"). This genre is related to other types of occasional poetry (the elegy, the birthday poem, the ode of welcome, and so on) in that its chief purpose is to praise and honor a person or event. Discuss specific techniques of laudation Spenser uses in the poem.

Answer In the first place, the whole narrative strategy of recounting the preparations, rites, and festivities of the wedding day is laudatory in effect, constituting a pageant which honors Spenser's bride. The poet also praises his beloved by description of her attributes, so endowing her with value and significance. Spenser uses the *blazon* detailing physical beauties and spiritual virtues to make a concentrated statement of all that is praiseworthy in his bride. In lingering tenderly over each feature, comparing the lady's physical attributes to the bounties of nature, Spenser combines erotic appreciation with religious reverence. The attitude of reverence continues in the description of the bride's inner radiance, her purity, chastity, and modesty, and in the depiction of the sacramental ritual, which binds the couple in "endless matrimony." The descriptive and narrative threads converge in stanzas 12 and 13, which describe the church ceremony, from the entrance of the bride to the priest's performance of the nuptial rite.

From the specific wedding day, Spenser moves to praise of marriage as an eternal bond, an "endless monument" of mortal life. Again both narrative and descriptive techniques contribute to the encomium, with the blessing on the marriage bed at nightfall serving as both a dramatic and rhetorical climax in the poem. Spenser invokes supernatural forces as a way of stressing the naturalness, fruitfulness, and godliness of marriage by calling on the deities connected with each of these qualities. The religious imagery, both here and in the earlier scene in the church, suggests that love and marriage possess the ultimate sanction and the final attribute of praise in that they represent God's plan. Love, marriage, and procreation constitute a divinely ordained pattern which issues forth in an eternity of saved souls.

Calling on the universal order, from angels to beasts, to celebrate with him, Spenser creates a dual sense of "marital" occasion. The poem is, in part, a memento of a particular occasion: June 11, 1599, Spenser's own wedding day; it is also, in part, a meditation on a universal human blessing: the sacrament of marriage and its holy consummation in the fruitful union of man and woman.

11.8   Analyze the use of invocation in the poem.

Answer   Spenser begins the *Epithalamion* with the conventional invocation of the Muses, requesting "Ye learned sisters" to "Help me mine own love's praises to resound." This is only the first in a long series of requests, invitations, commands, and prayers which create a continuous thread of direct address throughout the poem. Stanza by stanza Spenser calls on a vast range of beings, both supernatural and earthly, to join him in praising his beloved and celebrating his marriage. This swelling chorus of voices, he suggests in the refrain, will reverberate through all of nature to create a cosmic harmony: "The woods shall to you answer, and your echo ring." The idea of a responsive universe, a natural order which "echoes" and reflects the human order, permeates the poem. Thus, not only does Spenser "call on" the world around him, but the world answers.

The invocations differ subtly in purpose and tone, from the imperatives commanding the village youths and maidens to prepare for the festivities (stanza 7), to propitiatory incantations warding off evil (stanza 19), to prayers for fruitfulness and happiness (stanzas 21–23). At times, Spenser strikes the homely, personal note of a fussy bridegroom worrying over the details of the ceremony or the humorous stance of a superstitious villager invoking magic and ritual to ensure good fortune. But the closing stanzas, addressed to Cynthia, Juno, Genius, and "ye high heavens," move toward religious meditation as Spenser prays for a blessing "over the marriage bed," thus recalling the literal Greek meaning of *epithalamion*.

Throughout the poem, the reiterated direct address produces a tone which is intimate yet formal; Spenser, the private man, shows himself engaged in a social event which is also a sacramental occasion. The final six lines of the poem, the *tornato*, have a distancing effect as Spenser concludes with an address to the song itself. The song becomes a completed artifact, an ornament or gift for the bride and a commemoration ("an endless monument") of the occasion. Here Spenser formally adopts the role of poet and a self-conscious, self-assessing tone to complete his poem of personal celebration.

Thus the technique of invocation is Spenser's means of conveying his own intimate involvement with the occasion as earnest bridegroom, devout believer, and poetic celebrant.

11.9   Kenneth Hieatt's study of the *Epithalamion*, titled *Short Time's Endless Monument: The Symbolism of the Numbers in Edmund Spenser's Epithalamion* (1960), offers evidence for a complicated astronomical and numerological scheme in the poem, symbolizing the progress of time. For example, the 365 long lines in the poem correspond to the days of the year; the twenty-four stanzas parallel the hours of a day; and the shift at the sixteenth stanza from day to night reflects the number of daylight hours on Spenser's wedding day, June 11, the summer solstice.

Discuss other evidence in the poem of Spenser's preoccupation with time.

Answer   The most obvious indication in the *Epithalamion* of Spenser's concern with time is the narrative sequence of the poem, which documents, hour by hour, the events of the wedding day: the awakening of the beloved at dawn, the villagers' preparations, the bride's stately entrance, the performance of marriage rites, the postnuptial activities, and the final going to bed. The allusions to planetary deities—Aurora, Phoebus, Hesperus, Cynthia—contribute to the impression of the slow wheeling movement from day to night, as does the marked shift in the refrain in stanza 17, which invokes night's silence ("The woods no more shal answere, nor your echo ring").

Beyond the literal chronology of the poem, Spenser develops the implications of time in his treatment of marriage as a temporal event which paradoxically transcends time. The marriage sacrament joins the partners not just for a day, or even for a lifetime, but for all eternity: "The sacred ceremonies . . ./ The which do endless matrimony make." Spenser builds upon this relatively conventional idea in his closing prayer to Genius, the patron of fecundity and birth, and to "ye high heavens," that is, the stars and angels dwelling in the mansions of heaven. Through procreation, marriage empowers people to transcend their own brief time on earth, their children surviving them as a kind of legacy. Furthermore, Spenser alludes to the literal immortality of all these new-created souls in the kingdom of heaven: "And for the guerdon of their glorious merit/ May heavenly tabernacles there inherit" (lines 421–422). Repeated puns on the word "timely" ("timely seed," "timely fruit," "timely joys") reinforce the theme of transcending time through a "luck" which is, in fact, the natural blessedness attending on marriage.

Finally, Spenser emphasizes the patterns within change which make the mutable partake of the eternal. As Spenser describes the single day, the "short time," of his wedding day, he creates the impression of ordered design through allusions to the planets—sun, moon, stars—which mark out the diurnal round. Implicit in the passing hours of a single day is the patterned revolution of seasons and years:

> But first come ye, fair Hours which were begot
> In Jove's sweet paradise of Day and Night,
> Which do the seasons of the year allot,
> And all that ever in this world is fair
> Do make and still repair.
>
> (lines 98–102)

The processes of generation and renewal, in the rebirth of spring, in the reproduction of the human species, and in the resurrection of the saved soul, all express providential design. Thus, continual change symbolizes not destructive chaos but an eternal pattern, and the "short time" of a day, a season, or a life becomes the stuff of an "endless monument."

The Faerie Queene

11.10 What are the genre and form of *The Faerie Queene* as a whole, and what part in that form do Books I and II play?

Answer In an introductory letter to Sir Walter Ralegh, Spenser outlines his intended structure for *The Faerie Queene*: twelve books, each devoted to one of the twelve moral virtues and each comprising a kind of miniature epic. There are to be twelve epic heroes, one for each virtue, and a central protagonist, the "magnificent" Arthur, who will appear in each book and whose quest for Gloriana will provide a unified center for the whole.

But this methodical organization, with its numerical patterns and systematic relationships, can hardly be felt in the six books of *The Faerie Queene* which Spenser completed. The narrative lacks the orderly, coherent design that Spenser seems to have intended. Rather, it is characterized throughout by the abruptness which, in the letter to Ralegh, he acknowledges to be a feature of the beginning of the work. The first line of the epic, "A gentle knight was pricking on the playne," is only the first of a myriad of instances in which a scene or picture seems to loom up out of nowhere. The names of the actors in these scenes are often withheld for many stanzas, so that the action seems dreamlike and disconnected. A certain anonymity pervades the landscape as well, for the places of Faerie Land seem unmapped, existing in a world without geographical relationships. Juxtapositions of places, events, and characters are capricious rather than sequential or chronological, and the narrative seems to proliferate rather than develop.

The episodic nature of the narrative derives in part from Spenser's use of romance materials. Behind *The Faerie Queene* are the conventions of medieval romance, including the central motif of a chivalric knight embarked on a spiritual or amorous quest; the overall picaresque structure, with adventure following adventure in casual, rather than causal, order; the theme of combat with dragons, giants, and other fantastic creatures; and the theme of erotic intrigue and betrayal. Combining these traditions with certain epic conventions—the idea of a national hero, the theme of "magnificence" or "great doing," the elevated style—and drawing as well on the models of the great Renaissance epics written by his Italian contemporaries Ariosto (*Orlando Furioso*) and Tasso (*Gerusalemma Liberata*), Spenser composed his own rich, sensuous, leisurely narrative, with its proliferating tales and meandering development. Thus, both the Red Cross Knight (Book I) and Guyon (Book II) are knights with heroic missions to fulfill (the slaying of the dragon and the destruction of the Bower of Bliss); both are continually distracted from the objects of their quests by random combats and temptations.

However, it is not only the generic influence of medieval romance that accounts for the disconnected narrative of *The Faerie Queene*. Rather, Spenser seems to have chosen his method of composition with a particular aesthetic purpose in mind. Thus in the letter to Ralegh he defends the apparent disorder of his work, specifically its lack of chronology, by distinguishing between poets and historiographers:

> For the Methode of a Poet historical is not such, as of an Historiographer. For an Historiographer discourseth of affayres orderly as they were donne, accounting as well the times as the actions, but a Poet thrusteth into the middest, even where it most concerneth him, and there recoursing to the thinges forepaste, and divining of thinges to come, maketh a pleasing Analysis of all.

Spenser's intention is less to tell a story than to analyze a theme, and thus the emphasis is on logical and rhetorical processes of comparison, cause and effect, etymology, and definition rather than on such narrative structures as climax and denouement or suspense and revelation. The analytic intention explains the narrative's tendency toward redundancy, digressiveness, rhetorical profuseness, and static pictorialism. Thus Red Cross's combats with Sans foy and Sans joy and Guyon's with Pyrochles and Cymochles do not advance the "story" but illustrate a subject through repetition and variation. The numerous inset tales, for example, the stories of Fradubio and Trevisan in Book I or the stories of Amavia and Phedon in Book II, are not truly digressive because they contribute to the analysis of holiness and temperance by exhibiting their opposites. The rhetorical set pieces of Despair (Book I) and Mammon (Book II) slow up the story while once again illuminating theme. In these cases, Spenser uses the devil's mouthpieces to play devil's advocate, offering arguments against faith and continence and defining them through their chief antagonists. In a similar way the House of Pride and the House of Holiness (Book I), and Medina's house and Alma's (Book II), illustrate the chief concepts of the two books even as they inhibit the forward thrust of the narrative.

If something is accomplished, finally, in Books I and II of *The Faerie Queene*, a dragon killed and a bower destroyed, it is not precisely true that these ultimate actions constitute the climax of each story. The story as Spenser tells it is not the construction of a plot or the development of a character, but the growth of an idea. His analysis of theme is multivalent, syncretistic, cubistic: he views the central idea first from one angle, then from another, offering similitudes, opposites, examples, causes, and effects. Thus the structure of *The Faerie Queene* consists of the proliferating symbols, pictures, stories, and words with which the poet examines his central concept.

11.11 Discuss the function of the "doubles" in Book I of *The Faerie Queene*.

Answer The doubling, and sometimes tripling or quadrupling, of similar characters, places, and incidents is part of Spenser's general rhetorical strategy of amplification and copiousness. Dealing with the theme of faith's conquest over evil, the poet multiplies instances and examples to illustrate the many varieties of sin and error people are likely to encounter in their pilgrimage on earth. The didactic effect of these moral illustrations derives partly from the narrator's explicit commentary but partly from the very fact of repetition. Like a preacher delivering a sermon, Spenser says, in effect, look at this, and now this, and now this, to drive home his cautionary message. Man must know what evil is, and what it looks like, in order to defeat it.

Thus there are three "paynims," the brothers Sans foy, Sans loy, and Sans joy; four dragons, Error in Canto i, the beast Lucifera rides in Canto iv, the seven-headed monster Orgoglio gives to Duessa in Canto vii, and the dragon ravaging the kingdom of Una's parents in Canto xi; two figures associated with pride, Lucifera and Orgoglio; two betrayals engineered by Duessa, Red Cross's of Una and Fradubio's of Fraelissa; two "despairs," Sans joy and Despair himself; and three representatives of ignorance, Abessa (superstition) and Corceca (blind devotion) in Canto iii and Ignaro, keeper of Orgoglio's castle, in Canto viii.

In addition to the didactic import of all these related figures and episodes, a further effect of the repetitions is to provide a sense of dreamlike interrelationship, in which images are linked through their unexpressed symbolic connections. The device of pairing and multiplication thus contributes to thematic unity and coherence in a work which, on the narrative level, is an intricate labyrinth of disconnected adventures. It is the dream scenario, as opposed to the complex and meandering plot, that conveys the allegorical significance of Red Cross's pilgrimage. What the dream suggests is the fecundity of evil, the proliferation of nightmare encounters documenting the unceasing struggle of the Christian to conquer the enemies of faith. Beheading one dragon is not enough, for three others are waiting in the wings; escaping from one kind of pride may lead to one's easy capture by another kind. The very copiousness of the Red Cross Knight's combats suggests a kind of mechanical substitution, with one foe replacing another in an endless chain. This in turn suggests a fundamental kinship among all types of evil, a kinship literalized in the portrayal of the brothers Sans foy, Sans loy, and Sans joy. Despite their slightly differing narrative functions, they are essentially an interchangeable fairy-tale trio like Cinderella's wicked steprelatives.

In other instances the repetitions seem designed to distinguish among evils, to contrast them and probe their subtle differences. Thus the double treatment of pride in the persons of Lucifera and Orgoglio represents two of the possible guises, or disguises, of a single abstract vice. Lucifera is undoubtedly the more attractive or seductive of the two, "A mayden Queene, that shone as Titan's ray/ In glistering gold, and peerelesse pretious stone" (I.iv.8 meaning Book I, Canto iv, stanza 8). The lady's glittering surface is associated with vanity, exhibitionism, and the empty splendor of court life. That Lucifera's radiant beauty is only a "false semblant" becomes immediately clear through the comparison to Phaeton (a type of Lucifer symbolizing satanic *hubris*) and through the descriptions of her dragon (the beast of Revelation), her mirror (emblematic of self-love), her lineage (daughter of Pluto), and her "six wizards old" (the other six of the seven deadly sins).

In Lucifera Spenser approaches pride from an external or social perspective, providing attributes and glosses which allow the reader to penetrate beneath appearances to her true significance. In Orgoglio, on the other hand, he makes appearance and reality coincide, providing a graphic rendering of pride as physical deformity. The giant is "this monstrous masse of earthly slime,/ Puft up with emptie wind and fild with sinful crime" (I,vii,9). Orgoglio's hideous corporeality directly conveys the idea that pride originates not in a temptation toward ornament or exhibitionism but in the fleshly human body itself. While Spenser's treatment of the two figures resists any exact dichotomy, the contrast between them is nonetheless instructive. It is clear at least that Orgoglio is a more nightmarish and active foe than Lucifera with her pictorial attributes. Furthermore it is the pride of Orgoglio, the internal, inescapable pride in the carnal self, rather than the vanity of Lucifera, to which the Red Cross Knight succumbs.

Thus the repetitions of Book I anatomize evil, both in the manner of a sermon and in the manner of a dream. The reiterated encounters with sin also say something about the nature of man's perceptions of evil. On the one hand, it is easy to see sin for what it is: the three Sarazin brothers blazon their names on their shields, the hideous serpent Error spits books, the House of Pride is built on sand. On the other hand, it is hard to see, as the doubling of Duessa for Una and of Archimago for the Red Cross Knight suggests. The fact that the hero and heroine of the story can be counterfeited by their opposites implies that evil is not only a pervasive phenomenon but a protean and insidious one. It is not always clearly something "other," existing outside the self and alien to it; rather, it can greet one like a friend or a lover.

11.12   The encounter between a Christian hero and a satanic foe constitutes the major symbolic action in Book I of *The Faerie Queene*. Focusing on Red Cross's joust with the dragon in Canto xi, discuss the allegory of combat and the relationship between this climactic battle and earlier armed encounters in the book.

Answer   One of the chief characteristics of the allegory of combat is its bloodiness. Blood flows, gushes, streams, dyes, stains; heads are cleft, limbs chopped, wings and tails hewn off. The battle scenes are full of violent and hyperbolic description, larded with similes which bring in the animal world (rams, gryphons, dragons, hawks, bulls) and the elements (Jove's thunderbolts, raging seas, crashing oaks, earthquakes, avalanches) to convey the enormous intensity and power with which the antagonists clash. The knightly combats (between Red Cross and Sans foy, Red Cross and Sans joy, Archimago as Red Cross and Sans loy, Satyrane and Sans loy) are on the whole less terrible than the fights with monsters, drawing as they do on the language and conventions of jousting, with blows exchanged, shields and helmets dented, passes made, and enemies unseated. However, all the battle scenes, to one degree or another, convey an image of violent grappling amid purple gore. The pictorial extremism implies the extremity of Red Cross's peril, as well as the extremity of his response. Each struggle is a life-and-death one for the Christian fighting his way toward his own salvation.

The three monsters in Book I are special cases in the general allegory of combat. These inhuman creatures embody the idea of sin in a way the nearly indistinguishable Paynims do not. The faithlessness of Sans foy remains an abstraction, while Error becomes a corporeal presence, a she-monster who vomits books and breeds baby errors. Like an allegorical woodcut, the serpent literalizes the concept of heresy as the vile regurgitation and reproduction of falsehood. Reminded by Una to "Add faith unto your force," the Red Cross Knight is suddenly able, after a few stanzas of scuffling, to behead the dragon with one decisive stroke. The denouement of the episode, in which the offspring of the serpent devour their dead mother, illustrates the Christian conception that sin is, in the end, self-consuming.

The net effect of this initial encounter is to suggest Red Cross's essential preparedness to do battle against the more overt "errors" which assail humanity in its pilgrimage on earth. He is, after all, dressed in "the whole armor of God" (Ephesians 6:11–13) and attended by Una, the one true faith of the reformed church. (I.i.2–4)

However, the general pattern described by the combats is a downward curve. If Red Cross can defeat Sans foy rather handily, once separated from Una he finds himself in progressively graver danger. The victory over Sans joy is not decisive, for the Sarazin is wrapped in a cloud and carried down to hell before Red Cross can deliver a death stroke. By the time he confronts the next monster, Orgoglio, he has been too long in the company of Duessa, the false Romish faith, and has drunk from a magically ill-fated fountain which weakens him. The allegorical suggestion is that Red Cross has been enfeebled by despair (Sans joy), misled by falsehood (Duessa), and tempted into spiritual lassitude (the drinking from the fountain of sloth). He is thus an easy victim of carnal pride as represented by the giant Orgoglio.

Rescue is accomplished by Arthur, who makes his first appearance in *The Faerie Queene* in his meeting with Una in Canto vii and his subsequent defeat of Orgoglio in Canto viii. The special significance of Arthur to *The Faerie Queene* as a whole is evident from the lengthy, almost hieratic description given him in Canto vii. Radiant with light, he wears the badge of Gloriana (the "Ladies head") on his breast and bears a veiled diamond shield with magical powers. In the person of Arthur a mythical and political strain enters the predominantly religious allegory of Book I. Arthur never seems in serious danger from Orgoglio, lightly sidestepping the giant's first murderous stroke and patiently hacking away at the enemy (first smiting off Orgoglio's left arm, then his right leg, and finally his head) until victory is achieved. The magic shield, accidentally uncovered when Arthur falls, releases a "blazing brightnes" which is partially suggestive of Christ's grace in the religious scheme of Book I. But the radiance also signifies the legendary magic associated with the magnificent, "great-doing" founder of the British nation, who in defeating Red Cross's captor saves the knight for his role as St. George, patron saint of England. Finally the shield's brilliance connotes the illumination of the one true faith, with Arthur as the national or Anglican church combating Orgoglio, who represents (according to some commentators) the Church of Rome. In this interpretation the piecemeal dismemberment of Orgoglio in a violent, bloody encounter symbolizes the slow but sure defeat of Catholicism in England. Whether as a symbol of Christ, of England, of the reformed church, or, as is common in Spenser, of all three, Arthur appears as an invulnerable hero who "Slayes the Gyant, wounds the beast/ and strips Duessa quight."

Violence, bloodiness, and dismemberment also characterize Red Cross's encounter, in Canto xi, with the dragon ravaging the kingdom of Una's parents, but Red Cross seems anything but invulnerable in the course of the combat. In fact this climactic confrontation seems to stress the vulnerability of the solitary Christian soul as represented by Red Cross. The dragon, his foe, is clearly connected with Satan, who since the Fall has held Adam and Eve (Una's parents) hostage to death. In contrast to the vomiting, spawning dragon of Canto i, this one spits fire, not books, and as the elaborate description of his scales, wings, tail, claws, teeth, and eyes makes clear, he comes to the battle formidably equipped. The hacking and hewing, the wounds and the falls, the "blood and gobbets" are described extensively, with Spenser detailing every stroke and counterstroke delivered over the three days of battle in order to magnify the ultimate encounter between frail man on the one side and the combined forces of sin, Satan, and death on the other. The sense of an elaborate parallel text beneath the narrative is evoked by allusions to the Old and New Testaments and by the insistent emphasis on Red Cross's deathlike falls and miraculous recoveries, on one occasion through a fountain (the Well of Life) and on the other through a balm (the wine-and-blood of the Tree of Life). The reference to Christ's baptism (the well) and Crucifixion (the tree) as the specific means by which Christ triumphed over sin and death, as well as the general action of falling to rise, conveys basic tenets of Christian thought and dramatizes the redemption and salvation of the soul.

But apart from the specific theological subtext, this last battle is like the other combats in Book I in its insistence on the violence and intensity of struggle. The final encounter is an amplification and extension of the motif of struggle, the great inequality between the contestants adding an element of suspense which is relieved only by the emphatically conclusive statement "So downe he fell . . . So downe he fell . . . So downe he fell . . . So downe he fell" (I.xi.54).

All the combats in Book I draw on romance conventions and motifs, from chivalric jousting to the slaying of giants and dragons, and they all illustrate the religious theme of the militant Christian pilgrim doing battle against sin. The final encounter differs from the earlier ones in the extent of its theological parallels and the elaborateness of its epic embroidery. It is climactic partly because of its religious significance, showing a Christ-like deliverance of humanity from sin, and partly because of its national significance, portraying the historical and legendary St. George slaying the dragon and, symbolically, all the foes of Britain.

11.13   Analyze Spenser's allegorical technique in the description of the House of Holiness in Book I, Canto x.

Answer   Canto x elucidates in diagrammatic form the central concept underlying the entire tale of the Red Cross Knight: the idea of holiness. The introductory quatrain emphasizes the didactic significance of the episode:

> Her faithful knight fair Una brings
> To House of Holiness,
> Where he is taught repentance and
> The way to heavenly bliss.

Spenser's technique in describing Red Cross's "education" in holiness is largely pictorial and static. Instead of using the conventions of medieval romance to create allegorical fable, as elsewhere in Book I, here the poet exploits the conventions of religious iconography to create doctrinal emblems.

The chief theological virtues, faith, hope, and charity, appear in Canto x as allegorical statues with symbolic attributes. Fidelia's cup and book, Speranza's silver anchor, and Charissa's brood of infants may all be glossed by reference to the New Testament, to traditional church icons, and to the emblem books popular in the Renaissance, which depicted moral truths in symbolic pictorial form. For example, Fidelia's cup containing a serpent is the chalice of St. John, containing a poisoned draft which does him no harm. Quotations from Numbers and the Gospel of John indicate that cup and serpent symbolize redemption from sin and specifically the sacrament of communion. (Works of art from this period use the same symbols with much the same meaning.)

The events of Canto x similarly have the aspect of static pictures which allegorize theological doctrine. The image of Patience as physician of the soul applying leeches and salves to Red Cross's sin-festered flesh portrays in homely terms the meaning of an abstract virtue. The stages of Red Cross's recovery, involving Penance, Remorse, and Repentance, are likewise rendered as symbolic episodes. Remorse's pricking of Red Cross's heart until it bleeds and Repentance's bathing of his wounds in salt water are clearly not naturalistic actions but rather concrete translations of metaphoric conceits or ideas similar to those in medieval and Renaissance emblem books.

Red Cross's vision of the New Jerusalem, the etymology of his real name (St. George), and his return to earth to perform his saintly mission in the temporal realm also have a diagrammatic and expository quality different from the looser, multivalent symbolism of the narrative episodes drawn from medieval romance. Spenser exploits traditional doctrine, allusion, and icon not only in Canto x, but in Canto iv, when describing the House of Pride and the seven deadly sins. Wherever it occurs, the pictorial, emblematic technique has the effect of emphasizing the allegorical and didactic significance of the dreamlike narrative as a whole.

11.14 Discuss the basic conceit, or metaphor, governing the description of Alma's Castle in Book II, Canto x, and the allegorical significance of Maleger's assault upon it.

Answer Alma's Castle, the House of Temperance, is described as analogous to the human body in shape and function. The geometric figures which constitute its frame—a triangle at the base, a rectangle in the center, and a circle on top— suggest certain philosophical ideas about the human powers of reason and sense as they were conceived in the Renaissance. The perfect, "masculine" circle is equivalent to the "rational soul," imposing form or pattern on the imperfect, "feminine" triangle, which represents the "vegetative soul." The rectangle symbolizes the "sensible soul" which mediates between pure intellect and pure body. Furthermore, the overall shape created by these figures is essentially that of a man, the circle the head, the rectangle the torso, and the triangle the feet.

Spenser extends the basic anatomical conceit into an elaborate catalog of physical correspondences. A playful spirit informs these analogies, which are surprisingly witty and apt. For example, the barbican with its sixteen warders represents mouth and teeth, the portcullis the nose with its ivy "mustache," the bellows and oven of the kitchen the lungs and stomach, and the tower chambers the ventricles of the brain.

This well-developed physiological metaphor suggests important connotations of the classical concept of "temperance." In its root sense signifying an inter-mixing or blending, temperance implies, in Renaissance medical and psycho-logical thought, the proper relationship or balance among the four physiological "humors": black bile, yellow bile, phlegm, and blood. The perfect equilibrium of these four disparate elements was the state of the virtuous and temperate person, while the predominance of one element over another produced specified character disorders. For example, too much black bile produced a melancholic temperament, too much yellow bile a choleric or irascible type, and too much blood a concupiscent, ambitious personality.

The notion of balance includes the idea of decorum in the relations among disparate parts or elements. Each room in Alma's Castle has its proper function, the harmony of the household deriving from the organized distribution of dif-ferent powers and activities which intermesh in an organic whole. A smooth integration of parts distinguishes Alma's Castle from Medina's, where the in-habitants are constantly warring, the "imbalances" of lust and violence only barely contained through Medina's strenuous efforts. Medina, or the "mean," is associated with the lesser virtue of continence or self-denial, which a person may cultivate as a form of self-control but which falls short of the perfect equilibrium of the genuinely temperate person.

Thus Alma's Castle, the House of Temperance, cannot be threatened from within, as Medina's can; however, it is clearly vulnerable to an assault from outside its walls. The storming of the walls by Maleger's monstrous retinue symbolizes first physical disease, and second the devil's deadly onslaught on the Christian soul in the form of the temptations of sin. As Maleger's name suggests, he is both a representation of the sickness by which sin reveals itself (*male* + *aeger*, "badly sick") and a bearer of evil (*male* + *gerens*, "evil-bearing"). The theological conception of sin as the lot of fallen man, a basic and unavoidable "distemper" against which he must do battle to win his salvation, goes beyond the pagan notion of a moral imbalance to be corrected by the rational will. That reason, faith, and grace are required to conquer sin is implied by the defeat of the satanic Maleger. This deathlike foe can be quelled only by the decisive intervention of Prince Arthur, who symbolizes both Christian grace and the perfection of all the human virtues combined.

11.15   In the course of Book II of *The Faerie Queene*, two strands of narrative are interwoven, one involving the exploits of Guyon and the other the adventures of Arthur. Compare the two strands, analyzing their allegorical significance.

Answer   Guyon is a pagan hero symbolizing the classical virtue of temperance. To achieve this ideal state of perfect harmony and inner balance, Guyon must rely on the palmer, who represents right reason, to guide him in his constant struggle for control over and containment of the passions, which would otherwise produce the distempered states symbolized by Pyrochles and Cymochles. To avoid such vicious imbalance, Guyon must strive for continence, not allowing violent emotion to overcome his rational understanding. The proper harmony depends not on repression of all emotion but rather on the establishment of a mean or measure among such passions as fear, anger, ambition, and lust. At the end of Book II, Guyon is sufficiently master of himself and his emotions to resist the blandishments of the beautiful Acrasia, who symbolizes incontinence, and to destroy the Bower of Bliss. His earlier adventures with Pyrochles and Cymochles and in the Cave of Mammon suggest both the efficacy and the limitations of pagan virtue, with its emphasis on rational control, in combating the moral vices of wrath, lust, and greed.

Book II, however, is not only a moral allegory illustrating a classical virtue but also a religious and political allegory illustrating the theological concepts of sin and grace and the themes of legendary history and national destiny. Arthur is the hero of this level of the narrative. According to Spenser's intention as set forth in his letter to Sir Walter Ralegh, Arthur's deeds were to be "applyable to that vertue which I write of in that book," Arthur himself representing the sum of all the twelve moral virtues, or "magnificence," that is, "great-doing." Thus in Book II Arthur represents the perfect temperance which Guyon has not yet achieved. As in Book I Arthur succors the hero at the moment of his greatest weakness or distress, saving the unconscious Guyon from being despoiled of his arms by fighting off Pyrochles and Cymochles just as he had earlier delivered Red Cross from a near-fatal imprisonment by vanquishing Orgoglio. Although he is injured in both combats, Arthur nonetheless decisively conquers the enemies of "holiness" and "temperance" by killing them once and for all. Arthur is thus linked to the moral scheme of Books I and II, while suggesting a perfected virtue which is dependent not only on human powers of reason and self-mastery but on something supernatural, beyond the realm of moral philosophy. In part his special abilities seem connected with Christian faith: operating in the realm of grace he is peculiarly chosen or blessed. In the fight with Pyrochles and Cymochles, a combat of two against one, he is helped by the fact that his own sword, fallen into his enemy's hand, "refuses" to harm him, as well as by the palmer's timely offer of Guyon's sword when he finds himself weaponless. In the combat with Maleger he is able to destroy the hags Impatience and Impotence as well as the "evil-bearer" himself through an insightful recognition of the sources of their power. Although there is no exact correspondence between any of Arthur's "great doings" and an allegorical scheme, the miraculous quality of his victories seems to derive from a spiritual understanding, as opposed to Guyon's rational comprehension. In Books I and II Arthur is a savior and even, at times, like Christ the Savior himself.

Arthur is also connected with the theme of British history and national destiny, as the lengthy chronicle of Canto x suggests. Canto x also implies a relationship between the "real" history of British kings (actually based on legendary material) and the antiquity of Faerie Land. Elfin history is quite brief in comparison with the tangled narrative of war, treason, betrayal, and murder which describes in mythic terms 700 years of British rule. It requires only six stanzas to trace Faerie Land's past from Elf, the Promethean originator of the Elfin race, to Gloriana, that is, Queen Elizabeth. Here the progression is orderly and rational as the various kings speedily subdue foreign enemies, build cities and monuments, and hand down the succession to offspring in "their due descents" (II.x.74). Thus Arthur, British king and seeker of Gloriana, becomes a link between the confused legends of British history and the philosophical ideal of a temperate, rational, Christian rule on earth which Elizabeth, as the Elfin queen, was meant to signify.

The relationship between Guyon and Arthur has multiple meanings. Guyon is an Elfin knight, a pagan hero attempting with the aid of the palmer Reason to wreak revenge on Acrasia ("incontinence"), who has had a destructive effect on the family of man (the Mortdant/Amavia story) and who exerts a Circean allure for knights-errant and all wandering souls (the Bower of Bliss). Guyon's partial victories over Pyrochles, symbolic of choler, and Cymochles, symbolic of sensuality, and his resolute destruction of the bower with all its temptations suggest the efficacy of self-containment or "continence." In contrast, Arthur is a Christian hero and a specifically British one. His relatively easy victories over Pyrochles, Cymochles, and Maleger indicate that his temperance is not so much an active struggle to master various emotional excesses as an inner condition, a state of grace. His serene power and self-assurance also suggest his role as mythic forebear to Gloriana and prophet of a national destiny.

In the relationship between the two heroes of Book II, Spenser draws on many definitions of temperance and continence, both classical and contemporary. He also brings into play notions of spiritual grace and imperial destiny, the physiology of the body and the psychology of the humors. The characterizations of Arthur and Guyon exhibit the syncretistic quality typical of *The Faerie Queene* as a whole, the tendency of the allegory to become many allegories and of "strands" of the narrative to become entangled in complex patterns which resist simple diagrams or formulas.

11.16 Discuss the significance of the following features of the Bower of Bliss (II.xii): the ivory waves sculptured on the gate; the golden ivy painted green; the Genius of the Bower; the descriptions of naked damsels and of Acrasia with Verdant; and Guyon's destruction of the bower.

Answer All these features suggest the negative connotations of Acrasia's beautiful bower. Although Spenser often treats beauty and art as emblems of spiritual value, in the bower he illustrates the moral ambiguity of aesthetic illusion. One of the methods he uses to convey the insidious evil of this false Eden is ambivalent descriptions of art and artifice. By emphasizing the intermingling of art with nature in the skillfully fashioned landscape, he suggests that this art is somehow suspect. At best, the art of the craftsperson can only imitate nature, the handiwork of God; but here art is not only imitative but a kind of blasphemous mimicry, a deceitful illusion concealing the distinction between the real and the false. Although the ivory waves on the gate "seemed a work of admirable wit" (II.xii.44), they are, in fact, an instance of overrefined artifice and seductive illusionism. Apparently undulating and alive, they are really a static imitation. The description of the golden ivy (II.xii.61) is even more clearly an indictment of false seeming, its green coloring a deceptive trick to make it appear "ivy true" and its "lascivious arms" a sensual snare for the unwary spectator.

The relationship between art and nature was a major topic in Renaissance writing, and Spenser is in part restating a commonplace when he connects art with falsehood and deceit. But the greatest authors of the period, including Shakespeare, implied more than a simple dichotomy between the realms of art and nature. For example, in *The Winter's Tale* Polixenes makes the argument that in the gardener's technique of grafting different stocks to produce hybrids, "the art itself is nature" (Act IV, Scene iv, line 97). Nature perfects itself by harnessing the art and science of humanity to its purposes. The reconciliation of the two terms is important as well in works of literary criticism such as Sidney's *Defense of Poesy*, where he maintains that God, the Maker of nature, has given the poet his "erected wit" or reason so that he may make a "second nature," a golden world which images the perfection of nature before the Fall. Art is thus God's way of perfecting nature.

In the Bower of Bliss, Spenser stresses the conflict between art and nature, but he implies that such strife between the two is itself unnatural:

> One would have thought (so cunningly, the rude,
> And scorned partes were mingled with the fine,)
> That Nature had for wantonesse ensude
> Art, and that Art at Nature did repine;
> So striving each th'other to undermine,
> Each did the others worke more beautifie;
> So diff'ring both in willes, agreed in fine:
> So all agreed through sweet diversitie,
> This Gardin to adorne with all varietie.
>
> (II.xii.59)

The language of this passage suggests that the contention between art and nature is a perversion of their proper relationship. Instead of participating in the ordered design of God's creation, with art in the service of nature, the two realms strive "to undermine" each other's place in the universal scheme. Although art and nature appear to have "agreed" in the end, issuing forth in "sweet diversitie," they produce only a false semblance of beauty, for the means themselves are corrupt. By focusing on the confusion and chaos of clashing "willes," Spenser implies the possibility of something better: a true concord yoking art and nature to God's will.

That Spenser can imagine "an art that nature makes" (*The Winter's Tale*, Act IV, Scene iv, lines 91–92), an art like Sidney's that mirrors divine truth rather than deceives the senses, is implied by his own activity as a poet. Furthermore, there are passages in *The Faerie Queene* that suggest an ideal union of nature and art. For example, in the Garden of Adonis (III.xii) nature is not raw and undisciplined, but symmetrical, ordered, harmonious, and formal. In the center of "that paradise" is a "stately mount," topped by a grove of myrtle trees that, without pruning or cropping, naturally make a "girlond" shedding "pretious deaw" (III.xii.43). Spenser goes on to describe the heart of the grove, "a pleasaunt arber, not by art,/ But of the trees owne inclination made" (III.xii.44), decorated with "wanton yvie" and various flowers connected with amorous myths. The idea of concentric circles produced not by any gardener but by the trees' "owne inclination" and the natural symbolism afforded by the ivy and flowers suggest "an art that nature makes": art in the service of nature, nature disciplined and perfected by art.

If Spenser at times affords a glimpse of a true Eden, a "second nature" which uses art to image forth perfection, the Bower of Bliss is emblematic of a fallen world where art and nature, intermingled and confused, subvert truth itself. The Genius of the Bower is the proper governor of a false Eden. Apparently a guardian of eternal bliss, he is actually

> The foe of life, that good envyes to all,
> That secretly doth us procure to fall
> Through guilefull semblaunts, which he makes us see, . . .
>   (II.xii.48)

The Genius represents a cosmic principle of false-seeming and deceit in the universe, offering a satanic invitation to mistake evil for good and good for evil. In the bower, the invitation to sin is couched as an assault on the senses, especially the sense of sight. Many of the descriptions have a titillating, erotic quality; Guyon finds himself in the position of a voyeur glimpsing sexually beguiling tableaux.

Thus the two naked damsels playing peekaboo in the waves of the fountain, exhibiting "lilly paps" and hiding "the rest" underneath the water, soften Guyon's "stubborne brest" (II.xii.65–67). Only the palmer's rebuke recalls his "wandering eyes" from the hypnotic spectacle. The description of Acrasia, posing on "a bed of roses" in a diaphanous gown, "her snowy brest . . . bare to readie spoyle/ Of hungry eies" (II.xii.77–78), again suggests the voyeuristic invitation of erotic art. With her sleeping lover by her side, she symbolizes the paralysis of lust which has emasculated the warlike Verdant and robbed him of all honorable ambition.

Guyon's destruction of the bower represents the efficacy of pagan virtue in combating the sensual vices of Acrasia and the moral confusions generated by the Genius. Guyon never sees through the beautiful appearances to the demonic, hideous reality beneath, for he lacks the spiritual insight with which Arthur confronts Maleger. Yet he fulfills his mission in accord with his moral code and his rational understanding, thus illustrating the value of temperance to the Christian in his worldly pilgrimage.

Guyon's pronouncement "Let Gryll be Gryll" indicates that the bower re-mains a perpetual possibility, for evil cannot be destroyed forever as long as human hearts seek it out. Evil consists not only of the external temptations of satanic forces like Archimago, Acrasia, and the Genius but of the internal desires and bestial passions residing within man. Although Guyon's moral virtue may temporarily defeat vice, only Christ's grace can permanently eradicate man's sins and redeem his soul.

B.S.

SUGGESTED READINGS

Alpers, Paul J., *The Poetry of The Faerie Queene* (1967).

Alpers, Paul J., ed., *Edmund Spenser: A Critical Anthology* (1969).

Berger, Harry, Jr., *The Allegorical Temper: Vision and Reality in Book II of Spenser's Faerie Queene* (1957).

Hough, Graham, *A Preface to The Faerie Queene* (1962).

Kellogg, Robert, and Oliver Steele, eds., *Books I and II of The Faerie Queene* (1965).

Nelson, William, *The Poetry of Edmund Spenser* (1963).

Roche, Thomas P., Jr., *The Kindly Flame: A Study of the Third and Fourth Books of Spenser's Faerie Queene* (1964).

Sale, Roger, *Reading Spenser: An Introduction to The Faerie Queene* (1968).

Williams, Kathleen, *Spenser's World of Glass* (1966).

WALTER RALEGH

CHRONOLOGY

1554 Probable date of birth, at Hayes Barton, Devonshire (some sources say 1552). Son of Walter Ralegh (or Raleigh), a country gentleman and landowner. Little is known of the poet's early life.

1567 Probably enters Oriel College, Oxford, around this time; apparently leaves without earning a degree.

1569 Serves as a soldier with the Huguenots (Protestants) in the French Wars of Religion.

1575 Is listed as a student of law at the Middle Temple of the Inns of Court in London.

1580 Around this time serves with Lord Grey's army in suppressing the Desmond Rebellion in Ireland; first attracts the notice of the royal court when he returns to London with dispatches concerning the fighting.

1582 By this date is known to be a leading figure at the court of Elizabeth I; will maintain this position for about ten years. His charm, personal beauty, intelligence, ambition, and pride are universally noted, though not universally admired.

1584 Ralegh is knighted.

1585 Given a royal patent to found a colony in Virginia. Later in the year is put in charge of preparations for an expected invasion of England by Spain.

1587   Arrival at court of the earl of Essex, who is to become Ralegh's chief rival for the favor of the queen. Ralegh named captain of the Queen's Guard.

1588   Active in the war against Spain; plays a part in the battle of Cadiz. Challenges Essex to a duel; falls briefly from the queen's favor; is restored, according to legend, after presenting her with a complimentary poem.

1589   Serves in Ireland, perhaps in part because of the uncertainty of his status at court.

1592   Is presented with Sherborne Castle by the queen and sent on an expedition to Panama to seize Spanish treasure ships there. However, is then accused of having "wronged" Elizabeth Throckmorton, one of the queen's maids of honor; is recalled from the expedition by the queen and commanded to marry Miss Throckmorton. Ralegh is imprisoned in the Tower of London; does not gain his release until late in the year, when the riches from a ship captured by the Panamanian expedition are used to purchase his freedom. (Ralegh's single most significant work of poetry, the long fragment known as *The Ocean to Cynthia*, was probably written during this imprisonment.) Even after his release, Elizabeth refuses to receive Ralegh at court again. During this same year, Ralegh's wife gives birth to a child, who dies in infancy.

1595   Leads a colonizing expedition to Guiana in South America, hoping to win back the queen's favor; however, he returns with little plunder and is not received by Elizabeth.

1596   Establishes a friendship with his old rival Essex. Leads a highly successful expedition against the Spanish at Cadiz; obtains permission to return to the court.

1597   With Essex, leads an expedition to the Azores, hoping to intercept Spanish treasure ships. The two men quarrel, and the expedition is a failure.

1599   Essex's rebellion against Queen Elizabeth.

1601   Essex is tried and convicted of treason; Ralegh gives evidence against him at his trial; Essex is beheaded. Ralegh later appointed governor of Jersey by the queen.

1603   Death of Queen Elizabeth; accession of James I. Ralegh is implicated in a conspiracy to make peace with Spain and bring England under a Roman Catholic monarch. (The charges were probably false; certain peace overtures had been made, but Ralegh does not seem to have been involved.) Ralegh is tried, convicted, and sentenced to be executed; however, at the last minute he is pardoned by the king, though he remains a prisoner in the Tower.

1604   Ralegh sets to work on his prose *History of the World*, beginning with the creation and extending to his own day. Also pursues scientific studies while imprisoned.

1612   Death of Prince Henry, who had favored Ralegh and might have won his release had he lived.

1614   Ralegh's *History of the World* published; notable for its clear, vigorous style and wide-ranging learning.

1616   Ralegh released from prison on the intercession of the earl of Buckingham; is sent as leader of an expedition to Guiana, with the understanding that this is his last chance to redeem himself. However, is charged to maintain peace with Spain, despite the fact that Guiana is claimed as Spanish territory.

1617   Ralegh falls ill during the expedition to Guiana; his second-in-command, Keymis, leads Ralegh's men into the country in search of a fabled gold mine. Keymis fails to find the mine but clashes with Spanish forces; in the fight, Ralegh's son is killed. Reproached by Ralegh, Keymis commits suicide.

1618   Ralegh returns to England, the expedition a failure. King James, who wishes to maintain peace with Spain, feels it necessary to sacrifice Ralegh for having allowed his men to fight with the Spanish in Guiana. The charges of treason first raised in 1603 are revived, and Ralegh is executed, making a courageous speech of self-exoneration on the scaffold. At his death, few of Ralegh's poems have appeared in print, though they have long circulated in manuscript form. Not until the nineteenth century will it be possible to establish the canon of his works.

ESSAY QUESTION WITH ANSWER

"The Nymph's Reply to the Shepherd"

12.1 Compare Marlowe's "The Passionate Shepherd to His Love" with Ralegh's "The Nymph's Reply to the Shepherd."

Answer Ralegh's lyric is a literal reply to Marlowe's poem: the nymph counters the seductive argument of the passionate shepherd with a somber refusal resting on the ideas of *tempus edax* ("devouring time") and *memento mori* ("remember death"). "The Nymph's Reply" answers "The Passionate Shepherd" not only thematically but stylistically, echoing the structure and imagery of Marlowe's poem.

The persuasive force of Marlowe's lyric derives mainly from its vivid evocation of physical delights and pleasures. Without resorting to elaborate metaphors or conceits, Marlowe suggests a golden world, a pastoral Eden, through allusions to rural woods and mountains, shepherds and flocks, flowers and May games. Cataloguing the gifts he will bring to his mistress, he sets the scene for an entirely "natural" seduction: a bed of roses, music provided by tinkling waterfalls and bird songs, beautiful garments wrought from wool and flowers, ivy and straw, coral and amber. In this innocent, green world, nature offers up its bounty for the enjoyment of young lovers. The first and last stanzas, inviting the mistress to "live with me and be my love," suggest an equation between living and loving, between vitality and pleasure, which underlies many amorous lyrics of the Renaissance.

By contrast, "The Nymph's Reply" emphasizes the transience of love and pleasure. By bringing time and its destructive effects into the pastoral scene, Ralegh shatters the perfect, unchanging springtime world of Marlowe's poem. He retains Marlowe's Edenic catalogue but subjects it to the malignant forces of seasonal change. Thus, time drives the flocks, flowers fade, and nature ripens only to rot. Death waits in the wings; not only fields and meadows but men and women must yield a reckoning to winter, and all living things relinquish "fancy's spring" to "sorrow's fall." The language may imply a Christian perspective, the "fall" an allusion not only to autumnal decay but to Adam's Fall, and the "reckoning" a reference to death, the wages of Adam's sin.

The framing stanzas shift Marlowe's whole argument into the realm of the hypothetical: "*If* all the world and love were young"; "But *could* youth last and love still breed." By using the subjunctive construction, Ralegh acknowledges the universal human wish for immortal youth and unending pleasure while discounting its possibility.

Neither poem can be said to win the argument. By focusing on vivid, natural details and invoking rural pleasures, Marlowe makes his amorous invitation highly persuasive. By echoing Marlowe but altering the details to fit a darkening, wintry landscape shadowed by time and death, Ralegh offers a persuasive counterstatement. Each poem speaks for an aspect of human feeling and thought: Marlowe's for youthful desire and natural impulse, Ralegh's for philosophical contemplation and spiritual insight.

B.S.

SUGGESTED READINGS

Greenblatt, Stephen, *Sir Walter Raleigh: Renaissance Man and His Roles* (1973).
Wallace, Willard M., *Sir Walter Raleigh* (1959).

PHILIP SIDNEY

C H R O N O L O G Y

1554   Born at Penshurst, Kent. Son of Henry Sidney and Mary Dudley Sidney, both of distinguished, ancient families; Philip's godfather was his namesake, King Philip of Spain.

1564   Enters Shrewsbury Grammar School in Shropshire.

1566   Visits the home of his uncle, the earl of Leicester, at Oxford; probably meets Queen Elizabeth.

1568   Enters Christ Church College, Oxford. Will leave without a degree three years later when a plague closes the colleges.

1572   Begins a three-year tour of Europe, during which he is received at courts in France, Germany, Italy, Poland, and Holland; makes powerful friends and impresses all by his charm, intelligence, and grace. At Frankfurt, meets Hubert Languet, who first impresses upon Sidney the idea of a league of Protestant nations, to which Sidney will devote most of his later political efforts.

1575   Returns to England; lives at court in London.

1576   Becomes cupbearer to the queen. Visits his father in Ireland, where Henry Sidney is lord deputy, accompanying the earl of Essex. Fights in Ireland alongside his father. Later is sent to Germany on diplomatic embassy.

1577   Travels extensively in Europe on diplomatic business; seeks support for the idea of a Protestant League among rulers in the German states and Holland.

1578	Sidney's courtly play *The Lady of May* is performed before the queen. Begins writing *Arcadia* (so-called *Old Arcadia*), a prose romance.
1579	Further diplomatic travels. Writes a letter to the queen opposing her possible marriage to the duke of Anjou; it is thought that her resentment of this advice may hinder Sidney's future advancement at court. Stephen Gosson publishes *The School of Abuse* (dedicated to Sidney), attacking the "immorality" of poetry.
1580	Probably finishes the *Old Arcadia* (five books). Begins writing *The Defence of Poesie*, a prose work replying to Gosson's attack on poetry, which will be a major statement of the Renaissance position on literature and an important early English work of literary criticism.
1581	Elected to Parliament. Begins work on his verse translation of the Psalms. Penelope Devereux, daughter of the earl of Essex, is engaged and married to Lord Rich, apparently against her will; Sidney falls in love with her, and she is thought to be the inspiration for his *Astrophil and Stella*, the sonnet sequence begun at this time.
1582	Travels to the Netherlands as part of an official escort for the duke of Anjou. Probably begins work on the *New Arcadia*, a revised and expanded version of the *Old Arcadia*.
1583	Knighted. Appointed assistant to his uncle the earl of Warwick, master of ordnance. Marries Frances Walsingham. Probably abandons work on the *New Arcadia*, having revised two books and a part of a third.
1584	Plans to travel to America with Sir Francis Drake; is prevented by the queen's appointing him governor of Flushing.
1586	Death of Sidney's mother and father. In September, Sidney is wounded by a musket ball in the battle of Zutphen. According to his friend Fulke Greville, refuses a drink of water while being borne off the battlefield, offering it instead to a dying soldier with the words "Thy necessity is yet greater than mine." Though nursed at Arnheim by Lady Sidney, dies twenty-six days later. Is mourned throughout Europe as a model of the Renaissance courtier.
1590	Publication of the *New Arcadia*.
1591	Publication of *Astrophil and Stella*.
1595	Publication of *The Defence of Poesie*.
1598	Sidney's "collected works" published by William Ponsonby in an edition dedicated to Sidney's sister, the countess of Pembroke, under the title of *The Countesse of Pembrokes Arcadia . . . with sundry new additions*.
1926	First publication of the *Old Arcadia*.

ESSAY QUESTIONS WITH ANSWERS

The Defense of Poesy

13.1 Sidney's essay appeared under two different titles: *An Apologie for Poetrie* (1591) and *The Defence of Poesie* (1595). Both titles imply that poetry is under attack and requires justification. Discuss the defensive attitude adopted by Sidney, explaining why it was necessary and how it is effective.

Answer In the sixteenth century, both humanist scholars and writers and Protestant religious reformers tended to be suspicious of imaginative literature. The humanists, despite their enthusiasm for the classics, cautioned against "lascivious" writers such as Ovid and Catullus and defended heroic writers like Virgil and Homer largely by "moralizing" their epic narratives as allegories. The Puritans attacked fiction as a form of lying and plays as an immoral influence; it was the fury of such attacks as Stephen Gosson's puritanical *The School of Abuse* (which, ironically, had been dedicated to Sidney) that most likely provoked Sidney to form a reply. Given the moral assumptions of the period, very few commentators acknowledged that literature could exist purely for amusement. Instead, they stressed the classical theory of *docere, movere, delectare*: the purpose of poetry is "to teach, to persuade, to delight," and the delight of poetry must always remain in the service of teaching and moral persuasion.

Sidney's defense of poetry (by which he means all imaginative literature, whether in verse or prose) is very much in the mainstream of sixteenth-century literary criticism in its focus on didactic and ethical issues. For example, in comparing poetry to the two other "moral sciences," philosophy and history, Sidney defends poetry on the basis of its superiority as a teacher of virtuous action. On the one hand, philosophy is too universal: with its generalizing arguments, it merely defines good but doesn't move the reader to do good. On the other hand, history is too particular: its specific examples of virtue and vice may move the reader, but since history is confined to facts, it is sometimes forced to show virtue punished and vice rewarded. Poetry, with its dramatic illustrations of ideal virtue, can consistently show the good, thereby inspiring readers to imitate it in their own lives. Poetry is morally persuasive *because* it provides delight. It is "a speaking Picture," which offers "foode for the tenderest stomacks" and a "medicine of Cherries." In short, the beauty of poetry seduces people to virtue.

Sidney's moral emphasis is effective because it answers his opponents on their own ground. Also effective is the form in which Sidney delivers his defense. The essay is structured like a classical forensic oration delivered by a clever lawyer in behalf of an unjustly accused victim. (In Sidney's time and until the nineteenth century, the study of the forms and rules of classical rhetoric was part of the education of any English gentleman.) As Catherine Barnes points out in her article "The Hidden Persuader," Sidney flatters the reader (or "juror") by treating him as one of a select group that understands the truth about "poore Poetry," the maligned innocent. At the same time, he blackens the accusers by insinuating that they are ignorant, foolish, malicious. He carefully establishes the "character" of the defendant by developing each of the *topoi* ("places" or headings) found in a classical laudatory oration and praising poetry under the topics of its antiquity, its universality, its etymology (that is, the honorable "names" given to poets), its comparative excellence in relation to other arts, and its superior kinds or genres. Finally, like a good lawyer, he directly answers the prosecution's charges that poetry is trivial, effeminate, false, and immoral. Thus Sidney takes the format of "defense" forced on him by the Puritan attack and turns it into a triumphant courtroom performance.

13.2 Sidney's *Defense* begins obliquely, with an anecdote about horses, and ends with a mild joke about the fate of poet haters. Why does a serious piece of literary criticism have such a casual introduction and conclusion?

Answer The *exordium*, or introduction, of a classical oration was supposed to win the goodwill of the listeners by either amusing them, flattering them, or agreeing with them. In the *Defense*, Sidney ingratiates himself with his audience by telling a comic story about Pugliano, the master horseman, whose defense of horses was so moving that "if I had not beene a peece of a Logician before I came to him, I think he would have perswaded mee to have wished myself a horse." The story is entertaining in itself, containing as well a pun on the author's given name (*Phil-hippi*, "lover of horses"); but it is also Sidney's way of sharing his hearers' skepticism. He is saying, "Yes, I know I am as foolishly infatuated with poetry as Pugliano was with horses, but hear me out." By anticipating a hearer's possible objection, he disarms criticism.

Although according to theory the exordium could be treated lightly, the *peroration*, or conclusion, was supposed to be an eloquent, impassioned summation of the oration's chief points. But Sidney's conclusion, too, is in a light vein. He promises exaggerated rewards to believers in poetry ("you shall be most fayre, most ritch, most wise, most all; you shall dwell upon superlatives") and offers a mock threat to unbelievers, who will fail in love "for lacking skill of a Sonnet" and will die forgotten "for want of an Epitaph."

Thus, in place of a conventional conclusion, Sidney disengages himself from his subject, moving away from earnest moral argument in behalf of heroic poetry to an apparently casual mention of sonnets and epitaphs. Still, he is not sabotaging his own essay by suddenly joking about it; rather he is again joining his audience by taking a more distant, skeptical view of poetry, as he did at the beginning. At the same time, he is displaying a courtier's artless touch, concealing the labor which he has lavished on his *Defense* by ending on a light and witty note.

13.3   Analyze Sidney's theory of poetic creation as presented in this passage:

> Neither let it be deemed too sawcie a comparison to ballance the highest poynt of mans wit with the efficacie of Nature: but rather give right honor to the heavenly Maker of that maker, who, having made man to his owne likenes, set him beyond and over all the workes of that second nature, which in nothing hee sheweth so much as in Poetrie, when with the force of a divine breath he bringeth things forth far surpassing her dooings, with no small argument to the incredulous of that first accursed fall of *Adam*: sith our erected wit maketh us know what perfection is, and yet our infected will keepeth us from reaching unto it.

Answer   Sidney's praise of poetry builds on the notion of the poet as a creator who improves upon the "brasen" (that is, bronze) world of nature, producing instead a "golden" world by means of his imagined "Idea or foreconceit." This analysis of the poetic faculty combines Christian belief with the Platonic philosophy of ideal Forms to explain the poet's ability to imagine a golden world. The heavenly Maker, God, has given the lesser maker, man, the gift of "erected wit," or reason. (It is significant for Sidney's argument that the word "poet" derives from the Greek word for "maker," and that a common Middle English word for "poet" was "maker.") This rational power of man enables him to imagine perfection, that is, the Platonic "Idea." But since the Fall of Adam and the loss of the original golden world, nature has been imperfect, or "brasen," and man has suffered from original sin, or "infected will." Thus, it is only by means of the rational soul that the poet can re-create the golden world, through his "fore-conceit" or imagined Idea.

The ultimate honor for the poet's creations, then, belongs to God, who has established the poet as the maker of a "second nature"—including not solely physical but human nature as well—consisting of an image of that ideal world of beauty and virtue lost to man when he was expelled from paradise.

It is significant that Sidney is implicitly referring to the Aristotelian doctrine of imitation while at the same time emphasizing the poet's ability to create the ideal Forms or essences postulated by Plato. The poet's imitation is not slavish or mechanical or trivial, for what he imitates is not mere images but the godlike and God-given function of creation. Because he is not merely copying down the physical world but projecting an idealized version of that world, the poet is not the mere "imitator of imitations" that Plato calls him. The "second nature" he creates as a "maker" in little is a realm of true being or essence, and his imitation is of the very act of "making," or imagining, perfection. By conflating Aristotle with Plato, Sidney is able to have his poet both ways: he is a creator and, in a special philosophical sense, an imitator too.

13.4 What standards of literary excellence are stated or implied in Sidney's *Defense?*

Answer Sidney finds much to criticize in the literature of his time. Writing before the publication of Spenser's *The Faerie Queene* and Shakespeare's plays, he expresses disappointment in the poetry being produced and discusses his own criteria of excellence. It is not clear that Sidney would have admired the great works which were to come at the end of the sixteenth century, for he criticizes the "old rustick language," or archaisms, of Spenser's early cycle, *The Shepheardes Calender*; and he attacks the mixing of genres (tragedy and comedy) and the failure to observe the classical unities (one time and one place) in contemporary plays. Spenser and Shakespeare were "guilty" on these counts.

Sidney also criticizes "scurrilous" and "doltish" comedy, founded on unnatural incongruity and breeding only laughter; he prefers comedy based on "a conveniencie to our selves or to the generall nature" and breeding delight. ("Nature," in this context, includes human nature as well as nonhuman creation. The appeal to "the generall nature" is an appeal to truth and lifelikeness.) Sidney further attacks the stale artifice of imitative sonneteers, praising instead the fresh invention of those writers who project emotional sincerity. In addition, he rejects artificial language: "farre fette words," heavy alliteration,

Ciceronian phrases, and strange similes and metaphors like those in John Lyly's *Euphues*.

In every case, Sidney's standard of excellence is truth to nature. The art of the praiseworthy courtier consists in "following that which by practise hee findeth fittest to nature"; art should conceal art, not exhibit it. This notion of art based on what is "natural" accords with the classical theory of decorum: language and genre should be suited to the matter. Thus, Sidney's theories of the appropriate subjects for tragedy and comedy and the appropriate language for pastoral, lyric, and epic poetry are "neoclassical," dependent on the underlying idea that nature dictates a fitting form of expression for each kind of human experience. How far Sidney's own poetic practice, or that of other Renaissance poets, accorded with this doctrine is another matter; but Sidney's reliance on "nature" and decorum is fully in accord with the generally accepted critical theories of his day.

Astrophil and Stella
Sonnet 1: "Loving in truth, and fain in verse my love to show"

13.5   What is the theme of the sonnet, and how does Sidney's poetic style embody that theme?

Answer   The poem is less about "loving in truth" than about being desirous "in verse my love to show." Although the poet begins with an allusion to his emotion, in the very next phrase he establishes his true subject, which is self-expression. Throughout the poem attention is focused not on love (or, indeed, on the beloved, the "dear she" who is mentioned only in passing), but on the question of how to write about it.

The concern with writing manifests itself in very specific allusions to rhetorical theory. For example, the basic doctrine of *docere, movere, delectare*, which postulates that the purpose of poetry is "to teach, to persuade, to delight," is incorporated in the first quatrain. The *gradatio*, or interlocking series of words, in lines 2–4 wittily rearranges the elements of this doctrine so that delight comes first ("pleasure might cause her read"), teaching second ("reading might make her know"), and moving or persuasion third ("Knowledge might pity win, and pity grace obtain"). Thus, Astrophil explicitly announces and analyzes the latent purpose of all love poetry, clearly acknowledging that the sonnet is a studied rhetorical composition designed to persuade the mistress.

Just how "studied" is apparent from the almost pedantic vocabulary the poet uses to describe his efforts to compose a poem. The word "invention," used three times, had in the sixteenth century the specific technical meaning of discovering or "finding out" ideas and subject matter for a composition. The theory of decorum, the fitness of style to matter and of both to nature, is alluded to in the phrases "fit words to paint the blackest face of woe" and "Invention, Nature's child." The puns on "leaves," referring both to vegetative growth and to the leaves of a book, and on "feet," referring both to people (rival poets) and to metrical feet, reinforce the tone of bookishness and learned wit.

The strategy of the sonnet is essentially paradoxical. The opening and closing lines establish the pretense that the poet's concern is with sincerity ("Loving in truth") and spontaneity ("look in thy heart"), while the intervening twelve lines imply that he is less concerned with the genuineness of his emotions than with the originality of his writing. The witty displacement of subject matter is evident in the allusions to emotion in the body of the poem. The poet refers not merely to his "woe" but to "the blackest face of woe," that is, not to what he feels but to what he can "paint" in "fit words." He is frustrated and "helpless in my throes" not over love, but over his inability to express himself. Thus the language of emotion is transferred from the experience of love to the activity of writing, just as the sonnet substitutes the latter theme for the former.

Sonnet 5: "It is most true that eyes are form'd to serve/ The inward light, . . ."

13.6 Discuss how the sonnet form works in sonnet 5.

Answer The sonnet form was developed by Petrarch in Italy in the fourteenth century in the *Canzoniere*, a cycle of poems to his mistress, Laura, and adopted later in France and England, often with variations in the rhyme scheme. Sidney usually uses the original Petrarchan sonnet form, consisting of an octave, rhymed *abba abba*, and a sestet, generally rhymed *cdecde*. In sonnet 5, however, Sidney's rhyme scheme is *abab abab cdcd ee*—that is, the so-called Elizabethan form used, for example, by Shakespeare.

The sonnet form, whether Petrarchan or Elizabethan, produces the expectation of units of thought corresponding to its structured patterns of rhyme. Very often a major logical division will occur between the octave and sestet of a Petrarchan sonnet or between the quatrains and couplet of an Elizabethan sonnet. For example, there may be a shift from one view to an opposing one, from a general statement to a specific application, or from a series of examples to a broad generalization. In Sidney's sonnet 5, the development of the thought plays off against the patterned form, producing a "surprise" ending.

The expected units of thought are stressed throughout most of the poem. The octave is neatly divided into two quatrains, each beginning with "It is most true . . ." The sestet is likewise divided into two triplets, each beginning with "True, that . . ." These concessions constitute steps in a logical argument which grants that earthly love is (1) irrational, (2) idolatrous, (3) impure, and (4) transient. The logical structure is emphasized by means of *anaphora*, the exact repetition of phrases at the beginning of each major unit.

In the last line of the poem, however, Sidney subverts both our expectations and his whole preceding argument. He adds one last "True," but then breaks the line immediately with a rebuttal: "and yet true that I must Stella love." According to the pattern established in the poem, the reader expects the last line, beginning once again with "True," to make a final concession to the foes of love. But Sidney instead overturns all his earlier propositions by insisting on the primacy of his passion for Stella.

The structure of thought displays a quickening tempo, with first four lines, then three lines, then two lines, then a single word in the last line devoted to each concession. The rebuttal runs absolutely counter to the concessions, though it is formulated in precisely the same language: "and yet *true*." Truth paradoxically collides with truth, but one truth is rational, ethical, and theological, while the other is emotional.

Sidney's confession of the truth of passion, interrupting the rigid steps of the logical pattern, is especially effective not only because it puts a halt to the accelerating concessions, but because it ends the poem; it has the last word. Sidney's structural tactics become a means of validating Astrophil's emotion and a way of complimenting the lady as well: Stella alone has the power to stem the tide of logic.

Sonnet 31: "With how sad steps, Oh Moon, thou climb'st the skies!"

13.7 Personification, whereby human qualities are attributed to an inanimate object or abstract thing, is an important feature of sonnet 31. Explain how the figure functions here, and analyze its effect.

Answer Astrophil addresses the poem to the moon, apostrophizing the planet ("Oh Moon") and posing questions to it. The melancholy lover com-

plaining to the heavens is a conventional figure, but Sidney transforms the
stereotype; with a kind of mocking self-awareness the lover projects his own
feelings onto the moon, transforming soliloquy into a bantering conversation
with his pretended alter ego. Thus Astrophil treats the moon as though it were
an extension of his own psyche: it too is a disappointed lover, with a slow tread,
a wan face, and a "languished grace." He wittily elaborates on the theme of
identification, assuring himself that his own experience (his "long-with-love-
acquainted eyes") allows him to "read" the moon rightly as a fellow in misfortune. In the sestet, especially, the poet, looking up from below, asking one
question after another, seems to be communing with, and complaining to, a
fellow self. ("Then, even of fellowship, Oh Moon, tell me . . ."). These lines
simultaneously convey a suggestion of looking into a mirror, as Astrophil asks
for a comparison between "there" and "here," above and below. The personification of the moon has the effect of half-playful self-portraiture, allowing
Sidney to dramatize "a lover's case" through a lively interplay between the
complaining lover and the mirror image he creates in nature.

13.8   What is the meaning of the last line of sonnet 31?

Answer   The last line of the poem—"Do they call virtue there ungratefulness?"—is somewhat puzzling. "They" refers to the proud beauties or, more
generally, to all moon-dwellers, those hypothetical counterparts of poor suffering
humanity; but *whose* virtue might they call ungrateful? In what sense is virtue
ungrateful?

The poet has just plaintively inquired of the moon whether women are cruel
and frivolous up above, too: do they, like earthly women, dismiss fidelity as
folly, are they proud, self-infatuated, and scornful? The last line, too, may refer
to the cruelty of the mistress. If we assume that normal word order is inverted,
the line may be read as "Do they call ungratefulness there a virtue?"—that is,
do cruel lunar maidens call their own "ungratefulness" (their coldness and
unyielding chastity) a virtue? The assumption of inverted order is plausible, as
it is a common feature in Renaissance poetry.

However, it is equally likely that the line merits a straight reading. In that
case the "virtue," in the sense of integrity and devotion, would belong to the
lover, and the "ungratefulness" would have the sense of "unpleasantness." The
line would thus be parallel with and analogous to the earlier "Is constant love
deemed there but want of wit?"—"Do they call devotion there unpleasantness?"

In either reading the final line remains consistent with the plaintive tone
of the sestet. There is a certain querulousness about the insistent and repetitive

questions at the end, as Astrophil elaborates on the injustice of cruel mistresses both lunar and sublunar. Ending with a question, the poem seems suspended, with no neat resolution of the tension of unrequited love in the reassuring cadences of a closed couplet.

Sonnet 74: "I never drank of Aganippe well . . ."

13.9   Discuss the persona with special reference to tonal shifts in the sonnet.

Answer   In the octave of sonnet 74, Astrophil denies any dependence on the Muses, on divine inspiration ("poets' fury"), or on imitation ("no pick-purse of another's wit"). By this protestation Astrophil is announcing his difference from the mass of sonneteers who either conventionally cited the gods or "fury" as the source of their poetry or, in fact, ransacked the works of others for ideas. Such a declaration of independence is itself a stock attitude, the lover stoutly maintaining that he requires no other inspiration than the lady herself to stimulate him to "turn sonnet." Sidney thus offers us, in Astrophil, the stereotypical lover stereotypically pretending to be entirely singular and unique.

But Astrophil *is* singular, if not in posture then in tone, for he delivers the standard sentiments with the equivalent of a knowing wink. There is sophisticated irony in the allusions of the ostensibly naive persona ("Poor layman I") to all the classical lore surrounding the art of poetry. Thus he is acquainted with "Aganippe well," Tempe, and the river Styx ("the blackest brook of hell"), as well as with the aesthetic theories of inspiration and imitation. This "layman" is as adept in the vocabulary and mysteries of the craft as any initiate. Thus the protestation of ignorance becomes a mock disclaimer, the downright, forthright tone of the octave with its ejaculations and colloquialisms ("God wot, wot not" and "pick-purse") adding to the witty pretense. Clearly Astrophil is only playing dumb.

The first half of the sestet represents a shift in tone to a more formal and musical style of utterance. These lines exhibit a perfectly regular iambic rhythm, a studied *gradatio* (a patterned repetition of words, advancing by "steps": "speak . . . speak", "verse . . . verse"), and double enjambment, whereby the sentiments flow across the ends of lines. They thus illustrate very precisely that smooth ease that Astrophil claims is the sign of his amazing, and puzzling, artistry. In the second half of the sestet we are back to the rude idiomatic vigor of the octave, with an animated mock-dialogue communicated in short lively phrases and colloquial monosyllables ("Guess we the cause. What, is it thus? Fie, no").

These tonal shifts allow Sidney to have it all ways. Astrophil is the conventional lover and sonneteer who rebels against mere rules, professing independence from all affectation and erudite formality; yet he is pedant enough to incorporate classical allusions, rhetorician enough to exploit *gradatio* and enjambment. The sonnet becomes a game with convention, working back and forth within the styles and postures associated with the genre. By using both colloquial spontaneity and polished rhetoric, Sidney makes Astrophil both naive and sophisticated, artless and artful. This playful fusion of styles works against the chiming predictability of the closing line, lending the persona the originality and authority that he claims for himself.

13.10 Compare sonnet 1 ("Loving in truth") and sonnet 74 ("I never drank").

Answer The sonnets are similar in theme, the former discussing methods of composing a poem (imitation, invention, study) and the latter sources of inspiration (the Muses, God, other poets). Both poems reject art in favor of the "natural" poetry produced by love itself.

They are also similar in technique. Sonnet 1 displays a "fine invention," that is, an ingenious, studied conceit, while making the poet's failure of poetic invention the ostensible subject. With witty irony, it narrates the search for an idea, turning the very lack of subject into the main theme of thirteen lines. The poet discovers his "true" subject—the image of the beloved, which, according to Petrarchan convention, was engraved in the lover's heart—only in the final line: " 'Fool,' said my Muse to me, 'look in thy heart and write.' "

Likewise, sonnet 74 is cleverly ironic in that the denial of any knowledge of art is conveyed through learned allusion and formal rhetoric. The intelligent discussion of theories of poetic craft is conducted by a supposedly ignorant novice ("Poor layman I"). Again, it is only in the last line of the poem that Stella puts in an appearance, as the answer to the puzzle of how excellent verse can flow from the pen of an artless writer.

Both poems rest on a pretense—"I have no ideas" (sonnet 1) and "I know nothing about poetry" (sonnet 74)—which the sonnets themselves undercut. The poems thus become games in which straw men are set up only to be knocked down and ostensible difficulties posed only to be swept aside. In these two sonnets, as well as in many others in *Astrophil and Stella*, Sidney seems to be flaunting his rhetorical mastery, displaying his ability to create poetry *ex nihilo* (out of nothing) and to sustain a verbal performance despite the apparent odds against it. Related to this game of style is a game with subject matter, for in these two instances Sidney is clearly substituting the themes of writing and the writer for those of love and the beloved. In sonnet 74 the name of Stella and in sonnet 1 the subject of love are brought in, at the eleventh hour and in the fourteenth line, as the solution to a compositional, not emotional, problem.

B.S.

SUGGESTED READINGS

Barnes, Catherine, "The Hidden Persuader: The Complex Speaking Voice of Sidney's *Defence of Poetry*," *PMLA*, 86 (1971).

Feuillerat, Albert, ed., *The Complete Works of Sir Philip Sidney*, Vols. I–IV (1912–1926).

Kalstone, David, *Sidney's Poetry: Contexts and Interpretations* (1965).

Ringler, William A., Jr., ed., *The Poems of Sir Philip Sidney* (1962).

MICHAEL DRAYTON

C H R O N O L O G Y

1563	Born at Hartshill, North Warwickshire. Parents unknown, though his father is thought to have been either a butcher or a tanner.
1573	Enters the service of Henry Goodere, Esq., at Polesworth Hall in Warwickshire; serves as a page. Goodere is a friend of Sir Philip Sidney, noted courtier and important poet.
1586	Death of Philip Sidney; Henry Goodere is one of the executors of his will. Drayton writes "The tears of the Greene Hawthorne Tree," an elegy on Sidney, and other poems at this time.
1591	Drayton's *Harmonie of the Church* published, his first printed work; a collection of undistinguished verse paraphrases of scripture.
1593	Publication of *The Shepheards Garland*, a collection of pastoral poems (called by Drayton "eglogs") roughly similar in style to Spenser's *Shepheardes Calender*. Drayton will later revise them substantially for inclusion in his 1606 volume of poetry. Drayton's career as a professional writer well under way by this time. Also by this time, Drayton is probably in love with Anne Goodere, daughter of his patron. Though marriage is out of the question because of Drayton's low rank, he will remain devoted to her throughout his life, visiting her each summer. Anne Goodere is the "Idea" (that is, the ideal beauty) after whom Drayton's sonnet sequence will be named.
1594	First publication of the sonnet sequence *Ideas Mirrour*, Drayton's greatest work. Characteristically, Drayton will continue to revise and tinker with

the sequence, sometimes known simply as *Idea*, for a series of editions over the next twenty-five years.

1595   Death of Henry Goodere; Drayton witnesses his will. Publishes *Endimion and Phoebe*, a verse recasting of a Greek myth, dedicated to Lucy, countess of Bedford, on her marriage; she is a well-known patroness of poets. In same year, Anne Goodere marries Henry Rainsford of Clifford Chambers, Gloucestershire.

1596   Publication of *Mortimeriados*, first poem printed under Drayton's name. By this time, Drayton is probably in London, earning a living as a writer and collaborator on plays. During the later 1590s, he is mentioned as a part author of almost a score of plays, of which only one, *Sir John Oldcastle*, has survived.

1597   Publication of *Englands Heroicall Epistles*, a series of historical poems in the form of fictitious letters by actual people; probably the most popular works of Drayton during his lifetime. Several enlarged editions appear within the next few years.

1598   Drayton is at work on *Poly-Olbion*, which he himself will regard as his most important work.

1600   Publication of *Sir John Oldcastle*.

1602   Publication of *The Barrons Wars*, another historical poem.

1603   Death of Queen Elizabeth; accession of James I. Drayton writes a commemorative poem, "To the Majestie of King James," which fails to mention Elizabeth; this oversight is widely criticized, and noble patronage, which Drayton has previously enjoyed, dries up. Writes *The Owle*, a satirical poem popular at the time but now little read, since its topical allusions are very difficult to interpret.

1605   Publication of the first collected volume of Drayton's poems.

1606   *Poemes Lyrick and Pastorall* published. Includes greatly revised versions of many of Drayton's early poems, a series of Horatian odes, and "The Ballad of Agincourt," a well-known patriotic poem.

1607   Drayton mentioned as part owner of the Children of the King's Revels, a theatrical company.

1608   New edition of Drayton's poems published; others will follow in 1610, 1613, 1619, 1630, and 1637.

1612   The First Part of *Poly-Olbion* published. Almost 30,000 lines long, this poem surveys the geography, history, and customs of England and Wales; full of information gleaned from reading and travel. Greeted on its publication by relative indifference, which greatly disappoints Drayton.

1616   According to legend (supported only by a book published almost fifty years later), Drayton, Ben Jonson, and Shakespeare have a "merry meeting" at which Shakespeare "dranke too hard" and "died of a feaver there contracted." Truth of this story not known.

1620   Drayton treated for ague by Dr. John Hall, son-in-law of Shakespeare.

1622   Publication of the Second Part of *Poly-Olbion*.

1627   Publication of a collection of poems by Drayton including *Nimphidia*, a pastoral romance which is among his more important later works.

1631   Death of Drayton. The night before his death is said to have written verses reaffirming his lifelong love for Anne Goodere Rainsford. Buried in Westminster Abbey.

ESSAY QUESTIONS WITH ANSWERS

Sonnet 61: "Since there's no help . . ."

14.1   Analyze the structure of sonnet 61, *Idea*: "Since there's no help, come let us kiss and part."

Answer   The major division in the sonnet, occurring between the octave and the sestet, signals a shift or development in the speaker's attitude. The first eight lines of the poem develop a single idea, as the poet says a literal farewell to his mistress. In the two quatrains, the poet offers a series of specific, realistic details—the final kiss, the last handshake, the studied neutrality—which outline the process of disengagement, a contract for undoing their love. The idiomatic language of the octet adds to the impression of a "real" situation. Thus, the pseudo-spontaneous interrupters "come," "Nay," and "yea," the contraction "there's," and the casual repetition in the line "And I am glad, yea, glad with all my heart" create a conversational tone, as though the poet is improvising his good-bye as he speaks it.

In sharp contrast, the sestet (beginning, "Now at the last gasp of Love's latest breath") presents an allegorical tableau. This is another depiction of love undone, but the elaborate portrayal of the deathbed scene, with last rites administered by personified abstractions (Faith, Innocence), has a tragic aura very different from the colloquial, matter-of-fact tone of the octave. Although Drayton is elaborating the same basic situation in both octave and sestet, he uses the formal division of the sonnet to dramatize a subtle psychological conflict within the lover. The frank disavowal of love is juxtaposed with an iconic scene which lingers over the dying emotion, thus suggesting bravado undermined by regret.

The word "Now" in line 9 emphasizes the shift between octave and sestet by immediately establishing a new plane of action in the sonnet, a departure from the realm of everyday social conversation. "Now" stresses the dramatic present, the moment of farewell which is the subject of the sonnet. The word thus conveys temporal urgency, the pressure of the ultimate moment before "death" comes. The phrases "last gasp" and "latest breath" reinforce this sense of a single final instant. At the same time, because the "Now" introduces a fixed allegorical tableau, it seems to point to an eternal present in which the abstraction Love lies dying.

The repetition of "Now" at the beginning of the closing couplet signals a final shift that knits the entire poem together. This "Now" combines the symbolic and realistic planes in a direct address to the mistress. On the allegorical level, the poet is asking her to act a part in the symbolic drama of the sestet: to play physician to the dying patient by seizing on the eternal "now" and retrieving Love from the borders of death. On the realistic level, he is simply asking, in the dramatic present of the sonnet, for a resumption of the love relationship supposedly abandoned in the opening octave.

Thus, the structural development of the poem, demarcated by octave, sestet, and the final couplet within the sestet, and emphasized by the repetition of the word "now," represents the unfolding of a psychological drama. In a series of discrete steps, the poet moves from colloquial resignation to elegiac regret to a final ironic reversal.

14.2   Drayton's sonnet is not only a picture of the lover's psychological conflict but a persuasive address to the mistress. What persuasive tactics does the speaker employ?

Answer   Only in the closing couplet ("Now, if thou wouldst, when all have given him over,/ From death to life thou mightst him yet recover") does the lover directly suggest to the mistress the possibility of her changing her mind, that is, resuming their relationship and resuscitating their love; and even here, he makes no definite appeal. Earlier in the sonnet, the poet simply describes the end of the affair, first in colloquial, conversational form and then by means of allegorical emblem. His only attempt at persuasion is the suggestion that their farewell be friendly ("come let us kiss and part"). Although the final couplet is reticent, coolly describing a possibility rather than heatedly urging a change, it nonetheless introduces an element of argument. On the surface the poem seems to contradict itself: the lover cheerfully agrees to "cancel all his vows," only to reverse himself at the very end by suggesting a renewal of love.

However, the octave and sestet may be interpreted as forms of persuasion which subtly prepare for the final couplet. The opening eight lines suggest a kind of reverse psychology designed to pique the lady's interest. The emphatic denial "Nay I have done, you get no more of me" and the emphatic protest "And I am glad, yea glad with all my heart/ That thus so cleanly I myself can free" may be read as attempts to elicit a response from the mistress in the form of a counterprotest. He is not simply saying good-bye but engaging in a kind of amorous duel. At the same time, he seems to be dueling with himself. The poet protests his indifference almost too much, thus betraying his feeling. In the sestet, the elegiac meditation on the poor victim Love, gasping out his last on his deathbed in the company of Faith and Innocence, may also be seen as an effort to evoke a response from the lady and to stir her to sentiment and pity.

Thus, the entire sonnet, although ostensibly a palinode, or poem of farewell, is in fact an attempt at persuading an unwilling mistress. Drayton modifies the conventional poem of persuasion by means of such disguised persuasive tactics as the amorous threats of the octave and the pathetic description of the sestet, before stating his restrained plea in the couplet.

B.S.

SUGGESTED READINGS

Newdigate, B. H., *Michael Drayton and His Circle* (1941).
Praz, Mario, "Drayton," *English Studies*, 28 (1947).

CHRISTOPHER MARLOWE

C H R O N O L O G Y

1564   Born at Canterbury. Son of John Marlowe, a well-to-do shoemaker, and Katharine Arthur Marlowe.

1579   Enters the King's School at Canterbury.

1580   Enters Corpus Christi College, Cambridge University, on a fellowship granted by Archbishop Parker to a scholar who, it is assumed, intends to enter holy orders; however, records show Marlowe as a student of dialectics (i.e., logic and argumentation).

1584   Receives B.A. During the next three years, studies on an irregular basis at Cambridge, with many long, somewhat mysterious absences, often spent abroad. It is rumored that Marlowe intends to join a Catholic seminary at Reims in France; more likely he is working for the English government as a spy among English Catholics in France.

1587   Marlowe petitions Cambridge for his M.A. degree, which is denied him. However, the Privy Council later issues an order directing that Marlowe be given his degree and stating that he has been "employed . . . in matters touching the benefitt of his countrie." Later in the year, Marlowe is in London; Parts One and Two of his play *Tamburlaine the Great* are performed there.

1588–   Marlowe is a working London playwright during this period, though he may
1593   also have been employed as a spy by the government. The works he produces during these five years include the narrative poem *Hero and Leander* and

the plays *Edward II*; *Dido, Queen of Carthage*; *The Massacre at Paris*; and *Doctor Faustus*. None of these works is published during his lifetime. According to some accounts, Marlowe is also the leading figure in a group of London writers known as the School of Night, including Sir Walter Ralegh and George Chapman; they were supposed to have pursued heretical studies. However, nothing is known of this group for certain.

1589   Marlowe and Thomas Watson, a poet and playwright, are arrested for killing William Bradley in a brawl. Marlowe remains in Newgate Prison for thirteen days; the charges against him are ultimately dismissed, but he is officially ordered to keep the peace.

1590   Parts One and Two of *Tamburlaine the Great* are published.

1592   Marlowe is apparently sent as a government messenger to the English troops at the siege of Rouen. Later in the year, two constables petition that Marlowe be sworn to keep the peace; they claim that he assaulted them. However, no record exists of legal charges being brought against him. Robert Greene attacks Marlowe (and Shakespeare) in his *Groatsworth of Wit*.

1593   The playwright Thomas Kyd is arrested on charges of heresy and treason. When papers are found in his rooms which are said to deny the divinity of Jesus Christ, he claims that they belong to Marlowe. Accordingly, Marlowe is ordered to appear before the Privy Council to answer a charge of heresy. (However, he is not imprisoned or tortured, apparently because of his status as "gentleman.") Twelve days later, Marlowe is stabbed to death at an inn in Deptford; among the three men present is Robert Poley, a notorious spy and *agent provocateur*. As a result of the shady circumstances of his death, speculation about Marlowe's employment by the government, his religious and political views, and the reason for his murder has continued until this day. There is no evidence, however, to support the fanciful belief that Marlowe's death was a hoax or that he survived to write the plays commonly attributed to William Shakespeare.

1594   Publication of the plays *Edward II* and *Dido, Queen of Carthage*.

1598   Publication of *Hero and Leander*.

1599   A translation of Ovid's *Amores*, evidently a second-rate juvenile work by Marlowe, is published; it is burned by church censors for its erotic content.

1604   Publication of *The Massacre at Paris* and *Doctor Faustus*.

1633   Publication of *The Jew of Malta*.

ESSAY QUESTIONS WITH ANSWERS

Hero and Leander

15.1 Analyze Marlowe's descriptive techniques in the initial portrait of Hero. What is the tone of the passage?

Answer Marlowe uses a pastiche of extravagant conceits and images to construct his portrait of Hero, in the process turning her into a kind of "love machine." Her comically elaborate costume suggests a figurine encrusted with decoration, an icon of love rather than a person of flesh and blood. By making each item of Hero's clothing and anatomy a literal picture of or analogue to a quality associated with love, Marlowe produces a mixed tone of satiric praise. Hero is both admirable, a source of wonder and amazement, and comical, a walking joke.

Hero is, in part, a feast for the senses, appealing to sight, smell, and taste. Her gorgeous array, sweet breath, and honey lips are so many attractions which suggest the marvelous allure of love. But the image of desirability tips over into comic hyperbole when Marlowe describes Hero literally fighting off the bees which swarm about her mouth in search of honey. Similarly, the idea of the impassioned devotion inspired by the beautiful woman is made absurdly literal in the description of Hero's kirtle, stained with the blood of despairing suitors who have slain themselves for unrequited love of her. Again, the intricate description of her "chirping buskins" employs a kind of straight-faced hyperbole to suggest that when love walks in, bells ring and birds sing.

Hero is also a saint of love, "Venus' nun" or priestess, and as such she possesses iconographic attributes. The joke is, of course, that her "holy" relics—the picture of her patron, the naked Venus, sporting with Adonis on the border of her sleeves and the naked babe Cupid at her breast—are in fact erotic and sensuous. (The very term "Venus' nun" was Elizabethan slang for "prostitute.") The whole description is a witty exercise in amorous symbolism delivered with a deadpan precision that simultaneously mocks and celebrates its subject; the tone is paradoxically both detached and earnest. Although sly wit and comic literalism inform the description, the portrait is also a marvel of fanciful detail and visual riches. Hero, then, is both an absurd caricature and an encomiastic emblem. The "jocoserious" tone Marlowe establishes in describing her becomes the keynote for the rest of the verse narrative.

15.2 What are the purposes of Marlowe's use of extended similes, inset tales, and digressions in the poem?

Answer Generally speaking, Marlowe uses these techniques of storytelling to expand and embellish his epyllion. (*Epyllion,* or "little epic," although not used as a critical term until the nineteenth century, is a useful descriptive label for a literary fashion of the 1590s practiced by Shakespeare [*Venus and Adonis*] as well as by many others. Based on Ovidian myths of metamorphosis, such narrative poems dealt with the amorous entanglements of gods and mortals and were characteristically ornate in style.) In *Hero and Leander* the inset tales of gods and goddesses provide the poem with a fanciful mythic embroidery. Furthermore, these tales and allusions elaborate on the theme of love by describing a variety of amorous situations and demonstrate Marlowe's rhetorical skill by amplifying and inflating the narrative with decorative arabesques.

Many of the "minimyths" Marlowe includes in the narrative constitute witty and ingenious explanations of natural or social phenomena. Thus, the reason night falls over half the globe is that Nature has put on mourning to show her grief over Hero's theft of her beauty. Similarly, the reason scholars are poor is that the Fates are out of sorts with Mercury, the patron saint of students. These fanciful myths of causation are offered with a broad wink at the audience; the latter especially is a kind of in-joke, applying to Marlowe's own situation as an impoverished university wit.

The long tale of Mercury's love for a shepherdess, Cupid's intervention, and the Fates' displeasure falls into the category of mythic embroidery: Hero and Leander are star-crossed because the Fates, angry at Cupid, refuse to smile on love. At the same time this complicated digression elaborates on the theme of love's pervasiveness and irrationality, describing how a god becomes infatuated with a mortal and how even that austere trio, Clotho, Atropos, and Lachesis, fall victim to Mercury's amorous charms. Finally, the tale demonstrates the poet's virtuoso "invention," his ability to spin out story after story with consummate ease.

Another instance of thematic and rhetorical amplification is the underwater ballet of Leander and Neptune as the youth swims the Hellespont to reach his beloved on the far shore. The comical picture of the great god of the sea hopelessly trailing after the innocent Leander suggests a topsy-turvy world of sexual confusion and role reversal. At one point Marlowe explicitly announces Leander's feminine allure: "Some swore he was a maid in man's attire,/ For in his looks were all that men desire." The pictures of Jove's amorous escapades carved in the pavement of Venus's church at Sestos similarly amplify the theme of love's "heady riot." In the world of the poem, the force of sexual attraction is both random and irresistible, with male pursuing male, god pursuing mortal, and even bees getting into the act in pursuit of the honey from Hero's lips.

From the briefest allusion to the longest tale, these "superfluous" stories are, in a sense, not superfluous at all. They are the very stuff of the epic, establishing the breezy, comic tone of the poem, developing the erotic theme, and working a rhetorical magic by making something out of almost nothing.

15.3 *Hero and Leander* is punctuated by *sententiae*, or moral "sentences," generalizations which comment on the topics of love, pride, virginity, spinsterhood, and so on. What is the significance of this strand of moralizing in the poem?

Answer The most famous of the "sentences" in Marlowe's epyllion, the line "Whoever lov'd that lov'd not at first sight?" (line 176), illustrates the basic function of generalization in the poem: to emphasize the universality of love as the most common of human experiences. Marlowe uses these detachable proverblike "sentences" to convey the familiar nature of the lovers' emotions. Love is irresistibly attractive, striking the victim "at first sight"; it can be delightfully mutual ("Sweet are the kisses, the imbracements sweet,/ When like desires and affections meet" [lines 513–514]); it can be cruel and voracious ("Love is not full of pity (as men say)/ But deaf and cruel when it means to prey" [lines 781–782]); it is emotionally transparent ("Love deeply grounded hardly is dissembled" [line 184] and "Affection in the countenance is discovered" [line 616]); and it is naively trusting ("Love is too full of faith, too credulous,/ With follie and false hope deluding us" [lines 705–706]). Other adages remark on the nature of pride ("for loftie pride that dwels/ In tow'red courts, is oft in shepheards cels" [lines 393–394]) and on spinsterhood ("Lone women like to empty houses perish" [line 242]).

All these judgments and observations constitute a background of commonplaces against which the amorous tale unfolds. Thus, Marlowe lessens the tragic uniqueness of Hero and Leander, emphasizing instead the common qualities of their experience. This mundane perspective on the drama of love contributes to the comic tone of the poem; the narrator views the lovers with a detached and ironic air as simply one more case of absurd innocence succumbing to histrionic passion.

The moralizings also suggest a kind of mock earnestness, a pretense of extracting deep philosophy from a frivolous and amorous tale. The *sententiae* are, in part, a parody of the whole didactic tradition of the serious epic, with the poet preserving a deadpan style as he composes his comic "little epic." (It should be pointed out that Marlowe completed only two sestiads of the poem; he was thus able to preserve a consistently humorous tone, for his death prevented him from reaching the tragic denouement of the tale. Most critics agree that the conclusion to the poem, written by Marlowe's contemporary George Chapman, is inconsistent in tone and inferior in interest to Marlowe's own work.)

Finally the *sententiae*, like the digressions, allusions, and similes, are a form of rhetorical decoration. These detachable one-liners embroider on the theme of love and create a running commentary and refrain for the various narrative developments of the poem.

15.4　Discuss the rhyme scheme and metrics of the poem.

Answer　The poem is written in heroic couplets, that is, paired iambic pentameter lines. Generally speaking, the regular alternation of stresses and the chiming of the rhymed couplets provide a smoothly textured verse, with the narrative moving forward in two-line "ripples." However, Marlowe at times employs the couplet to achieve the very different effect of halting the narrative flow by striking out an epigrammatic clincher. This effect of discreteness usually depends on a manipulation of the rhyme words, specifically the use of feminine rhymes, to provide a comic fillip for the couplet.

For example, in the following lines the wit derives not only from Leander's absurd ignorance of the anatomical facts of sex but from the complicated tri-syllabic rhyme at the conclusion:

> Albeit Leander, rude in love and raw,
> Long dallying with Hero nothing saw
> Which might delight him more, yet he suspected,
> Some amorous rite or other were neglected.
> > (lines 545–548)

The surprising match of polysyllabic words is an amusing display of the poet's ingenuity, producing a pleasure not unlike that which modern readers find in limericks or nonsense verse.

Other couplets are like captions, underlining the dramatic action by an emphatic and, again, complicated rhyme. The lines "By this, sad Hero, with love unacquainted,/ Viewing Leander's face, fell downe and fainted" (lines 485–486) create a kind of tension with the word "unacquainted," a tension which is nonchalantly and promptly resolved with the simple word—and action—"fainted." Similarly the poet wittily remarks upon Leander's dramatic plunge into the flood using a rhyme which plays with consonance and assonance:

> Leander stript him to the ivory skin
> And crying, Love I come, leapt lively in.
> (lines 637–638)

Though not a true feminine rhyme, "ivory skin" and "lively in" produce a similar effect of formal difficulty wittily overcome in the surprising chime of consonants and vowels.

Marlowe thus exploits the rhythmic properties of the iambic pentameter line to create a smooth narrative fabric, while at the same time he uses feminine rhymes and comic acoustics to underscore his witty observations on the pair of romantic innocents.

Doctor Faustus

15.5 Analyze the structure of the play.

Answer   The plot of the play consists of Faustus's descent from the pinnacle of success and renown to the abyss of hell. Although this descent conforms in part to the outlines of tragedy, with a fall from high estate, the *peripety*, or crisis, occurs not in the middle of the play but in its very opening scenes, when the aspiring scholar commits himself to the black arts and signs his pact with the devil. Consequently, the drama has a static quality, consisting of a series of set pieces or "shows" as Faustus exercises his demonic powers. The diagrammatic nature of the action is further enhanced by the ongoing *psychomachia*, the debate between good and evil angels, which constitutes a kind of thematic elaboration of the central situation.

The play's structure can be read as a parody or inversion of the pattern of a saint's life, itself a popular medieval literary form. The typical saint's life consists of a sinful youth followed by conversion to God, temptations by the devil, the performance of miracles, martyrdom, and finally the ascent to heaven. In *Doctor Faustus*, each of these phases is inverted: first we glimpse Faustus's upright early life, followed by his conversion to the devil, the "temptations" to repentance offered by the Good Angel, black miracles, death, and the descent into hell. It is the black miracles which provide the thin thread of plot in a string of farcical intrigues with the horse-courser, the carter, Robin, Dick, the Pope, Benvolio, and so on.

Both the traditional saint's life and the folkloric history of the infamous Faustus—Marlowe's two sources for the form of his drama—are, in a sense, exhibitions rather than dramas, with the outcome preordained from the moment of conversion. The only suspense derives from the temptations which test the hero's commitment. However, in *Doctor Faustus*, the Good Angel's exhortations are repeatedly countered by Faustus's rationalizations and Mephistopheles's distractions; thus the "temptations" to repent themselves become a predictable part of the expository structure of the drama rather than a means of complicating or deepening the pattern of tragic action.

The structure of the play has, perhaps, more in common with allegory or morality plays than with true tragedy as conceived by modern critics. Marlowe's main debt is to the medieval conception of tragedy as simply a fall from power and honor into poverty and disgrace caused by the arbitrary turning of the wheel of fortune. His main accomplishment was to add to this simple scheme a new emphasis on a specific tragic flaw and a focus on the grandeur of the protagonist's aspirations. Thus his play does not reveal the subtle evolution of character found in Shakespearean tragedy but illustrates, in strong, crude strokes, a stereotype—that of the overreacher.

15.6 What is the function of the comic scenes in the play?

Answer It is possible that the comic scenes in *Doctor Faustus* may have been added by a hand other than Marlowe's, either with or without his consent and either at the time the rest of the play was written or later. Nonetheless, we cannot eliminate these scenes from our reading of the play; the work as it stands forms a dramatic whole, and the comic scenes within the drama invite interpretation.

One of the effects of these scenes, the majority of which involve low-life characters, is to create an atmosphere of grotesquerie and macabre farce surrounding the dark tale of Faustus's fall. The buffoonery of Robin, Dick, the horse-courser, and the carter develops the theme of black magic in the light vein of folk superstition. The disappearances of the tavern cups, of the horses in midstream, and of the wain of hay, and the apparent dismemberment of Faustus, who "loses" his head and leg, suggest sixteenth-century lore of witches, elves, and demons, folktales which combine the humor of practical jokes with the thrill of ghost stories. Although the shift in tone between the terrifying spectacle of Faustus's fall and the subsidiary antics of the clowns may be disconcerting, the range of action implies the pervasiveness of devilish doings and suggests the folk origins of the Faust legend.

In a sense, though, the farcical episodes are integral to the main plot of the play. The episodes involving Wagner and Robin constitute an ironic comment on Faustus's tragic flaw of mounting ambition, with Wagner aping Faustus and Robin imitating Wagner in calling on the devil to gratify their petty wishes. A kind of pecking order of overreachers is thus established, revealing the universality of greed, lust, and sadistic will, as servant enslaves servant and conjuring becomes a means of pursuing even infantile gratifications.

Faustus himself is capable of childish buffoonery, for it is he who plays the farcical tricks on the horse-courser and the carter. The scenes at the papal court are farcical as well: Faustus's seizing of the Pope's meal from under his nose and his planting of horns on Benvolio's head are, like jestbook tales, mere practical jokes. The distance between these low antics and the choric description of Faustus mounted on a chariot drawn by dragons, surveying the cosmos, is far indeed. This gap between Faustus's original pretensions to vast knowledge and his later satisfaction in sadistic sport is one measure of his fall. His bargain with the devil has robbed him of his finer instincts and aspirations; he ends up driven by his own base appetites to seek distraction and frivolous mirth.

Thus the comedy in the play has two important functions. On the one hand, the comic grotesquerie creates an eerie atmosphere of superstition, with devils lying in wait everywhere to undo poor mortals. On the other hand, it elaborates the main theme of the play, Faustus's "bad bargain": with the selling of one's soul, life itself becomes absurd, nothing more than an empty joke.

15.7 What affinities does *Doctor Faustus* have with medieval drama? With tragedy?

Answer *Doctor Faustus* is the product of a mixing of the two influences, with certain aspects deriving from medieval morality and mystery plays and others from the genre of tragedy. The theological content of the play—the concern with salvation and damnation, grace and repentance, God and the devil, mercy and judgment—indicates the close connection with a drama like *Everyman*. The obvious difference from *Everyman* is that, instead of showing the salvation of a Christian pilgrim, the play is a kind of admonitory sermon diagraming a soul's descent into hell. The personified abstractions contribute to the diagrammatic, moralitylike quality of the drama, with the good and evil angels conducting a theological debate over Faustus's soul and Mephistopheles playing the role of the Vice from medieval drama. The setting of the play, which ranges between the heavens and earth and includes a trapdoor to hell, recalls the primitive stage sets of the mysteries with their suggestion of a tripartite division of the world. Finally, the parody of the main action by clowns and tradesmen, who imitate Faustus's conjuring tricks and ape his grandiose desires, is linked with the rough-and-tumble farce of miracle plays like *The Second Shepherds' Play*, where a mock-nativity is performed by the clownish Mak.

The extent to which *Doctor Faustus* resembles a tragedy depends almost entirely on the character of Faustus. In the opening scene Faustus's long soliloquy establishes his tragic flaw: his intellectual pride and overreaching ambition. This "aspiring mind" is not simply a personal vice; it is a flaw with universal scope and significance, a failing bound up inextricably with the greatness of human designs and efforts. Seeking a godlike omnipotence, Faustus rejects each worldly discipline and chooses necromancy, immediately arriving at the crisis, or peripety, of the action. The psychological groundwork has been laid for the signing of his pact with the devil and for his inevitable and fateful fall. This psychological determinism, with character creating its own destiny, is central to tragedy and colors the whole of *Doctor Faustus*, even when the plot momentarily descends into farce.

The language of the play also suggests a relationship with tragedy. Marlowe's swelling blank verse line and the richness of metaphor which characterizes some of Faustus's speeches and soliloquies create a heroic and larger-than-life image. Although the tone of the play fluctuates and varies, the moments when Faustus produces a flight of eloquence suggest his tragic longings and finely developed sensibilities. Thus Faustus's character and language together evoke the cathartic "pity and terror" of tragedy: his fall involves universal questions of character, sin, and evil, and his death creates a sense of loss and emptiness.

The hybrid nature of *Doctor Faustus* produces an interesting tension in the play. The tragic elements—the interior glimpses into character and the fateful choice—are partly at odds with the more narrow focus on salvation; and the farcical episodes, though integral to the theme, introduce an anomalous tone. The mix of elements creates a rich tapestry, with the figure of Faustus, the tragic individualist, placed against a brooding medieval background of sin and retribution.

15.8   What is the effect of the figurative language spoken by Faustus in the following speech?

Was this the face that launched a thousand ships,
And burnt the topless towers of Ilium?
Sweet Helen, make me immortal with a kiss.
Her lips sucks forth my soul, see where it flies!
Come, Helen, come, give me my soul again.
Here will I dwell, for heaven is in these lips
And all is dross that is not Helena.
                              (Act V, Scene i, lines 92–98)

Answer In this speech Marlowe uses figurative language, notably hyperbole and metaphor, to express in condensed form the chief themes of the play: overreaching desire and the striving for an omnipotence which exceeds human limits. The whole passage is colored by religious imagery, for in Faustus's imagination Helen becomes a saint of love, an intercessor who will satisfy his soul's boundless longings. In his address to the apparition of Helen, Faustus's hyperbole suggests precisely these longings, for he treats Helen as the epitome of all desire, endowing her with immense seductive power. She is capable of sending forth an entire armada, "a thousand ships," to destroy a whole civilization, "the topless towers of Ilium." The emphasis on her "face" calls up the image of a ship's figurehead, as though Helen herself were at the prow, forcing a passage through the seas.

The hyperbolic description of Helen establishes her as a transcendent object of desire. Faustus proceeds to pray to this image, calling on the temptress to "make me immortal with a kiss." The religious longing for salvation is thus transposed into the sexual realm, with the soul's consummation described as a physical kiss and heaven located in Helen's lips. The metaphoric language reveals the extent of Faustus's delusion; he speaks as though the spirit and the body were interchangeable. The implied pun on "dying"—in Elizabethan speech, it meant both literal death and sexual consummation—reinforces this confusion of realms of experience. Faustus's substitution of a physical avenue to "heaven" for the soul's passage from life to eternity derives from sinful appetite; his shortcut to heaven becomes, in the end, a transit to hell.

15.9 Discuss Faustus's final speech in Act V, scene ii, beginning with "O Faustus!/ Now hast thou but one bare hour to live . . ." (lines 135–190).

Answer This soliloquy constitutes an emotional climax, Faustus's final recognition that his hour has indeed come and that his debt to the devil has at last come due. The fact that eight of the fifty-odd lines begin with "O" suggests how continuously exclamatory this outburst is, how tormented and overwrought the speaker is in the last hour before the reckoning. The suspense of the approaching denouement, when the devils "exeunt with Faustus," is emphasized by the pointed references to time: "one bare hour to live" (line 136); "The stars still move, time runs, the clock will strike" (line 145); "O half the hour is pass'd! 'Twill all be pass'd anon!" (line 166); "It strikes, it strikes!" (line 183).

The numerous ejaculations and the reiterated allusions to time create an obsessive tone as Faustus, trapped in his own bad bargain, struggles with the consequences fast approaching him. But what is perhaps most significant about this speech is how similar it is, in theme and even syntax, to earlier speeches by Faustus. His last obsessions are like his first: the same wish to control time and the elements, the same fearful reading of signs and omens, the same vacillation between hope and despair, the same contortions and rationalizations in an effort to escape from pain and from his own troubled conscience.

Many of the lines are structured as imperatives or hortatory subjunctives: "Stand still, you ever-moving spheres of Heaven" (line 138); "Mountains and hills, come, come" (line 155); "Gape earth!" (line 158); "Now body, turn to air" (line 183); "O soul, be changed into small water-drops" (line 185). Faustus's initial wish to master the elemental powers of the universe has become a frantic desire to dissolve himself into the elements—earth, air, water—in order to hide from his approaching doom. The striving for omnipotence and the desire to impress himself upon the universe characterize both Faustus's beginning and his end.

The essentially static nature of Faustus's situation is evident as well in his inability to repent. The vision of Christ's blood streaming in the firmament and a "threat'ning arm, an angry brow" (line 153) recall Faustus's signing of the pact with the devil, when his blood congealed and the words "Homo fuge" appeared on his arm. "One drop of blood will save me," Faustus says, that is, Christ's blood will cancel his own bloody signature; but his resolution "Yet will I call on Him!" is immediately and ironically followed by a prayer not to Christ but to Satan: "O spare me Lucifer" (lines 149–151). The rejection of repentance has been a recurrent action in the course of the drama, this last instance only confirming the mixture of defiance and despair fundamental to Faustus's character.

Another characteristic of Faustus's personality recurs in this final speech, the ratiocination and intellectuality which drove him to embrace necromancy in the first place. Even in the moment before his doom Faustus pauses to consider the question of the soul's immortality, with learned references to "Pythagoras' metempsychosis": if he could become a beast, "a creature wanting soul," then he could truly die rather than "live still to be plagu'd in Hell!" (lines 172–179). As always with Faustus, theories and facts are drawn into his obsession with his own desires and his own fate.

If Faustus is learned, it is nonetheless striking how little he has learned in the course of the play. This last speech is not a recognition scene but rather a confirmation of the hero's fixed and ferocious desires. Cast as a series of exclamations and exhortations, the monologue dramatizes Faustus's emotions as he seeks, one last time, to make the world bow to his commands.

B.S.

SUGGESTED READINGS

Levin, Harry, *The Overreacher* (1952).
Lewis, C.S., *Hero and Leander* (1952).
Steane, J. B., *Marlowe: A Critical Study* (1964).
Wilson, F. P., *Marlowe and the Early Shakespeare* (1953).

WILLIAM SHAKESPEARE

C H R O N O L O G Y

1564   Born at Stratford-upon-Avon. Son of John Shakespeare, an alderman and later mayor of Stratford, and Mary Arden Shakespeare. Virtually nothing is known of the poet's early life or education, although it is likely that he studied at a grammar school in the area, learning reading, writing, grammar, rhetoric, some Latin, and a smattering of other subjects.

1582   Marries Anne Hathaway in Stratford by a special license (generally issued in cases where a marriage must be held without delay). Six months later (1583), Shakespeare's first daughter, Susanna, is born.

1585   Birth of Shakespeare's twin son and daughter Hamnet and Judith. Shakespeare's seven "lost years" begin, the period of his life for which there is no documentary evidence as to his activities. It appears, however, that by the late 1580s Shakespeare had become an actor in London and was probably beginning his literary career, perhaps as a collaborator in the writing of plays.

1590   Probable date of the writing of *Henry VI, Parts I–III*, usually considered Shakespeare's earliest works.

1592   Record of the performance of *Henry VI* by Strange's Men, one of the Elizabethan theatrical companies. Robert Greene alludes to Shakespeare as an actor and playwright in his *Groatsworth of Wit*. The London theaters are temporarily closed during an outbreak of the plague; the enforced absence from the stage may be one reason for Shakespeare's writing of the narrative poem *Venus and Adonis* at this time.

1593   *Venus and Adonis* published; its sensuous style and erotic content make it highly popular; it is reprinted fifteen times by 1640. Probable date of the composition of *Richard III.* Shakespeare is probably also writing the sonnets at this time (probably completed by 1600).

1594   Narrative poem *The Rape of Lucrece* published by Shakespeare; it, too, is successful, though less so than *Venus and Adonis.* The theatrical company known as the Lord Chamberlain's Men is formed; Shakespeare is one of their principal actors and a part owner of the company.

1595   The Lord Chamberlain's Men noted as having performed at court. Probable date of composition of *Two Gentlemen of Verona.*

1596   Death of son Hamnet. Shakespeare's father is granted a coat of arms, indicating that by this time the playwright is evidently a prosperous and well-known figure. Probable date of composition of *Romeo and Juliet,* Shakespeare's earliest tragedy.

1597   Shakespeare buys New Place, the second largest house in Stratford. Is mentioned in Francis Meres's *Palladis Tamia* as one of the greatest English poets; specifically, twelve of Shakespeare's plays are listed, as are "his sugared sonnets among his private friends" (indicating that at least some of the sonnets had begun to circulate in manuscript form by this date).

1598   Shakespeare is listed as a principal actor in Ben Jonson's comedy *Every Man in His Humour. Henry IV, Part I* (probably Shakespeare's greatest historical play) and *Love's Labour's Lost* are both printed in quarto editions. During the poet's lifetime, quarto editions of many of his plays will be their only publication; they are apparently pirated, unauthorized versions, produced to capitalize on Shakespeare's popularity.

1599   The Globe Theater is built; Shakespeare is listed as a one-tenth owner of the theater. *Julius Caesar* is produced. *Much Ado about Nothing* is probably written.

1600   *Henry IV, Part II; The Merchant of Venice;* and *A Midsummer Night's Dream* are all published in quarto editions. Probable date of composition of *Hamlet.*

1601   Death of Shakespeare's father. Probable date of composition of "The Phoenix and the Turtle," an allegorical poem on love.

1602   Shakespeare buys a cottage and a tract of farmland in Stratford. *Twelfth Night* performed.

1603   Death of Queen Elizabeth; accession of King James I, who becomes the patron of Shakespeare's company, now called the King's Men. *Hamlet* is published in quarto. Shakespeare makes his last recorded appearance as an actor, in Ben Jonson's tragedy *Sejanus*.

1604   *Othello* is performed. Shakespeare's great middle period, in which the famous tragedies will be written, is well under way.

1606   *King Lear* is performed before King James.

1607   Probable date of composition of *Antony and Cleopatra* and *Macbeth*.

1608   The King's Men take a lease on the Blackfriars Theater; Shakespeare listed as a principal shareholder. *King Lear* published in quarto.

1609   Shakespeare's sonnets are published by Thomas Thorpe, with the mysterious dedication to "Mr. W.H.," their "Onlie Begetter," which may imply either that W.H. inspired the poet in writing the sonnets or simply that he gathered the copies of the poems for use by the publisher. Shakespeare clearly did not supervise this publication; the order of the 154 poems is somewhat haphazard and illogical, making the development of their themes difficult to follow. *Pericles* published in quarto; this play will not be included in the First Folio of 1623, perhaps because it was written in collaboration with another playwright; it is usually included in the canon of Shakespeare's works by virtue of its appearance in the Third Folio (1664).

1610   Probable date of composition of *The Winter's Tale*. Shakespeare's final period, dominated by the so-called late romances, begins.

1611   *Cymbeline* and *The Tempest* are performed. The latter is often regarded as Shakespeare's last play, or at least as the last play he wrote independently; the central character, Prospero, is often considered autobiographical, his farewell taken as Shakespeare's own farewell to the stage. This is all conjecture, however.

1612   Shakespeare has evidently retired to Stratford by this time.

1613   The Globe Theater is destroyed by fire during the premiere of *Henry VIII*, probably Shakespeare's last play (evidently a collaboration with John Fletcher).

1614   The rebuilt Globe opens.

1616   Death of Shakespeare; he is buried in Stratford. His will reveals him a prosperous country gentleman. His sole bequest to his wife is their second-best bed, which some have speculated indicates the low esteem in which the poet held his wife, while others claim it is a sign of fondness, since the second-best bed would have been the married couple's own bed (the best bed being reserved for guests). Like most of the few facts known about

Shakespeare's life, this has been the source of voluminous speculation, little of it relevant to our understanding or appreciation of his works.

1623   Death of Shakespeare's wife. Publication of the First Folio, a one-volume edition of Shakespeare's works edited by Shakespeare's theatrical colleagues and containing thirty-six plays, the sonnets, and other poems, as well as a set of commendatory verses by Ben Jonson. Many other Elizabethan plays were published under Shakespeare's name, and scholars believe that Shakespeare may have at least collaborated on some of these (such as *Sir Thomas More*, a part of which exists in Shakespeare's own hand). However, these plays are counted as the "Shakespeare Apocrypha" and are not generally considered when the works of the greatest English playwright and poet are under discussion.

ESSAY QUESTIONS WITH ANSWERS

Sonnet 12: "When I do count the clock that tells the time . . ."

16.1 As one of the seventeen "procreation" sonnets which appeared first in Shakespeare's cycle, sonnet 12 is addressed to a young nobleman with the purpose of persuading him to marry and produce children. How does this unconventional rhetorical occasion influence the tone of the poem? How does the lyric differ from more typical Renaissance sonnets?

Answer The typical sonnet was either a witty compliment designed to win the favor of a disdainful mistress, or a psychological self-portrait designed to arouse the lady's pity or simply express a state of feeling. Although there are intimations of flirtatious gesture and personal confession in Shakespeare's address to his young friend, the sonnet's tone prevents it from being read as an overt declaration of homosexual love. The poet's analysis of the universal theme of time has a musing, contemplative quality, producing an effect of distance and disinterestedness which plays off against the inevitable intimacy of the situation.

Thus, in the first two quatrains the poet is pondering not only a single person but the world at large. He scans the book of nature for images of decline and decay, seeing a reminder of death in flowers, trees, and harvested crops. Only in the third quatrain does Shakespeare shift to the personal, directly addressing the young man ("Then of thy beauty do I question make") and applying the general moral lesson to an individual human case. Like flower, tree, and "summer's green," the young man will inevitably die with the passage of time. The couplet continues in this personal vein, offering a possible solution to the young man's dilemma in "breed," which transcends the limits of mortality.

Yet the solution, like the problem, is posed in abstract terms: "breed" as the answer to "time." Indeed a certain abstraction permeates the whole closing movement of the sonnet, with "thy beauty" absorbed into the general class of "sweets and beauties" and the pathos of "That thou among the wastes of time must go" balanced by the more impersonal time-breed antithesis of the couplet.

The sonnet acquires a poised tension through Shakespeare's manipulation of tone. Some emotional involvement or intrigue with the young man is implied by the very act of giving advice. There is the suggestion that the poet is an older man who admires the young man's beauty and wishes to counsel the heedless youth. However, the poet's substitution of philosophical reflection for impassioned confession makes the emotional bond with the young friend latent rather than manifest.

16.2 How does Shakespeare characterize time in sonnet 12?

Answer The three explicit references to time in the poem associate the concept with concrete images: a clock (line 1); a desert or, more generally, all of nature, destroyed by time's passage ("the wastes of time" [line 10]); and the Grim Reaper, death ("Time's scythe" [line 13]). All these images convey negative ideas, the tick-tock of the clock implying the reduction of life to monotonous chronology, the "wastes" connoting emptiness and futility, and the "scythe" suggesting destructive mortality.

But Shakespeare goes beyond this conventional imagery, which resembles that used in allegorical woodcuts, in his description of the destructive force of time. By cataloguing the specific effects wrought by time on man and nature, he turns the abstract and intangible into something concrete and active. Throughout the poem, he dramatizes time as a dangerous enemy who must be combated.

In the first quatrain, the images of fading flower ("violet past prime") and graying hair ("sable curls all silvered o'er") suggest that time's destructive power affects all natural creatures equally. In the second quatrain, the anthropomorphic image of the harvest as a dead man carried in a funeral procession ("summer's green . . ./ Borne on a bier with white and bristly beard") explicitly links the seasonal cycles of life and death with the ages of man. Just as summer dies in winter and day is overwhelmed by "hideous night," so life itself tends always toward death. Every part of the natural order becomes a lesson in mortality and an illustration of time's cruel dominion.

In the final sestet of the sonnet, Shakespeare turns from description to argument. He applies the lesson drawn from nature to the particular case of his young friend: "Then of thy beauty do I question make,/ That thou among the wastes of time must go." The couplet offers a specific solution to the problem of time. Against decay, waste, loss, and death, the poet poses "breed," or procreation. Only by reproduction can the young man defy his personal dissolution. Here the idea of personal combat is most fully realized, in the implied image of a confrontation between the Grim Reaper and Shakespeare's young friend.

Thus, by means of vivid imagery, Shakespeare personalizes the battle between the vital force of nature and the deadly effects of time in the dramatization of his young friend's dilemma in the sestet of the sonnet.

16.3   How is the word "brave" used in sonnet 12?

Answer   The word occurs twice in the poem, as an adjective in line 2 ("And see the brave day sunk in hideous night") and as a verb in line 14 ("Save breed, to brave him when he takes thee hence"). In the first instance, "brave" suggests its usual modern meaning of "courageous" or "valorous," implying the image of a battlefield on which heroic "day" is overwhelmed by his enemy "night." But in sixteenth-century usage, "brave" primarily signified "gorgeous," "beautifully arrayed," an exact antonym of "hideous." The word further contains a faint echo of "bravado," intimating a swaggering or defiant *display* of both courage and beauty.

These senses color the use of "brave" as a verb in the concluding couplet. The primary significance of "brave" in this context is "defy" or "challenge": the bearing of children ("breed") becomes a kind of heroic protest against the inevitability of personal mortality. Though time takes the young man "hence," bearing him away into the empty wastes, the victim "outbraves" his enemy through the defiant gesture of self-reproduction, which will carry on the beauty of the young man.

Sonnet 55: "Not marble, nor the gilded monuments . . ."

16.4   What is the main idea of the lyric? How does Shakespeare develop his theme?

Answer   The theme of the poem is commemoration of the beloved, a theme Shakespeare develops through an extended comparison between conventional physical monuments and the written word. Shakespeare praises the art of poetry in contrast to the lesser arts of sculpture and architecture, using images of vitality, brightness, and movement to honor both the power of words and, by extension, the person enshrined in words, the loved one.

Thus, in the first quatrain "this powerful rime" is described as "outliving" marble and gold: the poem Shakespeare is writing confers a kind of immortality on its subject, more so than a mere physical monument could. The words of the sonnet lend not only long life but brilliance to the beloved: "But you shall shine more bright in these contents/ Than unswept stone, besmeared with sluttish Time." The gilding of monuments is, by comparison with Shakespeare's glowing words, only tinsel, subject to the physical decay produced by time.

The effect of the first quatrain, then, is to imply that public monuments are fragile in contrast to words. After elaborating on the inevitable destruction of material monuments by war and disasters, posing against these dead ruins "the living record of your memory," the poet goes on to claim one further advantage for language: its power to convey the illusion of life and movement. On the stage of the sonnet, the loved one will "pace forth" like a living being. Punning on the idea of architectural space, Shakespeare suggests that the poem is a physical place, a room: "your praise shall still find room,/ Even in the eyes of all posterity." This suggestion of space continues in the last line of the poem, where it is implied that the sonnet constitutes a habitation for the beloved ("You dwell in this"), with future readers providing a place of residence *in perpetuum* ("and dwell in lovers' eyes").

Thus, the art of poetry preempts the native function of the rival arts of sculpture and architecture, the language of the sonnet offering the loved one enduring commemoration, a radiant and lively likeness, and even a permanent "place" on earth.

16.5 How and why does sonnet 55 refer to itself?

Answer In the first quatrain and the final couplet of the sonnet, demonstrative adjectives and pronouns point directly to the poem itself: "*this* powerful rime" (line 2), "*these* contents" (line 3), and "You dwell in *this*" (line 14). Other allusions to the writing and reading of the sonnet also occur: "The living record of your memory" (line 8), "the eyes of all posterity" (line 11), "and dwell in lovers' eyes" (line 14). Taken together, these allusions constitute a self-conscious commentary on the sonneteer's artistic process, his actual activity of writing down a sonnet. Furthermore, the self-references emphasize the materiality of the resulting composition: *these* words on *this* page.

The effect of this strategy of self-reference is complex. First, it is part of a witty rhetorical manipulation which creates a double focus: ostensibly written in praise of the beloved, the sonnet in fact emphatically praises itself. Although the poem is supposedly a love sonnet commemorating the beloved, the attention falls more on the process of commemoration than on the person of the beloved. Thus, the line "But you shall shine more bright in these contents" suggests that it is "these contents," that is, the poem, which create a brilliant setting for the loved one, who gains radiance from the verbal medium itself.

Self-reference serves the further purpose of enforcing the poet's argument that his language is more enduring than material monuments. Against the vague generalities of "marble," "gilded monuments," "statues," and "masonry" the poet pits the specific words that he is writing: *this* rhyme, *these* contents, the *living* record. By insisting on the particular—sonnet 55 itself—Shakespeare strengthens his case for the efficacy of poetry. We, the readers, are "the eyes of all posterity," and the fact that we are reading the poem attests to its survival. The insistence on the actual words of the sonnet also conveys a sense of the poem's vital existence as an artifact, a thing made out of words. It becomes a kind of monument in its own right, capable of competing with the "gilded monuments/ Of princes." It is in fact superior to any physical object, for its immateriality makes it indestructible.

Thus, the self-reference in the sonnet serves as a means of shifting the theme from private emotion to the larger philosophical concerns of art and mutability. In addition, the self-quotation becomes a persuasive argument in favor of poetry, with Shakespeare pointing to his own words as he celebrates the power of words.

16.6
Two grammatical peculiarities occur in the poem. First, the line "Nor Mars his sword nor war's quick fire shall burn" yokes the two nouns "sword" and "fire" with a verb properly applying only to the latter. Second, the phrase "all-oblivious enmity" apparently reverses the proper positions of adjective and noun, since "oblivion" would normally be characterized as hostile, not "enmity" as oblivious. Comment on these peculiarities of usage.

Answer   These phrases are not errors of usage but deliberately crafted figures of speech. Figurative language by definition involves some departure from conventional usage, in order to draw the reader's attention to the heightening of verbal significance. The figures of speech used here are technically known as *zeugma* (the yoking of two nouns with a single verb) and *epithet* (an unusual adjective-noun combination). Both figures produce an effect of intensification through condensation.

In the line "Nor Mars his sword . . .," Shakespeare emphasizes the destructiveness of war by treating it as an indiscriminate conflagration, fusing subject and predicate by means of the strong final verb "burn." The "sword" of Mars, the god of war, becomes absorbed into the still more vivid and apt image of a raging war fire, from which Shakespeare's poem, not being a physical entity, miraculously escapes.

Similarly, "all-oblivious enmity" constitutes a fusion or condensation of several ideas into a single phrase. "All-oblivious enmity" suggests a sweeping antagonism, which is "oblivious" in two senses: it is unmindful and heedless, a blind and unconscious force; and it leads to oblivion, wipes out the record of former times. The adjective "all-oblivious" thus has the effect of a pun or a portmanteau word, and the beloved's "pacing forth" becomes especially miraculous in the face of a doubly malevolent foe.

In these two instances Shakespeare manipulates language to provide heightened significance. Both the image of fire and that of a hostile, obliterating horde contribute to the sense of miracle in the lyric, with the beloved—and the poem—triumphantly surviving these agents of holocaust.

Sonnet 73: "That time of year thou mayst in me behold . . ."

16.7 How does the structure of the sonnet relate to the logical progression of its argument?

Answer The logical development of the poem coincides with the rhyme pattern of this typical Shakespearean sonnet; it unfolds in three distinct statements (the three quatrains) with a concluding summation (the final couplet). The poem offers a series of three detailed images or conceits, relating autumn, sunset, and a dying fire, respectively, to the central idea of approaching death. The couplet shifts the focus from the aging poet to the beloved, describing the loved one's response to the spectacle of the poet's decline.

This structure, three variations and a conclusion, is tightly interwoven on both the verbal and thematic levels. The triple repetition of "in me" ("in me behold," "In me thou seest," "In me thou seest") binds the quatrains together by locating each different image within the poet, creating a continuous landscape of subjective feeling. A similar cohesive effect is achieved by the reexamination of the theme of aging through three differing metaphors which create a dense texture of cross connections. In the first quatrain the poet describes himself as a leafless tree in a winter landscape, as he regretfully muses on the loss of his youth: "Bare ruined choirs where late the sweet birds rang." The decline of the year from spring to autumn finds a parallel in the fading of day into twilight in the second quatrain, both the annual and diurnal cycles suggesting the stages of mortal life. In the third quatrain the poet poses yet another variation on the theme of aging in the image of a dying fire, "Which on the ashes of his youth doth lie."

All three images represent senescence as a deprivation and a dwindling, especially of heat and light. The "boughs which shake against the cold" in the first quatrain are related to the cold bed of ashes, the fire's "deathbed," in the third quatrain. Similarly, the "fading" of the sunset in the second quatrain is connected with the "glowing" of the dying fire in the third quatrain.

Another unifying pattern consists of allusions to youth and death. In the first quatrain the poet looks back on his "green" youth, when "late the sweet birds sang." In the second quatrain he looks forward to his end, with "black night" representing "Death's second self." In the last quatrain he combines the two perspectives, specifying the exact relationship between maturation and decline: the dying fire ("Which on the ashes of his youth doth lie,/ As the deathbed whereon it must expire") signifies that growth and decline are inextricably linked, each moment of progress simultaneously a moment of decay. The blaze is "nourished" by the flames of youth at the same time as it is "consumed" by them to dead ash.

The elaborate pattern of parallels and variations in the quatrains culminates in the couplet, which is both a summary and a request. With the phrase "This thou perceiv'st," the poet alludes to the preceding description of himself as aging, fading, and expiring. The consequence for the beloved, the poet suggests, is (or should be) a new intensity of feeling for the relationship. Thus, the structural tactics of the poem involve a shift of ground, from the impressionistic self-portraiture of the quatrains to a kind of *carpe diem* argument in the couplet. The poet's picture of himself becomes a piece of evidence proving the justice of his claim on the love of his beloved.

16.8 Paraphrase the final couplet and comment on its significance.

Answer In plain prose, the final couplet means roughly, "You see that I am growing old, and thus you love me more intensely, cherishing that which you must soon relinquish."

The final couplet functions both as summary and argument. The poet refers back to his impressionistic self-description in the three preceding quatrains, the "this" in "This thou perceiv'st" alluding to the images of himself as autumnal tree, dying sunset, and fading fire. This self-portrait then becomes the foundation of his final statement: "which makes thy love more strong/ To love that well which thou must leave ere long." This last declaration is on one level simply an assertion ("You see that I am dying; thus you love me") and on another level a plea or argument ("You see that I am dying; thus you must, or should, love me"). The pleading quality is reinforced by the use of the active verb "leave." The poet implies, somewhat oddly, that the beloved is going to leave him, rather than that he himself is going to leave the beloved when he dies.

In its active connotation, "leave" suggests not merely "relinquish" but "abandon." After the slow, meditative movement of the main body of the lyric, the couplet sounds like a lover's urgent plaint: "I am dying; so cherish me while you can, and do not abandon me until you must."

The almost desperate tone of the couplet suggests the further possibility that the lines should be read as ironic. The whole sonnet works against the convention of love as a youthful, passionate, springtime phenomenon; there are no "rosy cheeks and lips" in this poem. In the couplet the poet seems to acknowledge, beneath the overt sense of the words, that his young lover will *not* find him more attractive because of his imminent death. Thus the lines may be read as a bitter indictment rather than a passionate plea.

16.9 Compare sonnet 12 with sonnet 73.

Answer Both sonnets deal with the theme of time, cataloguing its destructive effects and attempting to find some compensation or remedy. The poems share certain images of temporal decline: the autumnal trees "barren of leaves" in sonnet 12 are paralleled by the bare, wintry boughs in sonnet 73, while "the brave day sunk in hideous night" (12) has its counterpart in the fading day "Which by and by black night doth take away" (73).

However, the poems differ in their rhetorical strategy, their tone, and the specific nature of the solution to the dilemma of time that the poet offers. In sonnet 12, the poet's persona is that of an objective spectator who sits back and "counts the clock," observing from a removed perspective the changing landscape around him. The poet scans the book of nature ("When I behold," "When . . . I see"), gathering evidence of the universal process of gradual decay. From the data of fading flowers and whitened hair he draws a logical inference; he then applies this moral to the case of his young friend ("Then of thy beauty do I question make"). In sonnet 73, the poet's gaze is directed not outward to the world but inward to his own situation, even his own body. He draws on nature only for illustrative purposes, using the imagery of autumn, sunset, and fire to depict his personal deterioration. Thus, the "landscape" in 73 is not objective but subjective, and the poet's tone, in contrast to the somewhat remote, musing quality of sonnet 12, is sorrowful and bitter. The "moral" the poet draws from the spectacle of his decline is not logical but psychological, not a deduction but a plea: he says, in effect, that his beloved must love him because he is dying.

To the young man in sonnet 12, the poet advises "breed" as a way of circumventing mortality and personal extinction. To the beloved in sonnet 73, he urges seizing the moment, fully experiencing the emotion of love, as a way of combating death and decay. These two solutions to the problem of time differ precisely as the analysis of time differs in the two sonnets. In sonnet 12 time is seen as a cycle of repetitions and substitutions: "Since sweets and beauties do themselves forsake/ And die as fast as they see others grow." Nature functions according to a "timed" pattern, with dying things steadily replaced by new growth. Thus the poet persuades the young man to create his own "new growth," to replace himself in the scheme of nature by producing children.

In sonnet 73 time is seen not as chronological pattern but as an ironically self-consuming process. At the base of existence is the paradox that we begin to die as soon as we begin to live; the process of maturation is simultaneously a process of deterioration, and each vital moment is a fatal step toward extinction. Like the blazing log, alive with flame but crumbling into ash, man is "consumed with that which it was nourished by." This more complex view of time as an inescapable prison yields an emotive response, an urging of love's value despite the transience of its object.

Sonnet 116: "Let me not to the marriage of true minds . . ."

16.10 Sonnet 116 is structured as a logical argument. Discuss Shakespeare's argumentative technique and its effect.

Answer The sonnet has many features of a formal argument or deliberative oration, with opening thesis, definitions and illustrations, and a concluding syllogism. Shakespeare begins by announcing his intention to refute all "impediments," all obstacles or objections, to true love. His chief means of developing his case is the technique of definition: in the first and third quatrains he offers negative definitions of love ("Love is not love," "Love's not Time's fool") which draw distinctions between false love and true; and in the second quatrain he presents an illustration of true love in the form of an extended metaphor. He concludes his argument with a pseudosyllogism which seeks to use the evidence of common sense as proof of his definition of love.

Despite the apparent rigor of the argument, the logical apparatus is somewhat strained. For example, the opening statement ("Let me not . . .") is not a true thesis or proposition, for it is expressed in the subjunctive mood, as though the "marriage of true minds" were a hypothesis to be urged rather than a fact to be asserted. Many of the statements in the sonnet contain negative constructions, suggesting that the subject, true love, is resistant to affirmation and straightforward description. As we have seen, both of the literal definitions of love are stated in the negative, throwing significant emphasis on what love is *not*. A kind of stumbling in the language is particularly evident in the phrase "Love is not love," which sounds like a naked contradiction, an impossible paradox; the addition of the defining clause "Which alters when it alteration finds" gives the impression of a recovery, as though the poet has extricated himself from a semantic difficulty. The very first sentence in the poem also offers a kind of stumbling block, tripping up the reader in a double negative construction and thus offering its own kind of impediment. What could be stated in the affirmative, "True minds marry faithfully and forever," is phrased as "Let me not . . . Admit impediments," that is, let there be no "nots" in a marriage of true minds.

The sense of strain continues in the positive definition of love in the second quatrain, which begins, significantly, with "Oh, no," as if the impediments, all that love is not, require energetic opposition. Although this quatrain conveys the clear ideas of stability and immutability, it also offers the central paradox of the poem. The line "Whose worth's unknown, although his height be taken" suggests that Shakespeare's attempt to evaluate love's qualities, to go beyond sterile measurement to a more complete comprehension, is essentially a futile effort to define the indefinable. The conclusion also contains a sense of difficulty, using the twisted logic of a contrary-to-fact conditional clause to produce a *reductio ad absurdum* (absurd inference). If I'm wrong, Shakespeare says, "I never writ"—and yet we are reading his very words.

The net effect is of thorny argument, the forcing of ideas into a pattern of definition and proof which cannot quite contain them. Certainly the format is repressive of the emotion of love, even while it attempts to express its meaning. The hortatory, conditional, negative, and paradoxical constructions produce a sense of arduousness, of difficulty only barely overcome. The emphasis, perhaps unwitting, is on "impediments" rather than on "marriage."

16.11 In sonnet 116 the way words sound is an important vehicle of significance. Select specific words that illustrate this feature of Shakespeare's language and analyze their effect.

Answer A striking example of the relationship between sound and sense occurs in the first two lines of the sonnet, where the spondee "true minds," with its two long vowel sounds and strong accents, is immediately followed by the phrase "admit impediments," with its short rapid syllables and hard consonant sounds. The Latinate, polysyllabic "impediments" itself produces an impediment, an obstacle, in the line, tripping up the flow of the sentence and producing a complication of tone after the slow, strong, open stresses of "true minds." The line throws its emphasis on "impediments," thus sounding the major theme of the poem.

Similarly, in the third quatrain, the line "But bears it out even to the edge of doom" uses long vowels ("bear," "doom") to reinforce the meaning, the open sustained sounds suggesting that love sustains itself and endures. There is a knell-like quality to the slow beat of the line, as though this endurance were a grim and melancholy feat rather than a spontaneous gesture. Once again the final word in the line, with its drawn-out vowel sound, receives special emphasis. "Doom," like "impediments," is thematic, making love itself sound doomed.

Repetition is another means by which the poet underscores his theme. The statement "Love is not love/ Which alters when it alteration finds/ Or bends with the remover to remove" contains the pairs "love"/"love," "alters"/"alteration," and "remover"/"remove." The verbal pairings are examples of *traductio,* a musical figure of speech in which different forms of a single word are used. In sonnet 116 these patterned pairs enact a "mirroring," with the second word imitating the first. The significance here, as elsewhere in the sonnet, seems paradoxical or double. On one level the mirroring suggests the mutuality of affection, the responsiveness of a lover to his beloved; on another it implies fickleness or infidelity, a lover who changes or grows distant. The relatively abstract language seems to rebel against itself: Who "alters" and what is the nature of the "alteration"? Who is the "remover" and where is the "remove"? The sense of contradiction is as strong as the effect of harmony. Just as "love" and "love" clash in the clause "Love is not love," so the other paired words seem to clash as well as coincide. The impersonal diction makes it hard to visualize a real situation involving human lovers, but the *traductio,* with its chameleonlike mirroring of word roots, seems to point to some kind of whimsicality or instability in "real" love, which is mutual one moment and fickle the next. This instability is opposed to the "ever-fixed mark" of "true" love, which is beyond time and change.

Even so subtle a repetition as "bends" (line 4) and "bending" (line 10) has meaning in the poem. Love, which does not "bend," is the antithesis of time, with its "bending" sickle. The connotation of "bending" is not only that time's sickle is bent, or curved, but also that it actively "bends" "rosy lips and cheeks," that is, alters them forever. Furthermore, the murmuring repetition of the *com* sound in "bending sickle's compass come" implies the trancelike submission of youthful beauties to time. The hypnotic sway of time's "compass" is powerfully depicted, with the consequence that Shakespeare's denial of time's influence sounds defiant in the first half of the quatrain ("Love's not Time's fool") and grimly defeated in the second ("But bears it out even to the edge of doom").

Thus musical arrangements of vowels and consonants and stylized repetitions reinforce the semantic or figurative properties of the language. Shakespeare uses acoustic suggestiveness to allow the underlying themes of the sonnet—impediments, doom, fickleness, and mutability—to emerge.

16.12   Discuss the final couplet.

Answer   The conclusion continues the quality of quibbling paradox that pervades the whole sonnet. The if-then construction implies a logical connection between the parts, with a conditional clause ("If this be error") followed by its consequence ("I never writ . . ."). But the logic is strained and backward. The sonnet itself is evidence that Shakespeare has "writ" and thus, in an odd reversal, we must assume that the argument of the poem is *not* "error." The pseudosyllogism implies a desperate attempt at proof, Shakespeare's effort to sweep away all objections, all impediments, including his own. In fact, the couplet suggests an ironic admission of error: Shakespeare's marriage of true minds, his everfixed mark, his love that is not Time's fool and alters not, is wholly imaginary. Men never have loved in the way he has writ. The "false" love described in the first quatrain ("Love is not love/ Which alters") is all that human lovers are capable of.

As You Like It

16.13   *As You Like It* has a dramatic structure involving a movement from one "world" into another. Characterize the two very different worlds in *As You Like It*, analyzing the relationship of this structural division to the theme of the play.

Answer   The play opens in the ostensibly civilized French court of Duke Frederick. However, its urbane surface masks unnatural tensions: Orlando has been deprived of his rights by his older brother Oliver, and Duke Senior has been usurped by his younger brother Frederick. "Place" and power are the important stakes in this society, which is founded on rigid hierarchy and legality. Duke Frederick's irrational banishment of his niece Rosalind from the court reinforces the idea of a harsh authority which subverts natural familial bonds.

Rosalind, Celia, and Orlando all flee from the hostile court world to the forest of Arden, where Rosalind's father, the exiled Duke Senior, lives in rural simplicity with a band of merry young men. This forest retreat is a green and golden world, associated with nature and with Eden before Adam's fall and linked with dreams of perfect freedom and romantic love. In the green world, everyone is free to play any chosen role, no longer bound by a fixed social identity. Rosalind disguises herself as a boy, and Celia dresses as a shepherdess; Orlando dutifully adopts the role of a student of love, and Duke Senior and his men play at being outlaws.

Thus the forest is a world of romantic illusion, festival release, and, ultimately, magical reconciliation. The series of wooings are like a set of games, with players who mistake each other's identities, burst into song, write verses, and deliver speeches. In these games the folly of love is expressed, with passionate outpourings punctuated by the comments of a chorus of "critics"—Touchstone, Jaques, and Rosalind herself. The forest of Arden is romantic in the sense that it is a setting for spontaneous emotion and liberated impulse, a place where desires are expressed and satisfied.

However, certain aspects of this rural paradise suggest that human beings can never fully escape the dark side of their own nature. That freedom can degenerate into license, or licentiousness, is hinted at in Touchstone's preoccupation with the flesh; and that holiday make-believe can rigidify into a habit of imposture is suggested by the fake "pastoralizing" of Phebe and Silvius and the obsessive melancholy of Jaques. It is only by virtue of Rosalind's presence that the green world of Arden preserves its function as a necessary phase, a retreat or release, in the progress toward reconciliation and clarification. Rosalind has the poise which comes from keeping one foot in each world, the real one of fact and the ideal one of romantic passion. While participating in the games of folly, she is also a representative of the everyday world to which the other characters must return; indeed, by her words and actions, she helps to ready them for that step. Thus Rosalind guarantees the ending of the play, which celebrates the happy resolution of passion in the domestic bond of marriage.

At the end of the play, with romantic love thus domesticated, social relationships can be reestablished on a firmer and more natural basis. Both sets of brothers are reconciled, and the court is reintegrated, with Duke Senior in his rightful place. The masque led by Hymen symbolizes the renewal of an ordered society through love. The movement from court to country and back to court constitutes the play's comic myth, from rigid law through festival release to social reintegration.

16.14 Both Jaques's speech beginning "All the world's a stage" (Act II, Scene vii) and Macbeth's statement that "Life's but a walking shadow; a poor player,/ That struts and frets his hour upon the stage, . . ." (Macbeth, Act V, Scene v) use a theatrical metaphor to express a view of human life. What is the difference in effect between the two speeches?

Answer Macbeth's soliloquy, which he delivers on hearing the news of his wife's death, is a profoundly pessimistic statement of the meaninglessness of human life. The reiteration of the word "tomorrow" in the opening line of the speech suggests a vision of time as mechanical repetition; and the statement that life is "a tale told by an idiot . . . signifying nothing" implies that human life is a meaningless dumb show masking an essential emptiness. Macbeth's tragedy is that the evil he has wrought has drained life of its significance. His words here illustrate the profound alienation of a man from all that is natural and fruitful.

Jaques's speech is vastly different in effect, primarily because his pessimism is not a tragic surrender to despair but an *idée fixe*, an exaggerated and all-encompassing philosophy. Throughout the play, Jaques flamboyantly plays the self-chosen role of the melancholy, cynical traveler who is merely passing through life. Himself a stereotype, he sees all life as a succession of stereotyped roles, from the mewling infant to the toothless, doddering old man. Playing with the Renaissance fondness for patterned progression, he sets forth the ages of man like cutout dolls: the lover sighing like a furnace, the justice equipped with a round belly and a stock of wise saws. Jaques, by assuming a distance from life, makes human existence into a comedy of types.

The itemization of stock types infuses the speech with an almost playful satiric energy. At the same time, Jaques's own fixed role as the melancholy man in a green world of freedom and folly makes it clear that he is neither Shakespeare's spokesman nor the play's. Unlike Macbeth, who stands at the center of the tragic universe he has created, Jaques is on the periphery of Arden, his mock-pessimistic philosophy overshadowed in the end by the joyous resolution of the play.

16.15 Rosalind is the central figure in As You Like It: she not only has intrinsic interest as a character but also performs important dramatic functions in the play. What is Rosalind's role in relation to the play's structure and theme?

Answer Rosalind has a double role in the play. In addition to being one of the lovers with whose happy joining the play ends, she has a special role as one of Shakespeare's "stage managers," like the duke in Measure for Measure or

Prospero in *The Tempest*, who arrange scenes, comment on the action, and assure a happy ending. Masquerading as the shepherd boy Ganymede, she tutors Orlando, scolds Phebe, and ultimately arranges the appropriate marriage for each. The masculine disguise, presumably so impenetrable that even her father fails to recognize her, allows her the freedom to speak her mind candidly on the subject of love. In mocking the romantic excesses of Orlando as a stock lover and the scornful pose of Phebe as a cold mistress, she displays an objectivity about romantic passion, including her own, that sets her above most comic lovers.

Her comments often take the form of witty epigrams: "Men have died from time to time, and worms have eaten them, but not for love" (IV, i, 96–98, meaning Act IV, Scene i, lines 96–98); or "Men are April when they woo, December when they wed. Maids are May when they are maids, but the sky changes when they are wives" (IV, i, 134–136). Speaking the plain prose of everyday life, in contrast to Orlando's limping verses, she educates him—and reminds herself—about the domestic reality of marriage.

Although Rosalind is clearly an observer of love's folly, she is its victim too, and thus her stage managing is different from the duke's or Prospero's. The happy endings of *Measure for Measure* and *The Tempest* seem to some degree unreal and fantastic because the managing is like a *deus ex machina*, a godlike intervention from above or outside the human situation dramatized. In contrast Rosalind "manages" from within the dramatic situation, functioning as an intermediary between the romantic world of impulse and desire and the rational world of law and social duty. Her criticism of love is always half-rueful, for her barbs and epigrams are partly self-directed.

It is as observer and representative of the social world that Rosalind moves the play toward its natural resolution. She readies the lovers for their marriage vows and unmasks herself at the climactic moment, unraveling the mystery that she herself has created. But it is as a lover herself that she makes the happy ending seem believable. Her personal engagement with folly makes the final domestication of love seem a real outcome rather than a dramatic convenience.

16.16 The forest of Arden is unusually well populated for a rural retreat. Among the many characters wandering the woods are relatively minor figures like Touchstone, Phebe and Silvius, and Corin. What is the function of these lesser characters? What do they contribute to the play's theme?

Answer Touchstone is the court jester who follows Rosalind and Celia into the pastoral world of Arden. His running commentary reflects an urban, sophisticated response to rural life. His attitude is that of the wise fool who speaks ironically, deflating the pretensions of those around him. Touchstone is not motivated by the romantic passions which stir the other lovers in the play; instead, he makes a practical decision to satisfy his carnal desires by marrying the ill-favored Audrey. Thus, his function is to provide an ironic counterpoint to pastoral affectations, especially the excessive idealization of love.

As Touchstone's name implies, he represents a defined perspective against which the views of the other characters can be tested or tried. His own viewpoint errs on the cynical side just as Orlando's, for example, errs on the romantic. Another character who provides a touchstone in the pastoral world is the real shepherd Corin. He represents the unaffected virtues of the natural man. Content with simple country pleasures, he provides a positive contrast to the unnatural life of the court and to the dissatisfied, affected, "literary" shepherds, Phebe and Silvius.

Phebe, the stereotyped mistress scorning her suitor, and Silvius, the wretched, self-abasing lover, indulge in a pastoral idyll divorced from real experience. Furthermore, Phebe's infatuation with Rosalind disguised as Ganymede illustrates the blindness of romantic love. Although Rosalind too plays at pastoral games, she is observant enough to recognize that love is not just a "holiday humor" but a realistic choice.

Phebe and Silvius are not the only ones afflicted with a pastoral tic. Even the good Duke Senior is prone to a certain kind of literary eloquence which is indebted more to pastoral convention than to real experience. His sententious moralizings on the sweet uses of adversity, the sermons in stones, and the welcomeness of natural ills as opposed to human ones are the half-truths of commonplace and adage; they play on the standard pastoral antithesis between painted pomp and unvarnished nature, between the envious court and the simple honest countryside. The conventional rhetoric is explicitly noted by Amiens, who, after the duke's first major oration, says, "Happy is your Grace/ That can translate the stubbornness of fortune/ Into so quiet and so sweet a style " (II, i, 18–20). The style is, precisely, pastoral, and the stylization invites skepticism. The duke and his men are as deluded as the lovers, too preoccupied with idealizing their exiled state to attempt in a practical manner to end it. They too are on holiday.

Thus the minor characters contribute to Shakespeare's exploration of the themes of the play by offering a range of viewpoints on pastoral life and ideal love. Touchstone stands at the cynical extreme; Phebe and Silvius, as well as Duke Senior and his men, at the romantic extreme; and Corin in the center, rooted in the natural world.

Henry IV, Part I

16. 17   What role does the theme of impersonation and counterfeiting play in *Henry IV, Part I?*

Answer   Impersonation is pervasive in the play, both as comic disguise and as political role playing. The comic instances of impersonation demonstrate in humorous terms the self-interest which underlies all performances in life. In particular, Falstaff's repertoire of roles, as courageous highwayman, king of England, outraged and innocent victim, swaggering soldier, dead man, and, finally, heroic slayer of Hotspur, show a man adept not only at playacting but at playing for advantage. The use of impersonation to save one's skin and serve one's purposes is described in Falstaff's speech on counterfeiting, delivered at the moment of his comic "resurrection" (V, iv):

> . . . to counterfeit dying when a man thereby liveth, is to
> be no counterfeit, but the true and perfect image of life
> indeed. The better part of valor is discretion, in which
> better part I have saved my life.

"Life," enlarged, inflated, and full of fleshly appetites, is personified by Falstaff in all his disguises.

Prince Hal's impersonations have an additional, political motive. The frivolous practical jokes he takes part in—playing the robber of robbers at Gads Hill, manipulating Francis's parrotlike responses at the Eastcheap tavern, picking Falstaff's pocket—show Hal's relish for the festive games he plays with Falstaff. But Hal's involvement with the low-life characters has a serious meaning as part of his political strategy. At the end of Act I, Scene ii, after some raucous banter with Falstaff and Poins, Hal reveals his true motivations in a soliloquy. When he reforms his debauched life, he says it will be like the sun's breaking out from behind "the base contagious clouds." He emphasizes the public reaction to his sudden brightness, saying that he will be "wond'red at," and that

> My reformation, glitt'ring o'er my fault,
> Shall show more goodly and attract more eyes
> Than that which hath no foil to set it off.
> (I, ii, 201–203)

Thus Hal is playing a role, that of the prodigal son, with the most calculating shrewdness, in order to manipulate public opinion and ensure his future success as heir apparent. In this he imitates his father, King Henry IV, another consummate actor on the stage of history. Explaining the strategy which bought him the crown, Henry repeatedly stresses the awe he produced in the public by keeping himself distant and mysterious:

> By being seldom seen, I could not stir
> But, like a comet, I was wond'red at;
> That men would tell their children, "This is he!"
> (III, ii, 46–48)

Both father and son are adept at playing to an audience to win political advantage.

Impersonation extends even to the life-and-death struggle on the battlefield at Shrewsbury, not only in Falstaff's antics but in the missions of the surrogate kings sent out to attract Douglas's sword. Even Hal's newfound martial prowess has the quality of assuming a part in a historical drama. Vernon's description of him ("I saw young Harry with his beaver on . . . Rise from the ground like feathered Mercury" [IV, i]) shows him dressing for the part of epic hero.

Shakespeare's development of the theme of acting suggests a view of history as man-made rather than divinely ordained, a view fundamental to the presentation of history in Shakespeare's plays. Thus, Richard II had made the mistake of assuming his kingship was "real," not a role to be enacted but an office given by God. In contrast, the Bolingbrokes represent a new order, in which acting is recognized as a political technique, used to wrest advantage from the historical moment.

16.18   How is the character of Falstaff revealed?

Answer   Falstaff is associated with a number of stock folklore figures and literary types, among them the Vice of medieval drama, the Lord of Misrule who presided over riotous springtime celebrations, the braggart soldier, the buffoon, the drunkard, the glutton, and the court jester. In general his role as the agent of festival disorder provides a dramatic counterpoint to the serious political disorder prevailing in the realm. However, his character extends beyond stereotypical traits, suggesting the complexities of human nature in his comic foibles and poignant affections.

Falstaff's physical presence is an inescapable feature of his personality, not only in his mountainous bulk when seen on the stage but in the many references to belly, paunch, lard, and so on, scattered throughout the play. His huge belly becomes the sign of his office as the spokesman for appetite, egotism, and impulse, a literal rendering of the self-inflation and self-aggrandizement that characterize Falstaff.

Inflation is also the distinguishing characteristic of Falstaff's rhetoric. Like his corpulence, his eloquence becomes a means of extending the self and its desires in defiance of the restrictions that logic or reality would impose. Whenever Falstaff is confronted by an unpleasant truth, he takes refuge in words, if necessary redefining them for his own purposes. He defends his cowardly flight from the prince in disguise by invoking the magic of his "instinct," which signaled the nearness of majesty; he lends his thievery a kind of sanctity by calling it his "vocation"; and he rationalizes his playing dead by recourse to the idea of "discretion."

Mingled with these comic glosses and logical inversions are puns, imprecations, mock invective, ballad tags, parodic adages, colorful hyperbole, and elaborate epithets. With all these verbal techniques Falstaff creates his own world, a world of words which he keeps trying to substitute for the world of facts, often with success. The effect throughout is that of a jack-in-the-box who springs back automatically in the face of adversity, or of an artful dodger who endlessly wiggles out of tight corners. Falstaff's comic resurrection, the rising up from his "death" on the battlefield, is only the last and best illustration of his invincibility.

Falstaff's most important role is as Hal's boon companion and mentor. The guidance Falstaff offers the prince in the ways of the world and in the art of role playing suggests a paternal interest. He plays at being Hal's father in the skit of royal interrogation played out in the tavern and he is, in a sense, responsible for the educated sense of drama and irony Hal brings to the battlefield at Shrewsbury. Thus Falstaff and Hal are bound together not only by shared gaiety but by the claims of affection and indebtedness. Falstaff's genuine claim on the prince contributes to the pathos of Part II, when Hal ultimately rejects his old mentor in order to assume his royal mantle.

16.19 Comment on the contrasting views of honor in the play.

Answer Even before his first appearance, Hotspur is identified with honor as an aristocratic ideal, King Henry calling him "the theme of honor's tongue" (I, i, 81). Hotspur's "honor" involves not only personal courage but personal renown, the public "honors" won by a chivalric career of fearless rectitude:

> By heaven, methinks it were an easy leap
> To pluck bright honor from the pale-faced moon,
> .   .   .   .
> So he that doth redeem her thence might wear
> Without corrival all her dignities; . . . .
>   (I, iii, 201–202; 206–207)

In a mocking tavern parody, Hal captures both the obsessive drive and the hotheaded willfulness which characterize Hotspur's preoccupation with honorable exploits. The prince announces, "I am not yet of Percy's mind, the Hotspur of the North; he that kills me some six or seven dozen of Scots at a breakfast, washes his hands, and says to his wife, 'Fie upon this quiet life! I want work!' " (II, iv, 97–100). Hotspur is vulnerable to such caricature because an excess of irascibility, impetuosity, and self-aggrandizement compromises his code of honor.

It is precisely because Hotspur's concept of honor is too rigid and impatient for the diplomatic maneuvers of conspiracy that he is chastised by his more politic relatives, Mortimer and Worcester. His hotheaded aristocratic sensibilities suggest not only his purity of heart but also his absurd naiveté. In contrast to his father and uncle, practical politicians who aim to preempt Bolingbroke's move against them, Hotspur sees "honor" as the sole motive for insurrection. In Hotspur's view, King Henry's refusal to ransom Mortimer, Hotspur's brother-in-law, and his demand for Hotspur's Scottish prisoners break the feudal bonds of obligation which he owes to the Percys, those liege men who helped him gain the throne.

Hotspur's hotheadedness is in contrast to Falstaff's cool wits. If Hotspur makes honor his be-all and end-all, Falstaff turns it into nothing. Analyzing the abstraction "honor" by its effects ("Can honor set to a leg? No. Or an arm? No" [V, i, 131]), Falstaff concludes that it is only a word, a mouthful of air. Falstaff's self-serving skepticism reduces moral necessity to an absurdity through rhetorical play which insists on the verbal surface and denies the substance. Against the ideal abstraction of honor he poses the concrete sensations of existence. Looking on the corpse of Walter Blunt, who, disguised as the king, has sacrificed his life to save his monarch, he says, "I like not such grinning honor as Sir Walter hath. Give me life" (V, iii, 57–58). Falstaff turns honor and reputation into mere baubles which can be won by deceit; thus, a slash in the dead Hotspur's thigh, he believes, will "earn" him the good renown for which Hal has had to labor in deadly earnest.

Falstaff and Hotspur do not merely cancel each other out. Both contribute something to Hal's developing sense of honor. Falstaff sees only the playacting involved, while Hotspur is so convinced by his own role that he fails to see it as a role. Hal's sense of honor has some of the earnest conviction of Hotspur's aristocratic code and some of the healthy cynicism of Falstaff's rhetorical game. The prince knows he has a role to play, but it is a serious, historic one: that of the reformed prodigal assuming his position as loyal son and royal heir. With a calculating shrewdness worthy of Falstaff, Hal chooses the right time and place for his performance and dresses the part in glittering battle array. But Hal's conduct on the field at Shrewsbury is not, like Falstaff's, mere counterfeiting. His enactment of his role is genuine and grimly effective, for he saves his father's life by fighting off Douglas and wins the day by slaying Hotspur. Thus the prince is able to use the concept of honor without naively believing, like Hotspur, in its magical worth or automatic success and without blithely denying, like Falstaff, that it has any meaning at all.

16.20 *Henry IV, Part I* may be criticized as essentially undramatic, with many irrelevant episodes (the domestic scene between Kate and Hotspur, the flyting between Glendower and Hotspur, the petty arguments among the rebels, Hal's practical jokes, and so on) and an inconclusive climax. Can the play's structure and theatrical effectiveness be justified?

Answer   The somewhat static and inconclusive quality of the drama can be attributed, in part, to its place in the historical tetralogy (four-play series) that begins with *Richard II*, continues with the two parts of *Henry IV*, and ends with *Henry V*. Both plays involving the reign of Henry IV constitute a bridge between the tragic fall of Richard and the glorious apotheosis of Henry V. They demonstrate historical process and analyze a political moment, using techniques of social description and thematic elaboration. At the same time they document the emergence of Hal as a historic figure, illustrating the education of a Christian prince in preparation for his future greatness.

Thus many of the seemingly irrelevant scenes contribute to the development of the themes of the drama (love versus honor, order versus disorder, sincerity versus hypocrisy) or aid in the characterization of Prince Hal. For example, the domestic repartee between Hotspur and Kate shows the competition between private impulse and public motive, between the claims of love and the duties of war, as Hotspur defers affection and concentrates on the pressing demands of honor. An emphasis on honor also figures in the scene between Hotspur and Glendower (II, i), with young Percy quick to compete and argue with his fellow conspirator, posing his soldierly brashness against the Welshman's "effeminate" mysticism. In this same scene a squabble breaks out among the rebels over the potential division of the kingdom, paralleled by the later arguments in the rebel camp at Shrewsbury. This petty infighting undercuts the nobility of the con-spirators, whose interests are revealed as selfish and mercenary rather than patriotic.

The comic parallel to the disorder symbolized by the conspiracy is the falling out among thieves in the Eastcheap scenes. The farcical gambit at Gads Hill, Hal's practical jokes on Francis and Falstaff, and Falstaff's mock soldiering are not irrelevant distractions. They contribute to the social scheme of the drama, showing the earthy, bawdy life of the fringes of the lower classes; to the themes of the play, especially role playing; and to the portrait of Hal as a man able to incorporate all perspectives and to traverse social boundaries.

The battle at Shrewsbury, the ostensible climax of the play, may also be criticized as poor dramaturgy, for it is a false climax. Though Hotspur is dead, King Henry must immediately go on to do battle with Northumberland and Glendower. The insurrections of Act I, Scene i are matched by the rebel gatherings at the very end of the play, and the realm remains prey to unrest and disorder. This inconclusive ending reflects a moment in a larger historical process. Bolingbroke's sin in deposing Richard II is not yet expiated, for the cycle of redemption for England is completed only by his death (*Henry IV, Part II*) and by his son's glorious victory at Agincourt (*Henry V*).

Julius Caesar

16.21   What qualities of Brutus's character are suggested by his style of speech?

Answer   One of the striking characteristics of Brutus's speeches is his use of figurative language to argue for his opinions. The exploitation of simile and metaphor to paint a persuasive picture of things is a common rhetorical tool, but in Brutus's case it is also a symptom of his character. His tendency to substitute figurative language for literal, rhetoric for logic, and hypothesis for factual statement indicates a mind closed to political realities.

Thus, in his soliloquy in the orchard Brutus begins by leaping to a conclusion: "It must be by his death " (II, i). The rest of the monologue consists of his attempt to justify this decision by using metaphors which suggest the insidious growth of evil. The adder coming forth on a bright day, the ambitious man's scorning the rungs of the ladder, and the hatching of the serpent's egg serve as evidence against Caesar, despite Brutus's own admission that

> . . . to speak truth of Caesar,
> I have not known when his affections sway'd
> More than his reason.
>
> (II, i, 19–21)

Brutus's case is founded on imaginative projections and hypotheses and directed against what Caesar "may" do, what he "would" do if his power were augmented.

In his speech to the conspirators, Brutus again uses the power of metaphor to convince the band of the proper "method" of the assassination. Antony, "but a limb of Caesar," must be spared, for it would be too bloody "To cut the head off and then hack the limbs" (II, i, 163). He urges his fellows to approach their violent deed with fitting reverence ("Let's carve him as a dish fit for the gods,/ Not hew him as a carcass fit for hounds" [II, i, 173–174]), and he insists on the nobility of their purpose ("We shall be call'd purgers, not murderers" [II, i, 180]). Thus Antony is mistakenly discounted as harmless by the force of the analogy to the human body, and the brutal fact of the assassination is disguised by figurative language referring to rites of sacrifice and healing.

After the assassination, Brutus's speech to the mob uses repetition and parallelism in a strangely disjunctive way: "As Caesar loved me, I weep for him; as he was fortunate, I rejoice at it; as he was valiant, I honor him; but, as he was ambitious, I slew him. There is tears, for his love; joy for his fortune; honor, for his valor; and death for his ambition" (III, ii, 24–28). Like Brutus's figurative language, his use of schematic, patterned prose disguises the literal truth. Here the chiming phrases suggest a series of measured, parallel, and appropriate responses when, in fact, the final gesture ("I slew him") cancels all the preceding ones. The compartmentalized reactions (tears, joy, honor, death) become a means of psychologically isolating the violent act, splitting it off from the loving attitudes toward Caesar which Brutus claims to possess.

Finally, in arguing for an immediate attack on Philippi, Brutus uses the image of boats anchored in a bay: "There is a tide in the affairs of men . . ." (IV, iii, 218). His vivid metaphor of taking the flood and floating out on the current is so rich with connotations of success, release, and energy that Cassius immediately gives in.

Again and again, Brutus substitutes figurative language for literal assertion. He is not a master of rhetoric but a slave to it, blinding himself and others to the true significance of men and events by the force of metaphor.

16.22 What is the climax of *Julius Caesar*?

Answer Act III as a whole is the hinge of the action, with the first two acts showing the birth of the conspiracy and the last two showing its "death" in civil war. Although the assassination of Caesar in the Capitol (III, i) is the central action of the play, the twin speeches in the Forum immediately following it (III, ii) constitute the dramatic turning point. Antony's speech, especially, is climactic, in that it changes the minds of the masses and decides the future course of events: "Mischief, thou art afoot,/ Take thou what course thou wilt" (III, ii, 260–261). If the scene in the Capitol represents the death of Caesar, the funeral oration in the Forum provides his "resurrection," sending his spirit abroad in the world to do the work of revenge. Thus Act III constitutes a decisive moment of change, presenting in stark dramatic terms political act (assassination) and political interpretation (the address to the mob). Ironically, it is interpretation which proves most crucial for controlling history. Antony's speech demonstrates that persuasion is the most effective political "act," overshadowing the deed itself by determining the way in which it is viewed.

Antony's speech is also a thematic crux of the play, since it exemplifies the central motif of persuasion. In the opening scenes, we see Cassius persuade Brutus, Brutus persuade the other conspirators, Portia and Calphurnia attempt to persuade their husbands, and Decius Brutus persuade Caesar. In the climactic funeral oration, Shakespeare in a sense anatomizes the very act of persuasion, with Antony exploiting the entire rhetorical bag of tricks to accomplish his aim. He insinuates himself into the mob's confidence by beginning with an apparent concession ("But Brutus says he was ambitious,/ And Brutus is an honorable man"); then, by offering proofs to the contrary, he gradually makes that refrain devastatingly ironic. His metrical speech is more memorable than Brutus's plain prose, and his more frequent use of figures of speech (such as apostrophe, exclamation, climax, praeteritio, and disclaimer) plays on the feelings of the crowd. Most important, his manipulation of props adds to argument the force of dramatic spectacle. He uses the will of the dead Caesar to tantalize the plebeians, the torn mantle as a relic with which to re-create the assassination scene, and the body as a bleeding icon which he ritually displays.

Antony's heightened oratory underscores what is hinted at elsewhere in the play: that evidence and logic alone are insufficient to stir an audience or change a belief. The facts—that Caesar brought booty back to Rome, wept for the poor, refused the crown, and made the populace his heirs—must be embedded in a dramatic, emotional, hypnotic medium compounded of words and gestures to weigh with the irrational mob. Similar instances abound: to win their points, Cassius must rely on nasty tale-telling, Brutus on metaphor and hypothesis, Portia on emotional rhetoric and symbolic gesture, Decius Brutus on false interpretation. In all these cases, as in the climax of the play, Shakespeare portrays a politics of both the mind and the emotions, and an image of history as the product of human passions and prejudices.

16.23 Does the play have a hero?

Answer   The play lacks a genuine hero. There are in a sense too many candidates for the role (Caesar, Brutus, and perhaps Antony), so that the effect of a single fascinating character, separated from his peers and alienated from his society, is diminished. Furthermore, what Shakespeare emphasizes in the major figures in this drama is not a "tragic flaw," some powerful obsession which undoes a man of great worth and high stature. Instead he seems at pains to underscore the general fallibility of men acting in the political arena, carefully shading the portraits of all his major characters to suggest a complicated mixture of strength and weakness. Of course Caesar, the titular hero, possesses a historical stature which exists apart from whatever qualities the play actively dramatizes. In a certain sense he is a given, a great military hero and politician whose dominating personality threatens the future of the republic. At the same time, he is dramatically presented in the opening scenes as an arrogant, physically infirm tyrant. To be sure, in Caesar's brief appearances on stage before the assassination he demonstrates certain positive traits, such as his psychological acuity in reading Cassius's character and his kindness to Calphurnia; but in the main he exhibits blind pride and autocratic will, as when he quickly succumbs to Decius Brutus's flattery and harshly rejects Metellus Cimber. After his death, Caesar appears as a martyr. Antony's description of the slain leader's generosity and wisdom and Caesar's spiritual domination of the rest of the play (in the role of Nemesis) identify him as a just and capable ruler, wrongly victimized by a lawless conspiracy. But the Caesar we observe ourselves is a flawed, not deeply admirable, figure.

This two-sided portrait is matched by those of Antony and Brutus. Antony is first characterized as "gamesome," a frivolous and self-indulgent man dominated by whim and appetite. Brutus refuses to take him seriously, "for he is given/ To sports, to wildness, and much company" (II, i, 188–189). But with the death of Caesar he grows in stature, revealing his loyalty and love in his soliloquy over the corpse. His practical political skills emerge in the funeral oration and later in the meeting with Octavius; and his generosity of spirit appears in his moving epitaph for Brutus. However, there is no suggestion that Antony has the personal greatness to occupy a truly heroic role.

Brutus himself is most nearly the hero of the play; he is, by common consensus, "the noblest Roman of them all." Alone of the conspirators he approaches the assassination with pure motives: he loves Caesar, but he loves Rome more. Furthermore, his interior thoughts are given dramatic presentation in the soliloquies of Act II, so that we view him from the inside out. But apart from the brief realization that he is a divided man, as indicated in his speech about man as "a little kingdom" suffering an insurrection (II, i, 67–69), he never fully recognizes the self-love and moral rigidity which tinge his idealism. From Act III on, he appears in an external light purely as one more actor on the historical stage, revealing, for example, the priggish and willful facets of his character in the quarrel with Cassius. In the world of *Julius Caesar*, no figure fully rises above the political circumstances to achieve universal significance or genuine self-knowledge.

Thus *Julius Caesar*, unlike Shakespeare's greatest tragedies, has no single "hero." The meaning of the play resides in men's reactions and interactions in the political realm, rather than in the impact of one memorable character upon the world at large.

16.24 Discuss the significance of portents in the play.

Answer The portents, which include the disturbances in heaven and earth, the beast with no heart, Calphurnia's dream, Caesar's ghost, and the birds flying over the conspirators' camp, together suggest some supernatural influence operating in the affairs of men. Shakespeare uses the recurrent omens to create a cosmic parallel to the political world of the play. Not only human ambition and human will but providential design affect the outcome of historical events. The sense of a providential working out of destiny is especially evident in the second half of the play, with Caesar's ghost acting as Nemesis, or avenger, and, as Brutus says, turning the conspirators' swords into "our own proper entrails."

In addition to suggesting a cosmic fate which interlocks with human will, the portents contribute to the theme of interpretation in the play. The prophetic omens are signs which must be properly read, for their misreading can constitute a disastrous error. Thus Caesar, interpreting the sacrificial beast as a sign that he would be a beast with no heart, that is, a coward, should he stay at home, commits a fatal mistake. The two interpretations of the bleeding statue of Calphurnia's dream—her own fears that it is a symbol of assassination, and

Decius Brutus's insistence that it is an emblem for Caesar's role as a "fountain" of blessings—become a kind of case study of the uses of interpretation.

Finally, the portents contribute to dramatic irony. Throughout the first two acts, all the signs point to the assassination to come in Act III, and the audience is privy not only to the conspiracy but to the true meanings of the omens which Caesar ignores. After the assassination, the appearances of Caesar's ghost and the carrion-seeking vultures create for the audience a chilling foretaste of the inevitable doom which will befall the conspirators. The fact that, for the most part, the audience possesses greater knowledge than the characters has two effects. On the one hand, viewers are held in suspense, experiencing pity and terror as the actors move unwittingly toward their tragic destinies; on the other hand, viewers are placed "above" the action, their distance from the events allowing them to weigh and assess the underlying political motivations.

The portents, then, are not merely atmospheric. They add to Shakespeare's analysis of political behavior by implying the influence of fate and the effects of human blindness in the arena of history.

16.25   In several key instances, actions of importance to the drama are reported by a character rather than enacted on stage. What is the point of these reported actions?

Answer   Among events reported on in *Julius Caesar* are Cassius's anecdote about his swimming contest with Caesar; Casca's report on the mob scene in which Caesar is offered the crown; the discussion of unnatural occurrences and omens among Cicero, Casca, and Cassius; several accounts of the assassination; the report of Portia's death; and Pindarus's account of Titinius's reception by the troops.

In some of these cases, there are dramaturgic reasons for reporting events rather than showing them. In order to meet theatrical limitations of time and space, Shakespeare uses narration to condense the action and supply relevant dramatic facts without diverting the forward thrust of the plot. However, more important, the reported actions almost uniformly suggest the coloring of differing individual viewpoints. In a sense, the speaker's attitude toward the event is as significant as the event itself. Thus, Cassius's stories about Caesar are crucial for what they reveal not only about Caesar's physical weakness but about Cassius's malevolence and envy. Similarly, Casca's account of the offer of the crown to Caesar is colored by ill feeling, so that Caesar is portrayed as a buffoon performing antics before the mob. Mark Antony's presentation of the assassination shows how an event (one witnessed, in fact, by the audience) may be entirely transfigured in its description by the speaker's attitude. Through Antony's retelling of the tale, the political act becomes a kind of religious martyrdom and the victim a saint. The way attitude colors events is likewise the point of the account of Portia's death, which reveals Brutus's stoicism, and of the report on Titinius, which demonstrates Cassius's rashness.

Thus, Shakespeare uses reported actions to underscore the significance of viewpoint, interpretation, and attitude. In these narrative scenes, he demonstrates how human perspectives color and shape events and suggests that history is subject to the power of language.

Macbeth

16.26   Discuss the structure of Macbeth.

Answer   The structure of the play is expressed not only through act and scene divisions but through patterns of events and shifts in the relationship of the characters. The main action of the play describes an arc: Act I is devoted to the upward curve of Macbeth's fortunes as he is named thane of Cawdor; Act II, which includes both the murder of Duncan and Macbeth's coronation, is the zenith which implies descent, the peripety at which the man of high estate begins his fall. In Act III and Act IV, Scene i, we see an accelerating decline, as Macbeth arranges the murders of Banquo and Fleance and plans the attack on Macduff. Finally, in Act V, the arc descends to its nadir, the brief, splintered scenes showing Macbeth's flashes of martial defiance and nihilistic despair and ending with his last appearance as a traitor's head upon a stake.

Other structural elements contribute not to the action but to the themes of the play. The patterning of these themes, among them kingship and the state, fate and free will, lends coherence to the drama as a whole, absorbing all the various actions and events into a unifying framework. Thus Acts I and V provide a frame which emphasizes the political content of the play: in both acts, the rewards to liege men, the punishment of traitors, and the epic scenes of national battle all suggest the historical plane, with the life and continuity of the state embodied in the person of the king. Most of Act IV is given over to a formal discussion of kingship, as Malcolm tests Macduff's loyalty by presenting himself as the "negative" of the saintly Duncan.

The appearances of the witches constitute another design element with thematic importance. The weird sisters' prophecies of the future in Acts I and IV act as spurs to Macbeth's ambition, so that his personal will contributes to the fulfillment of impersonal fate. The encounters between the witches and Macbeth underscore the relationship between external temptation and inner character. Macbeth is ready to grasp for power at the slightest suggestion; thus he fulfills his necessary destiny by running headlong to meet it. The soliloquies spaced at intervals in the first three acts likewise reinforce the impression that Macbeth's course of action is determined by his psychology, as we watch his rationalizations, hallucinations, wishes, and fears lead him on to his criminal deeds. The soliloquies in Act V show Macbeth meeting the destiny he himself has created, as he recognizes the ironic emptiness and fruitlessness of his life.

Another pattern involves the role reversal of Macbeth and Lady Macbeth: at first Macbeth is the partner with the guilty conscience and overcharged imagination, his wife the "manly" instigator and agent; at the end of the play the burden of guilt has passed to Lady Macbeth, who performs an obsessive "atonement" in the sleepwalking scene, while her husband, without conscience, pursues his fortune to the bitter end. The punishment, like the crime, is equally divided between husband and wife.

The epic frame, the prophecies of the witches, the spacing of soliloquies, and the role reversal all superimpose thematic patterns on the main action of rise and fall. All the structural relationships in the play illuminate the problem of evil in the universe: how it originates, grows, disrupts the social and political orders, and shatters the "single state of man."

16.27   Reiterated imagery is important in *Macbeth* as a means of concentrating attention on key ideas. For example, the repeated images of blood reinforce the themes of violence and unnatural upheaval, while the many references to clothing suggest the distorted relationship between Macbeth's external role and his interior self. What is the significance of the recurrent references to time and growth in the play?

Answer   From the witches' first appearance in the play, when Banquo requests that they "look into the seeds of time/ And say which grain will grow and which will not" (I, iii, 58–59), Shakespeare establishes a concern with future time. Macbeth is from this point obsessed with the idea of controlling the future, on the one hand actively pursuing the fate the witches have predicted (his kingship) and on the other attempting to circumvent fate (the inheritance of that kingship by Banquo's sons, not his). He also wishes to escape the future consequence (literally, the "following after") of his actions, to avoid the punishment that his sins demand. Thus, contemplating the murder of Duncan, he wishes "to trammel up the consequence and catch/ With his surcease success" (I, vii, 3–4), that is, not only victory but control over the succession and the political future.

It is precisely because he is dissatisfied with the mere present—"the ignorant present," as Lady Macbeth calls it—that Macbeth plots Banquo's murder. Wishing to extend his control forward into time, he soliloquizes on the "barrenness" of his throne and on his having plucked Duncan's crown with an "unlineal hand." In his second encounter with the witches, he defiantly bids that "nature's germens," that is, the "seeds of time," should tumble in disorder rather than that he should live in ignorance of the future. The compulsive emphasis on *doing* ("If it were done when 'tis done" [I, vii, 1], "The flighty purpose never is o'ertook/ Unless the deed go with it" [IV, i, 145–146]) suggests Macbeth's wish for a headlong rush into the future and his attempt to achieve some kind of continuing security beyond the unstable present.

All of Macbeth's attempts to hurry time and disrupt the natural processes of growth end in the emptiness of the "Tomorrow and tomorrow and tomorrow" speech (V, v, 17–28). In trying to wrench the natural course of things to his own purposes, Macbeth has emptied life of significance, turning his days into a mechanical progression without meaning. In contrast, Malcolm's final speech, asserting that "The time is free" and promising to perform kingly duties "in measure, time, and place," reestablishes ordered time and lineal succession. Thus fate moves "in its own good time" to purge the universe of evil.

16.28 Is Macbeth a villain?

Answer   In certain obvious ways, Macbeth is a villain. His wickedness is established at the outset, when he immediately leaps from the weird sisters' prediction of his future greatness to the idea of murdering Duncan. He hesitates to do the bloody deed not out of conscience but out of fear of the consequences, and he lies glibly when Duncan's body is discovered. From Macbeth's murder of the king to his last desperate stand against Macduff, we see an acceleration of crimes as he seeks to prevent exposure and punishment. His cold-blooded use of a band of cutthroats to rid himself of Banquo and his bloody assault on Macduff's innocent wife and child emphasize his criminality.

However, although Macbeth commits villainous acts, he cannot be viewed merely as an abhorrent figure or a criminal, for the audience is from the beginning invited to identify with him. Through Macbeth's soliloquies, Shakespeare shows the process by which a noble thane, "Bellona's bridegroom," becomes a "butcher." Highly imaginative and sensitive to suggestion, Macbeth analyzes his own evil promptings and struggles with his impulses in soliloquy: "This supernatural soliciting/ Cannot be ill, cannot be good" (I, iii, 130–131) and "If it were done when 'tis done, then 'twere well/ It were done quickly" (I, vii, 1–2). His guilt projects itself in hallucination—the "air-drawn" dagger and Banquo's ghost—and punishes him with sleeplessness and fear ("Sleep no more!/ Macbeth does murder sleep" [II, ii, 34–35]). His increasingly frantic attempts to make himself secure lead to a kind of despair:

> . . . I am in blood
> Stepped in so far that, should I wade no more,
> Returning were as tedious as go o'er.
> (III, iv, 136–138)

Finally, the language of his musings characteristically involves an opposition between hand and eye (for example, "The eye wink at the hand" [I, iv, 52]), suggesting Macbeth's psychological disintegration, as the self which acts is split off from the knowing, conscious self.

Thus, the portrait of Macbeth is not a horrific caricature of monstrous villainy but a study of the psychological breakdown of a great man infected by evil. The thane of Cawdor has tragic dimensions precisely because of his complexity; he includes within himself both his initial role as an honorable man of high estate and his final role as a bestial traitor. Because we see into his inner being as it responds to the stresses of ambition and the temptations of fate, Macbeth's fall evokes pity as well as terror.

16.29 What is the significance of the witches?

Answer A seventeenth-century audience might well have interpreted the weird sisters as literal agents of the devil, since belief in witchcraft was common in the period. At the opposite extreme, a modern audience may be tempted to interpret them as psychological projections of Macbeth's inner wishes and fears. However, since Banquo is a witness, the witches must be to some extent "real." In a metaphoric sense, they are clearly representatives of evil in the universe: their plots against mortals suggest willful malice, while their appearances before Macbeth on the foggy heath and in the darkened cave signal moral obscurity and confusion. They speak with the "equivocation of the fiend," tempting Macbeth to meet his fate with promises true in letter but not in spirit. Yet though they incarnate evil, the "midnight hags" cannot be viewed as responsible for Macbeth's fall. His vivid imagination and "vaulting" desires make him quick to seize on their promises: "murther" is in his mind almost simultaneously with the witches' prediction, and the plot against the thane of Fife is already hatched before the admonition in the cave. The riddles about "no babe born of woman" and the moving of Birnam Wood function only as malicious prods to the tyrant's already proven willfulness and vanity.

Neither simple fiends nor psychological hallucinations, the witches inhabit a crossroads between the natural and supernatural realms. They contribute to the play's examination of the metaphysics of evil by representing the subtle suggestion or temptation which unleashes it on the world. Thus Shakespeare uses the "machinery" of the weird sisters to show how character, meshing with external circumstances, produces tragic destiny and to suggest the unnatural, mysterious quality of evil.

16.30   What is the dramatic function of Lady Macbeth in the play?

Answer   Not only her husband's partner in crime, Lady Macbeth is almost literally his alter ego or "other self." She at first adopts a masculine role, invoking the powers of darkness to "unsex me here" and accusing Macbeth of womanish fears and compunctions. In discarding her feminine self, she does not hesitate to pervert her maternal role as well, claiming that she would pluck her infant from her breast and dash his brains out rather than falter in her ambitions. At this phase of the action, Macbeth's guilty, startled, fearful behavior suggests, if not femininity, at least the emotional sensibility traditionally associated with women. The confusion of traditional roles is one manifestation of the disruptive force of evil operating upon the hero. The very concept of manliness becomes associated with criminal and perverted acts, and "womanliness" is a term of opprobrium.

By the time of the sleepwalking scene, however, Lady Macbeth has become like the Macbeth of Act II: guilty, troubled, sleepless. If Macbeth has "murdered sleep," it is Lady Macbeth's sleep that he has murdered. She is visited by his former remorse: he had cried, "Will all great Neptune's ocean wash this blood/ Clean from my hand?" (II, ii, 59–60), and now she exclaims that "all the perfumes of Arabia will not sweeten this little hand" (V, i, 47–48). As Macbeth grows callous and "manly" in his desperate exploits and stratagems, Lady Macbeth assumes the burden of conscience. Husband and wife are so closely associated in evil that the one's madness is, in some sense, the other's as well.

Lady Macbeth serves the further function of bringing into the national and political arena of the play certain domestic and familial themes. Though Macbeth and his wife seem in fact to be childless, the dialogue between them is studded with allusions to children. For example, Lady Macbeth claims, "I have given suck, and know/How tender 'tis to love the babe that milks me. . . ." This reference and others, like Macbeth's reference to pity as a "naked newborn babe," invoke the strength of the natural bonds that are so violently disrupted in the drama. The ideas of procreation and natural succession lie behind the central action of the play: the regicide is followed by the return of the rightful heir to the throne and the future is promised to Banquo's line.

Lady Macbeth, then, contributes both to the psychological drama of crime and punishment and to the themes of natural growth and fruition that underlie the play's action.

16.31 Analyze Macbeth's "Tomorrow and tomorrow and tomorrow" speech.

Answer The speech is an ironic fulfillment of Macbeth's own prophecy. After witnessing Duncan's body in Act II, Scene iii, Macbeth speaks a lie which turns out to be the truth. Expatiating on his "sorrow," he says,

> Had I but died an hour before this chance,
> I had lived a blessed time; for from this instant
> There's nothing serious in mortality. . . .
>   (II, iii, 87–89)

The "Tomorrow" speech proves that, for Macbeth, there is indeed nothing "serious" in human life: existence is itself reduced to absurdity. "Tomorrow" suggests only an empty mechanical progression, and the past, "all our yesterdays," constitutes only an avenue to death. The "syllables of recorded time" are an idiot's babblings, and all action is reduced to puppetlike histrionics, so many "struts" and "frets" upon a stage.

Macbeth's allusions to temporal progression and to theatrical display are coldly nihilistic. Preoccupied with controlling the future, he has succeeded only in robbing it of any meaningful pattern. Concerned throughout with being a doer, an actor, he has made his life into an empty show, a thin illusion. The crucial act of murdering Duncan "emptied" his life, precisely as he himself had insincerely avowed it would just moments after the deed. Thus, this final despairing statement demonstrates the reflexive effect of evil; crime is its own punishment, for instead of bringing a sense of fulfillment it creates a horrible void.

The Tempest

16.32 Discuss *The Tempest* as a traveler's tale.

Answer As critics have often noted, the play reflects various contemporary accounts of New World voyages. Early seventeenth-century pamphlets about a shipwreck in the Bermudas may have influenced Shakespeare's conception of the plot, as well as suggesting Ariel's allusion to the "still-vex'd Bermoothes" and some of Caliban's natural lore of "pignuts" and "marmosets." Montaigne's famous essay on New World cannibals lies behind Gonzalo's description of the perfect commonwealth as a natural paradise; it may also have suggested the name Caliban, which constitutes an almost perfect anagram for "cannibal." Gonzalo's discussion of incredible tales—mountaineers dewlapped like bulls, men whose heads stand in their breasts (III, iii)—derives in a more general sense from travel lore, that collection of "vouched rarities" and unverifiable wonders that men describe on returning from exotic lands.

Gonzalo brings up his folklore of dewlaps and sunken heads in an attempt to explain the visionary banquet Prospero conjures up for the court party. By adducing other examples of the strange and miraculous which yet proved true, he attempts to naturalize the supernatural vision before him. Earlier in the same scene Sebastian and Antonio make a similar effort to explain the illusory feast. Sebastian mentions unicorns and the phoenix, and Antonio says,

> I'll believe both;
> And what does else want credit, come to me,
> And I'll be sworn 'tis true. Travellers ne'er did lie,
> Though fools at home condemn them.
> (III, iii, 24–27)

The net effect of these allusions to travel lore and "unnatural" natural history is to underscore the strangeness of experience in distant places. Prospero's "new world," his island domain, challenges conventional notions of fact and fiction, truth and falsehood, natural and unnatural. Isolated and exotic, the island invites hypothesis and triggers fantasies, both noble and ignoble. A sense of freedom from the old world of fixed realities and certainties stimulates Gonzalo to imagine a perfect commonwealth and tempts Antonio to initiate a new conspiracy. The power of imagination is unleashed, a power which in its comic form issues in a series of mistaken identities. On the island everyone is dislocated, everyone a "foreigner." Thus Ferdinand imagines Miranda to be a goddess, Miranda calls

Ferdinand a "spirit," Trinculo thinks Caliban is a fish, Stephano thinks Caliban-cum-Trinculo is a monster with four legs, and Caliban is convinced that Stephano has "dropped from heaven." The new acquaintances wonder at and marvel over each other as supernatural, or subnatural, beings.

In general the travel theme has the effect of dislocating normal expectations and creating a new sense of possibility, including the possibility of miracle. It is something of an irony when the new world representative, Miranda, looks on the old world ambassadors and says, "O brave new world/ That has such people in't" (V, i, 183–184). Prospero emphasizes the irony by rejoining, " 'Tis new to thee." The old world of the court party is not only old but decadent, a fallen world of fratricide, usurpation, conspiracy. Only by exposing Alonso and the others to the exotic and the marvelous can Prospero shake the cynicism and skepticism which keep an Antonio shut away in isolation. The strange environment induces in the "travelers" a more open attitude to experience, for it is a place where anything can happen, including a resurrection of the dead. It is through credulity and wonder, the secular counterparts of faith, that men can find a way to build, in the real world, a brave new one.

16.33 *The Tempest* is a relatively static play, substituting for major crises and recognitions a series of games and spectacles. How can we account for the pageantlike quality of the play?

Answer *The Tempest* has, in part, the effect of a masque or spectacle, with Prospero playing both stage manager and magician. The complicated actions involving dancers and musicians, the many interspersed songs, Ariel's metamorphoses and disappearances, and the masque-within-a-play in Act IV all contribute to the pageantry of the drama, giving it a festival air. There are also many "games" in the play: all the characters seem to be participating in a game of blindman's buff orchestrated by Prospero, who seduces his victims with illusory banquets, strange music, and sleeping spells, or hounds them with fearsome noises, physical torments, and impossible tasks. In addition, when Ferdinand and Miranda are discovered by the others in Act V, they are playing chess. In the epilogue, Prospero "places" the play as spectacle and game by appearing as an actor and asking for a round of applause.

Undoubtedly Jacobean audiences enjoyed the spectacle produced by the play's elements of stagecraft, orchestration, and choreography. However, *The Tempest* is more than a spectacular masque or a summer pageant. The game playing is not merely play, for the trials of the characters have a serious outcome in a genuine change of heart, as sins are repented and old enemies reconciled.

Prospero's mock-chivalric test of Ferdinand ends in a true union between the lovers, while his manipulation of Alonso results in the latter's recognition of his sin. The symbolic or allegorical quality of the freakish misadventures experienced by the characters is evident in the whole shape of the action, for the accumulated mishaps have the effect of an education which issues in new self-awareness and new kinship. Only Antonio stands apart from the new community which grows out of the game, his role as outsider symbolizing the limitations of magic and of love.

The game played out on Prospero's magical island is an exercise in wisdom and charity, for Prospero himself writes the rules and oversees the action, so that no harm befalls anyone. Despite its strange atmosphere and mysterious inhabitants, the island is safe territory for the visitors, a magical domain in which they lose themselves to find themselves. It is only by playing out a drama of loss and bewilderment that the characters undergo a process of repentance and rebirth. Part of the point of the game is to reaffirm the sense of an ultimately beneficent power ruling human life. Like the festive pageants from which the play descends, *The Tempest* points to an order and meaning in experience which are rediscovered through mock rituals and games. Thus the drunken antics of Trinculo, Stephano, and Caliban, the confused wanderings of the court party, and the mock servitude of Ferdinand represent play of a serious kind, becoming part of a phase of release in which the world is turned topsy-turvy as prologue to a new order.

16.34 The characters in *The Tempest* have sometimes been interpreted as allegorical figures: Prospero = Art, Caliban = Nature, Ariel = Spirit, Miranda = Chastity, and so on. What in the play reinforces the impression of allegorical types and what works against this impression?

Answer In common with fairy tales and romances, *The Tempest* has a schematic quality. The plot is episodic and dreamlike, and the characters are to a large extent stereotypical (omnipotent magician, virtuous daughter, noble prince, wicked schemer, wise old counselor, drunken sailors, "a salvage and deformed slave"). Character development in the play seems artificial, resulting from manipulative magic, rather than realistic and psychological, issuing from natural events and interactions. Indeed the most "realistic" character in the play, Antonio, does not develop, steadfastly adhering to the personal creed of cynicism and materialism which led him to usurp his brother in the first place. With the exception of Antonio, characters are generally subordinated to the plot, or *mythos*: a dethroned ruler-magician punishes the wicked usurpers who robbed him of his kingdom, causing them (all but one) to repent and at the same time promoting the union of his daughter with a captive prince who is the son of one of his enemies. The importance of the fable is suggested by Gonzalo's speech toward the end of the play (V, i, 205–213), which begins, "Was Milan thrust from Milan that his issue/ Should become kings of Naples?" and concludes with a reference to a regaining of self-mastery: ". . . and all of us ourselves/ When no man was his own." On the one hand, the story is a fairy tale about the righting of wrongs, ending in a dynastic marriage; on the other, it is a parable illustrating the Christian paradox of the fortunate fall or *felix culpa* ("happy blame"). Gonzalo thus stresses that aspect of the story that is about "everyman" rather than a particular man.

The allegorical quality of the play is reinforced by the doubling of characters and plot developments, for the duplications suggest that individuals and their actions are less important than the ideas they signify. Thus the dramatis personae include two sets of brothers (Antonio and Prospero, Sebastian and Alonso), two sets of father and child (Alonso and Ferdinand, Prospero and Miranda), two low-life characters (Stephano and Trinculo), and two fantastic creatures (Ariel and Caliban). The characters are related in schematic patterns which express the themes of the play. Thus the two conspiracies (Antonio and Sebastian against Alonso; Stephano, Trinculo, and Caliban against Prospero) illustrate man's fallen nature, with original sin manifesting itself in the aristocratic Antonio as well as in the bestial Caliban. The marriage of the royal offspring symbolizes man's capability for regeneration through love, while the opposition between the nonhuman characters, with Ariel representing spirit and Caliban flesh, suggests the conflicting impulses inherent in human nature. Finally, in the contrast between Caliban, the natural man on whom nurture can never stick, and Prospero, the good magician whose illusions control and transform unredeemed nature, Shakespeare elaborates on the theme of nature versus art.

One last aspect of the play which encourages an allegorical interpretation is the tendency of characters to speak "out of character" in the interest of expressing the central themes. When Miranda engages in angry invective against Caliban (in a speech some editors attempt to assign to Prospero), she is speaking for the play rather than revealing a new and surprising facet of her personality. By giving Miranda lines which directly attack Caliban, Shakespeare reinforces the contrast between a royal nature gently nurtured and the base nature, immune to nurture, of a subhuman savage ("Abhorred slave,/ Which any print of goodness will not take" [I, ii, 351–352]). Similarly, Caliban's beautiful verse ("I prithee let me bring thee where crabs grow" [II, ii, 163–168] and "Be not afeard:

the isle is full of noises" [III, ii, 132 ff.]) has thematic significance, illustrating the "soft primitivism" of pastoral whereby natural man, unaided by the civilizing influence of art, has his own dignity and wisdom.

However, despite all the evidence for a reading of the play as allegory and of the characters as convenient symbols, certain of the characters retain a vivid individuality which resists such schematic analysis. The most obvious case is Antonio, whose recalcitrant silence in the last act indicates precisely his refusal to cooperate in the play's fable of fall and redemption. His choosing to be unredeemed is the mark of individual personality: unlike Alonso and Sebastian, his fellows in sin, he shows no sign of sharing the atmosphere of wonder and amazement which permeates Act V, his one remark in that scene of recognition and rebirth ("Very like. One of them/ Is a plain fish and no doubt marketable" [V, i, 265–266]) suggesting the casual cynicism which is his chief characteristic.

Although on some level the play may be about everyman, not every man in the play is the same. Thus the linguistic idiosyncrasies of subsidiary characters like Stephano and Trinculo, with their colloquial jokes and obscene puns, and Gonzalo, with his sententious moralizings and digressions, while in a sense reinforcing their stereotypical roles in the drama, at the same time establish the speakers as individuals, with individual reactions to the dream into which they have fallen.

But the most notable instances of idiosyncrasy are exhibited by two of the chief characters in *The Tempest*, Prospero and Caliban. The one is not as noble, the other not as debased as an allegorical interpretation would suggest. Prospero has an irascibility which partly supports Caliban's assertion that all the spirits at the magician's command "hate him as rootedly as I." His characteristic style of speech, toward Ariel as well as Caliban, is invective and imprecation, as he threatens to cast malignant spells which will torture any servant who dares to disobey him. That he is not solely wise and forgiving is implied by the torments he inflicts on the bewildered travelers, cruelly tantalizing the court party and playing practical jokes on the servants. Paradoxically it is Ariel who must remind Prospero of what it means to be human when he says that Prospero's "affections / Would become tender" if the magician could see the mournful sinners afflicted by his charm. Prospero says, "Dost thou think so, spirit?" and Ariel replies, "Mine would, sir, were I human" (V, i, 19–20). It is almost immediately after this exchange that Prospero recognizes that "The rarer action is/ In virtue than in vengeance" (V, i, 27–28).

Apart from the hints of intemperance and vengefulness in Prospero's character, there is a comic strain of the interfering busybody. In a congratulatory aside addressed to Ariel, he metaphorically rubs his hands in observing the young lovers succumbing, according to his design, to love ("It works" [I, ii, 494]). His stern paternalistic reminder to Ferdinand to respect the laws of chastity before the marriage ceremony, issued not once but twice (IV, i, 14–23; 52–54), has something of the same effect.

Like Prospero, Caliban is also humanized and individualized so that he becomes not a function, "this thing of darkness," but a recognizable human being. For example, when he says to Miranda, "You taught me language and my profit on't/ Is, I know how to curse" (I, ii, 363–364), he is not merely a mouthpiece for the theme of nature *vs.* nurture. He is expressing a sullen independence in resisting servitude, an attitude that is at least partly comic. Although he has deserved his punishment, his ill temper is at least understandable. His puppy-dog eagerness to please his mistaken idol Stephano is also appealingly human. Finally, his poetry on the natural wonders of the isle, while it can be interpreted as the "play" speaking, nonetheless feels like a stroke of characterization. It is hard not to hear this language as belonging to Caliban, and it lends him dignity and pathos as a man sensitive to and hungry for the beauty and wonder all about him.

If *The Tempest* is part fairy tale and part allegory, the characters compel more belief than is usual in such forms. We are on more intimate terms with Prospero, Miranda, and Caliban than with an Archimago, a Sleeping Beauty, or a Pan.

16.35   One distinctive feature of the language of *The Tempest* is the tendency of literal statement to function simultaneously as metaphor. Using examples, analyze the handling of metaphor in the play.

Answer   As Frank Kermode points out, metaphor in *The Tempest* "gleams momentarily, and is rarely extensive enough to be catalogued and analyzed" (introduction to the New Arden edition, p. lxxix). In a few cases metaphors can be isolated. For example, in Act II, Scene i, Antonio, conversing with Sebastian, metaphorically equates the fluctuations of fortune with ebbing or flowing water (II, i, 216–222) and employs an image of digestion and regurgitation to describe the court party's survival of the tempest ("We all were sea-swallowed, though some cast again" [II, i, 245]). But in this scene the unusually formal rhetoric seems to derive from the particular dramatic situation: Antonio, in much the same manner as Cassius in *Julius Caesar*, is attempting to persuade a friend to join with him in a conspiracy and thus exploits figurative language to help effect his persuasion.

Elsewhere in the play the "gleams" of metaphor have a very different effect from the studied image-making of Antonio. Many lines that sound figurative have, in context, a primarily literal significance—for example, Ariel's song to Ferdinand:

> Full fathom five thy father lies;
> Of his bones are coral made;
> Those are pearls that were his eyes.
>   (I, ii, 399–401)

On one level it is a factual description of the transformations wrought by water on a drowned man. The "sea-change/ Into something rich and strange" (I, ii, 403–404) metaphorically suggests, or anticipates, the "resurrection" of Alonso, but the words retain their literal import: the skeleton is becoming encrusted with coral, and oysters are bedding in its eye sockets. Here metaphor behaves in a distinctive and unusual way. Instead of simply substituting figurative terms for literal ones, the metaphor is a "gleam" of suggestiveness emanating from words that have a primarily factual reference.

Prospero's speech at the conclusion of the masque (IV, i) is a central example of the tendency of language to sound metaphoric although in context it is not actually figurative. The speech sounds like a figurative comparison between a theatrical pageant and the dissolving images of a dream:

> Our revels now are ended. These our actors,
> As I foretold you, were all spirits, and
> Are melted into air, thin air;
>   (IV, i, 148–150)

But in fact Prospero's "actors" are literally "spirits" who, according to the dramatic fiction, actually disappear "into air, thin air" when the magician breaks his spell. The statement

> We are such stuff
> As dreams are made on, and our little life
> Is rounded with a sleep.
>   (IV, i, 156–158)

again, like the earlier statement about the melting away of the actors, fuses literal statement with metaphoric suggestiveness. Literally, Prospero's actors are spirits who visit in dreams. At the same time, a comparison is hinted at, implying that all men are dreamers, all life a dream, and death a dreamless sleep.

A similar effect of fusion occurs in Prospero's soliloquy in the last act:

> But this rough magic
> I here abjure; . . .
>
> . . . .
>
> . . . I'll break my staff,
> Bury it certain fathoms in the earth,
> And deeper than did ever plummet sound
> I'll drown my book.
>
> (V, i, 50–51; 54–57)

On the literal level Prospero is renouncing the arts of magic and describing the specific operations necessary to do so. But the language sounds strangely non-literal, as though referring to something larger than the end of Prospero's career as a magician. It is possible to hear in these lines, as many critics have, Shakespeare's metaphoric farewell to his art or to read them as a renunciation of life itself. This latter interpretation is suggested by the echo of Ariel's "elegy" for Alonso ("Full fathom five") and by the repetition of Alonso's language when he determines on suicide ("I'll seek him deeper than e'er plummet sounded/ And with him there lie mudded" [III, iii, 101–102]).

Widening circles of reference seem to emanate from many plain statements in the play. When Prospero says of Caliban, "This thing of darkness/ I acknowledge mine" (V, i, 275–276), he is primarily distinguishing his own servant from the two others, Stephano and Trinculo, who belong to the court party; but he sounds as though he is claiming or admitting the base nature of Caliban as part of himself. When Miranda exclaims, "O brave new world/ That hath such people in't" (V, i, 183–184), she is merely remarking on the handsome appearance (the "brave" show) of human men, with whom, other than her father, she has had no acquaintance; but she sounds as though she is welcoming the advent of an earthly paradise. When Gonzalo recites what has happened in the course of the play (". . . in one voyage/ Did Claribel her husband find at Tunis,/ . . . and all of us ourselves/ When no man was his own" [V, i, 208–213]), he is merely summarizing certain surprising discoveries and recoveries, including the court party's group recovery of their lost senses; but he sounds as though he is speaking of profound spiritual recognitions.

This tendency of plain statement to develop metaphoric resonance derives in part from the play's genre. As a romance The Tempest does not belong, or at least not entirely, to the literal world of factual reality. Thus the language of the play has something in common with the language of dreams and fairy tales. A dream statement, which in context makes perfect literal sense, assumes symbolic import as soon as it is brought out of the dream into the waking world. Similarly, what is, in the context of the play, blunt reporting or literal naming acquires magical force when brought out of the magical universe in which it originates. Put another way, within the play metaphors become strangely literal. What in the "real" world would be only a comparison, a wish, or a figurative expression is actualized in the world of romance, where desires are magically satisfied and fantasies made flesh.

B.S.

SUGGESTED READINGS

Background:

Bullough, Geoffrey, *Narrative and Dramatic Sources of Shakespeare*, Vols. I–VIII (1957–   ).

Eastman, Arthur M., *A Short History of Shakespearean Criticism* (1968).

Schoenbaum, Samuel, *William Shakespeare: A Documentary Life* (1977).

Sonnets:

Booth, Stephen, *An Essay on Shakespeare's Sonnets* (1969).

Knights, L. C., *Some Shakespearean Themes* (1959).

Leishman, J. B., *Themes and Variations in Shakespeare's Sonnets* (1961).

Lever, J. W., *The Elizabethan Love Sonnet* (1956).

Smith, Hallett, *Elizabethan Poetry: A Study in Conventions, Meaning, and Expression* (1952).

As You Like It:

Barber, C. L., *Shakespeare's Festive Comedy: A Study of Dramatic Form in Relation to Social Custom* (1959).

Bethell, S. L., *Shakespeare and the Popular Dramatic Tradition* (1944).

Bradbury, M., and D. J. Palmer, eds., *Shakespeare's Comedies* (1972).

Frye, Northrop, *A Natural Perspective: The Development of Shakespearean Comedy and Romance* (1965).

Goldsmith, R. H., *Wise Fools in Shakespeare* (1955).

Henry IV, Part I:

Dorius, R. J., ed., *Twentieth-Century Interpretations of Henry IV, Part One* (1970).

Hunter, G. K., ed., *Shakespeare: King Henry IV, Parts 1 and 2* (1970).

Traversi, D. A., *Shakespeare: From Richard II to Henry V* (1957).
Wilson, J. Dover, *The Fortunes of Falstaff* (1953).

Julius Caesar:

Dean, L. F., ed., *Twentieth-Century Interpretations of Julius Caesar* (1968).
Frye, Northrop, *Fools of Time* (1967).
Palmer, John, *Political Characters of Shakespeare* (1945).
Ure, Peter, ed., *Shakespeare: Julius Caesar* (1969).

Macbeth:

Brooks, Cleanth, "The Naked Babe and the Cloak of Manliness," in *The Well-Wrought Urn* (1947).
Heilman, R. B., "The Criminal as Tragic Hero: Dramatic Methods," *Shakespeare Survey*, 19 (1966).
Knight, G. Wilson, *The Imperial Theme* (1931).
Spurgeon, Caroline F. E., *Shakespeare's Imagery* (1935).
Wain, John, ed., *Shakespeare: Macbeth* (1969).

The Tempest:

Curry, W. C., *Shakespeare's Philosophical Patterns* (1973).
Frye, Northrop, *A Natural Perspective: The Development of Shakespearean Comedy and Romance* (1965).
Kermode, Frank, *Shakespeare: The Final Plays* (1963).
Palmer, D. J., ed., *Shakespeare's Later Comedies: An Anthology of Modern Criticism* (1971).

Part Four

THE
SEVENTEENTH
CENTURY

T I M E L I N E

The Age

1574:	James Burbage receives license to open a theater in London
1588:	Defeat of the Spanish Armada; apex of England's power under Elizabeth I
1592:	Plague kills 15,000 in London
1595:	Irish revolt suppressed
1603:	Death of Elizabeth I; accession of James I
1618:	Thirty Years' War begins
1620:	Pilgrims sail to America on the *Mayflower*
1625:	Death of James I; accession of Charles I
1628:	Parliament submits Petition of Rights, outlining grievances against Charles I
1642:	English civil war begins. Theaters ordered closed by Puritan-dominated Parliament
1648:	Thirty Years' War ended by Treaty of Westphalia
1649:	Charles I defeated, imprisoned, beheaded; Commonwealth declared. Cromwell marches against rebels in Scotland and Ireland
1652:	War with Holland; victories of Admiral Blake
1658:	Death of Cromwell
1660:	Restoration; accession of Charles II

The Authors

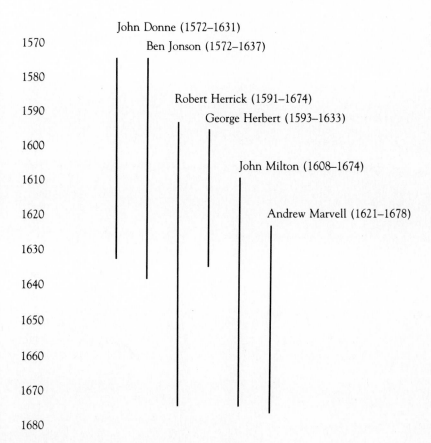

1570

John Donne (1572–1631)
Ben Jonson (1572–1637)

1580

1590

Robert Herrick (1591–1674)
George Herbert (1593–1633)

1600

1610

John Milton (1608–1674)

1620

Andrew Marvell (1621–1678)

1630

1640

1650

1660

1670

1680

JOHN DONNE

C H R O N O L O G Y

1572   Born in London. Son of John Donne, a London merchant, and Elizabeth Heywood Donne. His mother's family is remarkable for both literary achievement and religious faith; Elizabeth's father was John Heywood, poet and playwright; her great-uncle was Sir Thomas More, scholar, writer, statesman, and Catholic saint. Several members of the family were exiled or imprisoned for their adherence to the Roman church under Queen Elizabeth. John Donne will be raised as a Roman Catholic.

1584   Donne enters Hart Hall, Oxford University.

1587   Transfers to Trinity College, Cambridge University.

1589–   Donne may have traveled in Europe at this time.
1591

1591   Donne enters first Thavies Inn, then Lincoln's Inn, intending to pursue the study of law. Will continue these studies for about three years; is probably writing much of his early love poetry at this time.

1593   Death of Henry Donne, the poet's brother, while held in Newgate Prison for harboring a Jesuit priest (regarded at the time as treasonous, since Jesuits were assumed to be, and sometimes were, acting as spies in behalf of the Catholic powers of Europe).

1596–   Donne sails as a "gentleman adventurer" in two expeditions under Essex
1597   and Ralegh. The first expedition, to Cadiz, is successful; the Spanish stronghold there is sacked and looted. The second, to the Azores, is a failure.

| 1597 | Donne becomes chief secretary of Sir Thomas Egerton, lord keeper of the great seal. His holding of a government post indicates that he has become an Anglican by this time. |

1597   Donne becomes chief secretary of Sir Thomas Egerton, lord keeper of the great seal. His holding of a government post indicates that he has become an Anglican by this time.

1601   Donne secretly marries Ann More, daughter of Egerton's brother-in-law Sir George More. (Donne's low career status, and perhaps his Catholic background, would have made him a poor match.)

1602   Donne confesses the marriage; is dismissed from service by Egerton and briefly imprisoned for conspiring to marry without parental consent. Upon his release, Donne and his wife move to Surrey, where they live as guests of Ann's cousin. Most of Donne's secular poetry has probably been written by this date.

1606   Donne is working at this time for the Church of England as an anti-Catholic propagandist (until 1610).

1607   Seeks employment in the queen's household, in vain. Will continue to seek advancement in government service unsuccessfully until around 1615.

1609   Reconciliation with wife's family achieved; her father presents the couple with a belated dowry, thus effectively freeing the family from poverty.

1610   Religious polemic *Pseudo-Martyr* published. Donne receives an honorary M.A. from Oxford.

1611   *Ignatius his Conclave*, a prose satire against the Jesuits, published. Travels in Europe with Sir Robert Drury. Writes and publishes *The First Anniversary*, an elegy for Drury's daughter.

1612   Publishes *The Second Anniversary*, a further elegy for Robert Drury's daughter. Returns to England and moves with his family to a house on the Drury estate.

1615   At urging of King James I, is ordained deacon and priest in the Church of England. Appointed a royal chaplain, and receives an honorary doctor of divinity degree from Cambridge. Begins his career as England's most famous preacher with sermons before the king and queen.

1616   Presented with the livings of parishes in Huntingdonshire and Kent.

1617   Death of Anne Donne shortly after bearing a stillborn child. Donne continues his career as a prominent preacher.

1619   Travels in Europe as chaplain of a diplomatic mission; preaches before heads of state in Germany.

1621   Elected dean of St. Paul's Cathedral, London.

1622   Two of Donne's sermons published, the first of many to appear in print during his lifetime.

1624   *Devotions upon Emergent Occasions* published, a meditative religious prose work. Donne's divine poems have probably been written by this date.

1625   Donne probably writes his last poem, "An Hymn to the Saints." Death of James I; Charles I crowned, and Donne preaches the first sermon before the new monarch. Meets poet George Herbert.

1630   Donne falls seriously ill.

1631   Preaches his last sermon at court, published posthumously as "Death's Duel." Poses for a portrait in his burial shroud. Death of Donne; he is buried in St. Paul's.

1633   First collected edition of Donne's poems is published.

1640   A collection of eighty Donne sermons published; also Izaak Walton's *Life of Donne*, still a major source of information about Donne's life.

ESSAY QUESTIONS WITH ANSWERS

"A Valediction Forbidding Mourning"

17.1 Why does Donne's "Valediction" (a poem of farewell) forbid mourning?

Answer The occasion of the poem is the imminent, though temporary, separation of two lovers, an event which might ordinarily provoke strong expressions of grief. Yet the poet argues, paradoxically, both that their separation is too momentous for such trivial displays of emotion and that it is merely illusory.

In comparing their separation to a deathbed scene, stanza 1 implicitly accepts that their separation is a kind of death, a division of body and soul; in parting, each lover will be whispering farewell to his "soul," the other lover. Yet outcries and lamentations at a deathbed suggest the departure of a turbulent soul, resistant to God's will and possibly damned; the virtuous die at peace with themselves and hence quietly. A love which is serene and confident of reunion will suffer separation as calmly, indeed as imperceptibly, as the good man permits his soul to leave his body. A reverent hush, expressing awe at the mysteries of death and love, is the proper response to such moments, and this delicate respect for matters too sacred to be spoken of loudly controls the tone of the poem.

However, the notion that the affection of these lovers transcends the senses permits a subtle turn in Donne's argument. It is merely a physical separation which the lovers must endure; this would indeed be death to lovers whose bond is sensual, but to lovers who are "Inter-assured of the mind," the loss of "eyes, lips, and hands" is melancholy but not fatal. Since the lovers' souls "are one," they cannot genuinely be disjoined and hence, once again, there is no reason to mourn.

Moreover, the third stanza argues, events of cosmic magnitude—such as this separation—are not even perceived by the vulgar (that is, the "laity," who are uninitiated in the religious mysteries of love). To offer an analogy in contemporary terms, we feel the motion of a merry-go-round but not the rotation of the earth.

Thus the poet diminishes and magnifies the significance of the lovers' parting. In either case, he argues, the conventional reaction to parting—mourning—is inadequate to the occasion, because the understanding of love it implies is vulgar and hence irrelevant to the emotions and situation of a pair of lovers such as this.

17.2 The use of the conceit (an elaborately developed metaphor) as a basis for argument is one characteristic of Donne's metaphysical poetry. How do the conceits contribute to the argument in this poem?

Answer The poet's basic argument, that despite the lovers' physical separation their souls will be together, depends upon a series of carefully developed metaphors, or conceits. The poet constructs analogies between the lovers' parting and other examples of seeming separation which are not really separations at all. Thus, the strength of his argument to the lady depends upon the attractiveness, credibility, and intelligence of his analogies.

For example, he argues in the sixth stanza that what seems to be a breach between the lovers is really the expansion of their united souls, like "gold to airy thinness beat." The image of the thinnest gold foil, stretched to its utmost but never broken, represents the souls of the lovers maintaining their interconnection despite being separated by space. By comparing the souls to a precious metal, Donne emphasizes the value of their love, while the "airy thinness" of the gold foil suggests its ethereal, spiritual refinement.

Later the poet proposes an analogy between the lovers' souls and the legs of a compass. His "proof" that the relationship between the legs of the compass is like the relationship between the two souls provides another argument for the sympathetic connections between the lovers which exist while they are physically separated. The last three stanzas develop this analogy between every detail of the compass and the relationship between the lovers. The analogy culminates in the final two lines of the poem, where the poet suggests that, like the fixed foot of the compass, the lady's soul guides the poet's soul even in its absence, providing it with its center and home.

Although the compass was a standard emblem, or symbolic image, of constancy in the Renaissance, its intrusion into a love poem is still startling; its metallic coldness and the hardheaded, geometric vocabulary that comes with it seem at first encounter unsuitable for an emotional appeal. Donne means to surprise, of course; the improbability of the analogy is the source of its wit. His tone suffuses even this use of a mathematical implement with grave tenderness, but, more than that, the very absence of romantic associations works in favor of his argument: the assurance he is offering, it implies, is not a lover's hyperbole, but sober and definite, as capable of demonstration as a geometric theorem. Even in the most unlikely phenomena this love finds triumphant confirmation.

17.3   Paraphrase the following stanza of Donne's "Valediction":

> Dull sublunary lovers' love
> (Whose soul is sense) cannot admit
> Absence, because it doth remove
> Those things which elemented it.
> (lines 13–16)

Answer   In this stanza, the poet describes the plight of other, more ordinary and changeable lovers, who inhabit the "sublunary" world of matter and mutability. (In medieval and Renaissance cosmology, the region below the moon–including, of course, the earth–was thought to be the realm of change and decay, in contrast to the immutable, timeless region of the stars beyond.) They cannot tolerate separation because their very relationship is based on the senses, their direct, physical experience of one another. The parenthetical phrase "Whose soul is sense" refers to the physical basis of the relationship of these other lovers. The poet plays on the Latin derivation of the word "absence," meaning "without sense," thus reinforcing the idea that when ordinary lovers are parted, the basic "element" of the relationship is missing. The "things" which are "removed" by absence are the organs of the senses—the eyes, the lips, the hands of the lovers (mentioned in the following stanza).

"The Flea"

17.4   Describe the dramatic situation and the progress of the speaker's argument.

Answer   In a witty rhetorical exercise, the speaker tries to persuade his mistress to go to bed with him and to demonstrate that the reasons for her resistance are trivial. "Look at this flea," he tells her; "it bit first me, then you, and thus mingled our bloods. Is sexual intercourse anything more? Yet no one is going to call what the flea has done sin, or shame, or loss of maidenhead. The flea didn't even ask permission, as I do in wooing you."

Before the second stanza, the lady presumably lifts her hand to avenge herself by killing the flea, and the poet urges her not to strike: "Oh stay." In fact, he argues, she will commit a triple sin in killing the flea: it will be murder of the poet, since the flea contains his blood (though she's used to that murder, since she metaphorically kills him with her cruel resistance to his pleas); it will be suicide, since the flea has now become the vessel of her blood as well; and it will be sacrilege, since the flea's body ("these living walls of jet") has become the marriage temple in which their bloods are united. Line 10 says a third life is involved; it might be the flea's, but line 8 suggests that the flea is pregnant ("swells") with a new life, "with one blood made of two." Killing the flea would be a kind of abortion, a suggestion which is strengthened when the poet sub-sequently condemns the lady for shedding the "blood of innocence" (playing on the biblical slaughter of the innocents in Bethlehem).

The dramatic situation is redefined again between stanzas 2 and 3; the lady, "Cruel and sudden," has carried out the threatened action and her nail is purple with the flea's spilled blood. Yet the poet cheerfully abandons his recriminations after four lines to point out that she has just sacrificed a drop of her own blood and is clearly none the worse for it. He returns to the idea that no greater sacrifice of her "honor" will be involved if she complies with his desires. To mourn either the death of the flea or the loss of virginity would be hypocrisy ("false tears").

17.5   Discuss the tone of this poem.

Answer   The poet flaunts his ingenuity. He knows his argument is sophistic but, he implies, the arguments in favor of preserving the lady's virginity may be equally spurious. If she understands her honor as something more significant than avoiding the loss of blood, let her say so; if not, she is probably ripe for seduction in any case, and the poet's cynical tour de force will supply the pretext which she needs for surrender.

The poet's strategy is to trivialize phenomena such as love and honor by reducing them to a purely physical level. If the loss of honor costs only a minimal amount of blood, its significance surely cannot be very great. (The loss of blood may refer to either the puncturing of the hymen or the Renaissance notion that lovers actually mingled blood, with generative properties, in the act of inter-course.) Yet if love is a mere fleabite, why does the lover plead so urgently for this reward? By raising the issue of motive, it's possible to peer past the speaker's mask of dispassionate urbanity and observe the underlying sexual tension.

"The Canonization"

17.6   What is the dramatic situation in which "The Canonization" unfolds?

Answer   The speaker's words represent one side of an argument which began before the first line of the poem. The cause of his expostulation—"For God's sake hold your tongue"—is probably a friend's unsolicited advice about the poet's love for his lady. The poem begins as the speaker's retort; he tells his friend not only to shut his mouth but to tend to his own business, whether at court or in the world of commerce ("Observe . . . the King's real, or his stamped face"—stamped, that is, on coins). Later, particularly in stanza 5, he will contrast the friend's presumed worldliness with the withdrawal of the lovers from the world, to become "one another's hermitage" and celebrate the religious mysteries of love.

From the questions and imperatives of the speaker, one can deduce the kinds of objections to love which the well-meaning friend has offered. He seems to view the lover's passion as a kind of sickness or obsession which causes injury to the speaker and possibly to others around him. In reply, the speaker says, you can ridicule my infirmity ("my palsy, or my gout"), my age ("My five gray hairs"), or my poverty ("ruined fortune"), but leave my love alone; although the tears and sighs, the chills and fevers of passion may destroy *my* world, they are no cataclysm for the rest of the world. In stanza 2 he defends himself by saying he has injured no one's profits or property, and once again his emphasis on the acquisitiveness of others prepares an implicit contrast with the lovers' monastic aloofness from such concerns.

In the third stanza the speaker alludes to insults offered by the friend, saying, "Call us what you will." The friend has apparently compared the lovers to ephemeral flies, who live only for the brief present, or to candles ("tapers") consumed by fire, as the lovers "die" (consummate their sexual passion, as well as destroy themselves) by the heat of their own passion. Turning these insults into badges of honor, the speaker affirms these comparisons but adds some comparisons of his own which transform their significance. The lovers may consume themselves like tapers, but they will rise from their own ashes, renewed and youthful, like the mythical phoenix. Since the symbol of the phoenix was often associated with the death and Resurrection of Christ, its introduction here paves the way for the language of religion (or at least idolatry) in the final two stanzas.

In the course of stanza 3 the friend seems to fade from view. He has provided the occasion for the speaker's explanation of the sacred quality of his love, but as the self-canonization proceeds, the immediate occasion is almost forgotten. Indifferent to worldly gain or success, devoted solely to mutual contemplation, the speaker and his mistress have become not merely hermits but "saints" of love. This grandiose self-exaltation flirts with sacrilege, but for Donne's English

Protestant readers this conception probably seemed to parody Roman Catholic veneration of the saints rather than their own forms of piety. Despite this hint of superstition, the impression lingers that the speaker does indeed regard his love as sanctifying, and that the extravagance of the canonization expresses at least an emotional truth.

17.7 What ideas does the fourth stanza add to the development of the speaker's argument?

Answer The fourth stanza emphasizes the role of the poet's verses in making the lovers' "legend" not only sacred but enduring. It may be that the friend to whom the poem's opening outburst is addressed has condemned not only love but poetry as an unprofitable and self-destructive activity. If the lovers cannot "live by love" (that is, make a living out of it), poetry ("these hymns") will make them live in another sense.

If we cannot live by love, the poet says, we can at least die by it, punning on the Renaissance sense of "die" as "experience sexual consummation." In that case, one might suppose, the lovers' "legend" (that is, both "story" and "descriptive title") could adorn a tomb. However, grand, pompous "half-acre tombs" require precisely the material prosperity the lovers have scorned in neglecting worldly concerns; one can't even die ceremoniously, in a manner worthy of "chronicle," if one hasn't made a good living.

If the lovers' resources won't buy a magnificent funeral or the land for a large-scale monument, the poet can provide another kind of memorial, building "in sonnets [that is, lyric poems] pretty rooms." Here Donne puns on the meaning of "stanza," the Italian word for "room"; the memory of the lovers will inhabit only the space of a shapely and elegant poem ("a well-wrought urn"). Each of its stanzas, or "pretty rooms," will become a shrine to future lovers. The poet even designs the liturgy for such worship, offering in the final stanza of *this* poem a form of prayer for ritual invocations.

17.8 Discuss the use of meter in the poem.

Answer While the basic meter of the poem is iambic, the length of the lines varies between five feet (pentameter), four feet (tetrameter), and even, for the final line of each stanza, three feet (trimeter). (The pattern of feet per line in each stanza can be summarized as 5 4 5 5 4 4 5 4 3.) The effect of this variation is to give a rougher, more conversational tone to the poem, as though the flow of the poet's arguments and emotions is spontaneously transgressing metrical boundaries and breaking down neat parallel structure. The rhymes link lines of disparate length, for example, lines 2 and 3; two tetrameter lines (5 and 6) share a rhyme with the following pentameter line (7), and while the pentameter lines 1 and 4 rhyme with each other, they also rhyme with a tetrameter and a trimeter line (8 and 9). Enjambment (continuation of the syntax across the line breaks) also occurs (for example, at lines 7 and 8, 16 and 17, and 23 and 24) and enhances the general feeling that the poem is wrestling against its own form.

While the speaker's agitation is expressed partly through the unevenness of the lines, the *recurrence* of this irregular pattern in each stanza gives evidence of his underlying assurance, and consistency is conveyed in other ways as well, for example, by the use of the word "love" to end both the initial pentameter and the final trimeter line of each stanza.

Even within the individual line, Donne's colloquial, argumentative tone exploits the discrepancy between ordinary speech and regular poetic meter. Although the first line is basically iambic, the first four syllables ("For God's sake hold") seem to require an extra stress; the abruptness and emphasis of the imperative strain against the ordinary rules of scansion. (The colloquial rough-ness of Donne's verse was notorious among his contemporaries; Ben Jonson is reported to have said that Donne "for not keeping of accent, deserved hanging.") Donne may have learned from the Elizabethan dramatists the trick of violating strict meter in such a way as to suggest impassioned, energetic utterance while still giving the pleasure of poetic form. Donne's strongly dramatic conception of the lyric is one of the distinguishing marks of his poetry.

"Batter My Heart"

17.9 How does Donne use the formal divisions of the sonnet to develop his argument in the poem?

Answer In the complex and tightly woven argument of this sonnet, Donne makes strategic use of the two main kinds of structural divisions in the sonnet form: the break between the octave and sestet and the breaks between quatrains. The division between octave and sestet traditionally lends itself to a logical or emotional twist in a sonnet, and such a change of direction does occur in the ninth line. The quatrain is used by Donne to develop a series of metaphors which culminates in the rhetorical climax of the final couplet.

In the first eight lines of the poem, the speaker, with much agitation, sets forth his spiritual dilemma before God: although his desire to believe in and to submit to God is strong, his sins and weaknesses are stronger. In despair, he prays to God for radical help in overcoming his doubts. In the octave, then, the speaker emphasizes his own unfaithfulness.

In the ninth line, which initiates the sestet, it is as if the speaker *wants* to change emotional direction, in keeping with the formal division of the poem. The profession of love that begins the line ("Yet dearly I love you") indicates a change of emphasis; it seems as if the speaker will now concentrate on his love rather than his failure to love. But the tenth line returns us to the initial predicament of despair; the speaker finds that he cannot escape from the prison of his own unfaithfulness. He returns to his desperate plea to God to destroy his faithless self so that a new religious soul can emerge. Donne thus uses the traditional twist at the opening of the sestet in an interesting way: by acting out an *attempt* to change rather than a completed change, he mirrors in its structure the main theme of the poem, the inability of the despairing soul to change itself without God's help.

Donne uses the structural divisions of the quatrains to establish a series of interlocking metaphors. The exact nature and significance of the particular metaphors he employs in the poem have been hotly debated by critics, but clearly each quatrain introduces a different image for the relationship between the speaker and God. In the first quatrain, God, the Creator, is asked to "make" the sinner new, as if he were a metal object to be cast into the fire and reforged. In the second quatrain, the speaker imagines himself a city under siege and betrayed by its own ruler, the viceroy Reason, who should be faithful to God but is not. In the final quatrain, the image of the city under siege gives way to an image of the speaker as betrothed to God's enemy, Satan. Each quatrain, then, presents a different, disturbing image of the relationship between the poet and God, all of them connected to the central paradox of the poem: that the speaker must undergo a violent change to destroy his old self so that the new self can be born. The artifact must be reforged, the town recaptured, the woman seized and ravished—all by God.

The rhetorical climax of the poem takes place in the final couplet, in which the speaker encapsulates the central paradox he has been elaborating in the preceding quatrains: that freedom comes only from a total submission to God. Donne skillfully uses the tight structure of the final rhyming couplet to place side by side the antithetical words "enthrall" and "free," "chaste" and "ravish," in order to express one final time a central paradox of Christian freedom and love.

17.10 What is the meaning of the phrase "three-personed God"?

Answer The phrase refers to the concept of the Trinity: God is Father, Son, and Holy Ghost. It is possible that the three verbs used in the first quatrain, "knock," "breathe," and "shine" (which in line 4 become "break," "blow," and "burn"), each can be assigned to one of the persons of the Trinity. For example, the theory has been advanced that the knocking could originate with God the Father, the breathing with the spirit of the Holy Ghost, and the shining with Christ the Son (or Sun). However, although this reading may be plausible, it seems to limit the possible allusions in the case of each verb. For example, in the Book of Revelation, Christ stands at the door and knocks. He says, "If any man hear my voice and open the door, I will come in to him, and will sup with him, and he with me." Thus, scriptural allusion will support the reading that Christ (as well as God the Father) knocks at the door of the sinner's heart. The general reference to the Trinity should be felt and acknowledged without compelling an attempt to assign a "person" to each of the main verbs of the first quatrain.

The idea of the Trinity also seems to determine certain elements of the poem's design. For example, the three active verbs of lines 2 and 4 are followed by tripartite verb phrases ("seek to mend" and "make me new") which reveal or at least emphasize the significance of the first three verbs; similarly, the three persons of the Trinity find their most significant expression in the unity of godhead. The poem also offers three metaphors for the speaker's situation. He is first an artifact in the hands of a maker (the Father in his role as creator); next a town seeking restoration to its true lord (Christ the King, often portrayed as a knight or warrior); and finally a maiden longing for the embrace of her true bridegroom (perhaps the Holy Spirit, which "marries" the divine to the human). Again, the specific identification of these metaphors with persons of the Trinity is less important than the general pattern in which three coalesce into one—in this case, a single vision of renewal through the paradoxes of spiritual violence and violation.

K.L.

SUGGESTED READINGS

Carey, John, *John Donne: Life, Mind and Art* (1981).
Gardner, Helen, ed., *John Donne: A Collection of Critical Essays* (1962).
Kermode, Frank, ed., *Discussions of John Donne* (1962).
Leishman, J. B., *The Monarch of Wit*, revised edition (1962).
Stein, Arnold, *John Donne's Lyrics: The Eloquence of Action* (1962).
Tuve, Rosemond, *Elizabethan and Metaphysical Imagery* (1947).

BEN JONSON

CHRONOLOGY

1572   Born, probably in London. Son of a priest who died before his birth; adopted and raised by his stepfather, a prosperous London bricklayer and builder.

1583   Enters Westminster School in London, one of the largest and best schools of the day. Studies there for six years.

1589   May have attended St. John's College, Cambridge University, for a short time, leaving because of a lack of funds. In any case, soon begins to work as an apprentice to his stepfather.

1592   Around this time serves as a soldier, fighting with an expeditionary force against the Spanish in the Netherlands.

1595   Marries.

1597   Is mentioned as an actor and playwright in Philip Henslowe's company. Is imprisoned for sedition as a coauthor, with Thomas Nashe, of the satiric comedy *The Isle of Dogs* (now lost).

1598   Jonson's first notable comedy, *Every Man in His Humour*, is performed by Shakespeare's acting company; Shakespeare himself has a leading role. Jonson kills fellow actor Gabriel Spencer in a duel; is imprisoned, then released on the intervention of a friendly clergyman. Converts to Roman Catholicism.

1599	Comedy *Every Man out of His Humour* scores a major success; published the following year.
1600	Production of *Cynthias Revels*.
1601	Production of *Poetaster*, a satire ridiculing Johnson's literary and theatrical enemies; an episode in the so-called War of the Theaters.
1603	Death of Queen Elizabeth I; accession of James I, who is to become a patron of Jonson.
1605	Jonson is again imprisoned, this time for his collaboration on the satire *Eastward Ho*. Jonson's first court masque is staged; beginning of a long and lucrative association with the court of James I; until that monarch's death in 1625, Jonson will write about one masque a year. Publication of Jonson's first tragedy, *Sejanus*; now little regarded.
1606–1614	Jonson's main period of creativity: during this period, the plays *Volpone, Epicene, or The Silent Woman, The Alchemist, Catiline* and *Bartholomew Fair* are all produced.
1616	Publication of *The Workes of Benjamin Jonson*, containing Jonson's plays and masques and a collection of lyric poems under the title of *The Forrest*. The use of the folio format and the title "Workes," both of which had previously been reserved for classical authors, indicated Jonson's wish to challenge the great writers of Greece and Rome with his own productions in English. This publication may have inspired the posthumous publication of Shakespeare's plays in folio format; however, it also gained Jonson a good deal of mockery among his colleagues for his pretension. In this year, Jonson is granted a pension by James I.
1618	Jonson makes a walking tour of Scotland; meets poet William Drummond, whose record of their conversations will be published in 1711. They contain many pungent critical comments, including Jonson's famous disparagement of Shakespeare as wanting "art."
1619	Receives M.A. from Oxford University.
1623	Jonson's library is destroyed by fire. He publishes poem in praise of Shakespeare in the First Folio edition of Shakespeare's works.
1625	Death of James I; accession of Charles I. Jonson continues to write plays and masques, but his influence at court and his literary talents are both in decline.
1628	Jonson falls ill and is confined to his home. For the last decade of his life, he will be surrounded by his younger admirers, the "sons of Ben."

1630　　　*Workes of Benjamin Jonson* published in two volumes; the second volume contains, in addition to the plays and masques written after 1616, *Timber, or Discoveries*, a collection of often acute critical observations.

1637　　　Death of Jonson. Buried in Westminster Abbey under the epitaph "O Rare Ben Jonson," supposedly a stonecutter's error for the Latin "Orare Ben Jonson" (i.e., "Pray for Ben Jonson").

ESSAY QUESTIONS WITH ANSWERS

"On my First Son"

18.1 Ben Jonson's elegy for his son is based on the classical model of the epitaph, a brief poem commemorating the death of a personal acquaintance or public figure. How does this model influence the poem's tone?

Answer The classical influence can be felt in the restraint, brevity, and formality of the poem. Like the Roman epitaph, Jonson's poem has some of the qualities of an inscription on a tombstone: it gives the child's name ("child of my right hand," a translation into English of the Hebrew name "Benjamin") and his age ("Seven years thou wert lent to me") and offers a commonplace ("Rest in . . . peace"). Furthermore, the idea of death as the payment of a debt (lines 3–4) is common in epitaphs from ancient Greece and Rome. These features, together with the emphasis on impersonal fate, distinguish Jonson's poem from the typical Christian elegy, with its more impassioned consolations. This "farewell" has a ceremonial, formal quality.

However, there is some oscillation in the poem between the "public" tone of acceptance and resignation and the personal note of grief. The emotion lying just beneath the polished surface produces some of the poem's special poignancy. Although the poem has compression and restraint, typical of the classical epitaph, the occasion is personal, not public; the dead person is not a celebrated figure requiring ceremonial lamentation but the poet's firstborn son, only 7 years old. Thus there is an inherent irony and pathos in the discrepancy between the situation and the poet's treatment of it.

Furthermore, throughout the poem the poet seems to be struggling to maintain a public pose and to curb his personal emotions. The efforts to find comfort by insisting that fate is "just," that life is a debt to be repaid, and that death is an escape from the world's woes are like attempts to hold his grief in check. The exclamation "O could I lose all father now" is an outburst of grief; the attempt to distance himself from the personal relationship by choosing a dignified abstraction ("all father") only increases the poignancy of the outcry. The wish to let go of, and forget, his fatherhood implies the pain which it has brought him. Jonson's calling his son a "piece of poetry" likewise implies a subtle sense of loss and desolation. The epithet juxtaposes the idea of poetry as an activity of "making" (from the Greek *poesis*) with fathering as a similar activity, but creativity in the flesh, the begetting of offspring, is transient in contrast to the enduring creativity of the written word. Thus Jonson's lesser works, his actual poems, survive, while his masterpiece, his son, is lost to the world.

The poem ends with a rejection of personal emotion: "all his vows be such/ As what he loves may never like too much." The poet vows to detach himself, deliberately, from what he instinctively loves. This idea accords with the earlier sentiment "My sin was too much hope of thee, loved boy." "Too much" emotion, Jonson seems to be saying, is imbalanced, immoderate, at odds with a harmonious and measured life. Behind this view is not only Stoic resignation but a psychological defense against the pain of losing a loved one.

Thus the form of the epitaph, with its traditional brevity and cool restraint, helps to contain the poet's grief, making the personal sense of loss more powerful, more moving, precisely because it is understated.

18.2   Many of the sentiments in the poem are commonplaces: life is a vale of woe; fate is stern and exacting; the dead should "rest in soft peace." Furthermore, the style is relatively plain, without elaborate comparisons or descriptions. How does Jonson rescue the poem from triteness?

Answer   The epithet in the first line of the poem, "thou child of my right hand," is rich in connotation. It suggests, first of all, the homely idea of a "right-hand man," an indispensable partner in life. In addition, the words signify Benjamin's position as the poet's male heir, the eldest son who occupied the favored station ("right" having traditional associations with good fortune) of chief lineal descendant. Thus, Jonson immediately establishes, in this deceptively simple phrase of direct address, a sense of his son's precious significance.

The metaphor of life as something lent, again a very simple and commonplace way of expressing the idea of mortality, enriches the poem by its subtle introduction of Christian belief into an otherwise predominantly Stoic epitaph. The line "Seven years thou wert lent to me, and I thee pay" suggests a God-given life and a God-ordained death. Though Jonson calls the lender "fate," he seems to be alluding at the same time to Christian providence.

The idea of a Christian framework is reinforced by the pun on "just" in the phrase "on the just day." Here "just" seems to mean not only "precise" or "exact" but "fair." This "just day" is a day of justice adumbrating the Day of Judgment, when all Christian souls are called before their maker. The condensed language of the poem affords room for such complex notions as Stoicism and faith, even within the limits of a single word.

The final couplet of the poem appears to offer a neat, pointed conclusion with its patterned alliteration and antithesis ("As what he loves may never like too much"). But a subtle contrast is offered here, for Jonson takes almost synonymous terms ("love" and "like") and poses them against each other, creating a kind of puzzle or paradox where we might expect a simple summation. The "love" seems to refer to something abstract, impersonal, philosophical—perhaps the universal emotion felt by all fathers for all sons, or the Christian *agape*, which ideally exists among all living people. In contrast, "like" implies a more homely, personal, instinctive emotion. It is this latter feeling which the poet vows to reject, because it violates his Stoic moderation and because it has caused him so much pain.

The figurative language of the poem demonstrates that, though Jonson's style is simple and his thought unremarkable, the poem is not unsophisticated. Apparently simple statements enrich the emotional texture of the poem by introducing subtle connotations and tensions.

18.3 "On my First Son" is elaborately punctuated and phrased, containing many commas as well as rhetorical questions, direct address, and exclamation. Although many Renaissance texts were erratically punctuated by casual printers or editors, Jonson edited his works himself, lavishing care on such matters as commas and question marks. Analyze the significance of the forms of statement and of the punctuated rhythms in this poem.

Answer By means of punctuation and sentence structure, Jonson indicates how the poem is to be read in terms of rhythms and inflections, the punctuation marks serving some of the function of stage directions for a dramatic performance. Thus the rhetorical phrasings contribute to the ceremonial aspect of the poem as a formal elegiac oration and to its emotional resonance as the utterance of a grieving father.

The formal tone of a public speaker is suggested by such devices as the opening apostrophe of the dead boy ("Farewell, thou child . . .") and the rhetorical questions in the second quatrain ("for why/ Will man lament . . . ?"). These are the consciously dramatic techniques of public oratory. Furthermore, the lines move generally in the stately, pausing rhythms of formal speech. The short explanation ("O could I lose all father now") is effective partly because it disrupts the smooth controlled rhythm maintained throughout most of the poem.

Commas are also important as a means of introducing a personal tone, again by varying the rhythms. For example, the comma before "and joy" in the first line breaks the smooth flow of direct address, putting emphasis on a confession of personal feeling after the formality of the epithet. Likewise, the commas around "and asked" in the ninth line make the direct address truly direct after the stock imperative "Rest in soft peace." The word "asked" posits a relationship between the dead child and the reader or between the epitaph and the bystander. The child cannot respond to the question of the bystander but the epitaph answers for him, thus dramatizing the idea of child-as-poem, that is, a "piece of poetry." In general the pointing of the poem does just that, points up the competing rhythms of formal oratory and private lament, conveying complexity through changes in tempo and sudden pauses.

"To Penshurst"

18.4 "To Penshurst" was written to celebrate the estate of the Sidney family, who were members of the great landed aristocracy in sixteenth-century England. In praising the place and its inhabitants, Jonson uses the technique of the catalogue, itemizing at length the natural features of the estate, including livestock, game, and agricultural produce. What is the effect of this cataloguing?

Answer The most obvious effect of the cataloguing is to convey the idea of abundance. The good things which spring from the fruitful cornucopia of the estate are not merely plentiful but useful. The produce contributes to the gracious social life of the Sidneys in their hospitable feasts. Thus, the values associated with the wildlife and foodstuffs include not only abundance and richness, but human generosity and communal joy.

The many details drawn from nature combine to suggest a view of nature as responsive to human wishes and designs. The land overflows and teems with living things, providing food without labor to the dwellers on the estate. The partridge "is willing to be killed," carp "run into" the net, pike "themselves betray," eels "leap on land/ Before the fisher, or into his hand." Nature thus cooperates with man, offering up its plenty for his use.

A third aspect of the catalogue is its implicit suggestion of a natural order. The fruits do not merely accumulate on the boughs—rather, "each in his time doth come"; likewise the deer is "seasoned,"—comes in its proper season. This orderly progression of growth and activity, together with the cooperativeness of nature, evokes a classical, pagan idea of perfection: the golden age of natural virtue and natural harmony.

All three themes associated with the catalogue—plenty, usefulness, order—imply that Penshurst is a type of paradise, an Eden, where food comes without labor and a climate of festival joy prevails. Jonson praises this world not with empty generalization but with vivid particulars, giving us the sense of a world crowded with good things, from bullocks and kine to apples and cheeses.

18.5 Identify some of the classical allusions in the poem, and explain their function.

Answer The poem opens with a series of allusions to figures from classical myth: dryads (wood nymphs), Pan (the god of pipes and sylvan merrymaking), Bacchus (the god of wine), and satyrs and fauns (the goatish followers of Bacchus and Pan). All of these are deities, major or minor, who preside over the woods, engaging in the festive pastimes of eating, drinking, dancing, and music making. In the poem these references elevate the setting: Penshurst is an estate graced by spirits of joy and gods of festival. Thus, the allusions are a form of compliment which contributes to Jonson's general purpose of praising the Sidney family by eulogizing their estate. By showing that the gods themselves consort with the Sidneys, Jonson suggests that Penshurst and its inhabitants have achieved the kind of classical beauty, based on moderation, harmony, and gracefulness, thought to be characteristic of ancient Greece and Rome.

Jonson finds another means of complimenting the family by his graceful and subtle allusions to Sir Philip Sidney, the poet. He mentions in his catalogue of woodland beauties the tree planted "At his great birth, where all the Muses met" (line 14). The Muses have congregated at Penshurst as at another Mount Parnassus to consecrate the ground to poetry. Jonson also alludes to "many a sylvan," who, like the pastoral swains in Sidney's *Arcadia*, cut their names in the tree's bark. The "sylvans" thus evoke the golden world of natural perfection associated with the pastoral genre and, specifically, with Sidney's pastoral romance.

Finally, Jonson embellishes his account of King James's visit to the estate with an allusion to "thy Penates." The radiance and warmth of the blazing hearths at Penshurst are transferred metaphorically to the Roman household gods who preside there:

> . . . they saw thy fires
> Shine bright on every hearth, as the desires
> Of thy Penates had been set on flame
> To entertain them;
>
> (lines 77–80)

The reference to the Penates evokes the Roman ideal of hospitality, the extension of comfort and welcome to the *hospes*, the guest or stranger, who stops in his wandering at a place of rest.

The classical allusions are a means of introducing into the poem the ideals of beauty, poetic inspiration, natural perfection, and gracious conduct associated with the Greek and Roman worlds. Penshurst thus enshrines within its precincts all the best qualities of the classical past.

18.6 Discuss the structural and thematic significance of the following lines:

> Now, Penshurst, they that will proportion thee
> With other edifices, when they see
> Those proud, ambitious heaps, and nothing else,
> May say their lords have built, but thy lord dwells.
> (lines 99–102)

Answer These lines, which conclude "To Penshurst," mirror effectively the opening lines of the poem. At both beginning and end the poet directly addresses the estate and contrasts the purely architectural ornament of other great houses (which are built "to envious show" and are "proud, ambitious heaps") with the natural ornaments of Penshurst. In the opening lines, Jonson stresses the elemental virtues of the estate: "Thou joy'st in better marks of soil, of air,/Of wood, of water: therein thou art fair." These decorations, the handiwork of nature, exceed the artificial splendors of "polished pillars, or a roofe of gold."

At the end of the poem the contrast deepens, so that the antithesis is not merely between art and nature but between a sterile, external beauty and a creative, inner beauty deriving from the human inhabitants of Penshurst. The final line of the poem, "their lords have built, but thy lord dwells," poses the two sets of values against each other with epigrammatic brevity. The distinction is between a mere building, with its inanimate physical beauties of form and material, and a true dwelling, whose beauty radiates from the life lived within its walls. Thus, Jonson lays stress not only on the natural but on the specifically human "ornaments" of the estate: the virtues of warmth, hospitality, harmony, and spontaneity which, throughout the poem, have been amply illustrated through anecdote and description.

The conclusion of the poem suggests a moral polarity: pride versus humility, ambitious striving versus virtuous serenity. It also suggests a philosophical position, a view of life. The word "proportion" ("they that will proportion thee"), though in context simply a verb meaning "compare," suggests the connotations of the noun as well. The life of the Sidney family at Penshurst displays "proportion." Contained in the word are the ideas of harmony, order, balance, and moderation which Jonson, devoted to the classical idea of the "golden mean," so highly valued and often introduced into his poetry.

Volpone

18.7 *Volpone* has a complicated plot, with deceptions piling on top of deceptions as each fortune hunter falls into the hands of Volpone and his assistant, Mosca. The action of the play is consequently both episodic and farcical, consisting of a mad scramble on the part of the scheming pair to create the "scenes" which will serve their ends. Given its rather chaotic activity, how does Jonson manage to unify the play?

Answer   The unity of the play derives mainly from its thematic consistency, with certain recurrent ideas governing the entire action of the drama. For example, avarice is a continuous motif in the play: the motive of greed propels the action forward as the characters succumb, one by one, to their obsession for gold. Linguistically, too, *Volpone* exhibits an obsessive quality, the repeated references to gold and material riches binding together the disparate characters and episodes. Almost all the characters speak the same language and inhabit the same psychological territory. Gold, the "son of Sol" which animates all motion and activity, is at the center of the play's universe.

Another major theme in the play is acting and theatrical disguise. The sickroom with its curtained bed, the mountebank's stage, and the courtroom become stages for the enactment of plays-within-the-play. The many references to disguise and the actual costume changes of Volpone and Mosca reinforce the theatrical motif, which suggests that man is an actor, a role player, and a stage manager. In *Volpone* natural, spontaneous action is almost impossible; nearly everything is orchestrated and scripted according to the master plots of the two "directors." (Only Celia and Bonario act according to their own impulses, and in so doing they disrupt the schemes of Volpone and Mosca.) The idea of acting is thus associated with deception, "putting one over" on the audience, and also with obsession, the drive to repeat and even outdo a past performance. It is further linked with the idea of "playing," in the sense of make-believe and fantasy. Volpone and Mosca are not only consummate actors and con men but game players enjoying their sport and compulsively exhibiting their skill.

A final theme is bestiality, specifically the animal nature of human appetites and passions. Just as reiterated allusions to gold and playacting imply a kind of obsession, so the allegorical names of the characters project an image of man as controlled by and victim of animal instinct. Volpone the fox, attended by Mosca, his buzzing housefly, pretends to be a rotting carcass in order to attract, and despoil, the various birds of prey (Voltore the vulture, Corvino the crow, and so on) who flock around him. Volpone himself states this theme quite explicitly:

> . . . Now, now my clients
> Begin their visitation! Vulture, kite,
> Raven, and gorcrow, all my birds of prey,
> That think me turning carcass, now they come.
> (Act I, Scene ii, lines 87–90)

By focusing on the wiliness of the fox and the greedy hunger of the birds, Jonson reduces the complexities of human character to a few base motives.

Naming and reiteration lend the play the radical simplicity of an admonitory fable. Man is a lover of gold, a compulsive actor, an animal of one kind or another; and he will inevitably suffer the consequences of his obsessive follies.

18.8　In his preface to the play, Jonson apologizes for the unconventional ending of *Volpone* in the following way: "And, though my catastrophe may, in the strict rigor of comic law, meet with censure . . . it was done of industry . . . it being the office of a comic poet to imitate justice." In light of this statement, analyze the concluding scene of *Volpone*.

Answer　Jonson's stated intention is "to imitate justice." In the Renaissance all literature was, theoretically at least, didactic and moral; and the specific purpose of comedy, in Jonson's view, was to make vice abhorrent by making it both unattractive and ridiculous. In giving comedy this satiric role, Jonson felt he was following classical precedents; and the influence of models from closer to home, such as the medieval morality plays, may be discerned in *Volpone* as well. Jonson has written not a genial romantic comedy, gently mocking the folly of love, but a biting satire, teaching the dangers of avarice even as it entertains. Thus, the courtroom scene and the allotment of punishments to schemers and greedy fools express Jonson's ethical intentions in the play.

Of course the ending of the play is not merely an exercise in theory. Its harshness and aggressive energy exceed the formal rationale the playwright offers, betraying his temperamental bias and personal philosophy. Jonson's denouement is less moral or moralistic than it is profoundly pessimistic. In the final scenes he exposes humanity as fundamentally weak, dishonest, and grasping, with even the Avocatori compromised by their readiness to be swayed by Mosca's apparent wealth. The comedy of the play is not of the forgiving kind for, as the ending shows, every fool must pay the price of his folly.

It is the severity of Jonson's vision that leads him to violate "the strict rigor of comic law," that is, the conventional formula which demands a happy ending. In most comedies the ending consists of reconciliations between old and young, the banishment of villains, and the celebration of weddings. The courtroom scene with which Volpone concludes varies significantly from this formula, retaining only the usual punishment of villains—who in this case constitute practically the whole cast of characters. The final emphasis is on the negative aspects of human nature, so much so that recognitions and unions would seem implausible among these characters in this setting.

Though we have laughed at the characters in the course of the comic proceedings, the grim sentencing at the end brings us back to the moral universe. The punishments meted out are intended to fit the crimes. Mosca, the parasite, pays for his slavish flattery and pandering by becoming a literal slave in a ship's galley. Voltore, who has betrayed the law, is disbarred; Corbaccio, who has betrayed his son, is sent to a monastery where he must renounce all worldly attachments; and Corvino, who has shunned the opprobrium of the cuckold, is condemned to the pillory to wear the cuckold's donkey ears. Volpone, who has fraudulently feigned sickness, is forced by the irons to assume the cramped and paralytic posture he has been pretending all along.

The young "lovers"—Bonario, the good youth, and Celia, the good wife—cannot wed. Celia must return to her father's house and to a life of celibacy. The world of Volpone does not permit young love and chivalry to flower into a fruitful union; rather, Venice in the play is a society based on barter and deception, which must be controlled (just barely, at the eleventh hour) by a court of law, a court which itself has been shown to be scarcely immune to the temptation of gold. The corruption of Jonson's Venice reflects the seventeenth-century English view of Italy as a sinkhole of vice. Italianate villains and "Machiavels," with their oily hypocrisy and fantastic intrigues, were considered the epitome of evil. But the dark vision of human nature expressed in the play goes beyond xenophobic caricature: these decadent Venetians implicate all of us, suggesting certain inescapable drives and passions which know no nationality.

The effect of the final arraignment is stern and abrupt; the audience is pulled up short by this serious judgment meted out to characters who have been amusing and entertaining. Indeed, Volpone and Mosca have been almost attractive, playing out their games with contagious vitality and energy. The end of the play thus emphasizes the didactic and allegorical quality of *Volpone*, which, though present throughout, has been submerged at times by the surface farce. Jonson's harsh ending accords with his austere conception of the comic poet as a judge of humanity, expressing at the same time his pessimism about human nature and his acute sense of human limitations and liabilities.

18.9   Mosca, in Act III, Scene i, appears on stage alone and delivers a self-congratulatory soliloquy, part of which goes as follows:

> Success hath made me wanton. I could skip
> Out of my skin, now, like a subtle snake,
> I am so limber. O! your parasite
> Is a most precious thing, dropped from above,
>
> . . . .
>
> . . . your fine elegant rascal, that can rise
> And stoop, almost together, like an arrow;
> Shoot through the air as nimbly as a star;
> Turn short as doth a swallow; and be here,
> And there, and here, and yonder, all at once;
> Present to any humor, all occasion;
> And change a visor swifter than a thought,
> This is the creature had the art born with him.
>   (lines 6–9; 23–30)

Analyze the language of this soliloquy. What is its thematic significance?

Answer   The reference to "a visor" at the close of the quoted passage alludes to the idea of playacting, so strongly represented throughout *Volpone*: Mosca's ability to mask himself at will makes him a quick-change artist, a master of disguise and impersonation. But the other images in the soliloquy suggest not just impersonation but metamorphosis, not just a talent for false appearances but the power to *be* an entirely new creature, in the process transcending the limitations of reality and giving form to fantasy.

The simile of the snake, for example, suggests the idea of shedding a self just as a snake discards its skin. The phrase "dropped from above" suggests a godlike incarnation; and the comparisons to an arrow and a star evoke the image of an Ariel-like sprite, untrammeled by the laws of physical nature and free to traverse time and space at will. Thus Mosca's fantasy is one of omnipotence, omnipresence, omniscience: he can be everywhere at once, in any guise he chooses.

These "overreaching" fantasies make the scheming servant a vital and attractive figure, for he represents the wish to play at life, freed from the bondage of dull reality. At the same time the fantasies of omnipotence and metamorphosis are sinful, deriving from egomania and linked with the vices of avarice and pride. They are also, of course, comic in their extravagance, especially in the mouth of Mosca; for all his boasting, he remains nothing more than Volpone's parasite, a contemptible figure. In the end, Mosca is shown to be not the god of all he surveys but the slave of his own passions.

18.10 *Volpone* has many subplots, including Volpone's attempted seduction of Celia and the bartering of Bonario's inheritance by his father, Corbaccio. The subplot least connected to the legacy hunt is that centering on the activities of Sir Politic and Lady Wouldbe, the English visitors to Venice. What is the contribution of the Wouldbe scenes to the play?

Answer The Wouldbe scenes, though only loosely connected to the "avarice" plot, are closely linked to the larger theme of human folly and vanity. They play out the game of delusion and fantasy in a lighter key, contributing comic byplay and topical satire to Jonson's fable of greed.

As pure comedy, the interchanges between Lady Wouldbe and Volpone and between Sir Pol and Peregrine constitute an absurd drama of cross-purposes. The foolish lady, with her *sententiae*, maxims, and pseudo-learned quotations, outwits the clever fox, becoming the innocent instrument of torment to the schemer who torments all others. Sir Pol, repeating parrotlike the gossip of Continental spies and scandal in high places, parades foolishly before Peregrine, the sharp-eyed hawk and ironic commentator. In both cases the language becomes a vehicle for satire, Lady Wouldbe's endless adages revealing the pretensions to learning of the upstart gentry, Sir Pol's tales of espionage mirroring the patent absurdity of the seventeenth-century press.

But beyond the incidental humor and satire which the Wouldbes introduce, the so-called English subplot is a variation on the major themes of delusion and metamorphosis, albeit played out at the bottom end of the comic spectrum as slapstick farce. When Lady Wouldbe, told by Mosca that her husband has been seen in a gondola with another woman, assaults Peregrine as the guilty female, she is acting the part of the deluded gull. Although her mistaking a man for a woman is entirely ludicrous, her error reflects the human propensity for delusion based on fantasy and fear.

Sir Pol's comeuppance likewise reflects a central theme, that of metamorphosis. Told by Peregrine that he himself has been named as a spy by the high court of Venice, he promptly adopts the disquise of a tortoise, lying flat on the ground and kicking his arms and legs beneath his "shell." The wish to slip out of one's skin, to change shape at will, to make one's fantasies flesh through disguise or transmutation is here given a ludicrous treatment.

Thus the Wouldbe subplot is not irrelevant decoration. Indeed the farcical doings of the unfortunate English pair enrich the play, clarifying its major issues through cartoon sketches.

B.S.

SUGGESTED READINGS

Barish, Jonas, ed., *Ben Jonson* (1963).

Herford, C. H., and Percy Simpson, eds., *Ben Jonson's Works*, Vols. I–XI (1925–1952).

Kernan, Alvin B., and Richard B. Young, eds., *The Yale Ben Jonson* (1962–   ).

Levin, Harry, *Ben Jonson: Selected Works* (1938).

Trimpi, Wesley, *Ben Jonson's Poems: A Study of the Plain Style* (1962).

ROBERT HERRICK

C H R O N O L O G Y

1591	Born in London. Son of Nicholas Herrick, a goldsmith and banker and a member of a distinguished family of Leicestershire landowners, and Julian Stone Herrick.
1592	Nicholas Herrick dies in a fall from a window only two days after making his will. He has been known to be ill and despondent; suicide is suspected. However, it is not proved, so his property, which might otherwise have been subject to seizure by the government, passes to his heirs.
1607	Robert apprenticed to his uncle, Sir William Herrick, a noted London goldsmith. Nothing is known about his previous schooling.
1613	Abandoning his apprenticeship, Herrick enters St. John's College, Cambridge University, as a fellow commoner (a student of means).
1617	To reduce expenses, Herrick transfers to Trinity Hall, Cambridge. Receives B.A.
1620	Receives M.A. May have returned to London at this time and joined the circle of young scholars, poets, and wits around Ben Jonson (the "sons of Ben").
1623	Is ordained as deacon and priest in the Church of England.
1627	Travels as chaplain to the duke of Buckingham in an expedition to capture the Ile de Rhé from France. However, the expedition ends in complete failure, dashing Buckingham's hopes for advancement at court and probably

dooming any such hopes Herrick may have entertained; a year later, Buckingham will be assassinated.

1630   Appointed vicar of Dean Prior by King Charles I; it is a small country parish in Devonshire, where Herrick will serve for most of the rest of his life. Themes of rural life will figure prominently in his poetry.

1640   Returns to London briefly, bearing with him a collection of his poems. Under the name of *Severall Poems* it is registered for publication but not printed at this time. Herrick returns to Dean Prior.

1642   Outbreak of English Civil War. Herrick is a royalist; however, the people of his parish are predominantly antiroyalist.

1647   Herrick is removed from his post as vicar because of his royalist sympathies. Probably returns to London and lives there with relatives until 1660.

1648   *Hesperides*, Herrick's single volume of poems, is published. Although he will live for a quarter of a century longer, his poetic career is probably over; only a handful of poems other than those in *Hesperides* have ever been attributed to him. *Hesperides* is not frequently reprinted in the years just after its first publication, but this may be because the first printing was unusually large.

1660   Restoration of the monarchy under Charles II. Herrick petitions successfully to have his vicarage at Dean Prior restored; he returns there and remains for the rest of his life.

1674   Death of Herrick. He is buried at Dean Prior, evidently in an unmarked grave; the exact location of his remains is therefore unknown.

ESSAY QUESTIONS WITH ANSWERS

19.1   Like Andrew Marvell's "To His Coy Mistress" and Ben Jonson's "Come, My Celia," Herrick's "Corinna's Going A-Maying" exemplifies the *carpe diem* motif. *Carpe diem*, a phrase from Horace's Latin *Odes*, means "seize the day"; in a *carpe diem* poem, someone, usually a virgin, is urged to realize the pleasures of the present moment because youth, beauty, and life itself are so brief. In Herrick's poem, Corinna is urged to come "a-Maying" with the poet. What is involved in this activity?

Answer   The traditional May Day festivity, in which boughs of white haw-thorn blossom are brought indoors, has its roots in pagan rituals celebrating the return of spring and the rebirth of the earth's natural vigor. As "each field turns a street" (that is, becomes as populous as a city thoroughfare) and "each street a park," the fertility of nature renews not only the woods and meadows but even the life of the town and its citizens.

In Herrick's poem, this renewal is seen as almost a consecration of everyday existence; to be absent from this ceremony would be to sacrilegiously deny the potency and beauty of the natural world: " 'tis sin,/ Nay, profanation to keep in." Although Herrick was a priest of the Church of England, the religious terminology ("hymns," "Devotion," "An ark, a tabernacle") seems to acknowledge the legitimacy of the kind of pagan nature worship to which this observance harks back, as though Herrick, unlike his Puritan contemporaries, wanted to incorporate in Christianity, not exclude, the energy and wonder of the ancient ritual.

Like other *carpe diem* poems, "Corinna's Going A-Maying" implies that a full response to the natural world includes enjoyment of one's sexual vitality. Like spring itself, the boys and girls who pair off in stanza 4 are "budding." Corinna, who like the sun or Aurora (the goddess of dawn) must rise from her bed, will assume not merely her clothes but her "foliage," and emerging from her house, she will be "like the springtime, fresh and green,/ And sweet as Flora" (the Roman goddess of flowers). She becomes not merely the audience of the poet's admonition but an embodiment of the very qualities she is urged to honor and enjoy.

19.2 Many *carpe diem* poems seem to threaten as well as cajole. In Andrew Marvell's "To His Coy Mistress," for example, harrowing images like "Time's winged chariot" and "deserts of vast eternity" serve as dark reminders of the pressures of time and death. Do any such reminders and undertones exist in Herrick's treatment of the *carpe diem* theme?

Answer   The tone of "Corinna's Going A-Maying" markedly differs from that of such poems as Marvell's; for most of the poem, the tone is playful without being sardonic. A kind of good-humored hectoring goes on, as the poet issues a series of imperatives to the lady: "Get up," "see," "come," "wash," "dress," "mark," "take," and so on. He instructs her in the urgency of nature's claims by playfully calling her a "sweet slug-a-bed." Even the accusations of "sin" and "profanation" are cushioned by the humorous reversal of Christian terminology and by the reassuring chime of the couplet (" 'tis sin,/ Nay, profanation to keep in" [lines 11–12]).

The last stanza of the poem does, however, convey a sense of the darker awareness that lurks beneath the cavalier attitude of the poet. For in this stanza, the poet seems to admit that his flirtation with paganism is a "harmless folly" in the face of the process of time and death. It is in this stanza that the poet reminds us (and Corinna) that we can never halt the processes of decay, that eventually "All love, all liking, all delight/ Lies drowned with us in endless night" (lines 67–68). And in this stanza, the comforting effect of the earlier couplets' rhymes is disturbed by a more sinister final rhyme: "decaying/ a-Maying."

Unlike the previous stanzas' final couplets (such as "day/ May," "praying/ a-Maying," and "staying/ a-Maying"), this final rhyme emphasizes the darker side of the link between humanity and nature, which elsewhere in the poem seems a positive tie—as a part of nature, we, too, are subject to decay. In the midst of May, we are reminded of the inevitability of winter.

The poet does not dwell on this more ominous note. Yet this shift into the minor key makes it clear that the cheerful note of confidence in most of Herrick's poem does not depend on obliviousness to humanity's plight. The spirited affirmation of grace and pleasure becomes, if anything, firmer and more resonant through this hint of darkness.

K.L.

SUGGESTED READINGS

Braden, Gordon, *The Classics and English Renaissance Poetry: Three Case Studies* (1978).

Brooks, Cleanth, *The Well-Wrought Urn* (1947).

Moorman, Frederic, *Robert Herrick: A Biographical and Critical Study* (1962).

Rollin, Roger B., and J. Max Patrick, eds., *"Trust to Good Verses": Herrick Tercentenary Essays* (1978).

GEORGE HERBERT

C H R O N O L O G Y

1593	Born at Montgomery, Shropshire (near the Welsh border). Son of Richard and Magdalene Herbert, both of ancient noble families. His elder brother Edward will also be a notable poet.
1596	Death of Richard Herbert. After this time, George will live with his mother in Eyton, Oxford, and London.
1599	Probable date of meeting between Magdalene Herbert and poet John Donne, who will be a major influence on George Herbert's poetry.
1604	Enters Westminster School, where he will study until 1609; a good scholar, he will receive honors for his work.
1609	Magdalene Herbert marries Sir John Danvers, who will become a friend and patron of George. Enters Trinity College, Cambridge, where he will have a career spanning almost two decades.
1610	Sends his mother two sonnets proposing the love of God as the most suitable subject for poetry.
1612	Receives B.A. Writes Latin poetry in commemoration of the death of Prince Henry.
1614	Becomes a fellow of Trinity College. In 1617, he will become an assistant lecturer, and, in 1618, a full lecturer.
1620	Named public orator of Cambridge, a post calling for the composition and delivery of speeches and poetry on ceremonial occasions, generally in Latin.

The position is often a stepping-stone to political office; Herbert's predecessor became a secretary of state.

1623   Delivers an oration during a visit to the university by Prince Charles criticizing the current war with Spain. This may have damaged Herbert's chances of a successful political career.

1624   Serves briefly as a member of Parliament. Is granted a share in the living at the parish of Llandinam. Probably ordained deacon late in the year.

1625   By this date, Herbert has probably decided to abandon hopes of a political career and enter holy orders, perhaps influenced by the deaths, within two years, of the duke of Richmond, the marquis of Hamilton, and King James I, all of whom Herbert had hoped would support him. He is still officially the orator of Cambridge, although he is rarely in Cambridge.

1626   Granted the living of Leighton Bromswold parish; probably begins work on rebuilding the church there, which has fallen into disrepair, using his own funds and those of friends.

1627   Death of Magdalene Herbert. Herbert's Latin poems, *Memoriae Matris Sacrum*, are registered for publication, along with John Donne's sermon delivered at Magdalene's memorial service.

1628   Resigns oratorship. Probably lives with Henry Danvers, the earl of Danby, at his house in Wiltshire.

1629   Marries Jane Danvers, the daughter of the earl of Danby.

1630   Ordained priest. Appointed rector of Bemerton, a small country parish. Begins active life as rector, including the rebuilding of the rectory; gains local reputation as a deeply charitable minister. Also undertakes care of his orphaned nieces. Most of the poems in *The Temple* are being composed at this time.

1633   Death of Herbert. He gives his literary remains to his friend Nicholas Ferrar. Later in the year, *The Temple* is published at Cambridge.

1640   *Outlandish Proverbs*, an anthology of folk sayings from several European languages, probably compiled and edited by Herbert, is published.

1652   *Herbert's Remains* published, including *A Priest to the Temple, or the Country Person*, his manual for parish priests.

1670   Publication of Izaak Walton's *Life of Herbert*, which depicts Herbert as a greatly beloved, pious priest who abandoned a promising career in the "world" for a humble life of service; still the major source of information about Herbert's life.

ESSAY QUESTIONS WITH ANSWERS

"The Collar"

20.1 What is the basic dramatic situation of the poem? Why is the speaker so upset?

Answer Although the tone of Herbert's poetry is often exquisitely and subtly modulated, "The Collar" begins with a Donne-like dramatic gesture: the speaker pounds his fist on the table and declares his resolve to change his present unjust situation. However, it is probably more accurate to say that he dramatically narrates the tale of his rebellion, for the experience is cast in the past tense even as the recollected emotion is passionately reexperienced in the poem. The speaker reenacts for us his internal struggle: he feels that he has been chained to an ideal of service (his "cage" or "rope of sands") that has led only to misery ("no harvest but a thorn"). He tells his heart to rebel against this situation, to seek pleasure rather than duty, tranquillity (the tranquillity of the relaxed will, at least) rather than struggle. In fact, the title of the poem, "The Collar," supplies a general metaphor for the confining predicament the speaker feels he must escape.

The "collar" of the title, however, suggests not only a means of restraint but a clerical collar, like that which Herbert, as an Anglican priest, would have worn. The poem dramatizes not merely a rebellion against duty or a complaint about injustice but also the intense spiritual struggle of a poet-priest who feels that all his spiritual and creative endeavors have been ignored by God. He is sick of being one whose service brings no rewards, whether the "fruit" of material prosperity and pleasure (line 17) or the "bays" (line 14) of the laurel wreath which honors a poet's achievement. The laws of the church have imprisoned him, the speaker tells himself. The theological niceties of his calling ("Thy cold dispute") and its preoccupation with mortality ("thy death's-head") have consigned him to a mental prison, and he feels it is time to forsake the ties of the church. Denying his previous self-dedication, he reassumes the prerogative of choice and asserts that his "lines [of poetry] and life are free."

In the final four lines of the poem, however, the poet's angry argument with himself ends as another voice enters the poem. As the poet raves, he thinks he hears a voice calling him back to the fold. It addresses him with the utmost simplicity: "Child!" The nature of this call is ambiguous: it may rebuke the poet's unruly petulance, soothe his spirit with paternal solicitude, or even summon him to a renewal of his priestly vocation (literally, his "calling"). Yet the alacrity and sudden calm of the response, "My lord," suggest that, here at least, obedience is also love and that the poet has returned not only to God but to himself.

20.2 Discuss the relationship between structure and meaning in the poem.

Answer The poem can be divided roughly into three parts: the heart's angry questions and gesture of rebellion (lines 1–16); the poet's advice to himself to escape his bondage (lines 17–32); and the call of God and response of the poet (lines 33–36). These major divisions, in turn, correspond to particular types of sentences: the first section is rife with short questions; the second is composed largely of imperatives; the third is a simple declarative sentence.

The structure and sentence patterns mirror the flow of emotion in the poem. The heart's anxieties and grievances, conveyed in the rapid questions of the first section, give way to the imperatives of the assertive, rebellious part of the poet's nature (perhaps his will). The structural break before the final four lines of the poem reinforces the major change in the speaker's emotion. The poet now calls the questions and answers of the first two parts his "ravings"; the tone of the poem modulates into calm and quiet, just as the questions and imperatives are replaced by a simple description of a call and response.

The asymmetry of these structural divisions (thirty-two lines devoted to the speaker's "ravings" as opposed to four describing God's call) is also significant. It suggests how easily the simplest divine utterance, the power of God's love expressed by no more than a single word, outweighs the wordy and trivial grumblings of human desire.

20.3 The collar in the title of the poem is an image of both bondage and clerical service. How does this double symbolism of images appear elsewhere in the poem?

Answer Until the final four lines of the poem, it is possible to read "The Collar" as not specifically religious; the speaker's crisis or rebellion can be seen in more general terms. However, what is true of the poem's title is true of other images as well: the more obvious secular significance of certain images is shadowed by a less obvious religious significance. In fact, the speaker's apparent blindless to this dimension of meaning is in itself a manifestation of his wrongheadedness, a clue that he is misreading the signs of his own life.

For example, on the one hand, the metaphors of harvest in the poem's first section—the fruit, wine, and corn (the British word for "wheat")—create an image of a sumptuous feast that the poet feels he has been missing; the "board" in line 1 seems to be a dinner table upon which this feast might be served. But a second reading suggests another meaning, for the board is also the altar at which the eucharist is celebrated, and the corn and wine are symbols of the body and blood of Christ. The harvest of thorns lamented by the poet recalls the crown of thorns worn by Christ and thus conveys not merely sterility but tribulation as a passage to eternal life.

Thus, almost every image in the poem can be seen in two ways—as despairing evidence of the poet's outcast situation and as the very means of his salvation if he would only see beneath the surface to the redemptive potential which an allegorical reading of the image offers. The narrative of rebellion is also a narrative of potential religious salvation, and the sound of God's voice at the end of the poem is in fact anticipated in the double significance of the imagery.

"Jordan (I)"

20.4 "Jordan (I)" is a poem about poetry. What kind of poetry is Herbert criticizing? What kind is he advocating?

Answer In "Jordan (I)" Herbert questions both the style and the subject matter of his poetic contemporaries. Although conventional love poetry is his most evident target, the issues he raises strike at the very conception of poetry implied by the practice of other writers. The series of facetious (and rhetorical) questions in the first two stanzas implies his fundamental distaste for the styles and topics he evokes.

The specific poetic conventions he ridicules include complex, difficult syntax and structure (the "winding stair" of line 3), such as one might find in the poetry of Donne; the pastoral landscape and romance elements ("enchanted groves," "sudden arbours," and "purling streams"), which one might find not only in much Renaissance love poetry but also in Spenser's epic, *The Faerie Queene*; and the "veil'd" sense caught "at two removes" of allegorical poetry. The implied opposite of such poetry of artifice is a plainer, "truer" poetry which need not invent pastoral scenes to beautify its sense nor construct allegorical layers to enhance its authority. The empty, decorative beauty of conventional poetry is opposed to the beauty of simple truth, and the poet's question "Is there in truth no beauty?" implies its own answer: there *is* in truth a kind of beauty, quite different from the preciosity, prettiness, or needless complexity of artifice.

In the final stanza Herbert asserts the claims of a poetry which expresses love and obedience to God rather than infatuation with any earthly lover. Rather than bowing before the "painted chair" of stanza 1 (an earthly throne, whose worldly occupant may owe his dignity and glory to the "painting" of flattery), with humility and candor the poet praises God, the king whose "true chair" is the divine throne. (A Platonic argument against poetry also underlies these lines. In Book X of *The Republic*, Plato asserts that all earthly phenomena—including chairs, of course—are mere imitations of an unchanging eternal reality. The poet, concerned with appearances, is merely "painting," or imitating, imitations and hence presents the truth only "at two removes.") Simplicity and plainness are advocated on religious as well as aesthetic grounds: if it is merely vulgar to praise earthly love with elegant artifice, it would be almost sacrilegious to praise God in this trumped-up manner. The plain style is a correlative of the humility of the poet-priest: the abandonment of artistic subterfuge represents a gesture of sincerity and faith.

Nevertheless, the lingering question remains whether the beauty of truth needs poetry at all. If truth is most compelling in its utter nakedness, does it require any adornment or representation, even in a style as humble and self-abnegating as that which Herbert here espouses?

20.5   To what extent is "Jordan (I)" an example of the poetic simplicity Herbert praises?

Answer   At first inspection, "Jordan (I)" seems notably devoid of the frills and ornaments the poet decries. The sense of the poem seems straightforward and free of allegorical complication, while the rhetoric of pastoral allure is rehearsed only to be rejected. The five-line stanzas are fairly uniform and plain: in each stanza, four lines of reasonably regular iambic pentameter are followed by a shorter fifth line of iambic tetrameter.

On the other hand, the poem is by no means free of complication. The poetic inversion in line 2 ("Is there in truth no beauty?") introduces a double meaning; "winding stair" is a somewhat riddling metaphor; and as the discussion in the previous answer suggests, the antithesis between a "true" and a "painted chair" expresses "at two removes" several of Herbert's objections to conventional poetry. (The answer to question 20.3 concerning "The Collar" also has suggested how Herbert was able to use the doubleness of metaphoric language as a poetic resource.)

None of this should be surprising: a poet cannot merely and endlessly repeat "My God, My King" and remain a poet. Yet Herbert's skepticism about the decorative element in poetry commits him to questioning the status of his figurative language even as he uses it. Poetic language can bring one to the threshold of truth, but there it must surrender its power to the simplicity of truth itself: "My God, My King." In a similar way, the elaborate verbal structure of "The Collar," expressing the discontent of poet-priest, collapses like a house of cards before the single divine utterance "Child." While it is true that Herbert's diction and metaphors are usually less elaborate and gaudy than those of the contemporary metaphysical poets, the paradoxical relationship of his twin vocations as priest and poet is never fully resolved but finds varied expression throughout the body of his poetry.

"Love (III)"

20.6 Who is Love in this poem?

Answer   "Love (III)" is the final poem in *The Temple*, which collects nearly all of Herbert's English poems, and in the context of Herbert's poetry the association of Love with God, and perhaps specifically with Jesus, appears almost inevitable; the biblical text "He shall . . . make them to sit down to meat" (Luke 12:37) is particularly apt. God here seems to be welcoming the errant soul to his heavenly feast.

On the other hand, until the final stanza, when the speaker addresses Love as "Lord," the figure of Love is by no means clearly masculine, and the situation could be understood as easily in romantic as in religious terms—as if a mysterious and unexpectedly generous lady were offering a weary traveler repose and, perhaps, even sexual hospitality. Many of the epithets and actions ("quick-ey'd Love," "Drew nearer to me, sweetly questioning," "Love took my hand, and smiling did reply," "My dear") fit this interpretation, and Love seems alternately alluring, even seductive, and peremptory ("You shall be he," "You must sit down"). On the metaphoric level, the poet implies that God's relation to the human soul is one of both invitation and command, enticing persuasion and frank mastery.

The ambiguous presentation of God as Love frees the reader from conventional images of Christ and refocuses attention on the characteristics of love as it is presented in the New Testament. (Chapter 13 of St. Paul's First Epistle to the Corinthians is especially relevant: "Love is patient and kind . . . it is not arrogant or rude. Love does not insist on its own way; it is not irritable or resentful.") By suggesting in the first two stanzas a romantic situation, Herbert deliberately introduces secular associations with Love as well, as though to pose the question of how the erotic and religious experiences of love are related to one another. Bypassing such human images of God as white-bearded Jehovah or gentle Jesus in sky-blue robes, he presents a more indeterminate and enigmatic embodiment of divine love and magnanimity.

20.7 Why does the speaker resist Love's invitation, and how is his resistance finally overcome?

Answer Even though the speaker is being welcomed—to the communion feast and, ultimately, to heaven—and is thus presumably one of the blessed, he feels himself unworthy, stained as he is with both sin and the dust of mortality and worldly preoccupations. Love's authoritative "You shall be he" makes it clear that the host, not the guest, will decide who is worthy of the feast (compare the parable of the marriage feast, Luke 14:16–24). Perhaps the future tense ("shall be") also implies that the guest is not yet worthy while he still resists the liberality of the invitation.

The speaker renews his protest, accusing himself of ingratitude for the gifts he has already received; he is too ashamed even to raise his eyes to meet those of Love. Yet, as Love points out, he cannot very well withhold what Love itself has made; nothing the speaker possesses, including his guilt, belongs entirely to himself. Bit by bit, Love is cutting away the ground of separateness from the sinner.

In the third stanza the speaker offers his final reason for hesitation: he has "marred" (debased) the eyes (and, by extension, the whole being) which God has made, and this self-debasement deserves damnation. But, as Love reminds him by a rhetorical question, Christ (as the purest expression of Love itself) "bore the blame"; that is, through the Incarnation he assumed the burden of human guilt, and through the Crucifixion he paid its penalty. To refuse the feast which is offered to the guest is in effect to refuse Christ's sacrifice; indeed, the food which is offered is the body of Christ, as in holy communion. Thus, even the sinner's self-accusation is revealed as a form of *hubris*, a sinful insistence on his own otherness or individuality. At once humiliated by this catechism and joyful at its conclusion, the speaker acquiesces in the reward which he has not earned but which is nevertheless his: "So I did sit and eat."

K.L.

SUGGESTED READINGS

Charles, Amy, *The Life of George Herbert* (1977).
Fish, Stanley, *Self-Consuming Artifacts* (1972).
Harman, Barbara, *Costly Monuments* (1982).
Stein, Arnold, *George Herbert's Lyrics* (1968).
Vendler, Helen, *The Poetry of George Herbert* (1974).

JOHN MILTON

C H R O N O L O G Y

1608   Born in Cheapside, London. Son of John Milton, a scrivener (broker) by trade, also known as a musician and composer. The poet is educated at home by tutors and also attends St. Paul's School in London (exact date uncertain).

1625   Enters Christ's College, Cambridge University, under tutorship of William Chappell.

1626   Probably "rusticated" (suspended from the college) for some kind of disagreement with his tutor; allowed to return after several months under a new tutor.

1629   Receives B.A. Writes his first important work, the "Ode on the Morning of Christ's Nativity." Continues study at Cambridge.

1631   Writes "L'Allegro" and "Il Penseroso."

1632   Receives M.A. Returns to his parents' home in London, continuing private course of study.

1634   Milton's masque *Comus* performed at Ludlow Castle; it is published three years later.

1635   Milton retires to the country town of Horton in Buckinghamshire, where his father has a house; pursues a life of scholarship and writing.

1638   "Lycidas" published in an anthology of poems commemorating the death of Edward King, Milton's friend and a promising young poet. Milton embarks on a voyage of over a year, in which he will visit the major centers of learning in France and Italy.

1640   Back in England, settles in a large house in London, where he studies, writes, and works as a tutor; his pupils include several noble youths. Publishes *Epitaphium Damonis*, most famous of the many Latin poems of his early years.

1641   Publishes *Of Reformation* and two other strongly Protestant antiprelatic pamphlets; beginning of his long career as a writer of political and religious tracts.

1642   Publishes *The Reason of Church Government* and *Apology for Smectymnuus*, two more political-religious tracts. Marries Mary Powell. However, she leaves him within a few months and returns to her parents; he sends for her, but she refuses to return. (Political disagreements between Milton and the Powells may be part of the reason for the estrangement. In the civil war which had just broken out, Milton was strongly antiroyalist, while the Powells evidently supported the king.)

1643   Publishes *Doctrine and Discipline of Divorce*, the first of several tracts defending the practice of divorce, even for simple incompatibility; popularly assumed to be an outgrowth of his own troubled marriage.

1644   Publishes tract *Of Education*. His divorce tracts are publicly attacked in Parliament and elsewhere; attempts to suppress them are made. Publishes *Areopagitica*, his most famous prose work, a ringing defense of freedom of the press. Milton's sight begins to fail.

1645   Reconciliation between Milton and Mary Powell. In addition to two more political tracts, Milton publishes his first volume of poetry, *Poems of Mr. John Milton, Both English and Latin*.

1649   King Charles I is executed by the parliamentary forces. Milton publishes *The Tenure of Kings and Magistrates* in defense of this virtually unprecedented revolutionary act. He is appointed Latin secretary (roughly equivalent to foreign minister) under the government of Cromwell. Also publishes *Eikonoklastes*, an officially endorsed government response to *Eikon Basilike*, a royalist pamphlet.

1651   Publishes *Defensio pro populo Anglicano*, another tract defending the actions of the Cromwell regime.

1652   Milton is now totally blind. Birth of daughter Deborah, followed shortly by the death of Milton's wife and son.

1654   Publishes *Defensio Secunda*.

1655   Abandons governmental duties; devotes energies to private study and writing. Begins compilation of Latin and Greek dictionaries; writes the sonnet "On the Late Massacre in Piedmont"; perhaps begins work on *Paradise Lost*.

1656   Marries Katherine Woodcock.

1657   Fellow poet Andrew Marvell becomes Milton's assistant.

1658   Death of Milton's second wife and of his daughter Katherine. Writes sonnet "Methought I saw my late espoused saint," about either his first or second wife. Death of Cromwell.

1659   Publishes several important prose works, including *A Treatise of Civil Power* and *The Ready and Easy Way to Establish a Free Commonwealth*. Cromwell's son Richard abdicates, paving the way for the restoration of the monarchy. In the resulting repression of pro-Commonwealth leaders, Milton is arrested and imprisoned, and some of his works are burned. By order of Parliament, Milton is freed after about two months.

1663   Milton's third marriage, to Elizabeth Minshull. Is at work on *Paradise Lost*, probably dictated to his daughters.

1667   Publication of *Paradise Lost*.

1670   Publication of Milton's *History of Britain* (prose work).

1671   Publication of *Paradise Regained*, Milton's "short epic" about the temptation of Christ, and his moving, prosodically innovative "Greek tragedy" *Samson Agonistes*.

1673   An enlarged edition of Milton's 1645 volume of poems is published.

1674   Second edition of *Paradise Lost*, enlarged from ten to twelve books, is published. Death of Milton.

ESSAY QUESTIONS WITH ANSWERS

Sonnet 16: "When I consider . . ."

21.1 What is the problem faced by the speaker of the poem?

Answer On the most basic level, the speaker laments the blindness that afflicts him in middle age. His "light is spent"—he has lost the power of vision—and the world has thus become "dark" and "wide," devoid not only of physical light but of form and meaning. He feels isolated by literal darkness, but he also feels spiritual alienation: a loss of the guiding light of God.

God has endowed him with abilities, but seems to have deprived him of means to use them: "Doth God exact day-labour, light denied?" If the poet cannot expect the return of his sight, he may at least hope for the spiritual illumination which will direct his future efforts. (Up to this moment in his career, Milton had devoted himself not so much to poetry as to the service of Cromwell's Commonwealth, a regime which for its Puritan supporters seemed as much a religious as a political cause.)

The sonnet moves toward at least partial reassurance. Patience counsels the speaker that there are many forms of service. Deprived of his eyesight and therefore, perhaps, of some of the more active ministries available to God's servants, he may still serve God's purposes. God depends on the activity of no single man and knows the best uses of the gifts which He Himself has given (line 10). The poet may express his obedience, if not through action, at least by the readiness with which he awaits a deeper understanding of God's will. The speaker's spiritual confidence is thus restored, yet the tension of his situation is not fully resolved, and the poem ends on a note of indefinitely sustained expectancy.

21.2 Discuss the use of monetary imagery in the poem.

Answer The octave of the sonnet, especially, makes use of the language of monetary exchange: "spent," "talent," "account," "exact." This imagery derives from a parable in the New Testament (Matthew 25:14–30), in which a master gives three servants various quantities of talents (silver pieces) to see what they will do with them in his absence. After a certain time, the master returns to find that the good, industrious servants have used their money wisely and doubled its amount; the slothful servant has hoarded and hidden his money ("that one talent") and therefore has no increase to show his master, who rebukes him harshly. The parable expresses the central idea that *all* we possess in our earthly existence, our talents and abilities as well as our material possessions, is lent to us by God and must be husbanded wisely and fruitfully.

In the first quatrain of the sonnet, then, the speaker equates himself with the miserly servant who hides his talent and renders it useless. His capacities or talents are "spent," wasted; he has squandered his capital without spiritual fruit. This predicament seems especially ironic to the speaker, because he feels that his loss of vision comes at the very moment when he is most zealously inclined to serve God and so present his "true account," that is, establish his value and worth to God. His despairing questions in lines 7 and 8 continue this monetary imagery, for he sees the injustice of his situation in monetary terms— God seeks to "exact" payment that the speaker has been rendered unable to tender.

The absence of monetary imagery from the sestet of the sonnet helps to emphasize a major reversal in the poem: the poet realizes that one cannot bargain with God over the spiritual capital He has conferred, and the service He will exact may involve neither overt action nor measurable quantity. While "thousands" speed to carry out God's active ministries, there are others—by no means the least—whose very patience and spiritual attention are themselves a service.

21.3   How do structure and syntax contribute to meaning in the sonnet?

Answer   Both the structural division between octave and sestet in the sonnet form and the differences in syntax between them strategically emphasize the reversal of thought and feeling which occurs in lines 8 and 9. The whole of the first six lines of the poem forms a single dependent clause leading to the "fond" (foolish) question asked in lines 7 and 8 of the octave. A change of direction is then signaled in the "But" of line 8, and the clause which it initiates bridges, through enjambment, the octave and sestet, acting as a kind of hinge between the two major parts of the poem.

In the octave, the poet questions the unfairness of his predicament; in the sestet, his patience replies to the more restless, despairing part of his nature. The final line of the sonnet, which encapsulates this wisdom, is a smoothly flowing iambic line. Where the octave contains a long, difficult-to-grasp suspended clause and ends in a question, the sestet proceeds simply and directly to its final, decisive declaration.

Thus, the formal structure of the sonnet reinforces not only the reversal of thought and feeling, but also the basic structure of dialogue in the poem. The dialogue is internal; the poet counsels himself and quiets his own anger in the final 6½ lines of the poem.

"Lycidas"

21.4 "Lycidas" was written on the occasion of the death of Edward King, a friend and former classmate of Milton at Cambridge. To commemorate King's death, Milton chose to write a pastoral poem in which both he and King are transformed into rustic shepherds piping songs and roaming the fields. Why did Milton select this particular poetic genre?

Answer The venerable tradition of the pastoral poem provided Milton with images and themes relevant to the large issues he wished to consider in his elegy, such as death, consolation for loss, and immortality. The classical and biblical strains of pastoral afforded him a series of interlocking images with which to eulogize his dead friend and, at the same time, to create allusive patterns of ideas.

Through the conventional image of the shepherd piping his songs, Milton represented King in his twin roles as poet and minister; a minor poet, King was on his way to assume his pastorship—literally, the role of a shepherd—when he was drowned at sea. Using this stock figure out of classical pastoral, Milton was able to portray his friend as a virtuous and inspired poet. However, Milton also alludes to the Judeo-Christian figure of the shepherd, tapping the rich biblical symbolism of the shepherd as the pastor of souls. Images of the clergy as spiritual shepherds and of Christ as shepherd are juxtaposed in "Lycidas," as Milton leads the reader from classical images to biblical ones.

Thus the symbolic figure of the shepherd is used in the exploration of certain spiritual and philosophical issues. Milton first asks about the efficacy of poetry in providing consolation for death: "What boots it with incessant care/ To tend the homely slighted shepherd's trade,/ And strictly meditate the thankless Muse?" (lines 64–66). Can poetry help to console us in the face of such a loss? Poetry is defended by Phoebus, who insists that the gods recognize achievement and determine true fame. But the poet moves on to consider another question, related to another type of shepherd. In the second main section of the poem, he employs the image of the shepherd to castigate the corrupt bishops of the church, who "scarce themselves know how to hold/ A sheep-hook, or have learned aught else the least/ That to the faithful herdsman's art belongs!" (lines 119–121). These venial bishops, the poet says, prosper at the expense of others, ignore their flock, and pipe a corrupt tune—in short, they abuse their vocation as pastors. In the third main section of the poem, the central pastoral image of the shepherd finds its fulfillment in the representation of Christ, the shepherd of the New Testament, who leads young Lycidas to "other groves" and "other streams," where he hears "the unexpressive nuptial song" sung at the marriage supper of the lamb in heaven.

Rather than being mere repetition, this repeated use of the image of the shepherd suggests a certain kind of allegorical progression. Milton is relying here on the notion of scriptural typology, according to which an event or image in the Old Testament or even in classical literature is seen as anticipating or foreshadowing an event or image which fulfills it in the New Testament. Thus, medieval and Renaissance theologians read Virgil's Fourth Eclogue, with its account of a blessed child who would redeem humanity, as typologically pre-figuring the coming of Christ, and the erotic Song of Songs in the Old Testament as a type of the marriage of Christ and the church. By progressing from the image of the classical shepherd-poet through that of the spiritual shepherd to the fulfillment of the image (and of Christian pastoral) in the person of Christ, Milton creates a typological progression. The final eight lines of the poem return us to the classical pastoral; the "uncouth swain" or shepherd—the classical poet—finishes his "Doric lay" after the strains of religious poetry and prophecy have subsided. The poem ends quietly, back in the humbler poetic territory where it began.

21.5   Discuss the degree of success of Milton's use of the pastoral convention.

Answer   While the intellectual structure of "Lycidas" is comprehensible, its success in fusing classical and Christian elements has always been open to question. In 1779 Samuel Johnson complained in his *Lives of the English Poets* of Milton's mingling of the "trifling fictions" of the pastoral convention with "the most awful and sacred truths, such as ought never to be polluted with such irreverent combinations. The shepherd . . . is now a feeder of sheep, and af-terwards an ecclesiastical pastor, a superintendent of a Christian flock. Such equivocations are always unskilful; but here they are indecent, and at least approach to impiety, of which, however, I believe the writer not to have been conscious." To some extent, by the time Johnson wrote (nearly a century and a half after the composition of "Lycidas") the typological understanding of classical myth had begun to break down and was no longer as accessible or comfortable to most readers of poetry, but Johnson's complaint goes further. The pastoral convention, widely and mechanically used in his own time, struck him as stale and insipid—or rather, to use his own language, "easy, vulgar, and therefore disgusting: whatever images it can supply, are long ago exhausted; and its inherent improbability always forces dissatisfaction on the mind. . . . [What] image of tenderness can be excited by these lines!

> We drove afield, and both together heard
> What time the grey-fly winds her sultry horn,
> Battening our flocks with the fresh dews of night.

We know that they never drove afield, and that they had no flocks to batten; and though it be allowed that the representation may be allegorical, the true meaning is so uncertain and remote, that it is never sought because it cannot be known when it is found."

Johnson's thunderous objections have a certain common sense, and he is no doubt right that Milton's images convey very little sense of intimacy or personal tenderness toward King. On the other hand, King was not an especially close friend of Milton's, and in some ways Milton's grief is impersonal. "Lycidas" conveys the pathos of any life destroyed before its youthful promise can be fulfilled and a sense of frustration and even rage at the toll which chance and accident exact. The magnitude of such a loss can be measured by the need which the human community has for the abilities that have been squandered, and Milton sees his own society as critically wanting the consecrative powers of both poetry and selfless piety.

The pastoral convention, precisely because it can allude to the different metaphoric uses of the shepherd in the Christian and classical traditions, allows Milton to meditate upon King's dual vocation as poet and Protestant pastor. Milton does not ignore the disjunction between the different modes of poetry "Lycidas" yokes together—for example, he announces the return of the more classical pastoral by saying, "Return, Alpheus, the dread voice is past,/ That shrunk thy streams"—but the very breach of poetic decorum signals the urgency that underlies "Lycidas" and its questioning of human vocation and destiny.

21.6 Describe the structure of the poem and its relationship to the poem's meaning.

Answer   "Lycidas" can be divided into three main sections, together with an introduction and a conclusion. The fourteen-line introduction reveals the occasion of the poem and the dilemma that confronts the poet: Lycidas has died prematurely, and his death must not pass unnoticed; the poet, though aware of the immaturity of his own talents, pleads for inspiration to write a monody for his dead friend.

Each of the following three major sections of the poem begins with an invocation, mourns the loss of Lycidas, raises some problem or question, and offers some kind of consolation. In the first section, lines 15–84, the poet invokes the classical Muses (the "sisters of the sacred well" [line 15]), mourns the change in nature since Lycidas has died, asks what poetry can do in the face of such loss, and receives an answer from Phoebus Apollo, classical god of poetic inspiration. Phoebus's response, a strain "of a higher mood" than the poet's own, reminds him that fame is immortal. It is the gods who confer judgment on human deeds, not other people. This is the classical answer to a question asked in a classical context—an appropriate response at this stage of the poem, although it will be shown to be only provisional by the poem's conclusion.

The next section of the poem, lines 85–131, begins with an address, "O fountain Arethuse" (one of the traditional sources of pastoral poetry, associated with the Greek poet Theocritus), but it is not an invocation. Rather, both its spring and "smooth-sliding Mincius" (associated with Virgil's pastoral poetry) have been superseded by the higher strain introduced by Phoebus and developed by Neptune, Camus, and above all St. Peter; the purely pastoral mode of Arethusa goes underground until it returns with Alpheus in line 132. (According to tradition, the Arcadian river Alpheus fell in love with the nymph Arethusa and pursued her under the sea to Sicily, where she was transformed to a pool and their united waters rose as the fountain Arethusa. Moving from Sicily to Greece, Milton reverses the direction of the chase.) This section reiterates the fact of loss but also raises a question about justice and judgment. Why has Lycidas (King) been destroyed when, as St. Peter (the "pilot of the Galilean lake" [line 109]) points out, the church is overrun with self-seeking parasites, whose loss would matter so much less? Nevertheless, St. Peter indicates, earthly prosperity or misfortune—including premature death—does not provide the final measure of divine justice, and the fate of the corrupt clergy is already sealed: judgment will prevail, and the unscrupulous pastors will be punished by the "two-handed engine." Since St. Peter is the founder of the church and, by tradition, is said to hold the keys to heaven (lines 110–111), this section moves the poem forward to a Christian context.

In section three, lines 132–185, the poet returns again to the lowlier form of the classical pastoral with an invocation to Alpheus, reiterates the fact of Lycidas's death ("Ay me! Whilst thee the shores, and sounding seas/ Wash far away, where'er thy bones are hurled" [lines 154–155]), and then passes on to the final Christian consolation of the poem, beginning with "Weep no more, woeful shepherds" (line 165). Through the mercy of Christ, the poet says, Lycidas will be lifted up, "mounted high." The Christian paradox, that one dies to be born again, provides the final consolation; tears are no longer necessary, for Lycidas's spirit lives on. In the last eight lines, which frame the poem, the poet returns to the natural landscape of classical pastoral and to thoughts of life.

21.7 Why do the voices of Apollo (the strain of "a higher mood") and St. Peter (the "dread voice") interrupt that of the pastoral "swain"?

Answer   According to the classical notion of decorum in poetry, certain poetic forms are higher than others and are suited to higher themes. Among the classical genres, pastoral was considered lowlier than epic or tragedy; the pastoral poet, most often in reality a highly educated and sophisticated man, took on the person of the rustic shepherd, the "uncouth swain" piping his song on his natural oaten flute. When Milton begins his poem by saying, "Yet once more, O ye laurels, and once more/ Ye myrtles brown, with ivy never sere,/ I come to pluck your berries harsh and crude" (lines 1–3), he is confessing his own poetic immaturity, but, at the same time, he places himself within a long line of poets who have previously written pastoral elegies; and when he invokes the "sisters of the sacred well" (line 15), he invokes the same Muses who inspired Theocritus and Virgil, two masters of pastoral verse. (Since the time of Virgil, pastoral had also been regarded as the appropriate genre for the young, untried poet, who might eventually try to scale the heights of epic. As Virgil's *Eclogues* and Spenser's *Shepheardes Calender* were seen as rehearsals for *The Aeneid* and *The Faerie Queene* respectively, so "Lycidas" could be regarded as part of Milton's preparation for writing *Paradise Lost*.)

But a series of loftier, interrupting voices intrude upon the traditional pastoral dirge. Through these interruptions the poem itself enacts the process of grace descending. First, Apollo answers the poet's complaint and question, reminding him of the immortal source of fame. His voice represents a "higher mood" because it is the voice of a god, however pagan or metaphoric. Neptune (god of the sea which has shipwrecked Lycidas) and Camus (a *genius loci*, associated with Cambridge, which nursed King's promise and where the two young poets

met) continue the procession of classical deities, but their questions are interrupted, this time by St. Peter's stern judgment on the corrupt clergy. His voice
lifts the poem once more to heaven, but now a decisively Christian heaven.
The harshness of his prophecy leads the poet to describe his voice as "the dread
voice . . ./ That shrunk thy [Alpheus's] streams"; the voice of the founding
bishop of the Christian church predicting judgment and doom in the midst of
the poem awes and diminishes the classical Muses. The list of flowers that
follows presents a respite ("so to interpose a little ease" [line 152] from the
darker subjects considered in the poem.

Finally, the poet incorporates into his poem the message of Christ, through
whose "dear might" Lycidas is raised on high. This time we do not hear the
voice directly, for it is inexpressible in human speech. Lycidas, we are told by
the poet, "hears the unexpressive [that is, inexpressible] nuptial song,/ In the
blest kingdoms meek of joy and love" (lines 176–177).

Whether or not the Christian and classical elements of the poem have
successfully fused, they have, by the end of the poem, become thoroughly
intermingled. Lycidas has become at once "the genius of the shore" (the tutelary
deity of the pastoral setting) and a participant in the heavenly love feast where
all tears are wiped away. The Christian "strain" is no longer perceived as a
"dread voice" which intrudes upon the song of the swain but as a message of
consolation; and heaven, a landscape of "other groves, and other streams," is
a transfiguration of the shepherd's natural realm.

Paradise Lost

21.8   In the following passage from Book IX of *Paradise Lost*, Satan approaches Eve alone in the garden. Discuss the relationship between theme and
imagery in the passage.

> He sought them both, but wished his hap might find
> Eve separate, he wished, but not with hope
> Of what so seldom chanced, when to his wish,
> Beyond his hope, Eve separate he spies,
> Veiled in a cloud of fragrance, where she stood,
> Half spied, so thick the roses blushing round
> About her glowed, oft stooping to support
> Each flower of slender stalk, whose head though gay
> Carnation, purple, azure, or specked with gold,
> Hung drooping unsustained, them she upstays
> Gently with myrtle band, mindless the while,

> Her self, though fairest unsupported flower,
> From her best prop so far, and storm so nigh.
>   (IX, 421–433, meaning Book IX, lines 421–433)

Answer   The dominant simile in the passage, which makes Eve both gardener and the "fairest unsupported flower," heightens our anticipation of the impending Fall by suggesting the dual aspect of Eve's position: her dominion and her vulnerability. Immediately preceding this passage, Adam has warned Eve of the danger of wandering off alone. The passage confirms Adam's fear of Eve's susceptibility to temptation when divided from his support.

Eve is, of course, the gardener, the occupation with which God entrusts Adam and Eve before the Fall. In paradise, their work is their pleasure; they willingly tend the vegetation that grows plentifully and wild. The harmonious relationship between mankind and the rest of nature in paradise is expressed through the reciprocal benefits exchanged by Eve and the flowers: the roses veil Eve in a "cloud of fragrance," hiding her, at least in part, from Satan's view. Eve, in turn, supports the drooping heads gently, with "myrtle band."

The second part of the passage reveals that Eve, the supporter, is also Eve the "unsupported flower." Eve's vulnerability is, in fact, anticipated in the description of the heavy heads of the flowers, which hang "drooping unsustained." The simile here is more than a mere comparison, since nature in the garden actually corresponds to or sympathizes with the predicament of man. As Eve is to the flowers, Adam is to Eve: he is her "best prop." The natural drooping of the flowers presages Eve's Fall, which occurs when she lacks Adam's support. As Adam has earlier argued, he and Eve are in fact each other's best support, "Since reason not impossibly may meet/ Some specious object by the foe [i.e., Satan] suborned,/ And fall into deception unaware." Nevertheless, Eve attributes his caution neither to "tender love" (IX, 357) nor to suspicion of Satan's wiles but to mistrust of her. Feeling that compelled obedience will only alienate Eve more ("Go; for thy stay, not free, absents thee more" [IX, 372]), Adam reluctantly consents to their separation.

The comparison of Eve to a flower also recalls our (and Satan's) first glimpse of Adam and Eve in Eden in Book IV. There paradise is compared to "that fair field/ Of Enna, where Proserpine gathering flowers/ Her self a fairer flower by gloomy Dis/ Was gathered, which cost Ceres all that pain/ To seek her through the world" (IV, 268–272). The rape of Proserpina by Dis (or Pluto), the king of hell, here suggests Eve's coming seduction by another king of hell, Satan; the grief of Proserpina's mother—Ceres, the goddess of agricultural abundance— impaired the fertility of the natural world, just as the Fall of Adam and Eve will degrade the pristine harmony and innocence of Eden. Thus, Milton suggests, the central, sacred truths of Christian history are echoed in the myths and legends—partial truths—of other cultures and religions. Here, however, in Milton's narrative the later, pagan version of Eve's Fall serves to prefigure the actual event.

21.9 In famous comments on *Paradise Lost*, the romantic poets Blake and Shelley identified Satan as the real hero of Milton's poem. In Blake's words, Milton "was a true Poet and of the Devil's party without knowing it" (*The Marriage of Heaven and Hell*, 1793). To what extent is their interpretation supported by Milton's text?

Answer   Shelley and Blake's interpretation of Satan is in keeping with the romantic poets' fascination with the image of the hero as outcast (and, in Blake's case, with his heterodox celebration of evil as "the active springing from Energy. . . . Energy is Eternal Delight"). But while this response to Satan acknowledges his power and vitality, especially in Book I of *Paradise Lost*, it ignores his progressive degradation and his intellectual and emotional self-destructiveness.

When Satan first appears in Book I, as a military leader addressing his legions, he is meant to evoke the traditional response of admiration to an epic hero; his first speech to his fallen followers deliberately echoes a speech of Virgil's Aeneas in Book I of *The Aeneid*. But part of Milton's goal in *Paradise Lost* is to reveal the limitations of the earlier heroic code, replacing it with a Christian emphasis on passive endurance, "the better fortitude/ Of patience and heroic martyrdom." Blake and Shelley's comments imply that Milton's imaginative sympathies as a poet were at odds with this ideological goal and that in spite of himself he responded to the active energy of Satan. However, Satan's heroic presence in the opening books is short-lived. The reader soon encounters him peering, voyeurlike, at the happiness of Adam and Eve in paradise; "Squat like a toad" (IV, 800) at the ear of the sleeping Eve; and eventually slithering—grandly, but nevertheless on his belly—as a serpent toward Eve, the victim of his treachery. As Satan stealthily approaches Eden, the poet compares him to a "prowling wolf" (IV, 183) invading the shepherd's fold, to a thief climbing in the window of a rich burgher's house, and, perhaps most tellingly to Milton, to the "lewd hirelings" who have climbed into the church and so corrupted it. No longer a glorious rebel, Satan has become the archetypal outsider looking in, envious, sneaky, and intrusive.

Even in Book I, in the midst of Satan's seemingly persuasive, heroically phrased speeches to his followers, the poet warns us of the fallaciousness of

Satan's rhetoric, which "bore/ Semblance of worth, not substance" (I, 529). If we listen carefully to the speeches, we can perceive the shiftiness of some of the arguments and the wrongheadedness of Satan's conception of his own condition. For example, he first argues that the fallen angels are safe in hell, then tries to jolt them out of their despair by reminding them that their lethargy makes them vulnerable to God's avengers. In addition, he casts God in the role of tyrant ("farthest from him is best,/ Whom reason hath equalled, force has made supreme/ Above his equals" [I, 247–249]), interpreting God's actions in the false light of his own hunger for power. Moreover, behind the apparent solicitude of the leader for his men is an unquenchable thirst for personal glory and a disregard for danger inspired less by courage than despair. He volunteers to cross the unmapped abyss of chaos to newly created earth, but "the high repute . . . through hazard huge" (II, 472–473) which he seeks is implicitly contrasted with the genuine self-sacrifice of Christ, who in Book III (lines 227–265) offers to pay the penalty of man's guilt with his own death. By the beginning of Book IV, Satan's self-concern has become a prison more terrifying than hell itself:

> Me miserable! Which way shall I fly
> Infinite wrath, and infinite despair?
> Which way I fly is hell; my self am hell;
> And in the lowest deep a lower deep
> Still threatening to devour me opens wide,
> To which the hell I suffer seems a heaven.
>
> (IV, 73–78)

While the romantic poets might still have found a certain grandeur in the extremity of Satan's self-torment, by this point in the poem Satan's energies seem reduced and perverted; lacking a legitimate object, they become recklessly destructive, both to himself and to humanity. Although it is not until Book X that Satan is definitively transformed to a groveling snake, consuming dust and bitter ashes, the sterility and abasement of that destiny make themselves felt even while Satan still maintains the outward appearance of a tragic, if not epic, hero.

21.10 In *Paradise Lost*, God foresees the Fall and does nothing to stop it. Is man in Milton's scheme therefore fated to fall and so not truly responsible?

Answer Milton addresses this issue of free will several times in *Paradise Lost*, first in Book III. God there explains the difference between foreknowledge and absolute necessity. God is by definition omniscient and, knowing the future, foresees the Fall of Man, but he does not direct it: "Foreknowledge had no influence on their fault,/ Which had no less proved certain unforeknown" (lines 118–119). Since God has made mankind *Sufficient to have stood, though free to fall*" (line 99 [italics added]), his knowledge that humanity will misuse its freedom of choice does not in itself contribute to man's fall from innocence. Free will *must* be a power that can be used for evil or for good; otherwise it is not really free will.

In the same speech, God describes human free will, arguing that if obedience to God were not an *active* choice on man's part, it would be a specious, rather than sincere, allegiance: "Not free, what proof could they have given sincere/ Of true allegiance, constant faith, or love" (lines 103–104). According to Milton's theology, reason is choice: Adam and Eve choose to disobey God's injunction and to break the convenant he has established with them. Had God intervened to prevent the Fall, he would by that act have destroyed human free will:

> I formed them free, and free they must remain,
> Till they enthrall themselves: I else must change
> Their nature, and revoke the high decree
> Unchangeable, eternal, which ordained
> Their freedom
>
> (lines 124–128)

The concept of free will is also discussed by Adam in Book IX in his warning to Eve before she departs from him to journey alone. Adam counsels Eve to beware of temptation; God created man perfect, he explains, but left human reason free to choose a fate which would change that perfect state. Adam warns Eve: "But God left free the will, for what obeys/ Reason, is free, and reason he made right,/ But bid her well beware, and still erect,/ Lest by some fair appearing good surprised/ She dictate false, and misinform the will/ To do what God expressly hath forbid" (lines 351–356). Adam and Eve have been warned by Raphael of the approaching danger, and Adam accurately describes the nature of the impending temptation. Evil will appear as good, and reason, deceived by appearances, will "dictate false."

The notion that the reason and will must be tested and strengthened in their capacity to distinguish true good from apparent good underlies Milton's most famous prose writing, *Areopagitica* (1644), a plea for less restricted, though not unlimited, freedom of the press. "Good and evil we know in the field of this world grow up together almost inseparably; and the knowledge of good is so involved and interwoven with the knowledge of evil, and in so many cunning resemblances hardly to be discerned, that those confused seeds which were imposed on Psyche as an incessant labor to cull out and sort asunder, were not more intermixed." Human beings cannot, and should not, through prior censorship, be relieved of the burden of distinguishing good from evil. Virtue which has not confronted the possibility of evil is not true virtue: "I cannot praise a fugitive and cloistered virtue, unexercised and unbreathed, that never sallies out and sees her adversary, but slinks out of the race where that immortal garland is to be run for, not without dust and heat. . . . That virtue therefore which is but a youngling in the contemplation of evil, and knows not the utmost that vice promises to her followers, and rejects it, is but a blank virtue, not a pure."

To some extent Milton sees this situation as a consequence of the Fall, "that doom which Adam fell into of knowing good and evil, that is to say of knowing good by evil," but it is not unreasonable to apply this passage to the condition of Adam and Eve in paradise and conclude that Adam and Eve could not become capable of true virtue, rather than mere innocence and obedience—could not become fully human, as we understand the term—until they had been expelled from the garden of Eden. Contemplating the tragicomic fortunes of mankind in the historical world and, above all, the sublime mysteries of Christ's Incarnation and redemption of Adam's sin which the Fall set in motion, Milton may have shared the ambivalence of his readers about "man's first disobedience" and its consequences.

21.11   How are the conventions of classical epic used in *Paradise Lost*?

Answer   Milton is consciously challenging comparison with the achievements of earlier epic poets, such as Homer, Virgil, and (in the English tradition) Spenser. While earlier epics had narrated crucial moments in the founding or formation of particular civilizations or national communities, Milton chooses as his subject the moment of crisis when all of mankind first enters the historical world. The conventions of epic supply both Milton's poetic resources for this ambitious project and the means by which to emphasize his differences from his predecessors.

For example, just as classical epics, such as Homer's *Odyssey* or Virgil's *Aeneid*, call upon a muse or goddess, Milton too invokes inspiration. But although Milton addresses the "heavenly Muse" (I, 6) or later Urania (the ancient Muse of Astronomy; VII, 1), the context makes it clear that his muse is not so much a classical Muse as a Judeo-Christian source of inspiration: "The meaning, not the name I call" (VII, 5). This "heavenly Muse" is the same one who inspired Moses, the Old Testament prophet, lawgiver, and leader of the Jews, to write the Pentateuch, the first five books of the Bible. "Thou from the first/ Was present," Milton says to his muse, "and with mighty wings outspread/ Dove-like sat'st brooding on the vast abyss/ And madest it pregnant"; in effect, his muse is the creative principle of the Logos, or the Word which "was in the beginning with God" (John 1:1–3). Yet another name for this presence, the third person of the Trinity, would be the Holy Spirit, and not surprisingly some of Milton's contemporaries thought that this invocation bordered on sacrilegious presumption.

Milton's style, like that of earlier epics, is digressive and allusive, in order to enlarge its frame of historical, literary, and experiential reference; the epic form is almost by definition encyclopedic and aspires to present a total vision of the world and its possibilities. Epic similes are one of the most conspicuous means of introducing alternative realms of experience into an epic poem; as comparisons, such similes go far beyond the need to supply a clarifying analogy and develop into an almost independent picture, a vignette of a different reality which the main thrust of the narrative cannot easily accommodate. For example, by means of a simile, in the midst of incidents of terrifying slaughter Homer will suddenly shift to a pastoral scene of flies swarming about a pail of spilled milk. Milton compares the devils crowding into Pandaemonium for their first hellish council to bees in springtime, who

> when the sun with Taurus rides,
> Pour forth their populous youth about the hive
> In clusters; they among fresh dews and flowers
> Fly to and fro, or on the smoothed plank,
> The suburb of their straw-built citadel the hive,
> New rubbed with balm, expatiate and confer
> Their state affairs.
>   (I, 769–775)

In addition to the traditional epic function of diversifying and enriching the narrative, Milton's similes frequently seem to serve his purpose of justifying "the ways of God to men" (I, 26). The images imported by similes tacitly assert that from all of Satan's machinations and the conflict between heaven and hell emerges the goodness of the natural world—fertile, renewable, and as inexhaustible as divine grace. While not all Miltonic similes have the same design, most reinforce the larger themes of the epic, relating to human choice and the workings of divine providence. (For further discussion of this point, see Geoffrey Hartman's article "Milton's Counterplot," reprinted in Arthur Barker, ed., *Mil-*

ton: *Modern Essays in Criticism.*) Thus Milton stakes his claim to have written an epic not only larger in scope than those of his predecessors but also more philosophically coherent and profound.

21.12   One of the pervasive expressions of Milton's relation to the earlier epic tradition is the elevated language of *Paradise Lost,* emphasizing the extraordinary and majestic character of the events the poem narrates. While this language adds to the poem's grandeur, it is also one of the most frequent stumbling blocks to modern readers. Suggest a few of the ways in which Milton's language contributes to the effect of *Paradise Lost.*

Answer   The diction and syntax of *Paradise Lost* are particularly influenced by Latin precedents; at times it seems as though the style of the classical epic, as exemplified by Virgil's *Aeneid,* is wrestling in virtually every line of the poem with Milton's Hebraic subject matter. (And, as already suggested in the answers to questions 21.9 and 21.11, Milton wants to evoke the classical epic as much to challenge its ideology and literary achievement as to establish the genealogy of his own epic.) At the same time, this Latinate style provides Milton with different expressive possibilities from those of a more standard and colloquial form of English verse.

   Latin syntax has a less fixed word order than the ordinary English sentence. Milton adopts this freedom to place greater emphasis on certain words than conventional English syntax would allow. For example, writing of Satan's expulsion from heaven, he says:

> Him the almighty power
> Hurled headlong flaming from the ethereal sky
> With hideous ruin and combustion down
> To bottomless perdition
>
> (I, 44–46)

The initial placement of "Him," reinforced by the alliteration of "Hurld headlong" and "hideous," gives particular force and energy to the image of Satan's headfirst exit. The enjambment (the continuation of sense across the ends of individual lines) adds a sense that the falling motion goes on and on, renewing itself with each successive line. Subject-object inversion can also give special stress to the egoism of Satan, whether he is exalting himself among his followers ("Me though just right, and the fixed laws of heaven/ Did first create your leader" [II, 18–19]) or lamenting his self-entrapment ("Me miserable! Which way shall I fly . . .?" [IV, 73]). There is no fixed pattern to Milton's exploitation of Latin syntax, but he is always alert to the ways in which it can serve his expressive intentions.

Milton's acute awareness of the Latin etymology of English words—sometimes the reader may feel Milton is using words with more sense of Latin idiom than of English—often allows him to convey two meanings at once. For example, in Book VII (lines 19–20) he imagines being thrown from the Pegasus, or winged horse, of his imaginative inspiration:

> on the Aleian field I fall
> Erroneous there to wander and forlorn.

"Erroneous" here means both "wandering" (a Latin sense) and "straying from true wisdom." Other examples of such double meanings are "abject" (I, 312), meaning both "miserable" and "thrown down," from the Latin *abiectus*, and "voluble" (IX, 436), describing a snake that is both glib—"voluble" in the English sense—and rolling, as the Latin root *volubilis* suggests. Even the reader who does not know Latin is likely to feel, in the deviation from ordinary English idiom, the pressure of additional senses inhabiting the diction, as if Milton's story is so momentous that the resources of one language alone do not suffice for its telling.

Sometimes the very difficulty of Milton's language can contribute to the experience of the poem. Milton does not intend his verses to be read quickly, and the reader is frequently forced backward to sort out meanings only dimly apparent at a first encounter with the text. Moreover, the convoluted syntax (particularly among the devils in the first two books) can sometimes mirror contorted reasoning or the difficulty of coming to terms with some hitherto unknown phenomenon, for example, Death:

> The other shape,
> If shape it might be called that shape had none
> Distinguishable in member, joint, or limb,
> Or substance might be called that shadow seemed,
> For each seemed either; black it stood as night
> (II, 666–670)

While the topic of Milton's language is too complex for a brief exploration (Christopher Ricks's *Milton's Grand Style* is suggested for further reading), the disorienting features of his style should be recognized not as distracting archaisms but as essential elements of his storytelling, which upon further acquaintance reveal new dimensions of the epic's significance.

21.13   When Eve eats the forbidden fruit, she has been deceived by Satan, disguised as the serpent. Why does Adam eat the fruit?

Answer   Adam's fault is more conscious and deliberate and therefore, from a theological point of view, more culpable than Eve's. He knows that Eve has sinned, but instantly decides that he will share her fault:

> Some cursed fraud
> Of enemy hath beguiled thee, yet unknown,
> And me with thee hath ruined, for with thee
> Certain my resolution is to die;
> How can I live without thee, how forgo
> Thy sweet converse and love so dearly joined,
> To live again in these wild woods forlorn?
> (IX, 904–910)

(Note how expressively Milton's ambiguous syntax functions here. "Forlorn" presumably applies to Adam, deprived of companionship; but its placement subtly conveys that Eden itself, even untouched by consequences of the Fall, will become for Adam not merely "wild" but "forlorn" without the presence of Eve.) Presumably God can create another companion for Adam to replace the one he has lost in Eve, but Adam falls into the sin of loving the creature rather than the creator, placing his attachment to Eve above his obedience to God.

> Should God create another Eve, and I
> Another rib afford, yet loss of thee
> Would never from my heart; no no, I feel
> The link of nature draw me: flesh of flesh,
> Bone of my bone thou art, and from thy state
> Mine never shall be parted, bliss or woe.
> (IX, 911–916)

Yet it hardly seems adequate to see Adam's choice here simply as a sin. Accepting the fact of his own destruction, he acquires a tragic dignity. From the universality of a divine perspective one wife may well be as good as another, but attachment to the particular (in Adam's case, love for Eve, not love for woman in general) is part of what it means to be human. There is no reason to suppose that Milton does not perceive, and pay tribute to, Adam's nobility at this moment. It is only in the sequel—the shame and mutual recriminations of Book IX, which suggest a long epilogue in the subsequent history of Adam and Eve—that the noble act of Adam seems put in question; the highest human motives, untempered by a sense of God's prior claims, still produce a mixed crop of misery and blessings.

In a sense, Adam receives the reward as well as the punishment of his sin. He loses paradise, but retains Eve. At the end of the poem, as they leave Eden, they move tentatively toward reconciliation and receive the consolation of one another's society:

> Some natural tears they dropped, but wiped them soon;
> The world was all before them, where to choose
> Their place of rest, and providence their guide:
> They hand in hand with wandering steps and slow,
> Through Eden took their solitary way.
>
> (XII, 645–649)

21.14 Milton follows chapter 3 of Genesis in depicting shame, death, labor, knowledge, and exile as consequences of the Fall. However, he goes beyond his sources in exploring the consequences of the Fall for human sexuality. Discuss Milton's treatment of this topic.

Answer Shame and lasciviousness attend postlapsarian sex and distinguish it from the "Love unlibidinous"—innocent sexuality—of Eden before the Fall.

Just as nature itself "feels the wound" when Eve eats the fruit (when Eve goes to Adam, the roses in the garland he has made for her wither and die), Eve herself suffers a change of health: the perfect balance of her humors in the state of innocence is now disturbed, and the bodily imbalance is reflected in both Adam and Eve after their first sexual intercourse following the Fall. Here it is specifically related to the dominion of sensuality:

> Their inward state of mind, calm region once
> And full of peace, now tossed and turbulent:
> For understanding ruled not, and the will
> Heard not her lore, both in subjection now
> To sensual appetite, who from beneath
> Usurping over sovereign reason claimed
> Superior sway.
>
> (IX, 1125–1131)

It is not sensuality, but the *sovereignty* of sensuality, which distinguishes the fallen from the unfallen Adam and Eve. In effect, that dominance of sensuality trivializes sex, and that trivialization is reflected in the vocabulary of the poem, as words such as "dalliance" (1016), "play" (1027), "toy" (1034), and "disport" (1042) begin to be applied to Adam and Eve's newly inflamed desires. While sex seems to have become, in modern terms, more "fun," it has also become less satisfactory as an expression of mutual love.

It is also after the Fall that Adam and Eve first feel their own nakedness to be shameful and that they cover themselves with fig leaves: "O how unlike/ To that first naked Glorie," the poet says (lines 1114–1115). This shame in their own bodies ironically fulfills Satan's promise to Eve that her eyes will be opened; but instead of the wonderful, expansive knowledge to which Eve aspires, the shameful knowledge of fallen sexuality results.

K.L.

SUGGESTED READINGS

Barker, Arthur E., ed., *Milton: Modern Essays in Criticism* (1965).

Empson, William, *Milton's God*, Revised edition (1965).

Fish, Stanley E., *Surprised by Sin* (1971).

Frye, Northrop, *The Return of Eden: Five Essays on Milton's Epics* (1965).

Lewis, C. S., *A Preface to Paradise Lost* (1942).

MacCaffrey, Isabel G., *Paradise Lost as Myth* (1959).

Parker, William R., *Milton: A Biography* (1968).

Ricks, Christopher, *Milton's Grand Style* (1963).

Stein, Arnold, *Answerable Style: Essays on Paradise Lost* (1953).

Tuve, Rosemond, *Images and Themes in Five Poems by Milton* (1957).

ANDREW MARVELL

C H R O N O L O G Y

1621   Born at Winestead, near Hull. Son of Andrew Marvell, the parish priest, and Anne Pease Marvell.

1624   The senior Marvell is appointed lecturer at Holy Trinity Church in Hull and master at Hull Grammar School; family settles in Hull, where Andrew attends school.

1633   Enters Trinity College, Cambridge.

1637   Greek and Latin verses by Marvell published in *Musa Cantabrigiensis*, a volume by Cambridge students commemorating the birth of the daughter of King Charles I.

1638   Marvell receives B.A.

1639   According to some stories, Marvell is temporarily converted to Catholicism around this time and goes to live in London, until pursued by his father and returned to school. Truth of this incident is unknown.

1641   Death of Marvell's father by accidental drowning. Marvell leaves Cambridge.

1642   Marvell begins four years of travel in Europe, perhaps as tutor to Edward Skinner. Visits Richard Flecknoe in Rome, probably in 1645; writes *Flecknoe, an English Priest at Rome*.

1646   Probably writes "To His Coy Mistress."

1649   Two poems published: "To His Noble Friend Mr Richard Lovelace" and "Upon the Death of the Lord Hastings."

1650   Enters the service of the family of Lord Fairfax, a moderate leader of the parliamentary (i.e., antiroyalist) forces; Marvell's own political views, now and later, appear to be centrist. Lives at Nun Appleton House, the Fairfax estate in Yorkshire; writes *An Horatian Ode upon Cromwell's Return from Ireland*. Probably begins work on much of his lyric poetry.

1653   John Milton fails in attempt to win a governmental post for Marvell, who is later appointed tutor to Cromwell's ward William Dutton; settles in the house of John Oxenbridge at Eton.

1654   Writes *The First Anniversary of the Government under O.C.*, political poem; published anonymously the following year.

1657   Writes more occasional poetry dealing with political events, including "On the Victory Obtained by Blake over the Spaniards." Appointed assistant to Milton who was Latin secretary to the Council of State.

1658   Writes "A Poem upon the Death of Oliver Cromwell."

1659   Elected to Parliament from Hull; will remain a member of Parliament until his death.

1660   Restoration of the monarchy. Defends Milton in Parliament against charges of participating in regicide (i.e., the execution of King Charles I); helps win relatively lenient treatment for Milton.

1662   Travels for a year in Holland on a mission which probably includes both diplomacy and espionage.

1663   Travels in Russia and Scandinavia as part of the earl of Carlisle's diplomatic mission.

1665   Returns to England. His poem *The Character of Holland* is published anonymously.

1667   Politically active, speaking in Parliament against Lord Clarendon and other leaders of the court party. Also writes and publishes (anonymously) his most famous political satires, *Directions to a Painter* and *The Last Instructions to a Painter*. These and later political works will be the basis of Marvell's contemporary fame.

1669–   Marvell devotes his energies to a series of political-religious satires, most
1678   published anonymously.

1678   Marvell publishes the theological tract *Remarks Upon a Late Disingenuous Discourse . . . By a Protestant*. Death of Marvell.

1681   Most of Marvell's poems are published in a volume entitled *Miscellaneous Poems* by Mary Palmer, who claims to be Marvell's widow. In fact, she is probably a servant of Marvell's attempting to lay claim to his estate; Marvell was never married.

1689   Several of Marvell's political satires are published in *Poems on Affairs of State*. More are added to later editions of this anthology published between 1697 and 1716.

ESSAY QUESTIONS WITH ANSWERS

"To His Coy Mistress"

22.1 What is the theme of this poem?

Answer On the surface, the theme of this poem is love, its object seduction. The poet-lover attempts to seduce his lady by means of witty argument. Life is too short, he says, to delay the gratification of pleasure, as she seems to want to do. Advising her to act now while she is young and passionate, the speaker argues that sex provides a way to make the most out of life. But the darker subject of the poem is death, which underlies the unconventional aspects of Marvell's treatment of the traditional *carpe diem* motif.

It is in the middle of the poem (lines 20–33) that the subject of death is introduced. The "But" which begins line 20 suggests a logical turn in the poem: the poet, having lavishly described what he *would* do if he had the time, now shows that the time is lacking. Time, a somewhat sinister traditional figure, often depicted as armed with a scythe, enters the poem to remind the poet and the lady of their own mortality; here he seems to have taken over Phoebus's chariot, as though the progress of the sun itself were merely another expression of time's precipitous race toward the grave. The imagery which follows—the "Deserts of vast eternity" and the "worms" which invade the beloved's virginity—provide a macabre and graphic picture of death. In the midst of his seduction, the poet calls forth an image of death.

The conventional *carpe diem* poem does not include such a concrete evocation of death. Marvell's use of vivid, macabre imagery gives emotional intensity to these lines, as the playful, relaxed tone of the first twenty lines gives way to the more serious, gripping tone of the middle section. In the last section the speaker seems to recover his emotional balance. The imagery is vivid and the mood apparently brighter, yet there is a new intensity and urgency in the poet's tone. His pursuit of pleasure has become rapacious, almost desperate: "devour," "tear our pleasures with rough strife." This violent, willful immersion in the sensual seems a way of blocking out the disconcerting vision of mortality.

22.2   Discuss the poet's use of exaggeration in the first verse paragraph of the poem.

Answer   The poet begins his poem with a supposition: *if* he had enough time and space, he would patiently accept his lady's virginity and praise her virtues endlessly. This hypothetical condition enables the poet to indulge in praise so hyperbolic that it exceeds that of even the most ardent Petrarchan lover: "An hundred years should go to praise/ Thine eyes, and on thy forehead gaze;/ Two hundred to adore each breast." He would praise his lady, the poet says, from England to India and from the dawn of time to the very brink of the Last Judgment ("the Conversion of the Jews").

The exaggerations of the verse paragraph culminate in a final couplet: "For, lady, you deserve this state,/ Nor would I love at lower rate." The implied monetary metaphor in the last line makes an ironic comment on the quantitative praise employed by conventional love poetry. The implication is that there is something ludicrous in a love that can be reckoned.

This satirical note qualifies, but does not wholly dissipate, the poet's claim that only such extravagance will do justice to his lady's merits; although playfully, he is placing all of time and space at the lady's feet. If ordinary poets, with less deserving ladies, have cheapened the currency of more modest praise—so Marvell implies—only such inflationary rhetoric will now be adequate to the occasion. Even as he mocks the convention, the speaker outdoes his rivals—as much, presumably, as his mistress outshines theirs.

22.3   Comment on the imagery and tone of the following lines:

> And yonder all before us lie
> Deserts of vast eternity.
> Thy beauty shall no more be found,
> Nor, in thy marble vault, shall sound
> My echoing song; then worms shall try
> That long-preserved virginity,
> And your quaint honor turn to dust,
> And into ashes all my lust.
> (lines 23–30)

Answer   These lines present a picture of sterility and death: vast reverberating spaces in which nothing flourishes or even lives, except the worms who feed upon decay. The lady's refusal would deny life, both sexual fruition and generative possibilities, and inherit no future but silence and the grave. The "marble vault" of line 26 may suggest not only death—the lady's hollow funeral monument, in which no poet's "echoing song" disturbs the stillness—but also the barren womb of the mistress.

The lady's virginity, her "quaint honor," is presented as something merely physical, which worms will deflower; only in death will she "breed," or sustain new life. Although the imagery is ghoulish, the tone is dry and aloof, as though mocking the lady's fastidiousness, her "quaint" preservation of a commodity which will eventually profit no one. The same ironic understatement is continued in lines 31–32: "The grave's a fine and private place,/ But none, I think, do there embrace."

In the last two lines of the passage, a sexual image becomes an image of death: the fires of the poet's desire become the "ashes" of lust. The reference to ashes imports an echo of the biblical "ashes to ashes, dust to dust," and the poet remembers his own mortality as well as the lady's. Her "coyness" wastes his youth and animal vitality as well as her own. In lines 35–36 the poet once again evokes the "instant fires" of physical health and sexual energy which the "willing soul transpires/ At every pore." He seems to imply that after his tour of eternity's barren wastelands it should be clearer than ever that this glow, the radiance of "all our strength and all/ Our sweetness," is too precious to squander.

"The Garden"

22.4 What values or qualities are evoked by the image of the garden in Marvell's poem?

Answer Various stanzas of the poem depict different types of gardens. For example, in stanza 3, the garden is presented as a superior substitute for sexual love; in stanza 5, the poet paints an image of a sensual, richly natural garden; in stanza 6, he describes a solitary, contemplative garden, a garden of the mind. The major antithesis in the poem, however, depends upon the distinction between the active and the contemplative life. The garden of the title is primarily a garden of solitude and reflection, to which the male poet retires from society (and women) to meditate (and, perhaps, as the fruit of his meditation, to create poetry).

The first and second stanzas introduce this antithesis. Whereas other men vainly "amaze" themselves (that is, become frenzied) to win a garland which is the emblem of their success in the world, the poet can retire to nature and the country, there to find not only an abundance of real flowers but also quiet and innocence for his rewards. Wittily he contrasts the "single Herb or Tree" which crowns the poet, athlete, or politician with the wealth of plant life which shelters the contemplative man. Peace is mistakenly sought, he says, in the "busy companies of men." Society is "rude/ To [compared to] this delicious solitude," the poet says in stanza 2, thereby reversing the conventional association of civility with society.

This garden of solitude and contemplation excludes not only society in general but women in particular; the couplet which ends stanza 8, "Two paradises 'twere in one/ To live in paradise alone," is a witty (and misogynistic) twist on the image of the paradise of Adam and Eve. Eden, the poet says, would be so much greater without the distracting presence of Eve. On the other hand, the images of sensual ripeness in stanza 5 ("luscious clusters of the vine," "melons," "ripe apples," and so on) suggest that the garden may after all be suffused with a kind of feminine presence and that the poet, like the frustrated gods he recalls in stanza 4, has at most "sublimated" his desires. Perhaps sexual pleasure is not so easily renounced as the poem's explicit argument asserts. Can one finally imagine a garden of Eden without an Eve?

22.5   What is the meaning of the lines "Meanwhile the Mind, from pleasure less,/ Withdraws into its happiness"?

Answer   The two opening lines of stanza 6 are ambiguous. On the one hand, the lines may refer to the mind's becoming self-absorbed in savoring the pleasure of the garden. On the other hand, they may mean that the mind withdraws from lesser pleasures (those of the senses) into contemplation. The latter reading is attractive because it directly links this stanza with the preceding one: the natural, sensual pleasures portrayed in stanza 5 represent "lesser" pleasures than those of the mind. The first reading more directly links the lines with the remainder of stanza 6.

There the mind first discovers its own plenitude as an "ocean" which contains images of all things in external nature (just as medieval and Renaissance zoology proposed that the ocean contained an aquatic creature corresponding to every terrestrial one). However, the imagination, transcending the world of the senses, goes further, to "create" from its own resources "Far other worlds and other seas." Thus it "annihilates" the created world; that is, it extinguishes the image of the real world and substitutes instead a world of the imagination, a garden of the mind. Both the world that's "made" and the "green Thought" are creations—the first, God's creation; the second, the poet's.

22.6 What is the significance of the bird in stanza 7?

Answer The bird is a symbol for the poet's soul, preparing to take flight in mystic contemplation. The soul "sings," that is, expresses its desires and longings; it grooms itself, perhaps, for its final flight to God (the "longer flight" of line 55). The feeling of the seventh stanza is more mystical than that of the preceding stanzas, but it still retains a certain spirit of play. The bird/soul preening itself and waving its plumes in the light suggests a playful image of the poet singing his song or merely of the soul celebrating its own freedom. The metaphorical divestiture of the body in the stanza does not lead to asceticism for the poet, or a denial of earthly beauty; the poet's bird/soul can still delight in the play of the "various light" of this world on its feathers.

K.L.

SUGGESTED READINGS

Berthoff, Anne, *The Resolved Soul* (1970).

Carey, John, ed., *Andrew Marvell: Penguin Critical Anthology* (1969).

Colie, Rosalie, *"My Ecchoing Song": Andrew Marvell's Poetry of Criticism* (1970).

Friedman, Donald, *Marvell's Pastoral Art* (1970).

Leishman, J. B., *The Art of Marvell's Poetry* (1966).

Lord, George de Forest, ed., *Andrew Marvell: A Collection of Critical Essays* (1968).

Wallace, John, *Destiny His Choice: The Loyalism of Andrew Marvell* (1968).

Part Five

THE

RESTORATION

T I M E L I N E

The Age

1620:   Pilgrims sail to America on the *Mayflower*

1625:   Death of James I; accession of Charles I

1628:   Parliament submits Petition of Rights, outlining grievances against Charles I

1642:   English civil war begins. Theaters ordered closed by Puritan-dominated Parliament

1648:   Thirty Years' War ended by Treaty of Westphalia

1649:   Charles I defeated, imprisoned, beheaded; Commonwealth declared. Cromwell marches against rebels in Scotland and Ireland

1652:   War with Holland; victories of Admiral Blake

1658:   Death of Cromwell

1660:   Restoration; accession of Charles II

1685:   Death of Charles II; accession of James II, who favors the Roman Catholics; unpopular monarch

1688:   Protestant prince William of Orange invades England; James II escapes to France; "Bloodless Revolution"

1689:   William and Mary crowned

1694:   Death of Mary

1701:   Act of Settlement permanently excludes Roman Catholic descendants of James I from the throne

1702:   Death of William; accession of Queen Anne

1707:   Union of England and Scotland as Great Britain

1709:   First English copyright act

1714:   Death of Anne; accession of George I, Hanoverian (German) prince

1718:   England at war with Spain

1727:   Death of George I; accession of George II

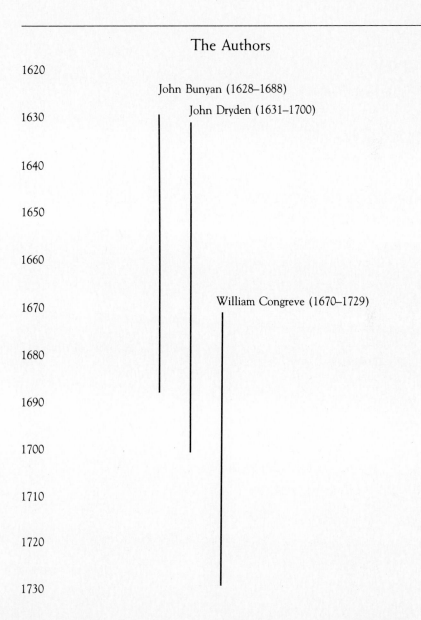

The Authors

1620

John Bunyan (1628–1688)

John Dryden (1631–1700)

1630

1640

1650

1660

1670   William Congreve (1670–1729)

1680

1690

1700

1710

1720

1730

JOHN BUNYAN

C H R O N O L O G Y

1628   Born in Elstow, near Bedford. Son of Thomas Bunyan and Margaret Bunyan, both from families of small tradesmen. Little is known of Bunyan's early life, although he probably attended grammar school in a nearby village.

1644   In quick succession, Bunyan's mother and younger sister die; his father remarries soon after. Bunyan is drafted, along with other young men of his village, into the Parliamentary Army then at war with the army of King Charles I; he is stationed at Newport Pagnell, about 12 miles from Elstow.

1647   Bunyan's regiment is disbanded; he returns home and takes up the family trade of tinker. He marries his first wife, about whom virtually nothing is known.

1650   Birth of Mary, Bunyan's daughter; she is blind from birth. Under the leadership of preacher John Gifford, the Bedford Separatist Church is formed; a nonconforming (i.e., non-Anglican) church close in doctrine to the Baptists, it will be a dominant influence in Bunyan's life.

1653   Probable date of the spiritual events Bunyan regarded as his conversion to Christ, as later described in *Grace Abounding to the Chief of Sinners.*

1655   Bunyan's family moves to Bedford; he is officially received into Gifford's Bedford church. Soon after, Gifford dies.

1656   Bunyan begins his career as a lay (i.e., nonordained) preacher; in the beginning, his preaching is probably done mainly in secret meetings, since lay preaching is officially outlawed in England. Bunyan also writes his first work, *Some Gospel-truths Opened*, a tract setting forth Bunyan's position in certain doctrinal disputes with the Quakers, another nonconforming sect.

1658   Death of Bunyan's wife, soon after the birth of son Thomas. Bunyan publishes *A Few Sighs from Hell*, one of the many sermonlike tracts he will write over the next three decades.

1659   Bunyan marries his second wife, Elizabeth.

1660   In the suppression of dissent initiated with the restoration of the monarchy, Bunyan is imprisoned for unlicensed preaching. He will remain in prison with only brief periods of freedom for twelve years; however, he continues to write, counsel, and even preach, both within prison and, on occasion, outside.

1666   Bunyan publishes his spiritual autobiography, *Grace Abounding*; after *The Pilgrim's Progress* his best-known work.

1671   Bunyan is allowed to leave prison occasionally; he preaches and writes.

1672   Ratified as pastor of the Bedford Separatist Church and soon thereafter licensed as a Congregational preacher. Finally released from prison under a royal Declaration of Indulgence. Ironically, Quaker leaders, whose beliefs Bunyan had often attacked in his writings, make a special plea that helps to obtain his release.

1674   Agnes Beaumont, a young woman in Bunyan's congregation, is accused of murdering her father, some say with Bunyan's help. She is cleared of the charge; however, for the rest of his life, Bunyan must defend himself against charges of sexual dalliance with his female followers.

1675   Royal proclamation issued enforcing attendance at Anglican churches; Bunyan is probably forced into hiding. By this time, he has published numerous tracts and has become a famous preacher, sometimes invited to preach in Pinner's Hall, a well-known London meetinghouse for dissenters.

1677   For failing to attend Anglican church services, Bunyan is imprisoned again; released after about six months. Probably writes Part I of *The Pilgrim's Progress* while in prison.

1678   Part I of *The Pilgrim's Progress* published.

1680   *The Life and Death of Mr. Badman*, an allegorical narrative in the vein of *The Pilgrim's Progress*, published.

1682   *The Holy War* published.

1684   Part II of *The Pilgrim's Progress*.

1685   Another wave of represssion against dissenters occurs, but Bunyan escapes
            imprisonment this time.

1686   Bunyan publishes *A Book for Boys and Girls*, a collection of brief, tender
            poems.

1688   On August 19, Bunyan visits Reading and there preaches his last sermon.
            He falls ill, aggravates the illness by exposure to cold and rain, and dies on
            August 31. Over the next ten years, more than a dozen of Bunyan's pre-
            viously unpublished works will appear, bringing to over sixty the total of
            his works.

ESSAY QUESTIONS WITH ANSWERS

The Pilgrim's Progress

23.1 John Bunyan's prose style is extremely simple; it employs the most basic verbs and nouns and tends to rely upon repetition. What is the effect of this narrative style?

Answer Bunyan's style is closely associated with that of biblical narrative, which likewise relies on a condensed, abrupt, repetitive mode of representation. Erich Auerbach, in Chapter 1 of *Mimesis: The Representation of Reality in Western Literature*, discusses how the abstraction and discontinuity of the bible produce a "background" quality: the alternation between general obscurity and moments of focused intensity suggests the influence of a background of unexpressed connections and correlatives which require interpretive commentary.

It is this mysterious background effect that Bunyan's narrative style creates. In the first paragraph of *The Pilgrim's Progress*, for example, Bunyan sets his dreamer in "a certain place" and the dream figure in "a certain place." We are thrust abruptly into an allegorical landscape quite different from our ordinary world. (Of course, the dream format itself suggests a symbolic plane. In western society, dreams have traditionally been thought to have moral or prophetic significance, and the use of the literary dream as a device for presenting a symbolic narrative is an old one.) As the dream begins, Bunyan provides, instead of realistic naming and factual description, an obscure, undifferentiated setting, a place lacking in geographical specificity and inhabited by people who are often without names. Christian, whose name is withheld for several pages, looms in front of this vague backdrop. His attributes—rags, burden, averted face, and book—acquire symbolic import partly because they are so carefully named by the dreamer-narrator.

The alternation between vague, abstract reference and intense focus on a few details creates an emblematic or synecdochic quality, with each significant feature standing for an unexpressed whole. Such a narrative technique is allegorical because it points to a suppressed narration, an implicit story to which the surface story alludes.

Bunyan points to the second level of meaning, the "true" story, in several ways. At key points he directs the reader to the scripture itself as a means of elaborating on the condensed images or utterances of his own narrative. Thus, the biblical citations which parenthetically follow the initial description of Christian as "a man clothed in rags" identify each feature of his appearance in relation to a scriptural reference point. His burden, for example, is glossed by Psalms 38:4: "For mine iniquities are gone over mine head: as a heavy burden they are too heavy for me." All of the citations taken together contribute to the portrait of a soul in crisis, awakening to a sense of sin and on the verge of detaching itself from such worldly possessions as house, clothes, and even family. Similarly, the scriptural footnotes to the "wicket gate" and "shining light," which the Evangelist points out to Christian as the destination of his journey, constitute a kind of shorthand exegesis of the meaning of and way toward salvation.

At other points in the narration Bunyan supplies his own exegesis. After offering the parable of the Slough of Despond in which Christian, almost sinking under the burden of his sins, is saved by Help, Bunyan explicates the story: ". . . it is the descent whither the scum and filth that attends conviction for sin doth continually run, and therefore it was called the Slough of Despond; for still, as the sinner is awakened about his lost condition, there ariseth in his soul many fears, and doubts, and discouraging apprehensions, which all of them get together, and settle in this place. And this is the reason of the badness of this ground."

Throughout the narrative, language is used as gesture, that is, as a means of pointing rather than directly naming or describing. Words are not solely references to or substitutes for the "real" world outside the text, but signs of something both unexpressed and perhaps even inexpressible except by symbolic means. For example, the Slough of Despond and Vanity Fair are both represented in the equivalent of sign language, a prose that lacks the coherence and connectedness of the realistic style. Although these places are described to a certain extent, the descriptions are selective and emphatic in ways that undermine objective reference. The miry bog named Despond into which the travelers "being heedless, did both fall suddenly" and the fair "of ancient standing" where lusts and souls are sold and "the ware of Rome and her merchandise is greatly promoted" clearly stand for something other than literal places. These images, of despair on the one hand and of worldly seduction on the other, are part of an unexpressed whole, namely the spiritual experience of a Christian in his pilgrimage on earth.

The sudden focus on a few vivid, concrete details is one way in which Bunyan makes language serve as sign or pointer. Another means he employs for activating the symbolic potential of words is repetition. For example, in his description of the Celestial City he repeatedly uses light imagery: "shone like gold," "shone as the light," "shone like the sun," "shining men." The insistent emphasis on shining links the city to the "shining light" (Psalms 119:105; 2 Peter 1:19) of salvation which the Evangelist pointed out to Christian at the outset of his pilgrimage. The reiterated imagery also brings into play all the possible associations of light, shining, and gold. Heaven is at once a source of spiritual illumination and a blinding vision: it is alluring but unreachable; translucent but, paradoxically, by virtue of its very brightness, opaque and somehow impenetrable. In a certain sense, Bunyan's language is ambivalent: heaven is as much armored in light as it is the bearer of it.

Bunyan's style, then, is, like the Bible's, anything but simple. By using a synecdochic and reiterative technique he compresses a large background of spiritual and scriptural history within his plainspoken narrative.

23.2 Analyze the description of Vanity Fair, comparing it with the final vision of the Celestial City.

Answer The name "Vanity" declares the fair's essential symbolic meaning: the word means "emptiness" and, as Bunyan implies, is associated with the qualities of "lightness" (in its seventeenth-century sense of "wantonness, frivolity"), weightlessness, and triviality. Although the town is a cornucopia of wares and possessions, of material things, its name suggests that it is in fact insubstantial and illusory.

In describing the town, Bunyan employs lengthy catalogues of nouns which stylistically reinforce the idea of material plenty. The fair is a marketplace which sells all the things of the world, from houses and pearls to titles, lusts, children, and even souls. In this carnival of merchandise, the pilgrims are seen first as foreigners, then as madmen who must be caged. They reject the offered wares, saying they will only "buy the truth." Christian is here an emblem of Christian folly, an innocence and truth which are martyred by the worldly sinners who are, of course, the real fools.

The idea of salvation, most fully expressed in the vision of the Celestial City is, perhaps surprisingly, conveyed through concrete imagery of wealth and riches not unlike that used to describe the fair. The streets of heaven are paved with gold, and the saved are dressed in raiment of gold, with crowns on their heads and golden harps in their hands. Thus, at least in part, the world is rebuked by heaven in the world's own terms. The illusory riches of Vanity Fair are exchanged for the genuine rewards of the Celestial City, and "truth" is revealed as a better bargain than all the kingdoms of the earth. The "bedlam" pilgrims are thus shown to be wiser than the savvy merchants of the marketplace.

This ironic reversal illustrates the essential Christian paradox: men must die to live again, rejecting earthly splendors for heavenly glory. But the vision of heaven is not unambiguously joyful. In part, the repeated emphasis on gold and splendid raiment, together with the incessant chorus of "Holy, holy, holy" with which the saved greet each other, makes heaven seem like a static and ecstatic state which excludes not only the dreamer ("after that they shut up the gates") but the reader as well. Heaven is a tantalizing prospect, an alluring vista beyond the reach of ordinary mortals. Vanity Fair is open to all, but heaven, clearly, is reserved for a chosen few. In this description Bunyan evokes the whole problem of election and the ongoing struggle of the individual Protestant to feel himself worthy of the golden crown and harp of the saved.

23.3   The story of *The Pilgrim's Progress* consists of the journey of the Christian soul through the temptations and trials of the world to a safe haven in the Celestial City. However, the story does not end on this happy note. In the final paragraph of the work, Bunyan describes the rejection of Ignorance at the same gates which have just opened to receive Christian and Hopeful. Discuss the effect of this episode and the logic of its placement.

Answer   The incident is especially significant because Ignorance is not an obviously villainous sinner but, rather, a fool whose error lies in a combination of dull passivity and obstinate refusal to accept the truth. His exclusion from heaven suggests the range of sins which are, literally, damnable. In the case of Ignorance, a kind of slothful ease attends his crossing of the river. Once at the gates of the Celestial City, however, he learns that although there are no shortcuts to heaven, there is a shortcut to hell. In accepting a ride across the River of Death with the ferryman Vain-Hope, Ignorance has evaded the necessary soul-searching which must precede salvation. The didactic import is that knowledge of God and the Bible is a prerequisite for salvation. The exclusion of Ignorance makes the point that not only willful sinners but the passive and the slothful will be turned away by the king.

This conclusion reinforces the homiletic quality of *The Pilgrim's Progress* as a whole. In the story of Christian's successful pilgrimage and the failure of others to complete the journey Bunyan pursues a hortatory purpose: to persuade the "congregation" of his readers to follow the path of faith and knowledge that will lead to the celestial gate. By ending with a pessimistic image, with the dreamer-narrator shut outside the gates and Ignorance thrown into hell, Bunyan places the reader beyond the pale as well. We are not welcomed in with Christian and Hopeful but excluded with the narrator. Furthermore, in Ignorance's fall we witness an ultimate exclusion. The effect is not solely hortatory, on the order of *memento mori* ("remember death"), but a dramatization of the reader's situation at the moment of his reading. Still in the midst of his pilgrimage, he is made to feel the peril and the promise that await him.

B.S.

SUGGESTED READINGS

Kaufmann, U. Milo, *The Pilgrim's Progress and Traditions in Puritan Meditation* (1966).

Talon, Henri A., *John Bunyan: The Man and His Work* (1951).

Tindall, William Y., *John Bunyan, Mechanick, Preacher* (1934).

Wharey, J. B., ed., *The Pilgrim's Progress* (1928; revised by Roger Sharrock, 1960).

JOHN DRYDEN

C H R O N O L O G Y

1631   Born in Northamptonshire. Son of Erasmus Dryden and Mary Pickering Dryden, both from families of small landowners. The Drydens are Puritans in religion and politics, and will side with Parliament against the king during the civil wars of the 1640s.

1642   Outbreak of first civil war. Closing of the English theaters under pressure from the Puritans, who decried the "immorality" of the stage.

1644   Dryden enters Westminster School in London, where he will study until 1650.

1649   Outbreak of second civil war; King Charles I executed; establishment of Puritan Commonwealth under Oliver Cromwell.

1650   Dryden enters Trinity College, Cambridge; receives B.A. in 1654.

1656   Settles in London, working as government clerk.

1658   Writes *Heroic Stanzas on the Death of the Protector*, commemorating Cromwell.

1660   Restoration of monarchy under Charles II, commemorated by Dryden in poem *Astraea Redux*. Reopening of the theaters.

1662   Dryden elected to the Royal Society, whose scientific publications help develop a new English prose style—clear, simple, strong—embodied also in Dryden's writings.

1663	Marries Lady Elizabeth Howard, daughter of a well-to-do royalist family. Produces his first play, *The Wild Gallant*; it is a failure.
1665	Dryden's career blossoms. "Heroic" plays *The Indian Queen* (written in collaboration with Sir Robert Howard) and *The Indian Emperor* (a sequel) are successes.
1666	*Annus Mirabilis*, political poem supporting the monarchy, published.
1667	Three plays by Dryden produced, including his adaptation of Shakespeare's *The Tempest*.
1668	On recommendation of King Charles II, Dryden receives M.A. from Cambridge. *An Essay of Dramatic Poesy* published; one of the finest early works of literary criticism. Appointment of Dryden as poet laureate.
1669	Dryden's comedy *An Evening's Love* produced, as is his heroic play *Tyrannic Love*; the latter features Nell Gwyn, mistress of the king, in a leading role.
1670	Production of *The Conquest of Granada*, Dryden's most famous heroic play. Appointment of Dryden as historiographer royal, which, with laureateship, carried an annual pension of £200.
1671– 1672	Three plays produced, including most notably the tragicomedy *Marriage à la Mode*.
1673– 1674	Among other works, Dryden writes *The State of Innocence*, an opera based on Milton's *Paradise Lost*. Engages in acrimonious "pamphlet war" with Elkanah Settle, a younger dramatist competing with Dryden for the favor of audiences and noble patrons.
1675– 1677	Plays *Aureng-Zebe* and *All For Love* produced; the latter, a version of the Antony and Cleopatra story, generally considered Dryden's best.
1678	Plays produced: *The Kind Keeper* (a comedy) and *Oedipus* (a collaboration with Nathaniel Lee). Writes *MacFlecknoe*, satirizing rival poet Thomas Shadwell.
1679	Writes essay "Remarks on the Grounds of Criticism in Tragedy," taking a strongly neoclassical stance, probably under influence of French critic Boileau. Beaten by hired thugs, probably because of false suspicion that he had written "An Essay on Satire," which had attacked the earl of Rochester and two of the king's noble mistresses.
1681	*Absalom and Achitophel*, great political narrative poem supporting the king; it is reprinted nine times in two years.
1682	*Religio Laici*, poem examining problems of religion and politics, supportive of the Church of England.

1683   Dryden embarks on a career as a translator, collaborating on an English version of Plutarch's *Lives*.

1684   Publisher Jacob Tonson issues first of several volumes of miscellaneous works by Dryden; it contains satires, prologues and epilogues to his plays, and translations. Dryden writes "To the Memory of Mr. Oldham."

1685   Death of Charles II; Roman Catholic James II accedes to throne; Dryden converts to Catholicism. Tonson publishes *Sylvae*, containing Dryden's translations from Latin.

1687   *The Hind and the Panther* published, a poem in defense of Catholicism.

1688   James II dethroned in favor of the Protestants William and Mary. Dryden refuses to take oath of allegiance to new monarchs, is ousted as poet laureate and historiographer royal in favor of his nemesis Shadwell.

1689   For financial reasons, Dryden returns to the stage with *Don Sebastian*. In later years, he becomes the first English author to depend directly on the public for his support.

1690–
1693   Several more plays produced, including *Amphitryon* (1690), an adaptation from Molière. Tonson publishes *Examen Poeticum* (1693), containing Dryden's translations from Latin and Greek.

1694–
1695   Death of Queen Mary. Dryden translates Virgil, other classic and contemporary writers.

1697   Dryden's *Works of Virgil* published; he vetoes Tonson's plan to dedicate the volume to King William, but Tonson alters the illustrations to make the hero, Aeneas, resemble the king. Dryden earns over £1200 from the volume.

1700   Dryden's *Fables* published, including translations from Chaucer and Ovid, verse adaptations of tales from Boccaccio's *Decameron*, and a notable preface. Death of Dryden.

ESSAY QUESTIONS WITH ANSWERS

"Song for St. Cecilia's Day"

24.1 Dryden's "Song for St. Cecilia's Day" is an occasional poem, written to celebrate the feast day of the patron saint of music. Appropriately, Dryden offers specific examples of the power of music to move its listeners. Discuss the language and the acoustic patterns which Dryden uses to develop this theme in the central section of the poem.

Answer Dryden relies heavily on acoustic patterns in the ode because he is trying, by an emphasis on sound itself, to make his poetry analogous to music. Of course, words differ from musical notes because of their semantic properties and their linear order; the verbal medium can produce neither pure sound nor an effect of simultaneity. However, despite the inevitable inexactness of the correspondences, Dryden seems to be trying to emphasize the musical qualities of words, attempting to capture the timbre, as well as the emotional resonance, associated with the notes of the lyre ("the corded shell"), trumpet, drum, flute, lute, violin, and organ. The organ has the climactic place in the catalogue partly because it is St. Cecilia's own instrument (Dryden attributes its invention to her) and perhaps also because of its richness of tone, which combines percussive and melodic qualities.

Dryden conveys the specific tonal quality of instruments through various sound patterns, including insistent rhythms, onomatopoeia, metrical pattern, alliteration, repeated cadences, and feminine (polysyllabic) rhymes. For example, the seven rhyming lines of stanza 2 focus attention on harmonic pattern, the similar sounds coming so rapidly that they produce almost the effect of a chord. In the third stanza, the trumpet's blare is described by the word "clangor," which both connotes a metallic ringing and, by its arrangement of consonants, partially echoes that sound. Dryden describes the drum with the adjective "thundering," but the steady iambic march of the line "The double double double beat" underscores the description by suggesting the rhythmic striking of a percussion instrument.

In the fourth stanza, the words "complaining," "dying," and "warbling" have semantic associations with singing (both plaint and bird song) and with cadence (literally, a "falling"). In addition, the reiterated *ing* sound makes its own music, producing a kind of chiming effect. The alliterative *w*'s add to the stanza's musical properties, their soft breathy quality drawing attention to the sounds apart from the connotations of words. In the fifth stanza Dryden describes the sharpness of the violins, attributing a special emotional resonance to the instrument by his allusions to "pangs," "fury," and "pains." Acoustic pattern further contributes to the idea of sharpness and discontinuity, the four-syllable words "desperation" and "indignation" creating a staccato effect as of plucked strings.

Again and again Dryden chooses words that allow him to exploit simultaneously their connotative and acoustic properties. In addition, Dryden supplies hints of different dramatic situations which are suitable to each instrument. Trumpet and drum are associated with warfare, flute and lute with hopeless love, and the violin with jealous passion. The organ is treated more elaborately, not by means of acoustic imitation but rather by a more fully developed narrative strand. Dryden alludes to the classical legend of Orpheus to suggest the miraculous power of music and then uses the saint's legend of Cecilia as an example of a specific miracle, the angelic sanction of the earthly music of the organ.

The descriptive and narrative elements in the poem portray a consort of instruments, but the emphatic use of acoustic patterns makes the poem itself into a harmony of sounds. Handel merely took the invitation implicit in the text of Dryden's poem when he created a musical score for the lyric in the eighteenth century.

24.2 What is the relationship beween the first and last stanzas of the poem?

Answer The first and last stanzas of the poem constitute an "overture" and "coda" for Dryden's song, initiating and concluding the development of its major themes. The movement from beginning to end also signifies the cycle of the universe from Creation to Apocalypse and a transition between the natural world and heaven. In both, music is the agent of change and development.

In the first stanza the metrical pattern, with its intricate, delayed rhyme scheme (*abcdefefcdababb*), embodies the slow emergence of order from the chaos of "jarring atoms" at the Creation. The repeated phrase "From harmony, from heavenly harmony," changing to "From harmony to harmony," reflects the resolution of dissonance in a "diapason," the full scale of an octave. Using musical imagery, Dryden establishes music as a symbol of natural law, that "tuneful voice" which calls dead nature into life. Through the harmonic powers of music, God orders and organizes the chaos of elements. The "diapason," or octave, "closing full in man," signifies the hierarchical pattern of the universe, with man occupying the highest natural place.

The highly regular metrical rhythms of the "Grand Chorus" which concludes the poem contrast with the complex syncopation of the opening, thus indicating the splendid order of the cosmic frame at the moment before its dissolution. (Paradoxically, the universe is at once an orderly motion of spheres and a "crumbling pageant," an imperfect, merely physical realm which shall be "devoured" at the Day of Judgment.) Instead of "jarring atoms" and scattered elements, Dryden presents in the "Grand Chorus" an image of moving spheres: the "sacred lays" of the angels impelled the celestial bodies (stars and planets) to move in patterns which produce a harmonious chord, the music of the spheres. Dryden thus poses a celestial unity against the chaos preceding Creation and the Apocalypse to come.

In the closing lines of the poem, Dryden emphasizes the permanence of pattern even as Judgment Day, "the last and dreadful hour," approaches. The biblical allusion to the final blare of the trumpet precedes a vivid use of paradox symbolizing the essential Christian mystery. The line "The dead shall live, the living die" embodies the paradox of eternal life through resurrection and the continuity of order even in the midst of apparent chaos, as the saved ascend from the natural world into heaven. In the final line of the poem, Dryden again uses music as the emblem of cosmic and religious transformation: music itself, the principle of harmony in the universe, is specifically named as the agent of dissolution. Furthermore, the phrase "untune the sky," containing within it the word "tune," suggests that the process of dissolution is somehow as harmonious, because divinely ordained, as was the process of creation in the opening stanza.

MacFlecknoe

24.3 How does Dryden establish the mock-heroic tone in his satire on Thomas Shadwell?

Answer Dryden's major rhetorical strategy in his satirical attack on Shadwell is to develop a parodic myth in which Shadwell is made heir to the imperial scepter of Flecknoe, a contemporary Irish poet known for his incompetence. By creating an elevated narrative involving Shadwell's "consecration" and "coronation," Dryden produces an ironic discrepancy between the lofty tale and the dubious "hero." Shadwell's inadequacies are thrown into high relief against this mock-epic backdrop.

Shadwell is dwarfed not only by the narrative but by the majestic style of the poem. The epic similes comparing Shadwell to famous Romans and the allusions to classical legends create a gap between the nobility of the ancients and the silly pretensions of Shadwell. Sometimes Dryden embroiders classical lore with comic variations, substituting, for example, a crown of poppies for the poet's laurel wreath (line 126) or an omen of drowsy owls for warlike vultures (line 129). Sometimes he inflates a classical parallel and then suddenly punctures it with a "punch line" which exposes Shadwell's ineptitude:

> As Hannibal did to the altars come,
> Sworn by his sire, a mortal foe to Rome,
> So Sh— swore, nor should his vow be vain,
> That he till death true dullness would maintain.
>   (lines 112–115)

Sudden deflation is also a mechanism operating in the mockery of encomiastic rhetoric which runs through the poem. Syntactic structure implying compliment is suddenly contradicted by Dryden's surprise offering of an insult where one expects praise.

> Sh— alone, of all my sons, is he
> Who stands confirmed in full stupidity.
> The rest to some faint meaning make pretense,
> But Sh— never deviates into sense.
>   (lines 17–20)

Behind the comic myth, epic allusion, and elevated rhetoric is the sustained pretense of praise. The myth of royal coronation is like a perspective trick which diminishes Shadwell by placing him in a vast heroic arena. The sudden drops in language shrink Shadwell to pygmy stature as the inflated diction collapses.

The mock-epic tone is thus Dryden's most effective weapon against Shadwell. By pushing his victim off such heights, blandly smiling all the while, Dryden demolishes him more thoroughly than he could with the direct violence of invective. With his deadpan praise, he makes of Shadwell something lower than a villain: a laughingstock.

24.4 Dryden's satire incorporates a wide range of topical references and classical allusions. Because many of these references may be obscure to a modern reader, it could be argued that the poem is a historical relic of only antiquarian interest. What is the effect of the references in the poem? Are they still effective for a modern audience?

Answer The classical allusions in *MacFlecknoe* are part of the mock-epic technique of the poem: the references to Augustus, Hannibal, Arion, Romulus, and so on create a heroic arena in which Shadwell appears much diminished. The contemporary references, too, diminish the poet; they provide a satiric counterpoint, moving Shadwell's kingdom from the Augustan realm down into the narrow crooked streets of seventeenth-century London.

The many topical references have the further effect of transforming the satire into a "scandal sheet"; the poem becomes a journalistic sally of immediate interest to a circle of Restoration literati who were knowledgeable about the rival poets, plays, and styles alluded to. However, the modern reader, who is not fully "in the know," can still pick up the gossipy, knowing air which hovers about the proper names and italicized titles. In addition, the information supplied in the footnotes to most modern editions of *MacFlecknoe* is sufficient to introduce a twentieth-century audience to the historical milieu of the poem. (Some knowledge of the people and events referred to is, of course, necessary for full enjoyment of the satire.)

Even when a specific allusion is obscure, Dryden's literary judgments emerge clearly. When he says that Heywood and Shirley "were but types of thee,/ Thou last great prophet of tautology" (lines 29–30), it is clear that he is incorporating contemporary writers into a biblical scheme. The two writers are, of course, bad writers (in Dryden's view) who, coming before MacFlecknoe's time, prefigured the great prophet himself, whose message is—redundancy. When Dryden alludes to Ben Jonson in Flecknoe's exhortation to his son ("Thou art my blood, where Jonson has not part" [line 175]), he elaborates on MacFlecknoe's lack of indebtedness to the great Jonson, listing as proof MacFlecknoe's many negative accomplishments. The reader is thus clearly invited to reverse the situation: Jonson, we understand, is the praiseworthy poet and MacFlecknoe, or Shadwell, the dunce.

The writers referred to come to stand for more than their particular names because Dryden incorporates them into a general pattern of literary vice and virtue. The sheer number of allusions makes any particular identification less crucial, as the poet constructs an opinionated, exaggerated, satirical universe in which literary wits square off against literary dunces and bores.

Thus the allusions are integral to the poem's success as a literary satire. The classical citations create a level of heroic parody, while the topical references create an air of scandalous gossip, as well as supplying a gallery of types for the failings of inarticulateness, stupidity, and tedium. Furthermore Dryden modulates from satire into pure criticism, indicating much about his true literary standards in the way he uses contemporary figures as comparisons damning to his opponent. Finally, the use of citations from Shadwell's works, including titles of plays and dramatis personae, constitutes a final satirical flourish: these references are Dryden's way of tweaking his enemy's nose by using his own words and phrases in a ludicrous context.

24.5 The satirical argument of *MacFlecknoe* is cast in the form of a narrative. Describe the plot of the poem, with special attention to the denouement.

Answer The poem describes the momentous occasion on which Flecknoe passes on his kingdom and scepter, symbol of his rule as the supreme poet of nonsense, to his heir MacFlecknoe ("son of Flecknoe"). This event comprises a series of rituals: Flecknoe's opening address to his son, a processional through the streets of London, the ceremonial transference of sacred objects, Flecknoe's farewell address, and his exit through a trapdoor to the realms below. The entire sequence is a parody of the rituals of a British coronation. By playing with the details of the true occasion, Dryden effects his major strategy of turning the world topsy-turvy: for glory and honor, he substitutes vulgarity and dullness. Thus, the mock-epic quality of the poem resides not merely in disparate allusions but in the parodic structure of the poem's narrative.

The final event of the poem is the appropriate climax to this upside-down coronation. However, it parodies not a state occasion but a biblical miracle, the ascent of the prophet Elijah in a whirlwind of fire. At the same time, it is a specific parody of Shadwell's use of a trapdoor as a comic device in one of his plays, a stratagem Dryden thought low.

> For Bruce and Longaville had a trap prepared,
> And down they sent the yet declaiming bard.
> Sinking he left his drugget robe behind,
> Borne upwards by a subterranean wind.
> The mantle fell to the young prophet's part,
> With double portion of his father's art.
>
> (lines 212–217)

Here Flecknoe experiences, in comparison with Elijah, an opposite, and apposite, fate. He descends rather than rises, thus manifesting his essential nature of flat and heavy dullness. The conclusion is an apotheosis in reverse.

24.6

> Thy genius calls thee not to purchase fame
> In keen iambics, but mild anagram.
> Leave writing plays, and choose for thy command
> There thou may'st wings display and altars raise,
> Some peaceful province in acrostic land.
> And torture one poor word ten thousand ways.
>
> (lines 203–208)

What do these lines imply about Dryden's poetic taste?

Answer In this passage, Dryden is using the technical terms for various verbal artifices to pass judgment on Shadwell. "Keen iambics" are associated with satire, which was traditionally written in iambic meter and connected with sharpness (the "cutting edge" of wit). Anagrams are puzzles in which the letters of a word are rearranged to spell another word. Acrostics are poems which spell out a proper name when the first letters of each line are combined. These latter two word games were popular semiliterary amusements in Dryden's day. The "wings" and "altars" refer to "shaped verses," which use typography to create such shapes on the printed page. By urging Shadwell to confine himself to "mild" anagrams, "peaceful" acrostics, and typographical trickery, Dryden is ironically commenting on the poet's boring literary productions and the dull "edge" of his wit. He is also expressing scorn: by making Shadwell king of "acrostic land," he relegates Shadwell to the level of mere verbal play, whereas Dryden himself (for example) wrote poetry which he hoped would influence the government of England.

Furthermore, Dryden implies in this passage the neoclassical view of poetic decorum. Decorum precludes excessive ingenuity, that is, a sterile and facile wit which is all on the surface. Anagrams and acrostics are two examples of such superficial wittiness, which resides in a mere design of scrambled letters. The last line of the passage, "And torture one poor word ten thousand ways," likewise refers to an elaborate trickery with words in ingenious punning. Homonymic variation approaches babble, just as play with letters veers toward doodle. Such play is "mere play," for the verbal manipulations constitute an evasion of the true task of literature, which is to imitate nature.

An Essay of Dramatic Poesy

24.7 Using Dryden's comparison between Ben Jonson and William Shakespeare, describe some of the norms he posits for literary excellence.

Answer In the *Essay* as a whole, Dryden employs the form of a dialogue among friends, which allows him to explore several differing points of view without imposing any single one. He uses the name "Neander," borrowed from Plato, to present his own viewpoint. The general effect of the dialogue format, as in Dryden's Platonic model, is to provide a tone of reasoned, moderate debate, inquiring and open-ended. In keeping with this tone, Dryden's comparison between Shakespeare and Jonson is a measured and balanced analysis of their different qualities. Instead of simplistically posing black against white, failure against success, Dryden recognizes the strengths and weaknesses of each writer and only at the end acknowledges his preference for Shakespeare.

Implied in the comparison between the two poets is a contrast between nature and art. Both of these are normative values for Dryden and indeed for the neoclassical period as a whole. Nature, Dryden suggests, is the greater value, for it incorporates not only the external world but inner human nature as well. The essential feature of Shakespeare's genius is his "wit," his "comprehensive soul," which not only grasps the physical forms of the universe but "looks inward" to discover the interior emotional life of human beings. (For Dryden, wit "is a propriety of thoughts and words; or, in other words, thought and words elegantly adapted to the subject." He thus associates wit with decorum or natural fitness.) Dryden condemns Shakespeare's occasional lapses into swelling bombast or comic punning ("clenches") precisely because both the highly rhetorical and the low comic styles violate Dryden's sense of what is "natural," decorous, and normative.

In contrast, Jonson's strength lies in his art or craftsmanship. Dryden praises him for his skill in classical imitation, which is not mere plagiarism but a masterly appropriation of a source to make it his own. Jonson is also adept at "humor" comedy, that is, the art of caricature which reveals types of men in broad outline according to their "humors," or obsessions. For Dryden, Jonson's weaknesses derive from his very strengths. The learning and wit Jonson brings to his craft can sometimes degenerate into pedantry; Latinate inkhornisms (words coined directly from Latin, created out of the inkwell or "inkhorn" rather than through idiomatic usage) and a certain frugality of invention (a sparing wit which matches words to subject with academic exactitude rather than natural ease) mar some of his plays.

Dryden's preference for Shakespeare rests on his belief in nature as the most fundamental criterion for art. In suggesting that literature should imitate nature, Dryden seems to consider human nature—the virtues, vices, passions, and beliefs of humanity—as the chief subject for the artist. Shakespeare's ability to treat an image so that "you more than see it, you feel it too" makes him a greater poet than Jonson, who, by comparison, seldom manages to gracefully "move the passions." Dryden is acknowledging Shakespeare's greater breadth of sympathetic human understanding when he says, "I admire him [Jonson], but I love Shakespeare." It is significant that in this preference Dryden departs from the stereotype of neoclassical doctrine, which values art over nature and the imitation of classical models over the inspiration of genius.

24.8 Dryden devotes much space in the *Essay* to an analysis of metaphor in the works of various writers, both classical and contemporary. Discuss his own use of metaphor in the *Essay* and evaluate his success or failure in adhering to the standards he sets forth for others.

Answer In characteristic fashion, Dryden defines the proper use of metaphor as a mean between extremes. One extreme is exemplified by the use of *catachresis*, an unnatural and farfetched metaphor which betrays the writer's laborious effort and excessive cleverness. Dryden refers to such metaphors as Clevelandisms, alluding to a poet of the previous generation known then, as now, as an untalented imitator of Donne. At the other extreme is a dull, flat style which Dryden characterizes by an allusion to the poet as "Leveler," playing on the name of an egalitarian political group which would "level" all class distinctions; the poetic version of the type is one whose flaccid wit creeps along as he fills out his line with droning syllables. This dull poet is incapable of making a fine distinction or of finding a rich conceit with which to express his meaning, just as the fantastic poet is always making unduly fine distinctions and forcing unnatural comparisons.

Between these two extremes lies the proper use of figurative language. Dryden says that "wit is best conveyed to us in the most easy language; and is most to be admired when a great thought comes dressed in words so commonly received that it is understood by the meanest apprehensions. . . ." He implies that common usage (that is, a standard language as defined by its best users, both speakers and writers) and common sense should dictate the poet's choice of image and metaphor.

Dryden's own prose in *An Essay of Dramtic Poesy* demonstrates, in the main, precisely those qualities of common sense and easy lucidity which he recommends to others. (It is true that Dryden is discussing standards for dramatic poetry, while his own essay represents a very different class of writing. However, the prescriptions for a natural, appropriate diction would seem to apply to all compositions, whatever their genre. Furthermore, the modern distinction between poetry and prose had less force in Dryden's time, when the word "poesy" applied to all verbal "makings" [Greek *poesis*], or compositions, both in poetry and in prose.) In the *Essay* Dryden's own metaphors are straightforward and apt; furthermore, they are functional, in that they do not call attention to themselves as verbal fireworks but serve to illustrate an idea.

For example, in describing the dull poet whose metaphors are thin and unimaginative, Dryden develops the image of a swallow swooping down to the surface of the Thames but never finally diving, and so never finally capturing a prize of any value. This image of a futile descent expresses vividly yet economically the notion of a limited and superficial wit which only "skims the surface" of its theme.

In describing Cleveland's tortured conceits and farfetched language, Dryden develops a metaphor of eating: the best meat, he says, is the most easily digested, but the diner will grimace at the fare offered by Cleveland. Dryden goes on to describe such poetry as a pill that is hard to swallow and a nut that is not only hard to crack but "without a kernel for our pains." He thus suggests that Cleveland's writing style resists the attempts of the reader to comprehend it and, worst of all, yields no significant truth once it has been comprehended.

Dryden's use of metaphor, then, conforms to his own criteria. He himself uses plain and lucid images which do not puzzle or repel the reader but invite understanding.

B.S.

SUGGESTED READINGS

Harth, Philip, *Contexts of Dryden's Thought* (1968).
Hooker, Edward N., and H. T. Swedenberg, eds., *Poetical Works of John Dryden* (1956).
Hume, Robert, *Dryden's Criticism* (1970).
Miner, Earl, *Dryden's Poetry* (1967).
Roper, Alan, *Dryden's Poetic Kingdoms* (1965).
Van Doren, Mark, *John Dryden: A Study of His Poetry* (1920).

WILLIAM CONGREVE

C H R O N O L O G Y

1670	Born in Staffordshire. Son of William Congreve and Mary Browning Congreve, both of the landed gentry. Congreve's relatively privileged background will distinguish him from the mostly middle-class denizens of London's literary society with whom he will later associate.
1674	Congreve's father is made a lieutenant and is sent to Ireland, where he and his family will live throughout his son's childhood, first in Youghal and then in Carrickfergus.
1681	Congreve enters Kilkenny College, where he meets Joseph Keally, who will be a lifelong friend, and probably Jonathan Swift.
1686	Congreve enters Trinity College, Dublin, where he shares a tutor with fellow student Jonathan Swift.
1688	James II dethroned; Protestant William of Orange becomes king. In Ireland, Protestants fear a massacre by the majority Catholic population, and many of them, including Congreve, flee to England. He visits Stretton Manor in Staffordshire, where he will stay for at least two years.
1689	Congreve writes *The Old Bachelor*, his first comedy.
1691	Goes to London, intending to study law; instead becomes involved in the literary world of the day. Writes his prose narrative *Incognita*, which is published early in 1692.
1692	Several translations by Congreve of classical poems are published in various

anthologies; he begins to develop a reputation as a wit and a writer. *The Old Bachelor* is revised by John Dryden and two other writers.

1693   *The Old Bachelor* is produced and runs for fourteen nights (considered very successful at that time); Congreve is now a celebrated young author. His second play, *The Double Dealer*, is produced (not so successfully). More poems are published. Congreve also meets actress Anne Bracegirdle, with whom he will have a long relationship whose degree of intimacy is unknown, though the subject of much conjecture.

1694   Among other poems, Congreve publishes "To Cynthia" and a "Prologue to the Queen."

1695   Congreve's comedy *Love for Love* is produced and scores a triumphant success. Among other poems, Congreve publishes an ode on the death of Queen Mary and another in compliment to the king; he is rewarded with a government post as a commissioner.

1697   Congreve's tragedy *The Mourning Bride* is produced.

1698   Jeremy Collier's tract *A Short View of the Immorality and Profaneness of the English Stage* is published; it attacks Congreve in particular. Congreve responds with his own essay, *Amendments of Mr. Collier's False and Imperfect Citations*.

1700   Congreve's last great comedy, *The Way of the World*, is produced. Congreve tours Europe. At this time, his health begins to decline; he will suffer from attacks of gout and increasing blindness during his remaining years, and his literary output will be relatively small.

1701   Libretto *The Judgment of Paris* performed.

1703   Congreve meets Henrietta, the duchess of Marlborough; they will virtually live together for most of the next two decades, apparently with her husband's acquiescence. Several poems published.

1704   The Kit-Kat Club, a literary and political society numbering among its members Addison and Steele and the publisher Tonson, establishes a new theater, the Haymarket, and appoints Congreve as one of its managers. However, it will prove a failure, and Congreve will drop out of the project after a year.

1706   Congreve publishes *Discourse on the Pindarique Ode* and a *Pindarique Ode Humbly Offer'd to the Queen*.

1710   Congreve organizes an edition of his collected works, published by Tonson. Also publishes a volume of poetry and a translation of the third book of Ovid's *Art of Love*.

1714   Appointed secretary to the island of Jamaica, a post which will support him for the rest of his life.

1717   Helps to edit an edition of Dryden's plays; further translations from Ovid published.

1723   Fathers Mary, daughter of the duchess of Marlborough.

1729   Death of Congreve.

ESSAY QUESTIONS WITH ANSWERS

The Way of the World

25.1   *The Way of the World* is not only the title of Congreve's play but one of its major themes. Discuss the significance of the title of the play.

Answer   *The Way of the World* implies a study of the regrettable tendencies of human nature. The title's ironic reference to human folly is borne out in the course of the drama, as characters dominated by various passions and obsessions scheme, plot, and deceive one another and themselves. Congreve seems more inclined to laugh at the ways of the world than to castigate them, only implying his moral bias in the play's resolution.

The two motives which dominate the action of the play are sexual appetite and greed. In Lady Wishfort, Congreve presents a stereotype of feminine vanity, endlessly pursuing her male quarry despite her own increasing age and fading beauty. Because of her ill-disguised sexual desires, she readily succumbs to Waitwell's impersonation of the noble "Sir Rowland." Similarly, Mrs. Marwood's sexual vanity leads her to take her best friend's husband as a lover and to seek vengeance on Mirabell for scorning her. Both these women, the one deluded and the other cynical, represent a sexually rapacious femininity which, Congreve seems to imply, is the rule among women rather than the exception.

Congreve's male characters fare no better. Fainall is the typical "man of the world," controlled not only by sexual appetite but by avarice. In his clubroom remarks to Mirabell he derides marital fidelity and treats his illicit liaisons as a matter of course. The only value he sees in marriage is financial, not emotional. His plotting with his coconspirator and mistress, Mrs. Marwood, demonstrates his amoral sophistication: he is quick to see his own advantage and seize it, careless of the injury he is doing to his wife, his mother-in-law, and his friends.

The eye for advantage is common to practically the entire cast of characters. As Lady Wishfort puts it, "Ah dear Marwood, what's integrity to an opportunity?" (III, iv, meaning Act III, Scene iv). Such a remark reveals the amorality and cycnicism of "the way of the world," but at the same time it illustrates its comic appeal. Lady Wishfort and the others are not only outrageous and indecorous but amusingly so. Overturning all the rules of moral conduct and polite

331

behavior, these characters deliver bon mots and epigrams that provoke laughter rather than scorn. For example, Mrs. Marwood, arguing for indulgence in love, asserts, "For my part, my youth may wear and waste, but it shall never rust in my possession" (II, i). Fainall, readying himself to falsely accuse his wife of infidelity, argues that his loss of reputation will mean nothing to him:

> . . . that's well thought on; marriage is honourable as you say; and if so, wherefore should cuckoldom be a discredit, being derived from so honourable a root? (III, iii)

The other "way of the world," the straight and narrow way of modesty, virtue, and prudence, is satirized in Lady Wishfort's earnest account of Mrs. Fainall's rigidly moral upbringing:

> . . . she would ha' shrieked if she had but seen a man, till she was in her teens. As I am a person 'tis true;—she was never suffered to play with a male child, though but in coats; nay, her very babies were of the feminine gender. Oh, she never looked a man in the face but her own father, or the chaplain, and him we made a shift to put upon her for a woman by the help of his long garments, and his sleek face, till she was going in her fifteen. (V, v)

The exaggeration makes prudence sound like prudery and turns modesty into a comic eccentricity.

If the characters in *The Way of the World* are for the most part vain and opportunistic, they express themselves in a witty, confident style that makes conventional morality seem dull and hypocritical and libertinism attractive. Millamant and Mirabell are the exceptions in this brittle, brilliant world, displaying fine natures and a capacity for genuine emotion in their courtship. Millamant is no mere coquette looking for a marriage of convenience; she is hesitant and thoughtful about seriously committing herself to her suitor. Mirabell, the reformed rake, is truly devoted to her and seeks a monogamous and permanent relationship.

However, they too are sophisticated and witty. Their verbal sparring is a variation on the battle of the sexes played out by Fainall and Mrs. Marwood, but Mirabell and Millamant play the game for different ends. Instead of playing hypocritically for sexual or economic advantage, they explicitly acknowledge the hypocrisy of manipulative courtships and convenient marriages. They even admit that their game is, in fact, a game. Millamant asks, "What would you give, that could help loving me?" and Mirabell replies, "I would give something that you did not know I could not help it" (II, ii).

At the end of the play Mirabell insists, in essence, that judgment and wisdom are a match for opportunism. He appropriates the play's title to describe the happy outcome achieved in the face of Fainall's "ways." He says, " 'tis the way of the world, sir," flourishing the decisive parchment before the discomfited villain. Thus he poses his own world view against Fainall's, countering cynical deceit with foresight and affection. Significantly, it is Mirabell who is triumphant. At the same time, there is a melancholy undertow at the play's end. Although she says little in the final scenes, Mrs. Fainall represents by her very fate the way in which "the world" callously dispenses injury and disappointment. Between the womanizing fortune hunter and the injured widow there can be no reconciliation, despite Mirabell's offer "to contribute all that in me lies to a reunion" (V, iii).

25.2 Millamant and Mirabell, as coquette and beau, engage in the witty sparring typical of the lovers in Congreve's Restoration comedies. However, their discussion of marriage strikes an unusually serious note. What is their concept of marriage?

Answer The courtship scene between Millamant and Mirabell (IV, i) begins with high-flown literary comparisons from a poem by Edmund Waller, a seventeenth-century poet: Millamant addresses her lover as "Phoebus" and Mirabell supplies the rhyming line, alluding to his mistress as "Daphne." They go on to argue playfully over whether Mirabell's solicitations of his lady are sufficiently "courtly." But as each diagrams his or her expectations in marriage, the conventional flirtation between the sexes is modified, and a more realistic, sober view of marital life is adumbrated. In part, Millamant is displaying her willfulness as she lists her "demands." However, when she rejects an entire list of endearments as "nauseous cant," criticizes the custom of amorous display in public, and requires that they be "strange" (reserved) with each other, she is satirizing the marriages of convenience common in Restoration society. She implies that married couples are often hypocrites, showering affectionate language on their partners as they commit infidelities in secret. Likewise, her rejection of public displays of affection is an attack on behavior that is all show and no substance. Finally, her insistence on politeness and respect between the partners distinguishes her definition of marriage from that implied by the casual, manipulative relationships which surround her.

Mirabell also satirizes the "way of the world" as manifested in the regrettable social customs of women. He attacks the vanity of using cosmetics; the immorality of wives who, with the protection of an intimate "she friend" or "duck decoy," go out on the town to meet their lovers; and the vice of drinking carried on under the guise of social tête-à-têtes. By criticizing these feminine vices, he indicates what he regards as virtues: simplicity, honesty, and self-restraint.

Although their tone is partly playful, both Millamant and Mirabell have strong, clear ideas about mutual respect and self-control. Through their dialogue Congreve introduces the idea of true marriage, a proper relationship between the sexes, in the midst of a world filled with casual betrayal and scandal.

The other marriages in the play demonstrate false marriage. Lady Wishfort, in her attempt to "buy" a husband, represents lust as opposed to love. The Fainalls are an illustration of a marriage of convenience, although the convenience seems all on the husband's side: Fainall married his wife for her money, and now keeps a mistress.

Thus it is in reference to the social abuse of the marriage tie that Millamant and Mirabell define their own position. Their articulation of "demands" and "items" signifies not only their wit but their wisdom in approaching the serious commitment of marriage.

25.3 Focusing on Act II, Scene i, discuss the concept of wit in the play.

Answer When Millamant makes her first entrance, encountering Mrs. Fainall, Mirabell, and Witwoud, she instantly becomes engaged in witty repartee with her friends. Witwoud especially provides a refrain of ingenious comparisons, provoking Millamant to exclaim "a truce with your similitudes." The scene as a whole consists of verbal fireworks, including not only Witwoud's similes but Millamant's and Mirabell's conceits, epigrams, and antitheses. The basis of all these rhetorical figures is, broadly speaking, comparison: characters find apt correspondences between unlike things and develop metaphors on the merest pretext. For example, Mirabell describes Millamant's entrance into the park as a ship proceeding under full sail, "and a shoal of fools for tenders." Millamant compares beauty to wit: "One no more owes one's beauty to a lover than one's wit to an echo—they can but reflect what we look and say; vain empty things if we are silent or unseen, and want a being." Witwoud is incessantly offering similes, describing suitors as moths about candles, wit as a blazing fire, and lovers as card-matches. The characters' pervasive self-consciousness about wit is implied in Witwoud's "scoring" of one of Mirabell's remarks. He congratulates him with the pronouncement "Hum, a hit, a hit, a palpable hit, I confess it."

Throughout the play men and women engage in verbal duels, using wit as a weapon of defense and attack, flirtation and deception. The play's social milieu is a world of words, in which Mirabell is the most sought after of men because of his quick tongue and Petulant and Sir Wilfull Witwoud are laughingstocks because of their literal-minded speech. Apart from its function in social relationships, wit contributes to the sheer comedy of the play, with almost every character capable of satirical epigrams and puns.

Wit, then, is generally for public exhibition, for scoring points before an audience. But a further dimension is suggested by the particular wittiness displayed by the hero and heroine. In private dialogue the two continue to play with words, but to a purpose, for together they develop a definition of true marriage. Though Mirabell cannot resist a figure of speech even in proposing marriage ("Well, have I liberty to offer conditions—that when you are dwindled into a wife, I may not be beyond measure enlarged into a husband?"), the conditions by which the lovers shall "dwindle" and "enlarge" are, in the end, bluntly named. Furthermore, at the denouement, Mirabell displays a wit that is not merely verbal, for it is his cleverness that saves the day: he foils Fainall's plot to gain control of his wife's fortune by means of an earlier contract. Thus Mirabell not only has the facile wit of a Witwoud but also has his wits about him. It is this latter quality of common sense that allows him a victory over the ways of the world.

25.4 The names of Congreve's characters are symbolic, linking each character with a specific idea or quality. Discuss the significance of this symbolic naming.

Answer The use of names to identify a character's humorous type or function in the plot is typical of comedy; it ensures a certain comic distance from the characters by suggesting an element of caricature and allows the audience to judge, as well as relate to, the actors. By means of symbolic names, Congreve "places" the characters so that the audience knows from the start what kind of antics to expect and can thus enjoy the spectacle of what the playwright has contrived to do with these familiar figures.

Thus Fainall, who feigns all, is a type of the hypocrite, constantly deceiving and scheming under a pleasant and witty facade. Mrs. Marwood "would mar," thus becoming the spoiler of the action and one of the villains of the play. Lady Wishfort is the type of the bawdy old dame, incessantly "wishing for" the gratification of her lust. Witwoud, who "would be witty," is the stereotyped fop showing off his pretensions to wit. Even the servants Waitwell and Foible have names which describe their functions as excellent manservant and capricious maid.

Mirabell and Millamant likewise have symbolic names which signal their roles as hero and heroine. Mirabell (*mira-belle*, wondrously handsome, or *mirabilis*, admirable) is distinguishable from the fops and cads around him not only because of his attractive appearance but because of his "admirable" character; Millamant, the coquette with "one thousand lovers," is an unquestionable object of desire.

Obviously the names imply not only dramatic function but also a moral judgment. The dominant "humors" or passions suggested by the names associate characters with such abstract vices as hypocrisy, vengeance, and lust. Thus Congreve's technique recalls that of Ben Jonson in *Volpone*, in which characters representing avarice are named for various birds of prey. The intellectual diagram supplied by the names underscores the moral basis of the comedy. Although *The Way of the World* is a social comedy of manners, relying on topical satire and scandal and celebrating the liberated wit of town gallants, the play also manages to suggest how character determines "manners" and how impulse and desire issue in behavior. Mirabell and Millamant constitute the play's center precisely because their behavior and manners are complex and spontaneous by comparison with the more fixed and predictable psyches of their friends. Unlike a Fainall or a Marwood, they transcend their names, and their types.

B.S.

SUGGESTED READINGS

Donaldson, Ian, *The World Upside-Down: Comedy from Jonson to Fielding* (1970).
Fujimara, Thomas H., *The Restoration Comedy of Wit* (1952).
Mueschke, Paul, and Miriam Mueschke, *A New View of Congreve's Way of the World* (1958).
Underwood, Dale, *Etherege and the Seventeenth-Century Comedy* (1957).

Part Six

THE NEOCLASSICAL AGE

T I M E L I N E

The Age

1660: Restoration; accession of Charles II

1685: Death of Charles II; accession of James II, who favors the Roman Catholics; unpopular monarch

1688: Protestant prince William of Orange invades England; James II escapes to France; "Bloodless Revolution"

1689: William and Mary crowned

1694: Death of Mary

1701: Act of Settlement permanently excludes Roman Catholic descendants of James I from the throne

1702: Death of William; accession of Queen Anne

1707: Union of England and Scotland as Great Britain

1709: First English copyright act

1714: Death of Anne; accession of George I, Hanoverian (German) prince

1718: England at war with Spain

1727: Death of George I; accession of George II

1739: Brief, unsuccessful war with Spain

1745: Unsuccessful attempt by Roman Catholic Charles Edward ("the Young Pretender") to conquer Scotland

1748: As part of general European war, England fights with France over North American colonies

1750: Founding of Methodism by John Wesley

1755: Publication of Johnson's *Dictionary*

1756: Outbreak of Seven Years' War

1757: Victory by Clive at Plassey secures English control of India

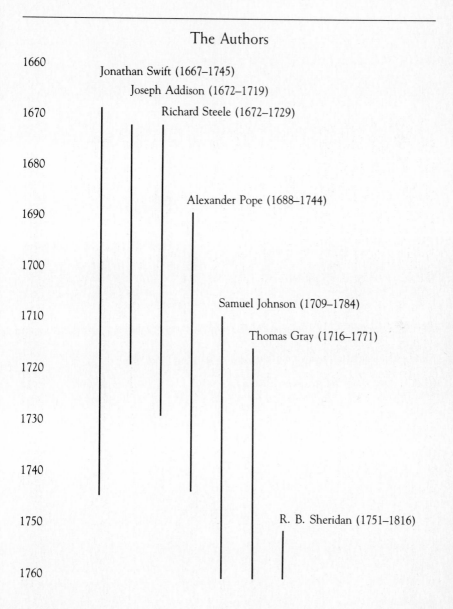

The Authors

1660

Jonathan Swift (1667–1745)

Joseph Addison (1672–1719)

1670   Richard Steele (1672–1729)

1680

Alexander Pope (1688–1744)

1690

1700

Samuel Johnson (1709–1784)

1710

Thomas Gray (1716–1771)

1720

1730

1740

1750   R. B. Sheridan (1751–1816)

1760

The Age

1760:	Death of George II; accession of George III
1763:	Treaty of Paris
1765:	Publication of Percy's *Reliques of Ancient Poetry*
1775:	Outbreak of American War of Independence
1783:	American independence won
1789:	French Revolution
1799:	Napoleon takes control of French government
1801:	Preface to *Lyrical Ballads*
1804:	Napoleon named emperor of France; war throughout Europe
1810:	George III insane; the Regency
1815:	Napoleon's final defeat at Waterloo
1820:	Accession of George IV

The Authors

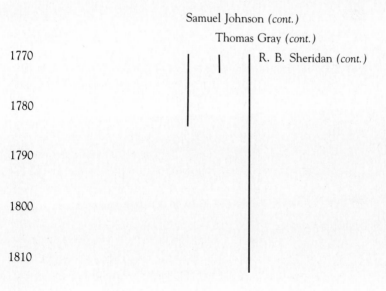

Samuel Johnson *(cont.)*
Thomas Gray *(cont.)*
1770   R. B. Sheridan *(cont.)*

1780

1790

1800

1810

1820

JONATHAN SWIFT

C H R O N O L O G Y

<table>
<tr><td>1667</td><td>Born in Dublin, son of English parents. Swift's father, the Reverend Thomas Swift, is a Protestant in a predominantly Catholic country and an active supporter of King Charles I in his struggles against the Puritans.</td></tr>
<tr><td>1673</td><td>Enters Kilkenny Grammar School, where he will study for nine years.</td></tr>
<tr><td>1682</td><td>Enters Trinity College, Dublin; receives B.A. in 1686.</td></tr>
<tr><td>1688</td><td>"Glorious Revolution" replaces James II with Protestant William of Orange. Violence breaks out in Ireland as a result, and Swift leaves for England, where he settles with his mother in Leicestershire.</td></tr>
<tr><td>1689</td><td>Becomes secretary to Sir William Temple, living in his household at Moor Park in Surrey, England. Probably meets Esther Johnson, the "Stella" with whom he will have a long, platonic love affair.</td></tr>
<tr><td>1690</td><td>Returns to Ireland; Swift's early poetry is being composed.</td></tr>
<tr><td>1691</td><td>Swift reenters Temple's service and takes up residence in England again.</td></tr>
<tr><td>1692</td><td>Receives M.A. degree from Oxford.</td></tr>
<tr><td>1695</td><td>Ordained as priest in Ireland, Swift is appointed to the prebend of Kilroot, near Belfast. He settles there and takes up his clerical duties, but finds this life lonely and unsatisfying.</td></tr>
<tr><td>1696</td><td>Returns to Moor Park, where he will work for Temple until the latter's</td></tr>
</table>

death in 1699. During these years, Swift writes A *Tale of a Tub*, a satiric attack on the dissenting English churches (not published until 1704).

1699   Serves as chaplain to Lord Berkeley in Dublin.

1700   Appointed rector of Laracor and two other country parishes in Ireland; then appointed prebend of St. Patrick's Cathedral in Dublin.

1701   Travels to England with Lord Berkeley. Swift's first political work published, *A Discourse of the Contests and Dissensions between the Nobles and the Commons in Athens and Rome*; it is a defense of certain out-of-favor Whig leaders. Returns to Ireland, settling again in Laracor.

1702   Receives doctor of divinity degree from Trinity College, Dublin.

1704   *A Tale of a Tub* published, along with *The Battle of the Books*, a literary satire supporting the scholars who defended the "ancients" against the "moderns."

1707   Sent as emissary of the Church of Ireland to seek remission of first fruits (a tax on Irish clerical incomes) from the English government. While in London on this mission, meets Esther Vanhomrigh, with whom he establishes a liaison lasting some sixteen years, though its degree of intimacy is unknown. Also writes various tracts on relations between church and state, including the ironic *Argument against Abolishing Christianity* (published in 1711).

1708   Publishes several poems, as well as *The Bickerstaff Papers*, a series of satirical articles ridiculing John Partridge, a contemporary almanac maker and astrologer; many prominent writers of the day, including Congreve, Addison, and Steele, join in the satire with articles of their own.

1709   Returns to Ireland, having failed in his mission for the church.

1710   Sent to England again, still seeking remission of first fruits; will remain four years, becoming heavily involved in the politics of the day. During this period composes the letters to Esther Johnson later published as the *Journal to Stella*. Meets Robert Harley, head of the new Tory government, who offers his support for Swift's mission; Swift joins the Tories and is named editor of *The Examiner*, a Tory periodical.

1711–   Writes many poems and pamphlets supporting the Tory ministry; becomes
1714   a leader of the "Tory wits" and a founder of the Scriblerus Club, devoted to mockery of false scholarship and pedantry. Installed as dean of St. Patrick's Cathedral in Dublin (1713).

1714   Returns to Ireland after the death of Queen Anne and the fall from power of the Tories. During the next three years, the Tories are under attack as suspected supporters of the Roman Catholic pretender to the throne; some are imprisoned, and Swift is under suspicion.

1720   Publishes his first important work on Irish problems, *A Proposal for the Universal Use of Irish Manufacture.* Begins work on *Gulliver's Travels.*

1724   *The Drapier's Letters,* a series of anonymous articles attacking English exploitation of Ireland, makes Swift, as the "Drapier," an Irish national hero.

1726   Finishes *Gulliver's Travels;* visits England, where he stays with his friend Pope at Twickenham. Publishes poem *Cadenus and Vanessa,* telling of his relationship with Esther Vanhomrigh, who had died three years earlier. Returns to Ireland; *Gulliver's Travels* published in London.

1727   Swift makes his last visit to England.

1728   Death of "Stella." Swift helps write and edit a periodical, *The Intelligencer,* with Sheridan.

1729   Publishes *A Modest Proposal,* his most famous satirical work; a savage attack on English treatment of Ireland.

1731   Writes *Verses on the Death of Dr. Swift* (published in 1739).

1735   Four-volume edition of Swift's *Works* published in Dublin; two more volumes added in 1738.

1742   Swift's health is in rapid decline; he is found to be "of unsound mind and memory" and is committed to the care of guardians. From this period grows the popular image of Swift as misanthropic, bitter, mad. Modern scholars have diagnosed Swift's malady as Ménière's disease, a nervous disorder.

1745   Death of Swift. He leaves most of his estate for the founding of a hospital for the insane. Buried in St. Patrick's Cathedral.

ESSAY QUESTIONS WITH ANSWERS

A Modest Proposal

26. 1   Two pages of Swift's essay elapse before the narrator explicitly identifies his "modest proposal." What does this long preamble contribute to Swift's satire?

Answer   The major function of Swift's lengthy introduction to the main proposal is to establish a persona with admirable qualities, a speaker in whom the reader can feel some confidence. Among these qualities are compassion, lucidity, logic, knowledge of facts and figures, impartiality, and public-mindedness. The writer begins his essay with the phrase "It is a melancholy object . . .," thus drawing attention to the pathos of the regrettable state of beggared mothers and children and eliciting the natural sympathy of the reader. He continues his argument by establishing a consensus on the ills which he intends to correct ("I think it is agreed by all parties") and by itemizing the advantages of his unnamed solution. Furthermore, he analyzes the extent and nature of the problem by bringing in a welter of what would today be called sociological facts and demographic statistics.

The effect of the preamble is to present an appearance of credibility and to seduce the reader into a cozy alliance with the writer. However, Swift scatters various hints of something bizarre in the persona's character throughout the apparently plausible opening section. For example, a subtle strand of animal imagery suggests that he looks at Irish beggars as less than human, using the phrase "a child, just dropped from its dam" and referring to wives as "breeders." Likewise, the insistence on statistical computation becomes dehumanizing, reducing the pitiful circumstances of men, women, and children to mere numbers ("I again subtract fifty thousand, for those women who miscarry"). Logical quibbles replace moral judgment when the persona argues about the appropriate age for a child to turn thief. Finally, there is a suggestion of self-congratulation in the narrator's stance when he alludes to the setting up of a statue for the solver of so complex a problem, for we know that he has himself in mind.

By the time the narrator announces his cannibalistic scheme, Swift's satiric intention is already obvious. By the discrepancy between the persona's humane, rational pose and his outrageous argument, Swift indicates that the modest proposal is a mock-argument. In his ironic treatment of a profoundly tragic situation, he heightens the reader's sense of its horror. The grotesquerie of the persona's sunny and methodical approach to human suffering becomes a comment on the behavior of officials and, indeed, of a whole nation (namely, England) toward the Irish poor.

26.2 Toward the end of *A Modest Proposal*, the author mentions other solutions to the problems of Irish poverty and overpopulation, prefaced with the phrase "Therefore let no man talk to me of other expedients." He then goes on at some length about these other expedients before rejecting them in favor of his own proposal. What is the point of this lengthy digression?

Answer The digression on other solutions is, in fact, the heart of the essay; it presents Swift's true proposals for solving the problems of poverty and over-population in Ireland. Motivated by his strong sense of Irish nationalism, Swift suggests taxes on absentee landlords, an end to foreign importation, a unification of Irish political factions, and a rebirth of virtue and patriotism. He makes it clear whom he blames for Ireland's ills in the allusions to luxurious women, cheating shopkeepers, foreign exploiters, ruthless landowners, and craven Irishmen willing "to sell our country and consciences for nothing."

Any one of these alternative proposals would be, of course, far more reasonable and persuasive than the option of butchering infants for food. Swift is careful to emphasize the reasonableness of these "other expedients" by wording them as truly modest proposals. For example, the expedient "Of teaching landlords to have at least one degree of mercy towards their tenants" is, one would think, a mild enough expectation in a nominally Christian nation. But the "other expedients" are rejected by the narrator as impractical and utopian. He concludes, "Therefore I repeat, let no man talk to me of these and the like expedients, till he hath at least a glimpse of hope, that there will ever be some hearty and sincere attempt to put them in practice." Rhetorically, this statement punctures the ironic pose of slightly insane optimism assumed by the narrator. In rejecting the practical solutions as impossible, Swift expresses his own anger and outrage at the apathy and cynicism of Irish citizenry and English landlords alike. He also indicates a didactic purpose, directly advertising the political and economic steps necessary for ameliorating Ireland's plight.

Thus, the digression reinforces the essay's main effect of educating the readers to the horrors of Irish poverty. By means of ironic indirection, the paragraph on "other expedients" offers a straightforward list of serious, plausible reforms and supports them by the implied contrast to the modest proposal. Swift cleverly makes his "other expedients" appear the only natural, human solution to the problem by implying that, if one is unwilling to take these steps, one might just as well advocate cannibalism.

26.3   Explain how the following features of the essay relate to Swift's satiric purpose: the title of the essay; the allusions to "my American friend"; the references to culinary methods; the digression on adolescents; and the narrator's final "autobiographical" remark.

Answer   All of these features help create an ironic discrepancy between the ostensible thesis of the essay and Swift's true intentions. From title to concluding line, Swift spins out a dazzling web of allusions and comparisons to create a smooth rhetorical surface which masks, and yet reveals, his moral indignation.

The long title of the essay, *A Modest Proposal for Preventing the Children of Poor People in Ireland from Being a Burden to Their Parents or Country, and for Making Them Beneficial to the Public*, parodies the titles of official tracts, evoking an air of authority, civic pride, and social concern. The proposal is described as "modest," a humble offering in the interest of public welfare. Both the exaggerated officialism and the mock humility subtly undercut the ostensible seriousness of the title.

The allusions to "my American friend," who is full of helpful suggestions on the preparation of infant flesh and the possible usefulness of adolescents as a kind of "venison," more dramatically puncture the persuasive surface of the argument. Although the references to the friend resemble the learned citations of authority found in many a serious tract, the actual opinions cited are horrifying. Thus the dual effect of superficial logic and underlying barbarity is created through the machinery of rhetoric.

The fact that the friend cheerfully recommends the cooking of adolescents makes him, in the view of the persona, barbaric in comparison with the "modest proposer." (The fact that the friend is American is undoubtedly relevant here.) The narrator himself makes a dim-witted distinction between the "cruelty" of roasting teenagers and the "humanity" of butchering infants, revealing his real moral insensitivity by the very absurdity of the moral lines he draws.

The running references to various culinary methods, beginning with the description of the delicacy of a young child "whether stewed, roasted, baked, or boiled; and I make no doubt that it will equally serve in a fricassee or ragout," again create an absurd discrepancy between the air of humane concern and the gruesome physical details.

The narrator's final remark, that he himself has no children of an age suitable for slaughter and that his wife is past breeding, might seem to violate the ironic pretense of the argument as a whole. This statement sounds almost like an admission of the barbarity of the modest proposal, with the speaker finally confessing that he himself will escape scot-free from the consequences of his insane proposition. However, he maintains the outrageous pose he has adopted from the outset by boasting that his personal situation proves that he is free of self-interest because, luckily, he has nothing to gain from his project. Although he is "lucky" to have no children to contribute to the scheme, he defines his luck according to the peculiar logic of his proposal. The topsy-turvy reasoning clinches the upside-down ethics of the whole essay, in which traditional human values disappear under a dehumanized brand of "morality."

Gulliver's Travels

26.4 At the beginning and end of each of the four books, Swift locates Gulliver's travels in a familiar world, full of exact geographical references, specific dates, proper names, and precise measurements. This "logbook" style infiltrates, to varying extents, the narration of Gulliver's actual adventures in Lilliput, Brobdingnag, Laputa and its environs, and Houyhnhnmland. What is the significance of this realistic style for Gulliver's Travels as a whole?

Answer The factual style is Gulliver's characteristic narrative mode, and the flat, literal-minded reporting establishes his persona: he is fastidious, precise, gullible, and so compulsively comprehensive that he seems incapable of editing or evaluating the data he is scrupulously recording. We hear about everything, from the exact height of the trees in Lilliput, to the number of inhabitants of Lorbrulgrud in Brobdingnag, to his inventive methods of performing bodily functions. Of course, Gulliver is not merely, or solely, a neutral reporter. He has opinions too, for example, his contempt for the treasurer of Lilliput (I, vi, meaning Book I, Chapter vi) or his disapproval of the Brobdingnagian king for refusing to learn the secrets of gunpowder (II, vii); but apart from momentary lapses into emotion and bias, he is primarily obsessed with "facts," what he can measure and describe.

One of the effects of the welter of description and quantification is, curiously, to render Gulliver's account suspect. Under the guise of extreme fidelity to the "truth" he is quintessentially unreliable, a naive witness to scenes and events whose import almost uniformly escapes him. The suppression of judgment and reflection in favor of record keeping creates an ironic doubleness, for there is a vast discrepancy between the overt story Gulliver tells and the underlying implications of that story.

The reader is directed toward those implications by the strangeness of the narration, its exaggerated completeness and its crucial omissions. In part the preoccupation with quantifiable phenomena and observed facts constitutes a parody of travel literature, with its cataloguing of exotic sights and unusual experiences. Such literature tells the reader both more and less than he wants to know. Gulliver's own references to travel literature reinforce the satiric emphasis on the amassing of circumstantial detail, as well as on the omnivorous self that does the amassing. For example, at the end of Book II, Chapter i, Gulliver's comments on his motives for writing (his concern for the public benefit and his interest in truth) and his compunctions about becoming "tedious and trifling" delineate him as a self-centered, self-conscious traveler who jots down his every action and opinion ostensibly for the greater good of humanity. Such a remark also serves to disarm criticism as Gulliver proceeds to belabor all his points at length, taxing the reader's patience and committing various assaults on decorum.

Thus, Gulliver tells us what he ate (the meals of 1728 Lilliputians per day), where he slept (the baby's cradle in Brobdingnag), whom he met (the *struldbruggs* of Laputa), and how he communicated (in snippets of foreign languages, of which he offers samples). But he never makes explicit the value or meaning of his experiences—that is, what these races and places signify—except in the case of Houyhnhnmland, where the extremity of his praise has the same suspect ring as the neutrality of his reports from the other lands. Like many a traveler before and since, Gulliver has the experience but misses the meaning, a meaning which Swift forces the reader to supply.

One of the ways in which Swift enforces an allegorical reading of the text is by the overt clash between fact and fiction. The realistic references begin to seem surreal, attached as they are to such fantastic subjects as pygmies, giants, mad scientists, and philosopher-horses. As in a surrealistic painting, surface appearances and circumstantial details clash bizarrely with the basically dreamlike landscape. For example, the discussion of the dust-licking ceremony before the king of Luggnagg (III, ix) is rendered in a generally neutral expository style, including such details as a description of the poison strewn as a means of executing enemies ("a certain brown powder, of a deadly composition, which being licked up infallibly kills him in twenty-four hours") and an account of an accidental murder when the page forgets to order that the floor be cleansed after a preceding execution ("by which neglect a young lord of great hopes coming to an audience, was unfortunately poisoned, although the king at that time had no design against his life"). The deadpan reporting and the suppression of all judgment on a ritual both absurdly fantastic and morally repugnant recall the style of Swift's "modest proposer," although Gulliver sounds more like a newspaper reporter than a public official. In both cases, however, there is a surrealistic gap between rhetorical form (ethical persuasion in A Modest Proposal, eyewitness account in Gulliver's Travels) and content. The reader cannot accept the Luggnagg account at face value and so begins to supply his own subtext on the vanity and treachery of absolute monarchs.

In general, the important facts of Gulliver's Travels are the ones that newpaper reporting and travelogue cannot accommodate. What comes through Gulliver's neutral style is that the Lilliputians are contemptibly small and the Brobdingnagians impressively, if grotesquely, big in comparison with himself; that the projectors of Laputa are lunatics and the horses of Houyhnhnmland egomaniacs. Confining himself to "certifiable" data, Gulliver gives us their measurements but not their measure.

In a sense, then, the realistic style determines the whole nature of the narrative: it establishes Gulliver as a limited, excessively naive observer, and creates the effect of discrepancy which is the basis for the satire.

26.5 Discuss the size discrepancies in Gulliver's Travels.

Answer   The perspective shifts associated with Gulliver's experiences in Lilliput and Brobdingnag convey a number of ideas about the fundamental nature of man. Inevitably the play on dimensions puts a major emphasis on man's physical being: his appearance, functions, instincts, and abilities. Swift's use of size as a theme may well have grown out of the new science of the day, which, with its telescope and microscope, had made obvious to people that there are other perspectives from which human life can be viewed, including that of the microbe and, conceivably, that of the superbeing from another world.

In Lilliput, Gulliver has, at least in part, the aspect of a kindly giant surrounded by petty, narrow-minded pygmies who represent the pretensions of their European counterparts. For example, the king of Lilliput is entitled "Golbasto Momaren Evlame Gurdilo Shefin Mully Ully Gue, most mighty Emperor of Lilliput, delight and terror of the universe, whose dominions extend five thousand blustrugs (about twelve miles in circumference) to the extremities of the globe" (I, iii). Thus, imperialist ambitions persist even when the empire is tiny. Despite his physical superiority, Gulliver's naiveté and generosity make him the pawn of power-mad factions and ministers, and he is ultimately forced to flee to the "enemy" Blefuscudians because of the malice of Skyresh Bolgolam. In the 6-inch Lilliputians, Swift makes diminutiveness a symbol of smallness of character and meanness of mind.

At the same time, this diagram is complicated by events and actions that make the Lilliputians seem admirable and Gulliver despicable. In the first episode of Book I, Gulliver confesses to an impulse to "seize forty or fifty of the first that came in my reach and dash them against the ground" (I, i). Thus he has a brutish and sadistic impulse to destroy at random when confronted by the insectlike Lilliputian population. His accounts of defecation and urination make him seem grotesque and even obscene, particularly in contrast to the delicate, almost microscopic physicality of the Lilliputians. (Indeed, the queen is so offended by Gulliver's means of dousing the fire in her palace apartments that she refuses ever to use them again.) Furthermore the Lilliputians, at least according to their original constitution, have a certain utopian grandeur. Some of their ancient traditions form a positive contrast, rather than a regrettable parallel, to European practices, so that such customs as the *Snilpall*, an honorary title rewarding obedience to the law, and the punishment of fraud and ingratitude by death attest to a moral rigor which does not fit with the degenerate rope dancing and intrigue of the court.

Swift's account of Brobdingnag is also a complex allegory which suggests some of the ambiguities of humanity's physical and moral nature. On the simplest level, in Brobdingnag Gulliver simply becomes a Lilliputian. He is comically inadequate to the simplest tasks and prey to the most ridiculous accidents, almost unable to make himself heard, nearly swallowed by a squalling infant, and tormented by flies, wasps, birds, and frogs. His boasts of English prowess and progress are deflated by the Brobdingnagian king's invective against such a vicious race of mortals. Thus Gulliver is "cut down to size," exposed as physically vulnerable and morally suspect. By comparison, the Brobdingnagians' learning and customs suggest a humanism founded on principles of reason, and their size seems a symbol of moral as well as physical strength.

Yet the Brobdingnagians have a negative side as well. The exploitative behavior of the farmer, Gulliver's first master; the malevolence of the court dwarf; and the exhibitionism of the maids of honor suggest that Brobdingnag, despite its rational principles, is not without such irrational passions as greed, envy, and lust. Furthermore, the physical disgust which the huge bodies and offensive smells of the giants evoke in Gulliver imply that man, whatever his size, is inescapably a creature of the flesh. The Brobdingnagians remind Gulliver of his own physical corruption, for he has been just such an ill-favored, noisome

monster in the eyes and noses of the delicate Lilliputians. The insistent grotesquerie of the descriptions of Brobdingnagian nipples, cancers, moles, and
wens is similar in effect to Gulliver's allusions to his own bodily functions in
Lilliput. There is a repellent quality to all these passages, which turn the human
body into an object of horror.

In general, the size discrepancies in Books I and II of *Gulliver's Travels* point
to the relativism of human nature. The same action, for example waving a
sword, seems magnificent and omnipotent when Gulliver is a giant in Lilliput
and toylike, mechanical, and insignificant when he is an insect in Brobdingnag.
The distortions up and down the scale point to the absence of the normative
and the normal in the human psyche. By showing the pathological relationship
obtaining between giants and dwarfs and by insisting on the grotesquerie of the
body, Swift satirizes the instability of human ethics and passions and the cor-
ruptibility of human flesh. If both Lilliput and Brobdingnag have their good
points, they nonetheless derive from a fundamentally misanthropic vision. Swift
observes one of the conventions of satire in treating humanity as malformed
and diseased, both in body and in soul. The satirist often performs the function
of a surgeon, dissecting, laying bare, anatomizing. Although Gulliver himself
is supposed to be a surgeon, he seems to suffer from the same diseases as the
races he encounters. Here it is Swift who wields the knife.

26.6 In *Gulliver's Travels* Swift employs a spectrum of satiric techniques,
including political allegory, invective, symbol, and irony. Illustrate each of these
devices with a specific example from the text.

Answer Political allegory, in the form of narrative incidents which are
analogous to real events and real people, is a significant feature in Book I of
Gulliver's Travels. Many of Swift's experiences as a Whig minister in the government of Queen Anne appear here in fictional guise. For example, one of
the chief entertainments at the court of Lilliput is the selection of new ministers
to government posts. A competition decides the election: the would-be minister
must dance on a tightrope, jumping high in the air without falling. Another
court entertainment involves ministers' approaching a stick held by the emperor
and either leaping over it or creeping under it. These court events parallel the
figurative ministerial acrobatics of Swift's own day, the vying for favor and the
political contortions engaged in by ambitious climbers such as Walpole and the
earl of Nottingham. These two figures, both Whig ministers, are specially al-
legorized under the names of Flimnap and Skyresh Bolgolam. The story line
involving Gulliver's betrayal by a faction of ministers led by Skyresh Bolgolam

closely parallels Swift's betrayal by the Whig party which led him ultimately to switch his allegiance to the Tories. Thus the political allegory in Lilliput is not merely a general assault on political double-dealing and dishonesty but a very specific account of Swift's own experiences in government.

Invective—that is, straightforward verbal denunciation—occurs less frequently than allegory in *Gulliver's Travels*, but it does appear, notably in the scene in Book II where the king of Brobdingnag closely interrogates Gulliver on his report of the English nation and its people. The questions themselves have a satiric purpose, in that they "needle" Gulliver, exposing discrepancies in his report and underscoring the negative truths implied in his panegyric of England. But the Brobdingnagian king concludes with a piece of very direct and violent invective against the English nation, pointing to the lawlessness masquerading as law, the falsehood masquerading as honesty. Finally he says, "I cannot but conclude the bulk of your natives to be the most pernicious race of odious little vermin that nature ever suffered to crawl upon the surface of the earth" (II, vi). Although we cannot assume that the judgment of the king is totally accurate, his invective is another means of satirizing English customs and practices as seen from an outsider's point of view.

Symbolism is like allegory in evoking a meaning beyond the immediate context, but symbolism does not, like allegory, depend on a particular structure of ideas latent in the text. A symbol does not "stand for" an idea but embodies it, bearing a significance which cannot readily be translated into other terms. In *Gulliver's Travels*, the Yahoos of Book IV have the aspect of a symbol. They do not so much point to or "stand for" the coarse and bestial side of human nature; rather, they constitute a vision or embodiment of man as viewed from a peculiarly austere and pessimistic perspective. It is significant that the Houyhnhnms regard the Yahoos as symbolic, using the word "yahoo" as an epithet to signify "evil," for which they have no other word. The word has entered our own language to refer to a vicious or degraded man, a fact that attests to the power of Swift's symbolism.

The vivid and repugnant physical descriptions of the Yahoos, with their yellow excrements, hairy bodies, and offensive smells, are, literally, a laying bare or exposing of humanity's essential bestiality and animal nature. Much is made in Book IV of Gulliver's clothes, a mysterious covering which superficially distinguishes him from other Yahoos. But a Yahoo is man stripped not only of clothes but of all the pretensions to reason, importance, virtue, and power which his pride engenders. When the female Yahoo attacks Gulliver while he is bathing, he is finally forced to abandon his own pretensions and reluctantly acknowledge kinship: "For now I could no longer deny that I was a real Yahoo."

Her sexual overture signifies her instinctual awareness that he is of the same species. The sense of a species, a real animal group with a characteristic biology and social order, permeates all the descriptions of the Yahoos in Book IV. The grinning, chattering, filthy, soulless herd, motivated by instinct, appetite, and will, is a more powerful symbol of man's degradation than any allegorical rendering of the seven deadly sins.

Finally, irony pervades *Gulliver's Travels*, in that there is always some discrepancy between the surface of the narrative and Swift's latent meaning. Throughout the book Swift invites a double awareness, using Gulliver's literal, fastidious persona to create a quality of strangeness and dislocation. One of the most effective uses of irony occurs at the very end of the work, in Gulliver's description of his state of mind and being on returning to England after his experiences in Houyhnhnmland. On the one hand, Gulliver describes the English people as Yahoos. Though he has returned to his native country and to "normal" life, he sees those around him as bestial, the society as vile and corrupt. On the other hand, Swift seems to indicate that in some ways Gulliver himself is the madman: he takes to neighing like a horse and stuffing lavender and tobacco leaves in his nose to help him tolerate the smell of his wife. The last paragraph of the work is the crowning irony. Here Gulliver attacks his native countrymen, those formless lumps of clay, for their pride, but in his rejection of his fellow human beings and his refusal to bear their company he exhibits his own excessive pride. Thus Swift uses irony to suggest that the question of who is mad is a matter of perspective, and that neither Houyhnhnm nor Yahoo is a true picture of man.

26.7 Compare Book II of Sir Thomas More's *Utopia* with Book IV of *Gulliver's Travels*.

Answer Both Swift and More use the form of a fictional travelogue to present blueprints of perfect societies. Furthermore, both Houyhnhnmland and Utopia are founded on the same general principle, which their creators would call natural reason. The inhabitants of each never-never land are rationalists whose customs, practices, and laws are naturally virtuous because they conform to the dictates of reason. Both societies banish irrational passion on the assumption that higher instincts naturally subdue baser ones.

Thus, in Houyhnhnmland marriages are arranged, while in Utopia they are a matter of rational choice, with a mandatory physical inspection of the prospective partner before the marriage contract is signed. Money is unheard of in both societies, since it is only an invitation to avarice and ostentation. In both countries, the economies are based on agriculture and barter, living arrangements are simple and humble, and only necessities are valued, luxuries having no place in these planned and rationalistic societies.

Both Utopia and Houyhnhnmland share certain humanistic features as well, including the mandatory education of women and government by a learned assembly of the wisest and best-educated members of the community. Thus, More and Swift seem to be envisaging similar ideal or perfect worlds.

However, these images of "perfect" worlds also have in common a certain ambiguity, since each displays features which could be interpreted as imperfections or drawbacks. In Utopia, there is a slave class drawn from the ranks of criminals; in Houyhnhnmland, genetically inferior horses of particular colors are designated as servants of the purebred horses. By most ethical standards, such subjugation of one group by another is inhumane and distasteful.

Furthermore, both societies appear to be limited with respect to religion. More describes the religious practices of the Utopians but indicates that theirs is a "natural" religion; reason leads them to believe in the immortality of the soul and the existence of a Creator. For More, who was a devout Catholic, this is a severely limited religion, which does not require faith and does not center on the revealed deity in the person of Christ. Swift, who was a dean of the Anglican church, rather strangely omits any mention of religion among the Houyhnhnms.

Both societies are also somewhat chilling in their portraits of "perfection." The eradication of all passion makes relationships cool, remote, and rationalistic. Although friendship, benevolence, and obedience are highly valued in both societies, the individuals seem to lack any warmly human bonds of love. The treatment of faith and emotion in both Utopia and Houyhnhnmland points to the inadequacy of pure reason as a guide to human life.

Eighteenth-century philosophy especially tended to pride itself on having developed to the highest point the Renaissance faith in reason as the distinctive quality of man. (It is this self-conscious, confident belief in rational principles that gives the period its historical labels of the Age of Reason and the Enlightenment.) By implying that their utopias are flawed, More and Swift illustrate the pretentiousness and folly of relying on reason as the sole criterion of value.

Finally, the Utopians' disdain for all other nations and the Houyhnhnms' distaste for the Yahoos and for the English nation which Gulliver represents suggest that these perfect beings are guilty of the sin of pride which, ironically, they pride themselves on subduing. The self-love of these utopian beings could be taken as another indication of the inevitable failure of pure reason when applied to fallible, fleshly creatures. No matter how idealistic and principled the Utopians and Houyhnhnms may be, they readily fall victim to the chief of the seven deadly sins, pride.

These, then, are complicated portraits. Swift and More have the stature of great satirists partly because they include complexity in their vision and raise troubling doubts in the mind of the reader. Their "utopias" thereby perform one of the major functions of great literature, to make the audience reflect.

B.S.

SUGGESTED READINGS

Davis, H., *Jonathan Swift: Essays on His Satires and Other Studies* (1964).
Price, M., *Swift's Rhetorical Art* (1953).
Quintana, R., *Swift: An Introduction* (1955).
Vickers, B., ed., *The World of Jonathan Swift* (1968).

JOSEPH ADDISON AND RICHARD STEELE

C H R O N O L O G Y

JOSEPH ADDISON

1672   Born at Milston, Wiltshire. Son of Lancelot Addison, a clergyman of modest means, and Jane Gulston Addison.

1683   Enters grammar school in Lichfield.

1686   Enters the Charterhouse School in London, where he meets Richard Steele. Remains there until 1687.

1687   Enters Queen's College, Oxford; he will receive his B.A. in 1691 and remain there as a tutor until 1698.

1694–   Produces his earliest literary works: the poem "To Mr. Dryden," published
1695   in an anthology; several poems in a *Miscellany* published by Tonson in 1694; and a "Poem to His Majesty" in 1695.

1699–   With the help of a grant obtained by several Whig political leaders, travels
1703   and studies in France, Italy, Switzerland, Austria, Germany, and Holland, in preparation for a political and diplomatic career.

1703–   Returns to England. Publishes *The Campaign*, a poem commemorating Marl-
1704   borough's victory at the battle of Blenheim; he is appointed commissioner of appeals as a result. Renews his friendship with Steele; both become acquainted with various "wits" and the literary and political figures of the day.

1705   Helps Steele in revising his comedy *The Tender Husband*; it is a failure when produced, however. Publishes *Remarks on Italy*.

1706   Appointed undersecretary of state, and travels in Europe on a diplomatic mission.

1707   Addison's opera *Rosamond* is produced; it runs only three nights. He lives with Steele for several months; writes political pamphlet *The Present State of the War*.

1708   Is elected to Parliament; also serves as secretary of the Irish government.

1709   Steele begins publishing *The Tatler* in April; starting with number 18, Addison is a frequent contributer.

1710   Publishes five numbers of his own journal, *The Whig Examiner*, in support of the government; however, the Whigs are ousted later in the year.

1711   *The Tatler* is concluded in January. Two months later, Addison and Steele begin *The Spectator* in collaboration.

1712   *The Spectator* ceases publication in December.

1713   Buys an estate in Warwickshire. His tragedy *Cato* is produced; it is a moderate success. Contributes fifty-one numbers to Steele's journal *The Guardian*, published from March to October.

1714   Serves briefly as secretary to the regency following the death of Queen Anne; with the accession of George I, is disappointed at being renamed secretary of the Irish government. With the help of Eustace Budgell, revives *The Spectator* for about six months.

1715   Appointed commissioner of trade. When the pretender James III invades Ireland, he begins the periodical *The Freeholder* in defense of King George.

1716   Marries the countess of Warwick. With Steele's help, revises his comedy *The Drummer*, which Steele produces; it runs three nights.

1717   Appointed secretary of state; it is the highest governmental post he will hold.

1718   Resigns his post because of ill health. Visits Bristol.

1719   Birth of Addison's daughter. Publishes *The Old Whig*, defending the Peerage Bill against attacks by, among others, Steele. Dies on June 17.

1721   Addison's executor, Thomas Tickell, publishes his *Works*.

RICHARD STEELE

1672   Born in Dublin. Son of Richard Steele and Elinor Sheyles Symes Steele, genteel but impoverished Irish Protestants.

1677   Death of Steele's parents. Until 1684, he will be educated at home by his uncle and guardian, Henry Gascoigne.

1684   Enters the Charterhouse School in London, where he will meet Joseph Addison in 1686. Remains there until 1689.

1689   Enters Christ Church College, Oxford; he will leave without a degree in 1692 and enlist in the duke of Ormond's Second Troop of Horse Guards, hoping for a military career.

1695   Publishes his first work, "The Procession," a poem on the death of Queen Mary.

1695–
1700   Serves first as ensign, then as captain, in the Coldstream Guards. During this period, he conceives a child by Elizabeth Tonson, sister of the publisher, whom he acknowledges and later helps to raise. Publishes a poem in praise of Addison (1700).

1701   Writes *The Christian Hero*, a small moral and religious manual, and a comedy, *The Funeral* (performed in 1702).

1703–
1704   Writes the comedy *The Lying Lover*; he has become a fairly well known author. He and Addison renew their friendship when Steele is stationed at a fort near London; they become members of the literary and political circles of the day.

1705   Addison helps Steele in revising his comedy *The Tender Husband*; it is a failure when produced, however. Steele marries Margaret Ford Stretch.

1706   Becomes gentleman-waiter to Prince George, the husband of Queen Anne; his wife dies.

1707   Lives with Addison for several months. Through his Whig friends, is appointed to the influential post of Gazetteer (i.e., editor of the government journal *The London Gazette*). Remarries; his second wife is Mary Scurlock.

1709   Begins publishing *The Tatler* in April; starting with number 18, Addison is a frequent contributor.

1710   The Whigs fall from power, and Steele loses his post as Gazetteer in consequence.

1711   *The Tatler* is concluded in January. Two months later, Addison and Steele begin *The Spectator* in collaboration.

1712   *The Spectator* ceases publication in December.

1713   Steele elected to Parliament. He publishes *The Guardian* from March to October (with fifty-one numbers contributed by Addison) and *The Englishman* beginning in October (terminated four months later).

1714   Publishes several anti-Tory periodicals and pamphlets, for which he is expelled from Parliament in March. However, with the return to power of the Whigs following the death of Queen Anne, is named manager of the Drury Lane Theatre in reward for his services.

1715   Elected to Parliament again; revives *The Englishman* briefly; is knighted by King George.

1716   Helps Addison revise his comedy *The Drummer*, and then produces it; it runs three nights.

1718   Visits Scotland as a government commissioner; his wife and son die.

1719   Attacks the Peerage Bill, which Addison strongly supports. Death of Addison.

1720   Engages in dispute with Lord Chamberlain Newcastle over the management of the Drury Lane Theatre; he publishes *The Theatre* to air his views. Is briefly relieved of his managerial duties.

1722   Elected to Parliament. His play *The Conscious Lovers* is a great success.

1725–
1729   Lives mainly at his wife's estate in Wales, for reasons of health and finances. Suffers a stroke (1726). Death of Steele (1729).

ESSAY QUESTIONS WITH ANSWERS

27.1 In many of their essays, Addison and Steele examine the relationship between manners and morals, relating social customs to serious ethical values. Using Steele's essay on dueling (*Tatler*, 25, meaning number 25) and Addison's on "party patches" (*Spectator*, 81), compare the two men's approaches to contemporary mores.

Answer Richard Steele handles the subject of duels, a common means of settling disputes among upper-class men in the eighteenth century, in the manner of a witty conversationalist taking part in a debate. Spurred on, as he says, by a letter from a young female reader, he takes on this instance of men's folly, vowing to strip it "of all its false pretenses to credit and reputation amongst men."

In his attack on dueling, Steele uses some of the techniques of formal proof, such as definition, example, and citation of authorities, but his argumentation is oblique, ironic, and amusing rather than logical and exhaustive. Thus he offers a satiric definition, rather than a serious analysis, of the phrase "a man of honor": "it is not to do handsome actions denominates a man of honor; it is enough if he dares to defend ill ones." Using the anecdote of an honest country gentleman challenged by a "modern man of honor," he points to the perversion of the word "satisfaction" to mean not pleasure or compensation but revenge: " 'This is fine doing,' says the plain fellow; 'last night he sent me away cursedly out of humor, and this morning he fancies it would be a satisfaction to be run through the body.' "

Steele also refers to examples and authorities, but his references are only hypothetical; he promises an argument rather than delivering it. Alluding to, rather than actually citing, elaborate historical evidence from "other ages and nations," he promises at some unspecified future time a "good history of quarrels" complete with "cuts" (woodcuts) to prove his case. His oblique allusions lend an appearance of proof by suggesting that he is armed with the required evidence, but at the same time they circumvent the tediousness of actual illustration. Steele's solitary quotation, from Swift's *A Tale of a Tub*, lightly embroiders on the contradiction in the phrase "giving a man satisfaction" by offering another instance, namely the pope's practice of issuing indulgences, in which blackmail masquerades as generosity.

Thus Steele appropriates the methods of formal argument but focuses more on the rhetoric than the logic of persuasion. His tendency to turn definition into bon mot, example into anecdote, and citation of authority into decorative embroidery is nowhere more evident than in the invented letter which closes the essay. His translation of the rhetoric of dueling into frank language is yet another step in his argument against the custom, but again it is a rhetorical proof, relying on linguistic effects. He lays bare the discrepancy between the pretended politeness of the challenge to a duel and its actual barbarity through a mock-invitation: ". . . I desire you would come with a pistol in your hand, and endeavor to shoot me through the head, to teach you more manners." By focusing on the comic contradictions in the language, he exposes the folly of the action.

Addison, too, uses an oblique approach to satirize social absurdities, but his strategy in his essay on "party patches" is more formal and elaborate than Steele's, his argument assuming almost the proportions of a mock-oration. His subject is twofold: feminine vanity in the use of cosmetics and the follies of partisan politics. Beginning with a mock-heroic description of a confrontation at the opera, he describes Amazon ladies drawn up in battle array on either side of him, displaying their "colors" in the form of false beauty marks placed on the right or left forehead to indicate their Whig or Tory allegiance. (This practice of "patching" was a common one throughout the late seventeenth and early eighteenth centuries.) Developing the irony inherent in this frivolous exhibitionism masquerading as political statement, he analyzes the motives behind patching, both capricious and principled; mentions two exemplars (the unfortunate Rosalinda and Nigranilla, whose natural marks are on the sides opposite to their actual political allegiances); and discusses the effects of patching, specifically the evil consequences of excessive partisanship. Addison begins to shift the tone of his essay at this point, as caricature yields to direct criticism:

> I have, in former papers, endeavored to expose this party rage in women, as it only serves to aggravate the hatreds and animosities that reign among men, and in a great measure deprives the fair sex of those peculiar charms with which nature has endowed them.

Addison's allusions to the Sabine, Roman, and Athenian women are not a mock-rhetorical ploy but a serious form of persuasion. Using classical illustrations, he holds up to the women of England an ideal of feminine conduct:

> As our English women excel those of all other nations in beauty, they should endeavor to outshine them in all other accomplishments

proper to the sex, and to distinguish themselves as tender mothers and faithful wives, rather than as furious partisans.

The proper role of the female sex is to promote peaceful accord and domestic harmony. Thus Addison's initial joke becomes the basis for a serious discourse on the role of women in society.

In part, the difference between these essays resides in the larger contrast between *The Tatler* and *The Spectator*, the former generally devoted to light social observations and the latter a forum for more serious ideas. But in part the difference derives from the characters and intentions of the two essayists. Steele cultivated a personal, chatty tone, partially concealing his moral message behind a witty facade designed, first of all, to entertain. Addison's wit was more formal, his firm intellectual and ethical aims giving his periodical sallies a weighty resonance less commonly found in Steele's.

27.2 In the second number of *The Spectator*, Steele sketched portraits of the fictional members of "The Spectator's Club." Addison later took over the character of Sir Roger de Coverley in a series of essays of his own. What techniques of selection and illustration do Addison and Steele use in sketching the portraits of these characters?

Answer In the fiction of the club, Steele offers a dissection of early eighteenty-century society. His cast of characters is ranked by social standing and wealth, beginning with "the first of our Society," Sir Roger de Coverley, and ending with the humble, unworldly clergyman. Each of the men described represents not only an individual or a social class but a specific personality type or "character." Thus, Sir Roger is the eccentric country gentleman of sanguine temperament and hearty disposition. The lawyer is a young urban wit, schooled not in law but in the ancient classics and the current drama. Sir Andrew Freeport represents the city merchant, a member of the rising middle class, with its virtues of frugality, prudence, energy, and optimism. Captain Sentry is a retired soldier whose modest inclinations make him a good coffeehouse companion, though he was an unsuccessful commander. Will Honeycomb, the town gallant or fop, and the simple clergyman, upright and earnest, complete the gallery of types.

In describing these men, Steele alternates between broad abstraction and specific detail. Though Sir Roger represents the stock figure of the good landholder, he is also a man haunted by disappointed love; the lawyer, though a scholar and an aesthete, has a nagging father who demands legal opinions of his son; and the captain, although a military type, is not the traditional swaggering and contentious soldier but a man of modesty and frankness. By enlivening caricature with deviations from type, Steele makes his characters seem both symbolic and individual at the same time.

From Steele's cast, Addison selects Sir Roger de Coverley and makes him the chief actor in a series of small dramas which reveal English country life as well as Sir Roger's own character. In his depictions of Sir Roger at church (*Spectator*, 112) and Sir Roger at the assizes (*Spectator*, 122), he shows the squire's amicable relationships with his parson and fellow parishioners and with his fellow justices and tenants. For example, the anecdote about the old retainer, now an innkeeper, who sets up a portrait of Sir Roger as an inn sign is not merely a comic tale but an illustration of the bond between landholder and servant. Thus these tales of Sir Roger are also small essays on the proper role of the English gentry in the life of the countryside.

Addison's elaboration of Steele's sketch of Sir Roger not only expands the moral implications of the type but fleshes out the character, giving him more weight and individuality. Some of Addison's stories have no strong ethical point, but are amusing, realistic glimpses of character in action. Sir Roger's "singularities" and the "mirthful cast in his behavior," briefly mentioned by Steele, are dramatized by Addison in a number of comic anecdotes. For example, Sir Roger at church is a good-hearted busybody:

> As Sir Roger is landlord to the whole congregation, he keeps them in very good order, and will suffer nobody to sleep in it besides himself; for if by chance he has been surprised into a short nap at sermon, upon recovering out of it he stands up and looks about him, and if he sees anybody else nodding, either wakes them himself, or sends his servant to them. (*Spectator*, 112)

Similarly, on the way to the county assizes, Sir Roger is a picture of genial befuddlement when approached by two yeomen to settle an argument about fishing rights. After a period of weighty deliberation, he delivers himself of the comically indecisive judgment "that much might be said on both sides" (*Spectator*, 122). This equivocation delights both parties, "because neither of them found himself in the wrong by it."

In these episodes Addison's technique approaches that of the novelist. What he gives the reader is not a moral essay on benevolence but a fully rounded character, engaged, in his idiosyncratic way, in benevolent actions. Fielding's Squire Western and Mr. Allworthy have their literary origins in the type of country gentleman which Sir Roger represents.

27.3 In *Spectator* number 70, Addison discusses the anonymous medieval ballad *Chevy Chase*. What criteria does Addison use in evaluating the poem, and how do these standards reflect the neoclassicism of the period?

Answer Addison's praise of *Chevy Chase* seems somewhat unorthodox for a critic of the neoclassical period. Medieval poetry as a whole was in relative disrepute in the early eighteenth century, partly for its failure to adhere to classical doctrine in such matters as imitation and decorum. In particular, ballads were often considered barbarous and crude because, as anonymous expressions of folk culture, they lacked formal classical antecedents. Although ballads like *Chevy Chase* sometimes dealt with patriotic or heroic themes, their rough and simple language was regarded as a violation of stylistic decorum.

It is true that in the second half of the eighteenth century there was a revival of interest in the medieval period. The gothic style, formerly viewed as extravagant and irrational, became a vogue in architecture and poetry; and, after the publication of Thomas Percy's edition of *Reliques of Ancient Poetry* in 1765, there was renewed interest in archaic language and older literary forms, including the ballad. But in the earlier Augustan period, appreciation of medieval arts and letters was relatively rare. Addison's essay, then, is anomalous.

In his critique of *Chevy Chase*, Addison's stance is thus, at least initially, defensive. What is interesting about his argument is that he uses neoclassical theory to answer the neoclassical objections to the older, native poetry. Invoking one of the chief critical criteria of the Augustan age, he points out that the popularity of ballads proves that they conform to and represent "nature," that is, the universal, permanent elements in human experience:

> . . . for it is impossible that any thing should be universally tasted and approved by a multitude, though they are only the rabble of a nation, which hath not in it some peculiar aptness to please and gratify the mind of man. Human nature is the same in all reasonable creatures; and whatever falls in with it, will meet with admirers amongst readers of all qualities and conditions.

Addison treats the style of ballads as the opposite of gothic extravagance and praises the "simplicity of thought" they exhibit. The reason for their universal appeal, he says, is plain, "because the same paintings of nature which recommend it to the most ordinary reader, will appear beautiful to the most refined." Addison goes on to cite the positive reactions to *Chevy Chase* of two earlier critics, Ben Jonson and Sir Philip Sidney (both classicists themselves, to varying degrees), as if to justify his own delight in the poem. Indeed, he seems to take the theme of his whole essay from Sidney's remark that the ballad's power to move and persuade is unimpaired by its "rude style." (Sidney says his heart was "moved" by the poem, "which being so evil apparelled in the dust and cobweb of that uncivil age, what would it work trimmed in the gorgeous eloquence of Pindar?")

Thus Addison concedes the stylistic imperfections of the ballad, resting his defense of the poem on the idea that its theme is moral, patriotic, and heroic, a true expression of the noblest impulses of human nature. He first emphasizes that *Chevy Chase* conforms to the neoclassical view that great literature must have didactic significance. Pointing out the analogy to Homer's subject in *The Iliad* and Virgil's in *The Aeneid*, he suggests that the poet's purpose in *Chevy Chase* was to deter men from the "unnatural contentions" of civil war by describing the blood feud between two earls, one English and one Scottish. He quotes the final four lines of the ballad as proof of the writer's moral intention, describing them as "a precept for the benefit of his readers":

> God save the king, and bless the land
> In plenty, joy, and peace;
> And grant henceforth that foul debate
> 'Twixt noblemen may cease.

The ballad is, according to Addison, not only morally instructive but, like the Greek and Roman epics, nationalistic and patriotic in emphasis. Addison cites evidence from the poem reflecting "a laudable partiality" to the English nation, in particular the English superiority in battle and the confident revenge the English take on the Scots for the slaying of Piercy. At the same time, he commends the poet for making Douglas, the Scottish foe of Piercy, noble and heroic. Quoting the challenge to single combat offered by Douglas to Piercy, Addison suggests that the whole of the poem is ennobled by the elevated level of the contest between the two protagonists.

In the closing section of the essay Addison points to various beautiful sentiments expressed in the ballad, comparing Douglas's dying words with those of Camilla and Turnus in *The Aeneid* and Piercy's lamentation over his dead foe with Aeneas's lament for Lausus. Although the language of the ballad is archaic and simple by comparison with Virgilian Latin, the nobility of the ideas expressed (the bitterness of dying in front of a rival, the encouragement of one's soldiers to continue the fight, the compassion expressed at the defeat of a worthy foe) transcends the stylistic naïveté and stands comparison with classical literature.

Thus Addison uses the neoclassical criterion of fidelity to human nature and the neoclassical definition of epic as moral, nationalistic, and heroic to defend

Chevy Chase against the charges of vulgarity and rudeness, using analogies and quotations from Homer and Virgil to lend classical sanction to his argument. Taking his hint from Sidney, he stresses the elevated themes and actions of the ballad while making allowances for the language. Toward the close of the essay he says:

> Earl Piercy's lamentation over his enemy is generous, beautiful, and passionate; I must only caution the reader not to let the simplicity of the style, which one may well pardon in so old a poet, prejudice him against the greatness of the thought.

In emphasizing the importance of the thought, Addison expresses the typical neoclassical taste for heroic sentiments, refusing to sacrifice his delight in such beautiful gestures on the altar of strict linguistic decorum.

Much of the essay is devoted to description of and quotations from *Chevy Chase* itself, giving the discourse the air of an "appreciation" rather than a rigorous critique. However, this aspect of the essay also contributes to Addison's thesis that the ballad has merit, for the descriptive sections are a means of "giving" the poem to the reader by conveying its tone and quality. Thus the paraphrases and citations are part of Addison's technique of recovering the poem from unjustified obscurity. His precise application of certain neoclassical standards of excellence and his willing suspension of others allow him to recognize a classic of a slightly unorthodox kind.

B.S.

SUGGESTED READINGS

Dobree, B., *English Literature in the Early 18th Century* (1959).

Graham, W., *The Beginnings of English Literary Periodicals* (1926).

Humphreys, A. R., *Steele, Addison and Their Periodical Essays* (1959).

Thorpe, C. D., "Addison's Contribution to Criticism," in *The 17th Century: Studies by R. F. Jones and Others in His Honour* (1951).

ALEXANDER POPE

C H R O N O L O G Y

1688   Born in London, son of elderly Roman Catholic parents. Year of the "Glorious Revolution," which replaced James II with the Protestant William III, leading to repression of Catholics in England.

1700   Family moves to Binfield in Windsor Forest, near London; Pope is educated mainly at home by family and tutors. Contracts tuberculosis, which will leave him deformed and frail for life; he is humpbacked and never grows beyond 4½ feet.

1702   Accession of Queen Anne, James II's daughter.

1705   Pope enters the literary society of London.

1709   Leading publisher Jacob Tonson publishes Pope's *Pastorals*, poems probably written when Pope was in his teens.

1711   *An Essay on Criticism*, Pope's first great poem, published anonymously. An elegant statement of neoclassical literary views, it will be reprinted at least ten times within a decade.

1712   First version of Pope's mock-epic masterpiece *The Rape of the Lock* published. Pope writes the *Epistle to Miss Blount*.

1713   Pope publishes *Windsor Forest*, poem commemorating the end of the War of the Spanish Succession.

1714   Greatly enlarged version of *The Rape of the Lock* published. Death of Queen Anne; accession of George I.

1715	The first volume of Pope's translation of Homer's *Iliad* is published, to immediate acclaim; his financial fortune is secured for life. The five succeeding volumes appear at intervals until 1720. Though Pope's *Iliad* is today considered more a reflection of neoclassical taste than an accurate expression of Homer's style, it is still regarded as a fine English poem.
1717	First collected edition of Pope's works published, including *Eloisa to Abelard*.
1718	Pope moves to Twickenham, 12 miles from London, where he builds his famous underground "grotto," lined with shells, glass, and semiprecious stones, as a private retreat.
1723	Pope's edition of the works of the duke of Buckingham (a friend of Pope's) is published; it is seized by the government as "Jacobite" (i.e., supporting Roman Catholicism).
1725	Pope's edition of Shakespeare published. The following year, Lewis Theobald will publish *Shakespeare Restored*, criticizing Pope (largely with justice) as a careless editor. For his pains, Theobald will be made King of the Dunces in Pope's *Dunciad*.
1728	First version of the *Dunciad* published (three books); a mock-epic satirizing Pope's personal enemies and all those who he felt degraded the world of literature, art, or scholarship. Also published: *Peri Bathous*, a satirical work probably written in collaboration with Jonathan Swift and other members of the Scriblerus Club.
1733	Pope's *Epistle to Bathurst*, *Imitations of Horace*, and *An Essay on Man* published.
1735	*Epistle to Dr. Arbuthnot* published; also Pope's versions of John Donne's *Satires*, in which Pope regularized Donne's meters in accordance with neoclassical taste.
1737	Pope's edition of his letters published; also his translation of the *First Epistle of the Second Book of Horace*.
1742	The fourth book of the *Dunciad* published.
1744	Death of Pope.

ESSAY QUESTIONS WITH ANSWERS

An Essay on Man

28.1 The following lines are from Pope's mock-epic *The Rape of the Lock*:

> Whether the nymph shall break Diana's law,
> Or some frail china jar receive a flaw,
> Or stain her honor or her new brocade,
> Forget her prayers, or miss a masquerade
> (Canto II, lines 105–108)

> Then flashed the living lightning from her eyes,
> And screams of horror rend the affrighted skies.
> Not louder shrieks to pitying heaven are cast,
> When husbands, or when lapdogs breathe their last
> (Canto III, lines 155–158)

What do these passages have in common with the following lines from Pope's meditative poem *An Essay on Man?*

> Who sees with equal eye, as God of all,
> A hero perish, or a sparrow fall,
> Atoms or systems into ruin hurled,
> And now a bubble burst, and now a world.
> (I, 87–90, meaning Epistle I, lines 87–90)

Answer   All the passages quoted illustrate Pope's technique of yoking highly disparate things in a single syntactic unit, often with an ironic effect. But the disparities in *The Rape of the Lock* have a comic quality, in contrast to the philosophical paradoxes in *An Essay on Man*, which have moral and metaphysical implications.

   Thus, the juxtaposition of moral virtue ("honor") and material possession ("new brocade") in the first passage quoted employs a discrepancy between profound and trivial to puncture, in a playful way, human illusions and pretensions. The delicate creatures, both male and female, who inhabit the fanciful world of the poem are continually equating minor events with major catastrophes, viewing the demise of a husband and that of a lapdog as equivalent and the snipping of a lock of hair as a brutal rape. Through these incongruous combinations Pope exposes the glittering social world of *The Rape of the Lock* as essentially amoral. The nymphs and gallants of the poem are preoccupied with pleasure, self-enhancement, and display; they are incapable of discriminating between material things and virtues precisely because they treat chastity, piety, and fidelity as "belongings" to be exhibited rather than attributes to be possessed. Although Pope's rhetorical presentation of this amoral indifference is pointedly satiric, his tone is relatively genial. Instead of savagely stripping away the social facade to reveal, like Swift, the Yahoo beneath the finery, Pope almost lovingly preserves the glittering surface. He offers us the brocade and the china jar—all the delicate, fragile beauty of social ritual and display—as well as pointing out the moral obtuseness that overvalues these merely material things.

The tone of *An Essay on Man* is generally very different. Once again Pope presents a series of contrasts, juxtaposing hero and sparrow, atoms and systems, bubble and world. But here the yoked items are not all drawn from a single frame of reference. In the *Rape*, honor and brocade, prayers and masquerade are all part of the human world (although some of these are more morally significant than others). In the *Essay*, the elements yoked together are drawn from the two different realms of microcosm and macrocosm, bubble and world. Such discrepant pairs suggest a cosmic rather than a purely social perspective and imply a providential pattern rather than the chaos of human callousness and misjudgment. The omniscient eye of God surveys the entire universal design, which incorporates all things from high to low, from trivial to profound. By insisting on the sweeping spectrum of created things, Pope attempts to convey the same sense of divine order as suggested in Matthew 10:29: "Are not two sparrows sold for a farthing? and one of them shall not fall on the ground without your Father."

Part of Pope's rhetorical strategy here, as elsewhere in the *Essay*, is to assert a harmony while documenting a discord. In attempting to "vindicate the ways of God to man" (I,16), he constantly has recourse to paradox and contradiction to explain apparent ills and evils in God's universal plan. Whatever seems unequal, unjust, or unkind is only an apparent wrong: "Respecting man, whatever wrong we call,/ May, must be right, as relative to all" (I, 51–52). Man in his ignorance perceives contradiction, while God in his wisdom comprehends and harmonizes apparent discrepancies in a providential scheme unknown to humankind:

> All Nature is but art, unknown to thee,
> All chance, direction, which thou canst not see;
> All discord, harmony not understood;
> All partial evil, universal good.
>
> (I, 289–292)

The paradoxes here come thick and fast, but the modifying clauses explain away the oppositions as superficial, a kind of optical illusion. Black is white, Pope says, if only we had the "equal eye" of God to see it. By shifting the ground of argument to the unseen realm of providence, fate, and "ORDER" (almost always capitalized in the poem), Pope defends God from the charges of callousness, indifference, and indiscriminateness. The deaths of heroes and sparrows, atoms and systems, bubbles and worlds may serve some larger purpose which man cannot see. Only the omniscient eye sees all:

> He, who through vast immensity can pierce,
> See worlds on worlds compose one universe,
> Observe how system into system runs,
> What other planets circle other suns,
> What varied Being peoples every star,
> May tell why Heaven has made us as we are.
>
> (I, 23–28)

Thus, Pope sets up his rhetorical situations very differently in the two poems in question. It is true that the figure of yoking occurs in both works, and that the use of the same figure of speech gives both poems a rather brittle, coldly intellectual, witty feeling. However, in the *Rape* the syntactical yokings have a mainly satiric effect, for there is nothing in the surrounding context of the poem to mitigate the sense of discrepancy. The paradoxes are a way of passing judgment on the "equal eye," or rather the myopia, of the nymph. In the *Essay*, however, the rhetoric of the poem in general is designed to override any sense of contradiction, to transcend it or deny it. The yokings thus have a witty, surprising quality without the deflationary irony of the paradoxes in the *Rape*. By constantly shifting the ground of the *Essay*'s argument from the particular to the universal, Pope makes the "equal eye" of God seem not nearsighted but farsighted.

28.2   Pope's major argument in *An Essay on Man* is summarized in the resounding phrase at the end of Epistle I: "Whatever is, is 'RIGHT'" (line 294). It might be argued that such a statement is facile, superficial, and even morally suspect, masking all the evils of the world by means of a simplistic tautology. To what extent can we defend Pope's philosophy of man and the universe?

Answer   Pope's philosophical position is not as facile as the closing line of Epistle I might suggest. Isolated from their context, many of the lines in the poem sound unduly simplistic or assertively optimistic: "Then say not man's imperfect, Heaven in fault;/ Say rather, man's as perfect as he ought" (I, 69–70) or "to reason right is to submit" (I, 164). But Pope's argument, taken as a whole, is a complex acknowledgment of and answer to the very evident imperfections and evils of the world. At the very beginning of the poem, he concedes the apparent disharmonies and inconsistencies which he must rationalize if he is to "vindicate the ways of God to man." Although he asserts that the "mighty maze" of the world is "not without a plan" (I, 6), his language conveys a sense of the evil lurking in nature. The world is a "wild, where weeds and flowers promiscuous shoot,/ Or garden, tempting with forbidden fruit" (I, 7–8). This earthly Eden has its serpent and its "promiscuous" disorder.

Pope's answer to the problem of suffering and chaos takes several forms. His poem is a rhetorical persuasion, shifting from defense to attack, exploiting analogy, commonplace, example, rhetorical question, admonition, exclamation, and epigram. A major part of Pope's vindication of God consists of an assault on the pride, narcissism, and blindness of man. For example, he points to the folly and querulousness of teleological questioning:

> Presumptuous man! the reason wouldst thou find,
> Why formed so weak, so little, and so blind?
> . . . .
> Ask of thy mother earth, why oaks are made
> Taller or stronger than the weeds they shade?
>   (I, 35–36; 39–40)

He goes on to expose the inevitable limitations of man's perspective (" 'Tis but a part we see and not the whole" [I, 60]); insists that ignorance is bliss ("O blindness to the future! kindly given" [I, 85]); and recommends hope and faith ("Hope humbly then; with trembling pinions soar;/ Wait the great teacher Death, and God adore!" [I, 91–92]). Pope also appeals to human egocentricity (Epistle I, section 5), which sees the world as a gratifying toy, both fit and natural, to persuade that all the things of the world, including human evil, are somehow fitting and acceptable.

By referring continually to God, order, heaven, and fate, Pope shifts the ground of the argument from the fallible human viewpoint to an absolute and omniscient perspective, where contradictions disappear and apparent ills are eradicated. Much of the argument is given over to a kind of admonitory hypothesizing: What if we had senses much more acute and refined than we now possess? Then we might "Die of a rose in aromatic pain" (I, 200). What if we tried to rebel against our station? Then "the Whole must fall . . . ./ Being on being wrecked, and world on world" (I, 250; 254).

Apart from the invective and admonition directed against man, Pope's vindication of God also takes the form of positive examples which illustrate an order and harmony in the universe. His description of "the scale of sensual, mental powers" (Epistle I, section 7) exemplifies God's benevolence and wisdom in giving to each creature its due. "The mole's dim curtain, and the lynx's beam," the "groveling swine" and the "half-reasoning elephant" suggest the plenitude and fecundity of God's creation and the subtle, just gradations of the chain of being. A similar effect of celebration is achieved through analogy. For example, in section 3 of Epistle I, the untutored Indian who glimpses the divine is evidence for the universality of God's grace, while the cavorting lamb illustrates the blessedness of man's ignorant state.

Finally, Pope advances his argument by straightforward assertion, often cast in the form of epigrams which coincide with the heroic couplets in which the poem is written:

> And who but wishes to invert the laws
> Of order, sins against the Eternal Cause.
> (I, 129–130)

> The general ORDER, since the whole began,
> Is kept in Nature, and is kept in Man.
> (I, 171–172)

> All are but parts of one stupendous whole,
> Whose body Nature is, and God the soul.
> (I, 267–268)

In these lines Pope offers no proof, as such, but argument by fiat. The line "Whatever is, is RIGHT," as well as the lines preceding it ("All Nature is but art, unknown to thee . . .") belong in this category. Part of the effectiveness of these epigrams derives from the features of antithesis, balance, and parallelism; they constitute "sentences," strikingly pointed phrases which linger in the mind. Furthermore, they derive resonance from the rhetorical strategy of the poem as a whole. Pope can afford these simple declarative statements against a background of subtle, shifting, concessive argument. They ring truer for the context in which they are embedded, conveying a sense of earned optimism and hard-won conviction.

The Dunciad

28.3   A convention of the epic genre is the opening invocation of the Muse. Pope begins Book IV of his mock-epic *The Dunciad* with a parodic invocation. Discuss these opening lines and relate this tactic to the rhetorical strategy of Book IV as a whole.

Answer   Pope's invocation is based on the technique of inversion. Instead of requesting divine guidance in the form of brilliant illumination and spiritual inspiration, Pope addresses as Muses "dread Chaos, and eternal Night," begging them to refrain from shedding total darkness until the poem is ended. He asks only for "one dim ray of light," conjuring up the obscure and murky atmosphere appropriate to his theme of dullness.

He continues with his parodic reversals in a backward version of Genesis: his satiric universe originates not with God's majestic commandment "Let there be light" but with the emergence of the offspring of the powers of darkness "To blot out Order, and extinguish Light" (IV, 14, meaning Book IV, line 14). That the world of Dullness is an upside-down one is shown in the allegorical portrait of the enthroned goddess: Science, Wit, Rhetoric, and Morality are enslaved and bound, while Sophistry, "Billingsgate" (fish market slang), Chicanery, and Casuistry bear the honors.

Likewise, at many junctures throughout Book IV, the grand pronouncements of the goddess Dullness are ironic reversals, substituting incongruous directives for sound advice. For example, her address to the two mad collectors (the botanist and the butterfly catcher) is a model of backward reasoning:

> "O! would the Sons of Men once think their eyes
> And reason given them but to study *flies!*
> See Nature in some partial narrow shape,
> And let the Author of the whole escape:

Learn but to trifle; or, who most observe,
To wonder at their Maker, not to serve."
(IV, 453–458)

The traditional exercise of reading the book of nature as evidence of God's art is inverted here, for the collectors are instructed to see only the book (or the "flies") and not the "Author." From their minute observations of the works of the Creator, these naturalists should learn to express not humility and reverence (the wish "to serve") but merely their shallow admiration or "wonder."

Another instance of ironic inversion, the apocalyptic vision which ends the poem, is the strongest and most compelling of all the reversals in Pope's parodic epic. As Dullness's reign began in dim obscurity, so it ends in pitch-darkness. In this passage Pope elaborates on the theme of darkness through imagery and metaphor, as well as through amplification in the form of a catalogue. As night descends on the realm, the poet describes the gradual darkening of the landscape:

Wit shoots in vain its momentary fires,
The meteor drops, and in a flash expires.
As one by one, at dread Medea's strain,
The sickening stars fade off the ethereal plain.
(IV, 633–636)

"Art after Art goes out," as Religion's sacred fires are quenched, and neither "public flame" nor "human spark" survives the encroaching dark. Here Pope's strategy is to oppose the imagery of light—fire, meteor, flash, star, flame, spark— with the image of night's shadow lengthening over the face of the earth, ob-literating every glimmer of light and reason.

The extensive development of the conceit of growing night gives the vision a comic quality, as we see one bright light after another succumb to the pervasive influence of Dullness, but also a kind of somber intensity as this malign influence creeps across the landscape like an eclipse. The apocalypse concludes with a final instance of inversion in a reversal of the Logos, that is, God's creative Word, "Let there be light." The "uncreating word" of the "great Anarch" plunges the universe into a black void, replacing the variety and wonder of the world with empty chaos. The unmaking of God's creation is presented as a natural outgrowth of the triumph of dullness in the arts and letters, for Dullness is the reverse of the traditional idea of the poet as a godlike creator.

This last instance is only the most elaborate and extensive example of Pope's general strategy of parodying the forms and conventions associated with the epic and with such rhetorical models as the didactic sermon or hortatory oration. The implicit reference to lofty literary traditions puts a sting in Pope's satire of Dullness. Appropriating the forms of moral persuasion, epic narration, and biblical allegory, Pope produces a sense of incongruity through a verbal technique involving inversion, contradiction, hyperbole, and understatement. The resulting parody is not only comic but critical, for the allusion to serious models reveals the debasement of Dullness and the corruption of the culture which makes her its goddess. The inversions constitute a measure of the distance between the elevated norms of the models and the decadence of contemporary society.

28.4   The targets of Pope's satire in Book IV include not only literary dunces but a vast range of social figures, including pedagogues, pseudoscientists, judges, lawyers, noblemen, clergymen, and politicians. What satiric techniques does Pope use in painting this gallery of types?

Answer   Pope uses highly selective detail to present stereotypes which expose the vices of men of various professions, ranks, and estates. In certain instances, he develops a full character sketch, complete with visual description and dramatic utterance. For example, his portrait of the Educator, although based on a historical figure (Dr. Richard Busby of Westminster School), is broadly drawn to caricature flaws and abuses common to many teachers. His sadism toward pupils is expressed in his allegorical garb, the "dreadful wand" and "birchen garland . . ./ Dropping with infant's blood, and mother's tears" (IV, 140–142) signifying corporal punishment inflicted in the name of education. This tyrant voices his twisted pedagogical theory, which values memorization and superficial verbal presentation over a grasp of meaning, in a series of ironic images involving imprisonment and constraint:

> We ply the memory, we load the brain,
> Bind rebel wit, and double chain on chain,
> Confine the thought, to exercise the breath;
> And keep them in the pale of words till death.
> (IV, 157–160)

The Educator, like many of his fellow dunces, is no passive disciple but an unabashed advocate of dullness, defending idiocy and obtuseness in his ringing speech. The lavish expenditure of rhetoric on the subject of dullness is witty and ironic, lending comic vigor to Pope's satiric attack.

In contrast to this elaborate portrait of a sadist, Pope uses brief allusion as well, dissecting the whole of society in a climactic catalogue of vices. In a grand benediction, Dullness addresses all of her "children," directing each class or group to indulge in its characteristic folly. Thus horse racing is the proper province of the duke, "his Grace"; sketching butterflies, the chief endeavor of the Baron; dancing and cricket, the respective "achievements" of the Judge and Senator; French cooking, the favorite amusement of the "sturdy squire"; and, in a pointed reversal, using princes as playthings is the special pastime of first ministers like Walpole. The frenetic series of images paints a picture of a topsy-turvy society. The verse sounds consonantally jangly, and the names and epithets are piled up rapidly, suggesting that the world is swarming with dunces.

Thus Pope damns his fools not with moral maxims and abstract allegations but with hyperbole, irony, and caricature, giving flesh and substance to the idea of dullness.

28.5 Analyze the yawn elaborately described in Book IV, lines 605–626.

Answer   The description of the yawn takes the form of a conceit, a metaphor extended over twenty-one lines. The conceit compares Dullness's gaping yawn to a contagion which infects every person, place, and thing in its path. The comic aspect of this yawn, which causes whole schools, churches, and armies to nod off gently, resides in its homely realism: yawns truly are contagious; watching someone yawn often does, in fact, elicit a yawn.

In this passage, yawning also connotes vacancy, as in a "yawning" abyss. As one institution after another sinks into somnolence, the land becomes a void, emptied of all activity and sensation:

> Lost was the Nation's Sense, nor could be found,
> While the long solemn unison went round.
>   (IV, 611–612)

This "unison" is a song of silence. The passage on yawning begins with a paralysis of speech ("More she had spoke, but yawned—All Nature nods:/ What mortal can resist the Yawn of Gods?" [IV, 605–606]). There is a latent allusion to sound, or rather the lack of it, in the verbs Pope uses to describe the creeping paralysis spread by the yawn: Dullness lulls, quiets, and entrances her audience, "'Till drowned was sense, and shame, and right, and wrong" (IV, 625). The yawn drugs all the faculties, not only sense but conscience. The passage ends, as it begins, in obliterating silence: "O sing," the poet begs the Muse, "and hush the nations with thy song!" (IV, 626). Pope uses this epic yawn to characterize the goddess Dullness and thus elaborate on his theme. Dullness is the great yawner and the great producer of yawns, who arrests all the activity of church and state and obliterates speech, the symbol of man's rational and moral nature.

The Rape of the Lock

28.6   Describe the specific features of Pope's poem which derive from the epic genre, analyzing the tone they produce.

Answer   The supernatural agents presiding over the beau monde of *The Rape of the Lock* correspond to the deities of mythology who controlled the course of events in the great Greek and Roman epics. However, Pope's "deities" are of diminutive size and nondivine status and, like elves or fairies, inhabit the four elements of fire (salamanders), water (nymphs), earth (gnomes), and air (sylphs). These invisible creatures, who constitute the epic "machinery" of the poem, interfere not in weighty affairs of state but in the social milieu of eighteenth-century parties and drawing rooms; for example, Ariel the sylph is Belinda's "good genius," protecting her from harm, while Umbriel the gnome is her "evil genius," inspiring her to wrath. (The use of invisible creatures or "gods" to explain human events and behavior is common in classical myth; for example, when a mortal falls in love, Cupid is to blame. Another source for these good and evil geniuses is the *psychomachia* of medieval morality plays, in which virtue and vice or good and bad angels contend for the soul of man.)

The distance between the sprightly elves of the *Rape* and the heroic gods and goddesses of myth is vast, this discrepancy contributing to the mock-heroic tone of the piece. In contrast to mythological deities, who symbolize human virtues like wisdom or vices like jealousy, the sylphs and gnomes represent minor feminine charms and foibles. The witty play on the theme of virtues and vices diminishes the fair Belinda, who is shown to be a coquette and a prude. At the same time, Belinda and her world have some of the delicacy and charm of a miniature. The abundance of lush, well-observed, precisely described details (for example, Belinda's toilet) make the admittedly trivial setting and activities seem somehow beautiful, and the delight in fantasy for its own sake softens the satiric edge of the mock-epic formulations.

The action of the poem, however, has a mainly satiric thrust, constituting an ironic contrast to the vast arena of epic poetry. The parallels to great events again contribute to the mock-heroic tone of *The Rape of the Lock*, the trivial social world of the poem diminished against the towering backdrop of epic allusions. Thus, the plot includes all the conventional features of epic: the omen or portent (Ariel's oracular pronouncements in Canto I); the arming for battle (Belinda's ritual toilet and the Baron's sacrifice on the altar); the preliminary battle (the skirmish at cards); the visit to the underworld (Umbriel's visit to the Cave of Spleen); the climactic battle (the drawing-room exchange of frowns and smiles, snuff and bodkins); and the metamorphosis of the lock.

The poem's parody involves a substitution of social conventions for epic ones, replacing the moral values of epic—patriotism, fraternity, altruism, honor—with social mores such as vanity, rivalry, reputation. Instead of arms and the man, Pope sings of "amorous causes" and "Belinda." By juxtaposing the masculine, military world of heroes and demigods with the feminine, social one of coquettes and fops, Pope exposes the superficiality and fragility of the latter. Thus the mock-epic allusions have the predominant effect of belittling the trivial obsessions of social butterflies.

What is remarkable is the extent to which the poem transcends its own parodic tendencies, the way in which Pope's mock-epic style manages to preserve some of the grandeur and pageantry of serious epic in the much reduced arena he marks out for himself. For example, Belinda's arming for battle at her boudoir is not solely a satire on the feminine obsession with conquest ("Now awful Beauty puts on all its arms") but a delightful description of the world over which she is rightfully the mistress:

> This casket India's glowing gems unlocks,
> And all Arabia breathes from yonder box.
> The tortoise here and elephant unite,
> Transformed to combs, the speckled and the white.
>   (I, 133–136, meaning Canto I, lines 133–136)

Even on a dressing table the spoils of empire retain some of their imperial grandeur. If Belinda's world is, by epic standards, disappointingly diminutive and fragile, it is, on its own terms, charming.

28.7 What is the theme of the poem and how is it expressed?

Answer The poem, Pope announces, is about "amorous causes," but the amorousness is of a particular kind. Pope's subject is not romantic love but rather sexuality and its social expression. Although the "rape" in the poem is a mock one and Belinda's chastity is never seriously threatened, Pope raises the whole question of sexual relationship in his mock-heroic treatment of a ravished maiden.

Thus chastity, "Diana's law" (II, 105), is a major motif in the poem; however, in keeping with the prevailing social and satiric emphasis, it is treated less as a moral virtue than as a social ritual. Many passages describe female "honor" in ironic terms. It is an attendant sylph, that is, the departed soul of a light coquette, who "guards the purity of melting maids,/ In courtly balls and midnight masquerades" (I, 72–73). Honor is preserved, paradoxically, by the very inconstancy of women, who cannot concentrate long enough on any one beau to surrender to him:

> With varying vanities, from every part,
> They shift the moving toyshop of their heart;
> Where wigs with wigs, with sword-knots sword-knots strive,
> Beaux banish beaux, and coaches coaches drive.
> (I, 99–102)

Honor and purity are the accidental by-products of obsessive coquetry. Furthermore, the appearance of honor is more important than the possession of it. As Thalestris says to Belinda, in admonishing her not to submit quietly to the rape of her lock, "Honor forbid! at whose unrivaled shrine/ Ease, pleasure, virtue, all, our sex resign" (IV, 105–106).

Vanity, too, plays a part in the preservation of virginity. The love Belinda feels on arising on the fateful day to prepare her toilet is, clearly, self-love ("A heavenly image in the glass appears;/ To that she bends, to that her eyes she rears" [I, 125–126]). As she displays her beauty to admiring onlookers, every eye is "fixed on her alone," but her own eyes are "quick" and "unfixed" (II, 6; 10). Intent on exhibiting her own beauty, she is as indifferent as the sun blazing in the sky: "Bright as the sun, her eyes the gazers strike,/ And, like the sun, they shine on all alike" (II, 13–14). The only suggestion that Belinda is in love in the usual romantic sense is the fact that she is abandoned by her sylph at the critical moment because he has glimpsed "An earthly lover lurking at her heart" (III, 144). If this lover is indeed the Baron, Belinda shows her willingness to sacrifice love for vanity (or "honor") in her subsequent treatment of him.

Thus Belinda, it would appear, is more interested in conquest than in love. The military terms in which Pope describes so many of the events in the poem suggest that the relationship between the sexes is warlike. Belinda's toilet is an arming for battle, while the Baron's comparable rite, the burning of French romances on a sacrificial pyre, ends with a prayer "Soon to obtain and long possess the prize." They are preparing, literally, to conquer each other. Thus, Belinda's hair is described as a labyrinth, a snare, and a bait (III, 23–28) and the Baron's reaction to the seductive tresses is a violent desire "By force to ravish, or by fraud betray" (II, 32).

Throughout the poem Pope focuses on the animosity and aggression underlying a certain kind of erotic desire. Although he constantly displaces the erotic content from the physical realm to symbolic arenas—a card game, drawing-room repartee, the "rape" of a lock—his language metaphorically implies that the sexual act is a siege or an assault. Belinda's petticoat is a fortification, a "sevenfold fence . . . armed with ribs of whale" (II, 119–120), that still must be guarded by fifty sylphs, so vulnerable is the spot. The scissors ("glittering forfex," "fatal engine") is clearly described as a phallic instrument. Even the conventional conceits describing the fatal power of glances and frowns ("O cruel nymph! a living death I bear" [V, 61]; "Chloe stepped in, and killed him with a frown" [V, 68]), as well as the pun on "die" to imply sexual intercourse ("Who sought no more than on his foe to die" [V, 78]), suggest a latent connection between sexual flirtation and aggression, a connection that goes back at least as far as early sonneteers like Wyatt.

In Canto IV, the description of the Cave of Spleen further emphasizes the dark side of "love." Here Pope catalogues the various forms of what we might call neurosis, generally female, engendered by sexual disappointment and jealousy. In the opening passage of the canto, Belinda's swelling wrath is compared to the ire of rejected lovers:

> Not scornful virgins who their charms survive,
> Not ardent lovers robbed of all their bliss,
> Not ancient ladies when refused a kiss,
>
> .   .   .   .
>
> E'er felt such rage, resentment, and despair,
> As thou, sad virgin! for thy ravished hair.
>   (IV, 4–6; 9–10)

Pope ironically hints that misery and regret await the likes of Belinda, who though now a scornful virgin will one day be an ancient lady. The hypochondria and hypocrisy of Spleen, Ill-Nature, and Affectation, the bizarre erotic fantasies which people Spleen's cave ("Men prove with child, as powerful fancy works,/ And maids, turned bottles, call aloud for corks" [IV, 54–55]), and the allusions to "vapors" and hysteria all suggest the perverted animus governing female prudery.

In his treatment of eros, Pope satirizes the sexual minuet of eighteenth-century society, exposing the narcissism and aggression which masquerade as flirtation and desire. There is an interesting, and comic, ambivalence in the poem about who the aggressor is: if the Baron has his forfex, Belinda has her bodkin, and it is the ladies, not the gallants, who fire off snuff and kill with looks.

28.8   Analyze the tone of The Rape of the Lock.

Answer   The tone of the poem is variable, modulating from the broadly parodic effect of a couplet like "A beau and witling perished in the throng,/ One died in metaphor, and one in song" (V, 59–60) to the somber intensity of lines like "The hungry judges soon the sentence sign,/ And wretches hang that jurymen may dine" (III, 21–22). The prevailing mood of the poem is lightly ironic and deflationary, with a characteristic tendency of elevated rhetoric to collapse into a comic anticlimax. For example, the whole of Belinda's overwrought complaint (IV, 147–176) is an exercise in lofty hyperbole undermined by prosaic commonplaces. As she bemoans "this detested day,/ Which snatched my best, my favorite curl away!" (IV, 147–148), she develops the serious *topos* of the advantages of the country over the court. She continues with a catalogue of "ominous" portents (for example, "Poll sat mute") and concludes with a bitter lament over her lost curl, as though the "rape" had been the most heinous of amputations:

> Oh, hadst thou, cruel! been content to seize
> Hairs less in sight, or any hairs but these!
>   (IV, 175–176)

The texture of the verse, deriving from a rhetorical strategy of deflation, incongruity, and discrepancy, is generally ironic and amusing. But other tonal values enter the poem at various points. The description of the sylphs attending Belinda on the Thames, for example, is not primarily comic but lyric and pictorial:

> Loose to the wind their airy garments flew,
> Thin glittering textures of the filmy dew,
> Dipped in the richest tincture of the skies,
> Where light disports in ever-mingling dyes,
> While every beam new transient colors flings,
> Colors that change whene'er they wave their wings.
>   (II, 62–67)

This passage is connected with others in the poem which portray the beautiful appearances of things. The visual charm of this miniature world, with its tortoise combs and ornamental bodkins, its japanned tables and resplendent playing cards, at times gives the poem the feeling of a celebration or encomium. The social setting is at once parodied and praised.

Pope also offers a serious moral statement in the form of Clarissa's admonition to the assembled company right before the drawing-room battle. Reflecting on the traditional moral theme of *tempus edax* ("time the devourer"), she urges upon her audience less vanity and more good sense:

> But since, alas! frail beauty must decay,
> Curled or uncurled, since locks will turn to gray;
> Since painted, or not painted, all shall fade,
> And she who scorns a man must die a maid;
> What then remains but well our power to use,
> And keep good humor still whate'er we lose?
>
> (V, 25–30)

These "sentences" strike a sober note, but Pope returns to his dominant key of comic irony in the couplet following Clarissa's oration: "So spoke the dame, but no applause ensued;/ Belinda frowned, Thalestris called her prude." The silence is both a comic comment on the risks of sermonizing and a satiric comment on the inadequacies of the coquettes: they are impervious to good advice, good sense, and good humor.

Pope again features the theme of the vanity of earthly things in the passage on the lunar sphere, whither the lock is thought to have fled "Since all lost things on earth are treasured there" (V, 114). The description of these "lost things" is laced with wit ("There heroes' wits are kept in ponderous vases,/ And beaux' in snuffboxes and tweezer cases"), but as the catalogue accumulates, a poignant vision of human waste emerges:

> There broken vows and deathbed alms are found,
> And lovers' hearts with ends of ribands bound,
> The courtier's promises, and sick man's prayers,
> The smiles of harlots, and the tears of heirs.
>
> (V, 117–120)

Carnal desire and mortal longings, avarice and ambition are as futile as "chains to yoke a flea" (V, 121). If Pope's major aim is to satirize sex and society, the poem also touches on the larger perspectives of transience and death.

The Rape of the Lock concludes by combining the mocking tone of the satirist with the solemn tone of the elegist. The apotheosis of the lock provides Pope with yet another occasion for mock-heroic rhetoric: "Then cease, bright nymph! to mourn thy ravished hair,/ Which adds new glory to the shining sphere!" (V, 141–142). But the tone modulates from parody to consolation, as Pope makes manifest the latent theme of death:

> For, after all the murders of your eye,
> When, after millions slain, yourself shall die:
> When those fair suns shall set, as set they must,
> And all those tresses shall be laid in dust,
> This Lock the Muse shall consecrate to fame,
> And 'midst the stars inscribe Belinda's name.
>   (V, 145–150)

Thus the poem has its own weight and seriousness. Not just an occasional piece or a sally of wit, it combines sharp satire and visual fantasy with a moralizing and contemplative background and goes far beyond its mocking premise to provide Belinda with her promised immortality.

B.S.

SUGGESTED READINGS

Brower, R., *Alexander Pope: The Poetry of Allusion* (1959).
Mack, Maynard, ed., *Essential Articles for the Study of Alexander Pope* (1964).
Tillotson, G., *On the Poetry of Pope* (1950).

SAMUEL JOHNSON

C H R O N O L O G Y

1709	Born at Lichfield, Staffordshire. Son of Michael Johnson, a bookseller, and Sarah Ford Johnson, of a middle-class landowning family. From infancy he is tuberculous and sickly, though large and of voracious physical and mental appetites.
1719–1725	Attends Lichfield Grammar School, where he forms lifelong attachments with Edmund Hector and John Taylor.
1725–1726	Attends Stourbridge Grammar School, Worcestershire.
1728	Enters Pembroke College, Oxford. For financial reasons, he will leave after three years without a degree.
1732	Serves as usher (assistant teacher) at Market Bosworth School, Leiches; leaves after a few unhappy months.
1735	Marries Mrs. Elizabeth Porter, a 47-year-old widow. First published work, a translation of Father Lobo's *Voyage to Abyssinia*; first of a long series of "hack" jobs by which Johnson will support himself for over a decade.
1736	Opens a school at Edial, Staffordshire; among his small group of pupils is David Garrick, who is to become the greatest actor of his day as well as a longtime friend of Johnson's. The school fails, however.
1737	Accompanied by Garrick, moves to London, later sending for his wife. Works on *Irene*, a tragedy.

1738 Becomes a contributor to Edward Cave's *Gentleman's Magazine*, one of the first modern periodicals. Befriends the dissolute poet Richard Savage, whose life he will later write. Publishes *London*, a satirical poem based on Latin poet Juvenal; it is widely praised.

1741– Along with other work, writes versions of the proceedings of Parliament
1744 for the *Gentleman's Magazine*, using the heading "The Senate of Lilliput" to evade statute mandating secrecy for parliamentary debates; this work amounts to about half a million words, written with incredible speed, fluency, and elegance.

1742 Catalogs the library of the earl of Oxford; excerpts later published as the *Harleian Miscellany*, with a scholarly preface by Johnson.

1743 Death of Savage.

1744 Publishes the *Life of Savage*, a forerunner of his later *Lives of the Poets*, combining biographical and critical observations.

1745 Publishes *Miscellaneous Observations on the Tragedy of Macbeth*, containing both textual and literary remarks; floats scheme for a new edition of Shakespeare, but a legal threat by publisher Jacob Tonson scotches the plan.

1747 Writes a prologue for Garrick's opening of the Drury Lane Theatre. Seven booksellers ask Johnson to prepare a new, authoritative English dictionary; the money they advance lifts him out of poverty; he hires six secretaries to help him and sets to work. Johnson also publishes his "Plan" for the dictionary, hoping to enlist the financial support of the earl of Chesterfield; embittered when that support does not materialize.

1749 *Irene* is produced by Garrick; it is a failure. Johnson publishes *The Vanity of Human Wishes*, in imitation of a satire by Juvenal; his major poetic work.

1750– Johnson founds a periodical, *The Rambler*, similar in form to Addison and
1752 Steele's *Spectator*; it runs for 208 numbers, all but four written by Johnson.

1752 Death of Johnson's wife. He meets and befriends Joshua Reynolds, greatest painter in England at that time.

1753– Johnson contributes two dozen essays to *The Adventurer*, a periodical begun
1754 by his friend Dr. Hawkesworth.

1755 Johnson's *Dictionary* published; immediately recognized as a monumental achievement. Its use of quotations from fine writers to illustrate the definitions is a major contribution to lexicography. It will remain a standard work in its field for nearly a century.

1756 Publishes *Proposals for Printing the Dramatick Works of William Shakespeare*, seeking subscribers and financial help for his scheme.

1758–   Johnson publishes *The Idler*, another periodical; writes 92 of its 104 numbers.
1760

1759   *Rasselas* published.

1762   Granted a royal pension of £300 annually by the newly crowned King George
          III.

1763   Meets James Boswell, thirty-one years his junior, whose *Life of Johnson*
          (1791) will be the first great biography and is still widely considered the
          greatest ever written.

1764   Johnson, with Joshua Reynolds, Oliver Goldsmith, Edmund Burke, and
          other leading figures of the day, founds the Literary Club for conversation
          and companionship. Johnson meets Henry and Hester Thrale, with whom
          he will live for most of his remaining years.

1765   Johnson's edition of Shakespeare published; its preface and critical com-
          mentary remain a classic of literary criticism.

1770   Publishes *The False Alarm*, one of several progovernment political pam-
          phlets.

1773   Tours Scotland and the Hebrides with Boswell.

1775   Publishes *A Journey to the Western Islands of Scotland*, a fine travel book on
          his 1773 tour, as well as the pamphlet *Taxation No Tyranny*, attacking the
          American rebels. Receives doctor's degree from Oxford. Visits France with
          the Thrales.

1779–   Publishes the *Lives of the English Poets*, a series of biographical and critical
1781   prefaces to the works of the English poets; a major critical and scholarly
          work.

1784   Death of Johnson.

ESSAY QUESTIONS WITH ANSWERS

Rasselas

29.1 The title of Johnson's poem *The Vanity of Human Wishes* expresses the theme of his philosophical fable *Rasselas*. Behind Johnson's artistic treatment of vanity is the Old Testament book of Ecclesiastes, whose refrain is "all is vanity." Compare the final chapter of *Rasselas*, "The Conclusion, in Which Nothing is Concluded," with the final verse of Ecclesiastes.

Answer A note of skepticism about all human dreams and desires pervades both the Old Testament book and the eighteenth-century philosophical tale. Both *Rasselas* and Ecclesiastes express the belief that the human condition is fundamentally one of frustration and unsatisfied desire. Ecclesiastes says, "For what hath man of all his labor, and of the vexation of his heart, wherein he hath labored under the sun? For all his days are sorrows, and his travail grief; yea, his heart taketh not rest in the night. This is also vanity" (2:22–23).

Although the poet-philosopher Imlac seeks to impress a similar view on the youthful protagonists of *Rasselas*, Prince Rasselas determines "to judge with my own eyes of the various conditions of men, and then to make deliberately my *choice of life*" (Chapter XII). Yet his quest and inquiries, corroborated by the separate experiences and reflections of his sister, Princess Nekayah, produce the disillusionment Imlac has foreseen. Even stoic goodness is only a partial response to the human condition. As Princess Nekayah says in Chapter XXVII: "All that virtue can afford is quietness of conscience, a steady prospect of a happier state; this may enable us to endure calamity with patience; but remember that patience must suppose pain."

Both Ecclesiastes and *Rasselas* offer religious consolation in the face of this human predicament, but whereas the former concludes with a "sermon" on the importance of faith, the latter ends on a much more ambiguous note. The poet of Ecclesiastes admonishes his listener, "Let us hear the conclusion of the whole matter: Fear God, and keep his commandments, for this is the whole duty of man. For God shall bring every work into judgment with every secret thing, whether it be good, or whether it be evil." Some biblical commentators have maintained that this final "conclusion" is a later interpolation which attempts to mitigate the pessimism of the original version of the poem. Nevertheless, the poem as we have it does offer conclusive and unequivocal advice on the nature of the good life to the listener.

On the other hand, after offering a discourse on the immortality of the soul, Johnson deliberately avoids any definite affirmation at the end of *Rasselas*. Indeed, perhaps in conscious response to the conclusion of Ecclesiastes, Johnson entitles his last chapter "The Conclusion, in Which Nothing is Concluded." He ends his fable with the bald statement that the prince, the princess, Imlac, and the astronomer realize the vanity of their wishes and decide to return to Abyssinia. The title of the chapter, along with this flat conclusion, suggests that no final decision can allay man's anxiety about his plight in the world. Thus, the final chapter of the tale deliberately resists our desire for closure.

29.2   "Imlac and the astronomer were contented to be driven along the stream of life without directing their course to any particular port." What is the significance of this sentence from the last chapter of *Rasselas*?

Answer   The metaphor of a ship drifting at the mercy of wind and tide conveys Imlac's passivity. The final message of the tale is that humanity is forever at the mercy of external forces over which it has no control: "Very few . . . live by choice," as Imlac earlier tells the prince and princess.

Imlac, the poet-philosopher, is Johnson's spokesman in the tale. His weariness and purposelessness suggest that the message of *Rasselas* is in some ways, a pessimistic one: humankind must suffer its fate in the world with resignation. "Human life is everywhere a state in which much is to be endured, and little to be enjoyed," Imlac says (Chapter XI), summing up the world-weariness that *Rasselas* expresses. People can expect from life only frustration of their desires. Pleasure is based on chimerical fictions and dreams invented by man to deny the pain of life. The human search for happiness and the pursuit of wealth, fleshly pleasures, philosophy, and solitude are revealed as a mere chasing after rainbows. All the supposed roads to happiness end in frustration.

The final description of Imlac reveals the paradoxical nature of his role as guide: he is a philosopher who reveals the delusions of all wise men, a guide who is himself content to be directed by external forces.

However, the image of Imlac as a ship drifting on the waters of life is susceptible of another, less pessimistic interpretation. As reflected in the philosophy of Imlac, the message of *Rasselas* is that since people cannot choose their condition in life, they must accept those joys and pleasures of life which do come their way. "While you are making the choice of life, you neglect to live," Imlac admonishes the prince and princess (Chapter XXX), suggesting that they are so preoccupied with their search for happiness that they miss out on the riches life has to offer. The consolation offered in *Rasselas* is twofold, reflecting a mixture of Stoicism and Christian theology: One must look to the afterlife for true happiness, as suggested by Imlac's discourse on the immortality of the soul, but while on this earth must accept whatever happiness comes along.

Thus in contrast to many other fables, such as those of Aesop, *Rasselas* presents an equivocal moral; its varied episodes and numerous debates admit of more than one interpretation. The quotation in question can be interpreted either as an image of passivity which reinforces the generally pessimistic cast of the work or as an image of an openness to life as opposed to the narrow pursuit of a specific kind of happiness.

29.3 To what extent can Happy Valley in Chapter I of *Rasselas* be seen as representing the garden of Eden?

Answer The very name "Happy Valley" immediately calls to mind the garden of Eden, and the physical description of the valley's verdure and fertility evokes Milton's description of the garden in *Paradise Lost*. Furthermore, the inhabitants of the Happy Valley, like Adam and Eve in Milton's Paradise, seem to be free from hardship and unpleasant labor, their "every desire" being "immediately gratified." Critics have interpreted Johnson's *Rasselas* as a fable of everyman's passage from innocence to experience; Rasselas and his entourage thus represent all mankind, embodied in Adam, destined to leave paradise and in consequence discover that man's lot in the fallen world is one of hardship and pain.

But to equate the Happy Valley with the biblical Eden is to ignore certain sinister details in its description. Phrases like "blissful captivity," "fortress of security," and "appearance of security" suggest that the bower of bliss is a place of delusion and ignorance. These phrases suggest that the valley represents man's predilection for self-deception, his immersion in the pleasures of life as a means of avoiding its pains. The image of the palace, "built as if suspicion herself had dictated the plan," symbolizes the barriers and defenses people erect to shut out pain. Furthermore, the boredom of life in the valley and the need there to "make seclusion pleasant, to fill up the vacancies of attention and lessen the tediousness of time" suggest a state of postlapsarian decadence rather than prelapsarian ease. Coupled with the freedom from labor in the Valley is the implication that its inhabitants work hard to be happy.

While Milton's representation of Eden does not suggest complacency or ignorance, it too conveys a certain ambivalence about virtue or contentment untested by experience (or, as Milton says in the prose tract *Areopagitica*, he "cannot praise a fugitive and cloistered virtue . . . that never sallies out and sees her adversary"). It almost seems as though the true value of Eden can be known only through its loss (and since Adam's Fall leads ultimately to mankind's redemption through Christ, the loss is from a Christian perspective in some sense "fortunate"). Milton and Johnson, as men of learning and experience, may feel nostalgic for an innocence or ignorance which they have lost (or, in the case of man's prelapsarian state in Eden, which they have never known), but neither can fully reject the knowledge and maturity which have, paradoxically, led them to value a less conscious but more innocent condition.

29.4 In his search for happiness, Rasselas encounters many different types of people. Discuss the symbolic significance of these other characters.

Answer Imlac, the Johnsonian spokesman in the tale, is a wise man because he recognizes that no particular kind of life leads to happiness. He introduces the prince and princess to different types of people who seem to possess answers to the fundamental human questions, only to show them that the so-called wise men have not solved the problems of life. As in his poem *The Vanity of Human Wishes*, Johnson presents in *Rasselas* a series of generalized portraits of representative "types," few of whom are even given names; satire and allegory converge to reveal the inadequacies and self-delusions that attend all roads to happiness. Successively, Johnson shows that the time-honored pursuits of sensual pleasure, moral philosophy, scientific inquiry, rustic simplicity, wealth, political power, and marriage cannot make people happy.

Perhaps the most consistently satirized posture in the tale is that of the man who isolates himself from the entanglements of life, by means of either physical seclusion (the hermit) or overintellectualization (the sage or academician). The hermit, whom the prince encounters in Chapter XXII, has retreated from the temptations of the world but has brought into his solitude "a thousand perplexities of doubt, and vanities of imagination," and his imagination "riots in scenes of folly." The shepherds, less voluntary exiles from the great world, are also preoccupied with what they lack; consumed with envy, they are too brutishly inarticulate even to give full expression to their desires, much less to recognize and acknowledge the advantages of their pastoral life.

The second group, the intellectuals, are even more bitingly satirized. The rationalism and philosophical detachment of the "wise and happy man" (Chapter XVIII), who exhorts humanity to triumph over its passions, are undone by the death of his daughter, and Rasselas is made to realize "the emptiness of rhetorical sounds, and the inefficacy of polished periods and studied sentences." The complacency and arrogance of the philosophers in Chapter XXII are revealed in Johnson's staging of a mock-philosophical debate on happiness; glibly passing judgment on the failure of the hermit's retreat from society, they offer arid, abstract advice about living in accordance with a vaguely defined "Nature." Although the questions debated are important, by the end of their pompous disquisitions Rasselas realizes that their supposed wisdom is so much empty talk and that "he should understand less as he heard [them] longer."

The philosophical perspective implied in *Rasselas* is profoundly skeptical about neat philosophical pronouncements or easy moral prescriptions. It uses the indirection of fable or parable to convey a complex and flexible vision of the human predicament.

Preface to Shakespeare

29.5 Samuel Johnson's criticism is generally described as squarely in the neoclassical tradition; yet his *Preface to Shakespeare* includes a well-known defense of Shakespeare against specific charges made by other neoclassical critics such as Dennis and Rymer. What are the neoclassical criticisms of Shakespeare, and upon what grounds does Johnson defend the playwright?

Answer   Dennis, Rymer, and Johnson all subscribed to the fundamental tenet that art is an imitation of life. In accordance with their understanding of this basic principle, neoclassical critics had prescribed certain rules governing dramatic composition. These included the so-called three unities of time, place, and action: the time of the dramatic action should be restricted to a single day; the action should be restricted to a single location; and one action, or plot, should dominate the entire drama. The neoclassical critics generally insisted on a unity of genre within a single play as well—comedy *or* tragedy, for example, but not both. In each case of disagreement with the neoclassical critics, Johnson accuses them of a too-rigid insistence on "rules" of composition which prevents them from recognizing the way life is lived.

For example, the logic of the neoclassical argument for the unities of time and place, based on the necessity of maintaining the credibility of the drama, is disputed by Johnson. Johnson defends Shakespeare's liberties with time and place by saying that the audience members always know that drama in itself involves pretense; they never truly believe that they are present in Venice, ancient Rome, or Cyprus. Therefore, if the fundamental unreality of drama is accepted, lesser unrealities, such as a span of years between acts, ought to be permitted. "Time is, of all modes of existence, most obsequious to the imagination; a lapse of years is as easily conceived as a passage of hours," he says. He goes on to say that "imitations produce pain or pleasure, not because they are mistaken for realities, but because they bring realities to mind." Johnson denies the claim of the unities to verisimilitude and bases his own claim on the way the imagination actually operates when it confronts dramatic art.

Similarly, his argument with the neoclassical rule of the unity of genre is based on an appeal to the basic nature of life. Whereas neoclassical criticism would proscribe the playwright's mixing of comedy and tragedy, Johnson argues that life itself *is* a mixture of high and low, tragedy and comedy, sadness and happiness. Shakespeare's hybrid forms exhibit "the real state of sublunary nature, which partakes of good and evil, joy and sorrow, mingled with endless variety of proportion and innumerable modes of combination." Again, the highest court of appeal for Johnson is life itself. Shakespeare is defended by an appeal to a commonsense judgment of the way life really is, not the way criticism says it should be.

Finally, the neoclassical critics attack Shakespeare for not conforming to the decorum of type in his portrayal of character. They accuse his Romans of not being "Roman" enough, his misers of not being niggardly enough. Again, Johnson's defense is an appeal to life: "His story requires Romans or kings, but he thinks only of men"; that is, his characters display a complex of traits rather than representing only one category or type.

The genius of Johnson's criticism stems, at least in part, from the freedom and range of his imagination; though in his criticism he expresses the beliefs of his age, he refuses to be straitjacketed by narrow rules. While literary taste has changed much since the eighteenth century, at least in part as a result of Johnson's own influence, such powerfully original essays as the *Preface to Shakespeare* exemplify the best of the English critical tradition and remain provocative and relevant assessments of earlier English writers.

Lives of the English Poets

29.6 Quoting Aristotle's definition of poetry (in the *Poetics*), Johnson defines poetry in "The Life of Cowley" as "an imitative art" and faults the metaphysical poets for a want of imitation. Later in the essay, however, he praises them for not being imitators: "No man could be born a metaphysical poet, nor assume the dignity of a writer, by descriptions copied from descriptions, [or] by imitations borrowed from imitations." What are the two different meanings of "imitation" being employed by Johnson? What is Johnson's attitude toward "imitation"?

Answer In the first instance Johnson refers to the classical concept of art as imitating life: the poet endeavors to copy truthfully the matter of nature or to represent the operations of the intellect. The imitation of these two "models" is directed toward the same end, that of representing in poetry the general truths of human nature, which is seen as operating at all times in obedience to certain constant laws. When Johnson says that the poetry of the metaphysicals is not "natural," he indicts these poets for producing the odd or unusual rather than representing the general, common truths of human nature. In this sense, the metaphysicals are to be condemned for their failure to "imitate" successfully.

In the second instance, Johnson refers pejoratively to a more limited sense of "imitation," tantamount to lack of originality. Although, throughout the essay, Johnson deprecates the perversity of the metaphysical poets' "wit," here he does acknowledge their originality, which distinguishes them from writers who merely copy others' inventions. "To write on their plan," he notes, "it was at least necessary to read and think." Judiciously, he weighs the value and limitations of their innovations: "their learning instructs, and their subtilty surprises; but the reader commonly thinks his improvement dearly bought, and, though he sometimes admires, is seldom pleased."

Despite this qualified praise of originality, it is important to emphasize that although Johnson disparages unthinking, mechanical imitation, he by no means criticizes writers for drawing upon the strengths of tradition. Implicit in his reference to Aristotle and his statement that "great things cannot have escaped former observation" is an emphasis on the importance of literary authority and models from the past. The great writers of the past were faithful to the truths of human nature, and in departing from their precedent and overvaluing novelty, the metaphysical poets made "a voluntary deviation from nature in pursuit of something new and strange." A literary (and political) conservative, Johnson was anxious to preserve the literary treasures of the past and to assert their relevance for contemporary writers. To the extent that even the most original contemporary poet must learn the resources of his art from predecessors, the "imitation" not only of nature but of literary models, the very core of a writer's apprenticeship in earlier centuries, remains important to Johnson.

29.7   Like all criticism, Johnson's *Lives of the English Poets* reflects certain cultural assumptions characteristic of its age. What are the central cultural assumptions, either explicit or implicit, in "The Life of Cowley"?

Answer   Although the immediate object of Johnson's attention in "The Life of Cowley" is a particular kind of poetry, the essay provides him with an opportunity to make distinctions and establish antitheses between good and bad art. These depend upon certain very basic neoclassical assumptions about the function of art.

The statement "Great thoughts are always general" asserts one of the most important values of neoclassicism. As Imlac says, in Chapter X of *Rasselas*, "The business of the poet . . . is to examine, not the individual but the species; to remark general properties and large appearances: he does not number the streaks of the tulip, or describe the different shades in the verdure of the forest."

This emphasis on the general involves more than avoiding an overly fastidious preoccupation with "minuter descriptions"; it also implies an approbation of the normative and appropriate as opposed to the idiosyncratic and shocking. For neoclassical critics, decorum and harmony should govern artistic representations of nature, including human nature. This eighteenth-century view of art (and, implicitly, of the world itself) underlies Johnson's negative evaluation of metaphysical poetry; the seventeenth-century poets, in Johnson's view, mistakenly strain for the unusual and surprising, when what they should strive for is a representation of the "natural," the uniform. As in his *Preface to Shakespeare*, Johnson praises the artist who can imitate the general truths of human nature so that we can recognize ourselves in his fictions. It is through an emphasis on the general, rather than the local and particular, that an artist achieves universality: "He must divest himself of the prejudices of his age or country; he must consider right and wrong in their abstracted and invariable state; he must disregard present laws and opinions, and rise to general and transcendental truths" (*Rasselas*, Chapter X). If Johnson strikes modern readers as limited by his historical period and cultural milieu, it is, ironically, precisely because he perceives the possibility of transcending them and insists so forcefully upon its importance.

Johnson's conception of general truths as the basis of art also has consequences for his definition of true and false wit, and hence for his judgment of wit as the central characteristic of metaphysical poetry. While he rejects Pope's definition of wit ("What oft was thought, but ne'er so well expressed") as reductive and "below the dignity" of poetry, he praises wit as that "which is at once natural and new, that which though not obvious, is, upon its first production, acknowledged to be just; if it be that, which he that never found it, wonders how he missed." He sees metaphysical wit, however, "as a kind of *discordia concors*; a combination of dissimilar images, or discovery of occult resemblances in things apparently unlike." While appropriate poetic images derive from natural comparisons, Johnson sees metaphysical "conceits" as "heterogeneous ideas . . . yoked by violence together." Writing close to a century and a half later, T. S. Eliot would praise this very heterogeneity, seeing in it a unification of sensibility—of thought and feeling—which later ages had lost: "A thought to Donne was an experience; it modified his sensibility" ("The Metaphysical Poets," 1921).

However, Johnson's resistance to metaphysical poetry is not solely a matter of his adherence to neoclassical decorum; Pope's view of wit, which he repudiates, is perhaps a purer expression of neoclassicism than one would find in Johnson's criticism. He complains that metaphysical poetry is "not successful in representing or moving the affections" and that its adherents were incapable of the sublime, "for they never attempted that comprehension and expanse of thought which at once fills the whole, and of which the first effect is sudden astonishment, and the second rational admiration." While earlier Augustan figures, such as Pope and Addison, had helped to renew interest in Longinus's conception of sublimity, Johnson's emphasis on affective response anticipates the aesthetic of the romantic era. For romantic poets and critics, the appeal to the sublime was part of a revolt against the neoclassical and its taste for well-formed and elegant beauty. Despite Johnson's conservatism, he was in significant ways a transitional figure, too astute to be pigeonholed according to the dogmas of any single school of criticism.

K.L.

SUGGESTED READINGS

Bate, Walter Jackson, *The Achievement of Samuel Johnson* (1955).

Bate, Walter Jackson, *Samuel Johnson* (1977).

Boswell, James, *Life of Johnson* (standard edition, ed. G. B. Hill and L. F. Powell) (1934–1965).

Fussell, Paul, *Samuel Johnson and the Life of Writing* (1971).

Greene, Donald J., *The Politics of Johnson* (1960).

Greene, Donald J., ed., *Samuel Johnson: A Collection of Critical Essays* (1965).

Wimsatt, W. K., Jr., *The Prose Style of Samuel Johnson* (1941).

THOMAS GRAY

C H R O N O L O G Y

1716   Born in Cornhill. Son of Philip Gray and Dorothy Gray, middle-class tradespeople.

1725   Enters Eton, famous English school. Meets Richard West, who will be his closest friend until West's death at the age of 26. Also begins a lifelong friendship with Horace Walpole, son of Prime Minister Sir Robert Walpole and a novelist and noted eighteenth-century character; Walpole's home, Strawberry Hill, was built as a miniature gothic castle. Gray studies at Eton until 1734.

1734   Enters Peterhouse College, Cambridge. As student and teacher, Gray will remain at Cambridge, on and off, for the rest of his life.

1738   Leaves Cambridge without a degree, intending to study law in London. Instead, he is invited by Walpole on a tour of Europe (paid for by Walpole); they embark early in 1739.

1741   While in Italy, Gray and Walpole quarrel; Gray returns alone to London. He works on a tragedy, *Agrippina* (later abandoned).

1742   Death of Richard West. Gray returns to Cambridge as a graduate student and instructor. He produces many poems, including the "Ode on a Distant Prospect of Eton College" and a sonnet in commemoration of West.

1743   Receives LL.B. degree.

1745   Gray and Walpole are reconciled.

1748   Several poems, including the Eton ode, are published in an anthology. Meets William Mason, who will later be Gray's biographer and his literary executor. Also meets the eccentric poet Christopher Smart, then a student at Cambridge.

1751   Gray's finest work, the "Elegy Written in a Country Churchyard," is published by a London bookseller, Robert Dodsley. It is an immediate public success.

1753   *Six Poems* published, with illustrations by well-known artist Richard Bentley.

1754   Writes his pindaric ode "The Progress of Poesy."

1756   Several Cambridge students, as a practical joke, raise a false alarm of fire under Gray's window. As a result, he transfers from Peterhouse College to Pembroke College.

1757   Gray's *Odes*, including "The Progress of Poesy" and "The Bard," published; the latter poem illustrates Gray's (and the age's) growing fascination with the medieval. Gray is offered the post of poet laureate; he rejects it with contempt, regarding it as suitable only for a nonentity.

1759   Moves to London, where he will stay for most of the next two years, engaging in historical and antiquarian research.

1760   Works on translations of ancient poetry from the Norse and Welsh languages. Also planning a *History of English Poetry* (never completed).

1768   Appointed to a professorship in modern history at Cambridge. *Poems* published by Dodsley.

1769   Gray's "Ode for Music" performed at Cambridge.

1771   Death of Gray from a sudden stomach complaint.

ESSAY QUESTIONS WITH ANSWERS

"Elegy Written in a Country Churchyard"

30.1 Thomas Gray's "Elegy Written in a Country Churchyard" closes with an epitaph of three stanzas "Graved on the stone beneath yon aged thorn" (line 116). Whose epitaph is it? How is it important to the structure and meaning of the poem?

Answer The epitaph is an imagined inscription on the poet's own grave; it constitutes a poignant conclusion to a poem devoted to elegizing the nameless dead in the country churchyard. It is also part of a crucial shift of perspective that occurs in the course of the poem. In the first stanza, the poet uses the personal pronoun "me"—"And leaves the world to darkness and to me" (line 4)—to establish a subjective stance in relation to the scene he is describing. As he wanders through the graveyard, he moralizes over the humble tombstones of the rustic poor, supplying his own eloquent epitaphs on their lives to supplement the rudely printed names and dates. These poetic inscriptions take the form of striking phrases, some of them now commonplaces; among them are such famous lines as "The paths of glory lead but to the grave" (line 36), "Some mute inglorious Milton here may rest" (line 59), and "They kept the noiseless tenor of their way" (line 76). These epigrams are, appropriately, more moving than the "storied urn or animated bust" which memorializes the rich and powerful.

Then, toward the close, the poet addresses himself in an imagined projection of his own inevitable death ("For thee, who mindful of the unhonored dead/ Dost in these lines their artless tale relate" [lines 93–94]). He creates a scene in which a "kindred spirit shall inquire thy fate," reporting the imagined answer of a rustic swain who has daily observed the poet's melancholy rambles through the churchyard. The swain describes the poet meditating by the brook and roving near the woods. Finally, he reads aloud the poet's epitaph. We learn from the inscription that the dead man was humble and impoverished, but learned ("Fair Science frowned not on his humble birth" [line 119]); prone to melancholy (a mark of a poet, in the view of eighteenth-century sentimentalists like Gray), he was nevertheless sincere, charitable, and compassionate.

The gradual shift from the subjective "I" to the objective "him" in describing the poet records the poet's growth in self-knowledge. He has learned how to die, and how to understand his own death, by meditating on the humble dead who surround him. By perceiving "their useful toil,/ Their homely joys, and destiny obscure" (lines 29–30), he comes to value his own simple virtues (knowledge, generosity, sincerity, compassion) without longing for ambition, power, and glory. His epitaph is a monument to his own self-acceptance.

30.2   Two clusters of images occur in Gray's "Elegy," one set involving silence and the other sound or utterance. Discuss the thematic significance of these contrasting sets of images.

Answer   The imagery of the poem is less visual than aural: though the graveyard scene opens in twilight, its most significant feature is its "solemn stillness," broken only by the drone of the beetle, the bells of the herd, and the complaint of the owl. These animal sounds merely increase the impression of a melancholy human silence. The deaf, mute sleep of the dead in the churchyard is posed against the animated sounds of day: the breezy call of morn, the twittering of the swallow, the cry of the cock, and the echo of the hunter's horn, all sounds which have no power to awaken the dead. Furthermore, the "dull cold ear of Death" is beyond the call of "pealing anthem," the stories of urn and bust, the voice of honor, or the murmurings of flattery (lines 41–44). Still another aural contrast is offered, between the "applause" and "threats" of the public forum and the "noiseless tenor" of country life (lines 61–66; 76).

All these antitheses suggest death's "dumb Forgetfulness" (line 85) and silent oblivion. Gray clearly suggests that the noisy pomp of proud memorials is powerless to prevent inevitable death or to alter fate. But he also implies that some commemoration of the dead, some "noise" or utterance, is appropriate. The rustic tombstones implore "the passing tribute of a sigh" (line 80): a sigh of sympathetic identification and a reading aloud of the *memento mori* (the admonition to "remember death" implicit in every graveyard). Indeed, the entire poem is the poet's means of posing words against the silence of the grave, of creating a meaningful epitaph for the dead.

30.3   To what extent does Gray's attitude toward death reflect a romantic sensibility?

Answer   Gray's "Elegy" is in many respects neoclassical, employing conventions drawn from ancient elegies and epitaphs. Among the conventional motifs of the poem is the theme of sympathy between the natural world and man. Thus, in the opening stanzas, Gray uses the darkness and "solemn stillness" of dusk and the owl and yew tree, traditional emblems of mourning, to imply a connection between nature and human mortality. An antithetical but, again, conventional motif is the contrast between nature and man implied in the stanza describing the "call of incense-breathing Morn" and the animated sounds of swallow, cock, and hunter's horn (lines 17–20): although nature reawakens each dawn, the dead shall wake no more. The classical theme of *memento mori* pervades the poem, from the line "The paths of glory lead but to the grave" (line 36) to the many passages reflecting on the hollowness of worldly grandeur, honor, and flattery. Finally, the poem offers the traditional encomiastic features of the classical elegy: the dead are remembered for their "useful toil" and their "sequestered" virtues and praised for their exemplary deaths, "That teach the rustic moralist to die" (line 84).

However, Gray's attitude toward death is to some degree novel, in emphasis if not in form. Rather than confining himself, in Stoic fashion, to the themes of the inevitability and universality of death, Gray stresses its poignancy and pathos. The whole poem is imbued with sentiment which, at times, verges on sentimentality. For example, the stanzas describing the imagined lives of the men now lying buried in the churchyard, with wives and children gathering about them and the fields, animals, and woods responding to their vigorous labors (lines 21–28), convey Gray's sympathetic identification with "The rude forefather of the hamlet." This sympathy becomes something like idealization as the poet speculates on the wasted potential of these humble lives:

> Full many a gem of purest ray serene,
>   The dark unfathomed caves of ocean bear:
> Full many a flower is born to blush unseen,
>   And waste its sweetness on the desert air.

> Some village Hampden, that with dauntless breast
>   The little tyrant of his fields withstood;
> Some mute inglorious Milton here may rest,
>   Some Cromwell guiltless of his country's blood.
>   (lines 53–60)

Gray thus adds the pathos of what-might-have-been to the inevitable sadness of death. He goes on to reflect that the humble station of these dead, although it may have kept them from illustrious achievement, may also have saved them from the temptations and crimes of the ambitious and proud. They are, then, perfect in their obscurity:

> Far from the madding crowd's ignoble strife,
>   Their sober wishes never learned to stray;
> Along the cool sequestered vale of life
>   They kept the noiseless tenor of their way.
> (lines 73–76)

Gray, "mindful of the unhonored dead" and bearer of "their artless tale" (lines 93–94), brings lavish emotion to the subject of death. His melancholy meditation on the evanescence of life is, in a sense, romantic: the wish to identify with spirits who have passed away, the longing to transcend the merely physical ("Even from the tomb the voice of Nature cries" [line 91]), and the willingness to imagine one's own death may all be seen as part of the gothic cult of morbid sensitivity which, originating in the late eighteenth century, surfaces later in some of the poems of Byron and Shelley. Instead of commemorating the dead in a ceremonial, impersonal mode, Gray attempts to merge subject and object, self and external world, joining with those he eulogizes by imagining his own obsequies. In tone and atmosphere, then, the "Elegy" marks a break from the more restrained mood of neoclassical elegy and a move, however tentative, toward the metaphysical strivings of romanticism.

B.S.

SUGGESTED READINGS

Hilles, Frederick W., and Harold Bloom, eds., *From Sensibility to Romanticism* (1965).

Jones, William P., *Thomas Gray, Scholar* (1937).

Ketton-Cremer, R. W., *Thomas Gray* (1955).

Martin, Roger, *Essai sur Thomas Gray* (1934).

RICHARD BRINSLEY SHERIDAN

C H R O N O L O G Y

1751   Born in Dublin, Ireland. Son of Thomas Sheridan, an actor, theater manager, and speech teacher, and Frances Chamberlaine Sheridan, an author and playwright. Thomas Sheridan's father, the Reverend Thomas Sheridan, had been a friend and biographer of Jonathan Swift.

1762   Sheridan enters the Harrow School, where he will remain until 1768. He will receive no further formal education, unlike his father, who holds an M.A.

1764   Under pressure from creditors, Thomas Sheridan and his family leave Ireland and move to France, leaving Richard behind at school. The family will return from France only after five years have passed.

1770   Thomas Sheridan brings his family to Bath, where he starts a school; Richard is an assistant teacher. The school fails, however.

1771   Sheridan moves to London; begins work on various literary projects, unsure of a direction for his career. With a boyhood friend, Nathaniel Halhed, he writes and publishes some verse translations from Greek; they are little noted.

1772   Sheridan meets Elizabeth Ann Linley, a professional singer famed for her beauty. Seeking to escape the attentions of a Captain Thomas Mathews, she flees to Calais, France, accompanied by Sheridan. Challenged by Mathews, Sheridan fights two duels; he wins the first, but loses the second and is seriously wounded.

1773   Sheridan is sent by his father first to Waltham Abbey and then to the Middle Temple to study law; he soon abandons this field, however. He marries Miss Linley; she gives up her professional singing career, although she continues to give private concerts at home, which may help to support the otherwise impoverished couple.

1774   Sheridan dabbles in a variety of writing projects, unable to settle on a suitable career.

1775   Completes his first play, *The Rivals*; it is performed at Covent Garden Theatre and is a failure. However, Sheridan revises it rapidly, and the improved version, which opens only eleven days later, is a great success. Sheridan is now a well-known young author, and he is lifted from poverty. Later in the year, his farce *St. Patrick's Day* is produced; so is an opera, *The Duenna*, which is very successful.

1776   Sheridan joins with several partners in purchasing from the retiring David Garrick a share in the Drury Lane Theatre, using mostly borrowed money. This begins Sheridan's increasingly tangled financial career. The Drury Lane opens under Sheridan's management in September.

1777   Drury Lane Theatre produces *The Rivals*; *A Trip to Scarborough* (an adaptation by Sheridan of a play by Vanbrugh); and *The School for Scandal* (Sheridan's greatest play, and an immediate triumph). Sheridan is elected a member of the Literary Club, a gathering of the age's greatest writers, intellectual figures, and wits.

1779   *The Critic* produced; a successful satiric comedy, it represents practically the end of Sheridan's brief dramatic career. He writes articles for *The Englishman*, a Whig periodical published in opposition to the government.

1780   Sheridan elected to Parliament, thus beginning his political career, which he himself will view as the most important facet of his life. Speaks in opposition to the war against the American colonists.

1782   Serves as undersecretary for foreign affairs.

1783   Serves as secretary to the treasury.

1788   Crisis over the illness of King George III; Sheridan becomes confidential adviser to the Prince of Wales, and speaks in Parliament in support of the prince's right to assume the Regency without the sanction of Parliament.

Also makes memorable speech at the impeachment trial of Warren Hastings, attacking British colonial exploitation of India; probably the high point of Sheridan's political career.

1791   Drury Theatre in such disrepair that it must be torn down and rebuilt.

1792   Elizabeth Sheridan dies.

1794   The New Drury Theatre opens. Sheridan meets, woos, and weds Miss Elizabeth Jane Ogle, daughter of the dean of Winchester. Continues to speak in Parliament as a prominent Whig leader. However, his friendship with the Prince of Wales has begun to cool, and his political star is fading; problems exacerbated by increasing debt due to extravagance and mismanagement.

1799   Sheridan writes *Pizarro*, an adaptation of a tragedy by August von Kotzebue; his last play.

1806   Treasurer of the navy.

1809   The New Drury Theatre burns down.

1812   Sheridan loses his seat in Parliament; makes his last speech on June 21; his political career at an end. Having left Parliament, he is no longer immune from legal proceedings due to his debts. The newly rebuilt Drury Theatre opens, but Sheridan is expressly forbidden to play any part in its management.

1813   Sheridan is arrested for debt.

1816   Death of Sheridan. Buried in the Poets' Corner at Westminster Abbey, in a funeral attended by many of the nation's leading statesmen and literary figures. He had hoped to be buried among the statesmen, however.

ESSAY QUESTIONS WITH ANSWERS

The School for Scandal

31.1 Sheridan's characters have descriptive names such as Mr. Snake, Lady Sneerwell, Mrs. Candour, and Sir Benjamin Backbite. What is the significance of these names?

Answer The entire cast of Sheridan's comedy consists of comic stereotypes, men and women whose ruling passions are accurately labeled by their names. The play is an exposé of social vice and hypocrisy in which the naming of characters contributes to both the comic and the moral dimensions of the drama.

One group of characters clearly represents the scandalmongering which forms the major activity of the play, their names revealing their various skills in the arts of gossip and slander. Thus, Lady Sneerwell is particularly gifted at subtle innuendo; her servant Mr. Snake, himself adept at slimy insinuation, compliments the "mellowness of sneer, which distinguishes your ladyship's scandal." Similarly, Sir Benjamin Backbite contributes his covert abuse, Mr. Crabtree his crabbed ill-humor, and Mrs.Candour her garrulous and damaging bluntness, masquerading as honesty, to the "scandalous college" over which Lady Sneerwell presides. Lady Teazle, distinguished by her sparring, "teasing" relationship with her much older husband, Sir Peter, is the newest pupil in this school for scandal, acquiring the urbane sophistication of her companions in killing off reputations.

The allusions to "Miss Prim" and "Miss Nicely" suggest a fleeting satire on social prudes—the word "nice" in eighteenth-century English conveyed the idea of "fussy, finicky"—while the figures of "Moses" and "Mr. Premium" similarly attack the practices of usury and brokerage. Indeed, almost every name in the play has its satiric point.

Perhaps the most significant name in the play is Surface, the family name of Charles, Joseph, and their uncle Sir Oliver. Distinguishing surface appearances from essential qualities is the whole purpose of Oliver's "tests" of his two nephews. Charles, the libertine, turns out to be a generous, openhearted young man, richly deserving his uncle's legacy. In contrast, Joseph, who by reputation is a man of high moral sentiment, reveals himself to be licentious, avaricious, and hypocritical.

The chief exception to the symbolic naming in the play is Maria, Sir Peter Teazle's young ward and the beloved of both Charles and Joseph Surface. ("Maria" may allude to the purity and innocence of the Virgin Mary, though a religious reference of this kind would seem to be on a very different level from the social satire of the other characters' names.) However one interprets her name, Maria represents true candor and levelheaded judgment in the artificial, brittle social world which Sheridan portrays. Refusing to participate in, or even listen to, the malicious gossip of the school for scandal, she steadfastly remains true to Charles, despite all "surface" evidence. In the end, she and Charles emerge as the proper recipients of a rich legacy which includes both love and money.

31.2 A contemporary critic complained of *The School for Scandal*, "Why don't all these people leave off talking, and let the play begin?" To what extent can the plot of the play be defended as interesting and significant?

Answer The talk of the scandalmongers is, in a sense, the major activity of the play. Whether the butt of the gossip is some nonentity like "Lady Dowager Dundizzy" or a well-established character like Charles Surface, the point of the scenes of gossip is to show malicious wit at work and to satirize "high society" as Sheridan saw it. However, Sheridan also employs a double plot of considerable intricacy, involving on the one hand the intrigues of the school for scandal and on the other Sir Oliver Surface's legacy to his nephews.

The plot centered on Sir Oliver is a farcical exhibition of the misjudgments which result from scandalmongering and belief in surface appearances. Sir Oliver, suspicious of Charles as a worthless libertine, is led by Sir Peter to believe that Joseph is a man of refined moral sentiment. The unraveling of these false conceptions provides the double climax of the play. In the famous "screen" scene, Sir Peter learns of Joseph's hypocrisy despite Joseph's attempts to keep Sir Peter securely in the closet, Lady Teazle safely behind the screen, and Charles's mouth discreetly shut. In the last scene of the play, Sir Oliver finally discards his disguises as "Mr. Stanley" and "Mr. Premium," disconcerting both brothers and entirely humiliating Joseph by exposing him as a hypocrite. Both of these recognition scenes employ comic and dramatic irony to make their satiric point: the audience knows more than the characters and so can enjoy the working out of the delicious twists and turns of the plot from the eminence of superior knowledge.

Thus, all the witty talk of the play is reinforced by the patterned action, with a denouement in which Lady Teazle and Joseph are chagrined and Charles and Maria rewarded. Indeed the "moral" of the play is, in part, that actions speak louder than words. Charles's affectionate, generous gestures—preserving his uncle's portrait or sending a hundred pounds to his poor relation, the real Mr. Stanley—weigh more, in the end, than all of Joseph's sanctimonious "sentences" and pious sentiments.

31.3 Throughout *The School for Scandal* there are many allusions to "sentiment." In the eighteenth century, "sentiment" referred to a refined moral perception combined with emotional sensitivity. "Sentimental" novels and comedies in which virtuous characters spoke in eloquent phrases and adages became a literary vogue in the middle of the century. How does "sentiment" figure in Sheridan's play?

Answer Sheridan's attitude toward "sentiment" is mainly ironic. By equating Joseph's sanctimonious platitudes and proverbs with "sentiment," Sheridan implies that the facile expression of moral ideas and tender feelings is suspect unless accompanied by genuinely moral actions and behavior. The vogue for literary "sentences" (that is, eloquent moral adages) is satirized in Joseph's hypocritical epigrams, which often comically contradict each other. For example, in a single breath he offers the following maxims on the subject of malicious wit:

> Certainly, madam; to smile at the jest which plants a thorn in another's breast is to become a principal in the mischief.

> To be sure, madam; that conversation, where the spirit of raillery is suppressed, will ever appear tedious and insipid.

He has a nugget of wisdom for every occasion, but his ethics are infinitely malleable according to the demands of the moment. When Joseph is finally revealed as the chameleonlike flatterer he is, Sir Peter reverses his judgment on the "sentiments" which he has previously so much admired. As the servant Rowley prepares to offer a wise adage, Sir Peter cuts him short with the remark that

> . . . if you have any regard for me, let me never hear you utter anything like a sentiment. I have had enough of them to serve me the rest of my life.

Sheridan's satiric treatment of the "sentimental" man is in part a reaction to the vogue of the period, which saw the word used as an almost meaningless term of approbation. In the negative meaning he attaches to the term "senti-

ment," he anticipates the nineteenth- and twentieth-century use of "sentimental" to mean "excessively or falsely emotional."

Despite Sheridan's ironic view of moral platitudes, he does not banish all
sentimental feeling from his drama. He attempts to distinguish the artificial
pathos expressed by the duplicitous Joseph from the honest feelings of such
characters as Charles and Maria. Motivated by true generosity and love, these
two are happily united in the denouement of the play, whose final lines consist
of Charles's own "sentimental" poem addressed to his beloved.

B.S.

SUGGESTED READINGS

Rhodes, R. C., *Harlequin Sheridan* (1933).
Sichel, W., *The Life of Richard Brinsley Sheridan* (1909).

Part Seven

THE EMERGENCE
OF THE NOVEL

T I M E L I N E

The Age

1660: Restoration; accession of Charles II

1685: Death of Charles II; accession of James II, who favors the Roman Catholics; unpopular monarch

1688: Protestant prince William of Orange invades England; James II escapes to France; "Bloodless Revolution"

1689: William and Mary crowned

1694: Death of Mary

1701: Act of Settlement permanently excludes Roman Catholic descendants of James I from the throne

1702: Death of William; accession of Queen Anne

1707: Union of England and Scotland as Great Britain

1709: First English copyright act

1714: Death of Anne; accession of George I, Hanoverian (German) prince

1718: England at war with Spain

1727: Death of George I; accession of George II

1739: Brief, unsuccessful war with Spain

1745: Unsuccessful attempt by Roman Catholic Charles Edward ("the Young Pretender") to conquer Scotland

1748: As part of general European war, England fights with France over North American colonies

1750: Founding of Methodism by John Wesley

1755: Publication of Johnson's *Dictionary*

1756: Outbreak of Seven Years' War

1757: Victory by Clive at Plassey secures English control of India

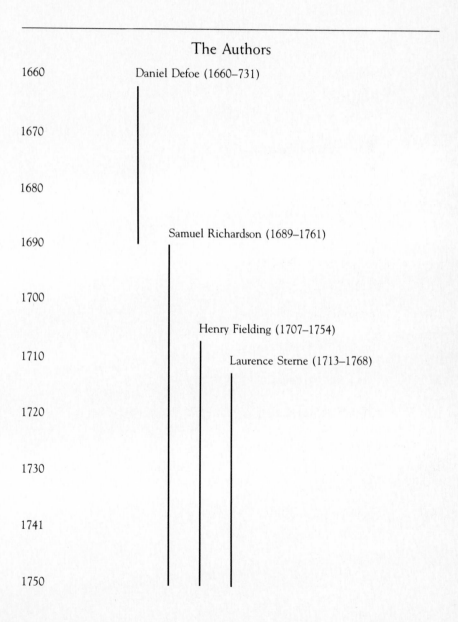

The Authors

1660	Daniel Defoe (1660–731)
1670	
1680	
1690	Samuel Richardson (1689–1761)
1700	
1710	Henry Fielding (1707–1754)
	Laurence Sterne (1713–1768)
1720	
1730	
1741	
1750	

The Age

1760:   Death of George II; accession of George III

1763:   Treaty of Paris

1765:   Publication of Percy's *Reliques of Ancient Poetry*

1775:   Outbreak of American War of Independence

1783:   American independence won

1789:   French Revolution

1799:   Napoleon takes control of French government

1801:   Preface to *Lyrical Ballads*

1804:   Napoleon named Emperor of France; war throughout Europe

1810:   George III insane; the Regency

1815:   Napoleon's final defeat at Waterloo

1820:   Accession of George IV

The Authors

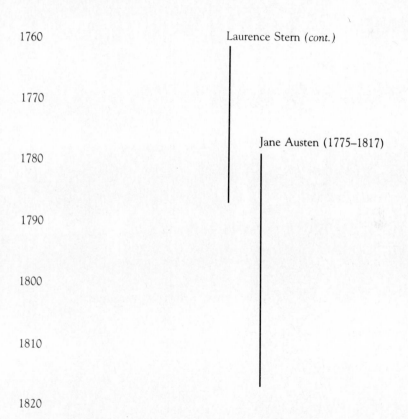

1760   Laurence Stern *(cont.)*

1770

                           Jane Austen (1775–1817)

1780

1790

1800

1810

1820

DANIEL DEFOE

C H R O N O L O G Y

1660	Born in London, son of James Foe, a chandler (candlemaker), and Alice Foe. Until 1695, Daniel will be known as Daniel Foe.
1662	Passage of the Act of Uniformity, which forces the Foe family to make a break with the Church of England and become Presbyterian dissenters.
1671	Enters school run by Rev. James Fisher at Dorking in Surrey. Studies there for three years.
1674	Enters the Reverend Charles Morton's school at Newington Green, a village near London; studies there for about five years, apparently in preparation for a career as a Presbyterian minister.
1682	By this date, has abandoned plans for the ministry; begins a decade as a merchant and businessman, trading in wine, tobacco, and hosiery and insuring ships. Travels widely in Europe on business. Also begins work as a writer, publishing several political pamphlets, first of hundreds that he will produce.
1684	Marries Mary Tuffley. Her dowry of £3700 helps establish the family as solidly middle-class. She will bear seven children.
1692	A series of business reversals bankrupts Foe; he soon rebounds, however.
1695	Foe is named manager and trustee of royal lotteries; he begins to use the name "De Foe."

1697   Begins work as an agent for King William III in England and Scotland. Publishes political tract *An Essay on Projects*, which wins him the favorable attention of several politically influential men. Establishes a brick and tile factory in Tilbury.

1701   Publishes *The True-Born Englishman*, a poem defending the policies of William III. It is enormously successful, selling more copies than any previously published poem in the English language.

1702   Publishes *The Shortest Way with the Dissenters*, a satiric attack on high church extremists within the Church of England. The controversy caused by this work, together with the death of Defoe's patron King William III, dashes his hopes for royal favor and leads to his imprisonment on charges of seditious libel in 1703.

1703   Is released from prison through the efforts of Robert Harley, Tory minister. For the next ten years, Defoe will be active in support of Tory policies as a journalist, adviser, and secret agent. Defoe's brick factory fails, leading to his second bankruptcy. A collected edition of Defoe's writings is published.

1704   Begins publishing *The Review*, a thrice-weekly periodical. He will publish it until 1713. It is one of over two dozen periodicals with which Defoe is connected during his career.

1707   Passage of the Act of Union between Scotland and England, which Defoe has actively supported.

1713   Defoe is arrested for debt, probably at the instigation of his political opponents; is soon released.

1715   Despite the fall of the Tories, Defoe continues to serve the government; works over the next fifteen years as a journalist and secret agent for several Whig administrations. Publishes *The Family Instructor*, a manual of conduct; it is popular, and a second volume is issued three years later.

1719   Publishes *Robinson Crusoe*, a tremendous popular success. It begets many imitations and spurious sequels; Defoe himself takes advantage of the craze by publishing the now little-read *Further Adventures of Robinson Crusoe*.

1720   Publishes *Captain Singleton*, another prose narrative mingling factual and fictional elements. Also yet another Crusoe title, the *Serious Reflections of Robinson Crusoe*.

1722   Publishes *Moll Flanders*, a fictional biography of a criminal; *A Journal of the Plague Year*, an imaginative reconstruction of events in London during the Great Plague of 1665–1666; and *Colonel Jack*, another fictional biography.

1724   Publishes *Roxana* and the travelogue *A Tour thro' the Whole Island of Great Britain*.

1725   Publishes the "self-help" book *The Complete English Tradesman* and more fictional rogue biographies.

1726   Publishes the satiric *Political History of the Devil*.

1727   Publishes the marriage manual *Conjugal Lewdness*.

1731   Dies in Ropemaker's Alley while hiding from debt collectors. Is buried in Bunhill Fields, the famous burying grounds for dissenters.

ESSAY QUESTIONS WITH ANSWERS

32.1 A major part of our enjoyment of *Moll Flanders* derives from our amusement at the heroine's criminal antics. Yet Defoe puts into her mouth numerous moralistic statements condemning the activities we find so appealing fictionally. Should Moll's moral reflections be taken ironically, or is the work a serious attack on the immorality of the criminal life?

Answer Various critics have taken widely differing stances in regard to this fundamental question concerning *Moll Flanders*. According to one view, far from being ironic, Defoe's novel is a serious indictment both of Moll as criminal and of the terrible social conditions prevailing among the lower classes in eighteenth-century England. Moll is first presented as a victim of social circumstances: her mother, a petty thief transported to the colonies, leaves Moll alone in the world, an orphan dependent on the parish church. Moll's impoverished position propels her into a career of immoral and criminal activities. Seduced by an elder brother, she descends into a life of sexual promiscuity involving bigamy, adultery, and incest. Furthermore, her abandonment by her own mother in childhood makes her incapable of maternal compassion for the many offspring she bears. Her attempts to live according to the moral code of the middle class are short-lived, the death or departure of a husband or lover forcing her to resort to petty thievery to sustain herself.

Not only personal misfortune but society at large dictates Moll's behavior: the undue severity of criminal law, the callous neglect of the poor and suffering, and the wretched conditions in orphanages and prisons actually create and foster the desperate class of thieves, whores, highwaymen, and pickpockets in which Moll lives.

Nonetheless, Defoe does not pardon Moll on the basis of what we might call psychological factors or socioeconomic necessities. He supplies a running moral commentary on the action in the form of Moll's penitent reflections, which are interspersed among the episodes illustrating her life of prostitution and crime. Thus Moll's confessions end, as all such moral sermons do, with what some critics consider an apparently genuine reformation of character. Her return to England symbolizes her own and her husband's shared resolution "to spend the remainder of our years in sincere penitence for the wicked lives we have lived." Thus, Defoe, according to this view, offers a complex analysis of the relationship between social forces and individual will in his portrait of a victim of society who ultimately becomes mistress of her own fate.

Other critics, however, refuse to accept Moll's penitence as serious. In their view, Defoe's portrait of Moll Flanders is a deeply ironic study of a character whose amoral strivings are masked by ethical platitudes. The author highlights the almost comic discrepancies between his heroine's successful, pleasurable exploits and her crocodile tears, mechanically shed at regular intervals in the course of events. Moll's character, in fact, reflects a larger cultural ambiguity which developed in the course of the eighteenth century: the Puritan moral code dictated both godly rectitude and mercantile self-advancement, two goals which were bound to clash as men sought to serve both God and Mammon.

Moll's moral reflections are contradicted again and again in the course of the novel. For example, when she robs a little girl of her necklace, she cavalierly rationalizes the deed, commenting that her robbery was a "just reproof" of the negligence of the parents in leaving the "poor lamb" to wander home on its own. This characteristic mixture of larceny and piety occurs everywhere in Defoe's ironic exposure of his deeply duplicitous heroine.

The whole structure of the book, according to this view, is founded on a major ironic discrepancy: it is Moll's vicious life of crime and promiscuity which has made her prosperous enough to afford the luxury of repentance. The novel contains no episode that shows the heroine developing in character through any difficult moral choice. Indeed, Moll has a kind of cartoon quality: like a cat, she continually lands on her feet, immune to the serious consequences of her immoral conduct.

Defoe's irony, in this view, is not merely a means of indicting Moll. The comic aspect of her ready pursuit of love and money puts her in a rather flattering light; her boundless vitality, energy, and individualism are somehow admirable, despite her lack of true moral fiber.

That Defoe's novel can support two such opposed interpretations—Moll as con artist, Moll as troubled soul finding relief in penitence—suggests a fundamental ambiguity in the narrative. At times, Defoe seems to judge Moll from a distant perspective, using incongruity pointedly to deflate Moll's sanctimonious platitudes or dramatic irony to criticize the social hypocrisy which surrounds her. At other points, the author seems closely identified with his heroine, imaginatively sharing her situation both as society's victim and as a self-confident, successful adventurer. Indeed, Defoe's own dual position as a devout dissenter and successful entrepreneur has been seen by some critics as in some ways parallel to Moll's life history.

Thus Defoe's narrative strategy seems to vacillate, sometimes offering an ironic assessment of the split between morality and worldly success and sometimes lapsing into naive sermons on ethical doctrine.

32.2   How coherent is the plot of Moll Flanders?

Answer   The plot of *Moll Flanders* consists of a series of adventures involving amorous intrigue and criminal exploits. Each brief episode recounts a separate vignette in the heroine's amazingly checkered career. Indeed, it is the attempt to reproduce a chaotic, disordered life, with all its inconsistencies and loose ends, that seems to dictate the apparently haphazard sequence of the narrative.

This type of fiction is often called a picaresque novel. The term connotes a chronicle generally written in a loose, purportedly autobiographical style by a rogue or low-life character, whose attention to detail and disregard for standard methods of story telling become the essence of the chronicle.

However, despite the apparent jumble of events, certain strands which suggest meaningful patterns do emerge in the story. The themes of identity and family run through the book from beginning to end: Moll's birth, her marriage to her half brother, and her final reunion with her family in Virginia suggest a search for security and connection through blood ties. The opening episodes, involving seduction by the elder brother and marriage to the younger, supply the symbolic motivation for Moll's erotic search throughout the book. The amorous theme is parallel to both the familial and financial themes, all involving a quest for a secure position and a stable identity. Another structural pattern develops from the bipartite division of the book, the first half dealing primarily with Moll's five marriages and the second with her life as a thief.

All of these structures hint at a submerged, almost mythic level, centering on the isolated and alienated individual constantly striving in the service of the self. Although Defoe's story has been criticized for its primitive technique and damaging incoherence, the rambling surface becomes a method of conveying the "felt life" of an individual, the submerged pattern a means of suggesting existential fable.

32.3   E. M. Forster called *Moll Flanders* a "novel of character." Analyze the

character of the heroine, touching on Defoe's use of first-person narrative, psychological realism, and the tradition of rogue biography.

Answer   The character of Moll Flanders might at first glance present difficulties in interpretation, primarily because she lacks the kind of interior life and explicit psychological motivation familiar to us from later fiction. Defoe's compelling use of the autobiographical "I" offers us Moll not as a self-examining thinker or sentimentalist but as an active agent, reporting her exploits without subtle explanation or introspection. Thus her "love" for various men inheres in the dramatic situations in which she finds herself; although the sheer number of these "loves" might lead the reader to suspect the depth of her emotion, Moll's own statements suggest that her affections are straightforward and sincere. Her character seems vividly realized, then, not because of its subtlety but because of its forcefulness; strong assertion and bold action replace psychological commentary in Defoe's handling of characterization. By placing his "autobiographical" heroine in a milieu rich in circumstantial detail and journalistic observation, the author further reinforces the air of reality surrounding both character and plot.

For example, when Moll first parts with Jeremy, in the hour of her deepest sadness, she is still able to catalog the value of the goods in her possession:

> Nothing that ever befell me in my life sunk so deep into my heart as this farewell. I reproached him a thousand times in my thoughts for leaving me, for I would have gone with him through the world if I had begged my bread. I felt in my pocket, and there I found ten guineas, his gold watch, and two little rings, one a small diamond ring worth only about £6 and the other a plain gold ring.

This type of detail and this sense of a mercantile (some might say mercenary) view of life is something the reader has grown to recognize as integral to Moll's personality.

Certainly the genre of rogue biography lies behind the autobiographical and confessional strategy of *Moll Flanders*. In these catchpenny tales of thieves and tricksters, dating from the sixteenth century, the rogue performs a series of practical jokes and criminal exploits as a kind of comic admonition to the average man to beware of the thief or trickster. Although Moll represents a significant advance over these stick-figure cartoons in the serious social and moral implications of her actions, she shares some of the scandalous vitality exhibited by the earlier rogues and *picaros*.

However, what takes *Moll Flanders* beyond these earlier efforts is in fact Defoe's narrative technique; his ability to create a concrete universe around a character whose energy, exploits, and experiences have a realistic basis provides a bridge between rogue biography and the novel form.

L.R.

SUGGESTED READINGS

McKillop, Alan, *The Early Masters of English Fiction* (1956).
Starr, G. A., *Defoe and Spiritual Autobiography* (1965).
Watt, Ian, *The Rise of the Novel* (1963).

SAMUEL RICHARDSON

C H R O N O L O G Y

1689	Born in Derbyshire. Son of Samuel Richardson, a joiner (that is, a cabinetmaker), and Elizabeth Lane Richardson.
1701	Probably enters the Merchant Taylors' School in London.
1706	Apprenticed to John Wilde, a London printer.
1715	Becomes a freeman of the Stationers' Company; is now qualified to set up his own printing business in London. Within four years is known as a successful printer.
1721	Marries Martha Wilde, daughter of his former master, John Wilde.
1722	Takes over the prosperous bookselling business of the Leake family; at that time, the printing, publishing, and bookselling industries overlapped, and one firm would usually combine these now-separate functions.
1731	Death of Martha Richardson; she had borne six children, all short-lived.
1732	Marries Elizabeth Leake, like his first wife the daughter of a highly successful businessman.
1733	Publication of the *Apprentice's Vade Mecum*, a short moral and instructional manual for boys entering an apprenticeship. Tradition has it that this is by Richardson; if so, it is his first published work.
1739	Two bookseller-publisher acquaintances of Richardson's, knowing of his literary abilities and piety, request that he write a collection of *Familiar*

Letters. These would be models of moral, polite correspondence for servants and other lower-class persons who knew the rudiments of writing but wanted guidance on the proper style, subjects, and form for letters. From this project will grow Richardson's interest in telling a story through the use of letters, leading to his career as a novelist.

1740	Opening of the first circulating library in London, indicating the growth at this time of a sizable middle-class reading public, one of the factors promoting the success of the novel as a literary form. Richardson, having conceived the story of *Pamela* and the device of telling the story through a series of letters, quickly writes his first novel; Volumes I and II are published by the end of the year.
1741	Volumes III and IV of *Pamela* are published. The novel meets with an unprecedented success. It is reprinted five times within a year, translated into several European languages, and made the basis of plays and an opera. All over England readers by the thousand, especially women, are fascinated by it; so real do Pamela's adventures seem that, according to legend, church bells are rung to celebrate her (fictional) wedding to Mr. B. Another side effect: publication of Henry Fielding's *Shamela*, spoofing Richardson's novel, and the beginning of Fielding's own distinguished career as a novelist.
1742	Publication of Fielding's *Joseph Andrews*, also begun as a parody of *Pamela* but developed into a comic novel in its own right.
1744	By this date, Richardson is at work on *The Lady's Legacy*, the novel ultimately to be known as *Clarissa*. In addition to being very wealthy, Richardson is now a literary lion, acquainted with such leading literary and artistic figures as the poets Edward Young and James Thomson, the actor David Garrick, and Dr. Johnson. Not all those who know him idolize him; he is considered vain and rather uncultured by many, and his vanity grows through the years.
1747–1748	Publication of the seven volumes of *Clarissa*, Richardson's greatest novel and, by some accounts, the longest novel in the English language. Like *Pamela*, it is written in epistolary form (as a series of letters), but it is far more sophisticated in its character and plot development.
1751	Richardson writes one number for Dr. Johnson's periodical *The Rambler*, evidence of the esteem in which he is held by the leading literary figure of the day.
1753–1754	Publication, in seven volumes, of Richardson's third and last novel, *Sir Charles Grandison*. Intended as a portrait of a good and pious man, to correspond to the portrait of the good and pious woman Clarissa, *Grandison*,

though widely read and often admired until well into the next century, is today almost universally regarded as insufferably smug and dull. During the last years of his life, Richardson gradually withdraws from literary society into a small circle of female admirers who dote upon and idolize him.

1761   Death of Richardson; he is buried at St. Bride's Church in London.

ESSAY QUESTIONS WITH ANSWERS

33.1 The full title of the novel is *Clarissa; or, The History of a Young Lady: Comprehending the most Important Concerns of Private Life, and particularly showing The Distresses that may attend the Misconduct Both of Parents and Children, in Relation to Marriage*. Discuss the significance of this title in relation to the moral and religious themes of *Clarissa*.

Answer Samuel Richardson's careful and pointed use of this elaborate title immediately alerts the reader to the moral basis of the novel. It serves as one beacon or guide for understanding and interpreting the pattern of events. In *Clarissa*, all the parties, both parents and children, behave improperly. Though Clarissa's parents have the right to forbid Lovelace's courtship, they are wrong in demanding that Clarissa marry Solmes, a man whom she actively dislikes and whom they favor for purely financial reasons. But Clarissa is wrong, too, in continuing to correspond with and see Lovelace. By maintaining their private relationship in defiance of parental authority, she invites the tragedy that occurs.

Because of these moral errors, all of the parties must be punished. The Harlowes take the back stairs for the rest of their lives to avoid passing Clarissa's room; both parents die in remorse a short time after their daughter's death; and her brother James and sister Arabella both have unhappy marriages. Clarissa's punishment is her death. The final third of the novel is concerned with her preparations for this event: her will, her coffin, even the embalming process.

This preoccupation with Clarissa's passage to the heavenly kingdom directly reveals the larger moral and religious focus of the novel: the existence of transcendental reward in a greater world than the earthly one. Clarissa writes to Lovelace shortly before her death, telling him that she will meet him in "her Father's house," a reference certainly not to Harlowe Place. Furthermore, Clarissa actively looks forward to her end. She writes to Belford, "How happily I die." By viewing the novel in this Christian context, the reader can interpret the ending of *Clarissa* as a happy one, for the heroine is granted her final wish, to leave behind her earthly sins and assume a place in heaven.

However, the "happiness" of the ending is not entirely that simple. The tremendous sense of tragedy of the final third of the novel cannot be so readily dismissed, particularly since Clarissa's Christianity, the sole foundation of the happiness, is itself so ambiguous. While Clarissa's faith is sincere and heroic, it is also tempered by pride, arrogance, and self-will which continue to her end. Furthermore, the final portion of the novel is virtually overwhelmed with all sorts of mortuary details, including embalming and burial, which certainly diminish for the reader Clarissa's notion of a "happy ending."

33.2 There are at least two possible views of the character of Lovelace. On the one hand, he may be regarded as the most interesting and vital character in the novel. Clarissa's flirtatious behavior with him invites her own disaster, and thus the reader cannot fully blame him for her seduction and death.

In another view, Lovelace is the villain of the novel. He seduces the innocent Clarissa, deceiving her into leaving home. Once they are in London, his evil practices continue, culminating in the vicious rape and death of Clarissa.

What evidence supports each of these interpretations? What should we conclude about the character of Lovelace?

Answer There is much textual evidence in *Clarissa* to support the first view. From the outset, Lovelace shines in contrast to the other male characters. Clarissa's brother James is a social climber; Solmes is rich but lowborn and mean; Mr. Hickman is weak-spirited and uninteresting. Lovelace, in comparison, is socially polite, considerate, and well educated. In an early episode, he shows his kindness by befriending Rosebud, his innkeeper's daughter, and then, rather than seducing her, secures her future by providing her with a dowry and arranging the girl's marriage to the man she loves. Furthermore, the early positive reactions of some of the characters to Lovelace heighten his stature in the reader's eyes. For example, Anna Howe recognizes Lovelace's personal power and encourages Clarissa in her attraction to him. In addition, the faults and failures of the other characters mitigate the reader's sense of Lovelace's guilt later in the novel. Certainly Lovelace's anger toward the Harlowe family is largely justified. The unreasonable jealousies which the Harlowes entertain are built on an obsession with social and class differences and have little to do with a desire to secure their daughter's happiness. And Clarissa herself can be seen as contributing to her own seduction: she allows Lovelace to continue their relationship and consents willingly to the disastrous rendezvous.

However, throughout the novel the authorial voice of Richardson urges the reader to see Lovelace as a villain. He is a direct descendant of the rakes of Restoration drama; like them, he is highborn, intelligent, and amoral in sexual matters, and, again like them, his name (which means "loveless") proclaims his character. His moral code and dissolute sexuality stand in contrast to the religious nature of Clarissa's character. His version of love is a degraded one, and he is unable to understand Clarissa's declaration "The man who has once been the villain to me that you have been shall never make me his wife." Richardson, afraid that readers would misunderstand Lovelace's attractive qualities, which a later age might call "Byronic," supplies an even stronger clue to the "correct" interpretation: he provides a series of footnotes, discussing and evaluating Lovelace's behavior, which reinforce the judgment of villainy. Later events in the novel bear out this judgment, as the reader is encouraged to see Lovelace as a menace to Clarissa's very freedom and ultimately as responsible for her death. Perhaps the most horrifying example of Lovelace's cruel character is his plot to kidnap and rape both Anna Howe and her mother—a detail which many critics have found excessive, but which Richardson evidently included in order to make clear the depth of Lovelace's villainy.

But almost in spite of Richardson's intention to portray Lovelace as an evil seducer, the character himself seems to rise above a one-sided interpretation. Lovelace succeeds as a fictional creation precisely because he is psychologically complex and because the many sides of his personality emerge so vividly in the novel.

33.3 *Clarissa* is an epistolary novel; that is, it consists of a series of letters. Discuss Richardson's use of this form and its contribution to the development of the genre of the novel.

Answer In his postscript, Richardson calls *Clarissa* a "dramatic narrative" and not a "history." This classification provides the essential clue to the epistolary method. As Ian Watt (*The Rise of the Novel*) points out, through the formal structure of letters, which record the minutiae of daily life virtually as they occur, the reader is able to enter the intimate private experience of the fictional character. In its length and detail the correspondence presents the kind of complete psychological self-portrait of a character that was not possible with earlier narrative techniques. The entire movement of *Clarissa* is, thus, toward discovering and revealing the characters' inward lives.

Furthermore, the fact that these letters are produced by two main sets of correspondents—Anna and Clarissa, and Lovelace and Belford—provides certain other advantages. First, it points up the differences among the four characters: Clarissa's uneasy, self-searching recitations are juxtaposed with Anna's secure, practical pronouncements; Lovelace's passionate variations of mood are contrasted with Belford's somber missives. Then, of course, one set is female and the other is male, providing yet another series of distinctions and emphasizing one of the book's underlying themes, that of the war between the sexes.

The use of this method also allows the author to alter the tempo of the action by merely switching correspondents. Perhaps the most dramatic example is the treatment of the rape episode. Lovelace tells Belford of the incident with a brief announcement: "The affair is over. Clarissa lives." But the reader's desire to know more, to hear from Clarissa, is held at bay for several hundred pages before Richardson supplies Clarissa's own account of the episode. This almost agonizingly slow presentation keeps the reader in a constant state of suspense and reinforces the sense of private torment which pervades the novel.

There are, of course, certain disadvantages to this type of narrative. The idea of Clarissa's spending hours in her "closet" writing each detail of her day's activities to Anna seems ludicrous and implausible. But the advantages of this method outweigh the seemingly excessive garrulity of the characters. No other early narrative formula allowed the reader the same type of familiarity with the fictional world or such a detailed entrance into the characters' consciousness.

33.4 *Clarissa* is concerned not only with the depiction of intimate private experience but also with broader social issues. Comment on the importance of the social setting for *Clarissa*.

Answer   The social environment of *Clarissa* provides a significant background for the events of the novel. From the outset, Clarissa is placed in an impossible situation: her grandfather's bequest to her has greatly angered her brother James, and her sister Arabella is incensed because Lovelace rejects her in favor of Clarissa. The Harlowes, though very rich, have noble relatives only on the mother's side, and they hope that, after consolidating the family fortune, they will have enough to buy James a peerage. Thus, they see marriage purely as a matter of economics, but, as Richardson says, "they are too rich to be happy." Lovelace, with his excellent family connections and good income, would seem an appropriate choice for Clarissa. But James, jealous of Lovelace's fortune and prospects, insists that his sister marry Solmes, a wealthy man but one who is lowborn and ill-mannered. All of this, the combination of social pressure and family alienation, serves to force Clarissa into Lovelace's waiting arms.

But Lovelace is waging his own battle with society. Furious at the Harlowes, he seems intent on debasing the "lily" of their house as a means of revenge. Furthermore, his allegiance to the moral and social code of the rake allows him to scoff at conventional marriage and practice a sadistic sexuality. What Lovelace represents for Richardson, then, is the degeneration of the chivalric ideals of courtesy and gallantry. These values were considered the basic code of the genteel classes, and certainly the middle-class Richardson (and his audience) would have viewed Lovelace's behavior as amoral.

Once Clarissa leaves the confines of the country, she becomes, almost immediately, Lovelace's victim. This gentle heroine is a stranger to the wicked ways of London—"Clarissa knew nothing of the town and its ways"—and is introduced to an evil society, that of the brothel keeper Mrs. Sinclair.

The introduction of London points up another antithesis in the novel, that of city versus country. The country, while not wholly depicted as a pastoral ideal, is still a safe, protected ground. London, on the other hand, is a city of shadows where Clarissa's life is in constant danger. The very diverseness and anonymity of the urban setting suggest the disruption of the eighteenth-century ideas of order and rightness on which the middle class depended.

The social setting, then, functions almost as a mirror for the action of the novel. The upheaval in Clarissa's life operates on two levels: the public level of the social universe where the Harlowes and Lovelace cruelly crush Clarissa's individuality, and the private level, where Clarissa fights with the demons which control her emotions.

The modern reader may become impatient with Clarissa's predicament, wondering why she doesn't run away from those oppressing her. What must be stressed here is Clarissa's entrapment both by the legal status of women in her day and by the social and moral conventions of her class. Legally, Clarissa doesn't have any power. Despite inheriting her grandfather's fortune, she lives in a society founded on the principles of male primogeniture; her father or her husband have complete power over her life. Furthermore, Clarissa doesn't recognize her own abilities to correct the wrongs being heaped upon her. She is literally helpless. Richardson's feelings for his heroine indicate his concern for woman's position in his time as well as his understanding of the social and legal realities she faced.

L.R.

SUGGESTED READINGS

Van Ghent, Dorothy, *The English Novel: Form and Function* (1961).
Watt, Ian, *The Rise of the Novel* (1957).

HENRY FIELDING

C H R O N O L O G Y

1707   Born at Sharpham Park in Somerset. Son of a distinguished general; raised as a country gentleman.

1719   Enters Eton, most famous public school (that is, private boarding school) in England; studies there for five years.

1728   Publishes poem *The Masquerade*; his first printed work. His first play, *Love in Several Masques*, is produced at London's Drury Lane Theatre. Enters the University of Leyden as a student of literature.

1729   Leaves Leyden and settles in London to pursue his career as a playwright.

1730   Begins his seven-year career as an author of over twenty comedies and burlesques for the stage. Plays produced this year include *The Temple Beau*, *The Author's Farce*, *Rape upon Rape*, and *Tom Thumb*, the last probably his most famous and popular play.

1731   Publication of *The Tragedy of Tragedies*, a revised version of *Tom Thumb*, with satiric annotations by "H. Scriblerus Secundus." Several more comedies produced and published during the year, most notably *The Grub Street Opera*.

1732–   Several more plays produced, including *The Lottery* and the farce *The Mock*
1733   *Doctor*, adapted from the French playwright Moliere.

1734   Marries Charlotte Cradock. Two more plays produced, one of which, *Don Quixote in England*, suggests Fielding's admiration for Cervantes, whose work will later influence Fielding's novels.

1735–1736	Several more comic and satiric plays produced.
1737	Production of satiric play *The Historical Register for the Year 1736*. Passage of the Stage Licensing Act, which makes it virtually impossible to produce satiric plays without being subject to government prosecution. This law practically ends Fielding's career as a playwright. He enters the Middle Temple to study law.
1739	Edits *The Champion*, a political periodical opposing the government (until 1741).
1740	Is called to the bar. Samuel Richardson's novel *Pamela* is published, to great public acclaim.
1741	Fielding publishes *An Apology for the Life of Mrs. Shamela Andrews*, under the name of "Conny Keyber." This parody of *Pamela* is mainly a satire on what Fielding sees as Richardson's shallow moral sense; it also directs side-swipes at the much-derided poet Colley Cibber. During this year, Fielding breaks his allegiance to the opposition and sides with Robert Walpole's administration.
1742	Publishes *Joseph Andrews*, his first true novel, avowedly "in Imitation of the Manner of Cervantes." The book begins with several scenes designed to parody *Pamela* again, but soon develops into a picaresque, comic tale that stands on its own. *Joseph Andrews* is highly successful, reprinted twice within a year. Walpole's government falls.
1743	Fielding's play *The Wedding Day* is produced. Three volumes of *Miscellanies* are published; this work includes *Jonathan Wild*, a satiric work combining fact and fiction; *A Journey from This World to the Next*, a fantasy modeled on the Roman author Lucian; and many poems, plays, and essays.
1744	Death of Charlotte Fielding.
1745	Edits the promonarchist periodical *The True Patriot*. Also publishes several pamphlets supporting the Hanoverians against "the Young Pretender," Charles Stuart. Is probably at work on *Tom Jones*.
1747	Marries Mary Daniel, formerly his housekeeper; she will bear him several children. Richardson's *Clarissa* is published; Fielding admires it and writes to Richardson to say so.
1748	Named justice of the peace for Westminster.
1749	Commissioned magistrate for the county of Middlesex; is absorbed in problems of justice, crime. *Tom Jones*, Fielding's greatest work, is published; four editions appear within a year.

1751   Publishes *An Enquiry into the Causes of the Late Increase of Robbers*, an important work of what would today be called legal sociology. Also publishes his last novel, *Amelia*, a work in the "sentimental" vein of mid-eighteenth-century fiction.

1752   Edits *The Covent-Garden Journal*, his last periodical.

1753   Publishes *A Proposal for Making an Effectual Provision for the Poor*, another social tract. Devotes himself to reducing crime in London; is widely known as a dedicated, honest, humane administrator of justice.

1754   Falls ill; journeys to Lisbon, Portugal, for his health. Revised version of *Jonathan Wild* is published. Death of Fielding in Portugal.

1755   Posthumous publication of *The Journal of a Voyage to Lisbon*.

ESSAY QUESTIONS WITH ANSWERS

34. 1   A major role is played in *Tom Jones* by what some critics have called the subplot of the novel: the author's introductory chapters, essayistic digressions, and other intrusions into the narrative. Discuss how this elaborate verbal apparatus affects the reader's experience of the novel.

Answer   The narrative flow of *Tom Jones* is continually interrupted by the author's "essays" on abstract themes and aesthetic principles. Fielding constantly interrupts his story to advise the reader of his mental processes and narrative intentions. At the very outset, Fielding makes a contract with his readers, offering to please their appetites with a well-designed feast (I, 1, meaning Book I, Chapter 1 [the "Bill of Fare"]) and to "make their Interest the great Rule of my Writings" (II, 1). In the later chapter, Fielding also clearly announces his aesthetic principles; he discusses his free manipulation of time, of verisimilitude, and of verbal style.

The net effect of the author's asides to the reader is to produce a comic sense of distance from the story. The reader takes on Fielding's omniscient perspective and is continually aware that the story is a fiction, an artifact rather than a slice of reality. Every time the reader begins to become sympathetically engaged with the characters and the drama they are enacting, he or she is pulled back from this identification by the author's wry explanations of his craft. This abrupt undercutting sets *Tom Jones* apart from many novels, in which the narrator deliberately remains an unobtrusive presence.

The intrusion of the voice of the narrator carries over from the rhetorical apparatus into the body of the story, as the author delivers comic generalizations on human nature and satiric remarks on human affairs. The reader thus derives a sense of relationship to an individual man who is telling the tale. This man, Fielding's surrogate, is worldly, amiable, wise, witty, and tolerant. He provides the sense of benevolent control and sound judgment necessary to Fielding's comic morality tale.

Thus, the digressions do constitute a kind of subplot, one centering on the writer's relationship with his text and with his audience. In the introductory chapter of Book XVIII, the last book of the novel, Fielding says a formal good-bye to the reader in preparation for concluding his work. He refers to his audience as "fellow-travelers in a stagecoach," with whom he has formed a warm, if temporary, bond. He again makes explicit that one of the bases of novel writing is the human act of communication, of meaning expressed and received between two cooperative parties. It is through the persuasive flow of his digressive rhetoric that Fielding forges this affectionate bond with his readership.

34.2 Fielding refers to his novel as a "comic epic in prose." Analyze the methods he uses to create this hybrid genre.

Answer Fielding borrows some of the conventions of the classical epic to create a comic effect. By magnifying characters and events with heroic comparisons and epithets, he ironically emphasizes their all-too-human failings. This strategy of inversion and incongruity is at work from the very beginning, when the hero makes his first appearance: Tom Jones, whose name suggests a sort of eighteenth-century John Doe, is introduced as a young man "certainly born to be hanged." The whole notion of bastardy seems to fly in the face of epic conventions of noble birth and high station. However, it was a frequent mark of the mythic hero (Oedipus and Perseus, for example) that the facts surrounding his birth were mysterious and obscure.

In addition, the plot parodies heroic actions of all kinds: Tom's "knightly exploits" for his lady, Sophia, involve the farcical pursuit of her little bird and the comic mishap of the broken arm, while the "battles" waged turn out to be cat fights between Molly and the village women and Tom's scuffle with Blifil and Thwackum when caught *in flagrante delicto*. In presenting these sorts of escapades, Fielding owes a debt to Cervantes's *Don Quixote*, which satirized romantic conventions while following the adventures of its hero.

Elevated language also contributes to the mock-epic quality of the whole, with the inflated prose creating a sense of comic discrepancy between style and content. Fielding draws attention to his linguistic strategy in chapter headings such as "A short Hint of what we can do in the Sublime," "A Picture of formal Courtship in Miniature, as it always ought to be drawn . . .," or ". . . a very full Description of the Battle of Upton." The description of Sophia, an anatomical catalogue rendered with exaggerated poetical flourishes (IV, 2), and the exhaustive invocation of Fame, Fortune, Genius, Learning, and Experience (XIII, 1) are only two examples of Fielding's use of tongue-in-cheek stylistic inflation. Homeric metaphors also abound, particularly in the battle scenes, where the animal imagery of predator and prey suggests the style of classical works like *The Odyssey* and *The Aeneid*.

The effect of the epic allusions is generally ironic, exposing the social pretensions of the various characters in the novel. However, the deflationary irony creates an air of genial comedy rather than of harsh satire; the literary borrowings from the epic suggest the heroic aspect of every man's wishes and desires, and in that sense are an affectionate tribute to the human nature Fielding has chosen to portray.

34.3 Despite its philandering hero and its reputation for bawdiness, *Tom Jones* is a novel about moral goodness. Not only the hero himself but a host of minor characters are the materials for Fielding's dissection of human nature and true virtue. Discuss the relationship between Fielding's use of characterization and the moral standards implied by the novel.

Answer In a novel concerned with human nature in a social context, the themes of illusion and hypocrisy have special significance. Entering a world fraught with vice and corruption, Tom Jones is the naive innocent whose essential goodness is insufficient to save him from misfortune. His imprudence and his failing in chastity are flaws which do not seriously mar his inner virtue but nonetheless cause him endless trouble. As Fielding says, "Prudence and Circumspection are necessary even to the best of Men. . . . It is not enough that your Designs, nay that your Actions, are intrinsically good, you must take Care they shall appear so" (III, 7). Here and elsewhere, the author's commentary links moral standards and social decorum, as well as emphasizing the theme of appearance and reality.

But the most important of Fielding's methods for distinguishing true goodness from surface virtue is the presentation of paired characters. Tom and Blifil are, of course, the chief instance of paired opposites, with the former's frank honesty and generosity contrasting sharply with the latter's sanctimonious, pious pursuit of self-interest. The sinking fortunes of Tom and the rising star of Blifil constitute a fable of "True Goodness blackened by False Appearances." But the narrative drive of the novel is constantly to inform the reader of the true moral balance existing beneath the surface.

The two country squires, Allworthy and Western, form another pair, though certainly not as direct a contrast as Tom and Blifil. The affection of both men for Tom suggests their alliance with good, but both have significant failings. Allworthy's "all-worthiness," or benevolence, is marred by his naive readiness to believe the best of everyone. This undiscriminating kindness leads him,

finally, to assess Tom's character wrongly under Blifil's malign influence. Western is more clearly a humorous caricature, with his appetites and self-interest
always ready to override his finer instincts.

Square and Thwackum, an obviously paired Tweedledum and Tweedledee
of hypocrisy, both fall on the bad side of the balance sheet. The philosopher
shrouds his ill nature with the "Rule of Right," the divine with the trappings
of religion.

Though Sophia is not paired with any single character, she stands in implicit
contrast to a whole gallery of female characters, ranging from the vulgar Molly
Seagrim to the worldly Lady Bellaston. All these women are sexually impure,
but the society dames are more particularly the targets of Fielding's satiric barbs,
because they disguise their lascivious appetites with an elaborate masquerade of
polite manners. Sophia, on the other hand, represents all that is good and true
about womanhood. Her chastity is one of both mind and body, and she stands
for the qualities of loyalty and honesty.

In some ways, the novel has the appearance of an amoral tale of sexual
adventures. Certainly, though Fielding praises chastity, Tom does not really
suffer much for his promiscuity, and sexual sins are treated with amusement
(unlike, for example, hypocrisy and greed). It often seems as though the narrator
is winking at Tom's lapses and assuring the reader that they will not really harm
our hero. But despite its lusty and brawling canvas, *Tom Jones* remains a moral
novel, both because of the narrator's ethical judgments throughout and because
of the conclusion of the story. Tom must undergo a reformation before he can
enter Paradise Hall as its rightful heir. His "luck" in the chance discovery of
his true birthright can come only after the sobering recognition of his misconduct.

34.4   Poet and critic Samuel Taylor Coleridge said of *Tom Jones*, "What a
master of composition Fielding was! Upon my word, I think the *Oedipus Tyr-
annus*, *The Alchemist*, and *Tom Jones* the three most perfect plots ever planned."
How does Fielding construct his "perfect plot"?

Answer   The sense of *Tom Jones*'s "perfect plot" derives in part from the
symmetry of the novel, with three sections of six books each, devoted, respectively, to life in the country, life on the road, and life in the city. The novel
has a momentum which extends through these subdivisions, following the prodigal son's adventures on the path toward reform and reconciliation.

Thus, the first section establishes the impetus of the narrative in setting
forth the central mystery of Tom's birth and establishing the dawning love

between Tom and Sophia. A host of subsidiary characters are introduced, most of them reappearing in the latter sections of the book. The first six books also present a coherent view of English country life, showing the benevolent though sometimes strained relations between gentry and villagers and the lusty emotions which are constantly breaking through the restrictions imposed by religion, education, law, and polite society. Tom's expulsion from this essentially Edenic setting creates a narrative tension which is not resolved until the final pages of the novel, when he is readmitted into "Paradise."

On the road to Upton and beyond, the panorama widens as the naive hero encounters new segments of society, including a band of soldiers, a woman of shady reputation, and an itinerant barber. Fielding uses coincidence to forge narrative links, for these last two turn out to be none other than Tom's reputed parents, Jenny Jones (later known as "Mrs. Waters") and the schoolmaster Partridge. Coincidence also provides the mad convergence at Upton Inn, which occurs almost at the center of the novel. Here Tom beds the mysterious Mrs. Waters; Sophia and her maid arrive, only to be disappointed by Tom's infidelity; and Squire Western appears in hot pursuit of his missing daughter. These narrative threads continue into the final section of the novel, where the fact of Tom's "incest" with Mrs. Waters, the injured retreat of Sophia, and the continued watchfulness of Squire Western sustain the comic complications of the plot.

Another convergence occurs in London, the scene of the last third of the novel. Here Tom pursues Sophia, who is herself pursuing Tom, while specifically urban characters are introduced, including Mrs. Miller the landlady and Lord Fellmar the fop. All the necessary characters from earlier sections of the novel are likewise brought on stage for the final revelation: Squires Western and Allworthy, Blifil, Square, Thwackum, and Mrs. Waters, who alone is in possession of the facts of Tom's birth. Urban society is represented, in the form of masquerades, courtly stratagems, and middle-class romances, to complete the tripartite dissection of English life. At the same time, the plot arrives at completion, with Tom revealed as the son of Bridget Allworthy and thus Squire Allworthy's true heir. With the marriage of Sophia and Tom and the return to Paradise Hall—a movement back to the land and to the more natural rural life—the book is resolved with the sense of a full circle.

The unity of the plot is maintained not only through its complex division into country, road, and city but through Fielding's use of a variety of other techniques. The frequent changes of location, character, and even novelistic pace help the reader to maintain interest by variety and surprise. Then, too, the constant interweaving of stories and characters brings a sense of unity to the picaresque form, which in previous novels had been merely a series of disconnected episodes.

Perhaps most important, these seemingly disparate elements of a long and elaborate narrative are carefully and cheerfully resolved so that evil is exposed and punished and virtue rewarded. Thus Fielding manages to suggest the work- ings of a divine providence which is directing all things in his comedic universe ultimately toward good. Finally, though, the "perfection" of the plot lies pre- cisely in the novel's complexity and ingenuity and in the considerable pleasure the reader derives from watching Fielding play the role of master juggler.

34.5 *Tom Jones* ends with a perfect marriage. However, throughout the novel, marriage is presented as a highly imperfect institution. Discuss Fielding's handling of the themes of love and marriage in *Tom Jones*. Is the ending of the novel ironic?

Answer   Among the unhappy marriages in the book are Squire Western's, Bridget Blifil's, Mr. Partridge's, and Mrs. Fitzpatrick's. These negative instances, together with the narrator's generalized comments on shrewish wives and faith- less husbands, suggest a jaundiced view of the marital state distinctly at odds with the blessings promised to Tom and Sophia. Indeed, Fielding's world seems singularly lacking in models of wedded happiness, with the exception of Squire Allworthy, who, Fielding tells us, "married a Beautiful Woman for Love." Yet here too, Fielding's very realistic view of the world provides the keynote. Though Mrs. Allworthy is dead, Mr. Allworthy continues in his steadfast love for her and expects to rejoin her when both are in heaven. "Sentiments," the narrator informs the reader, "for which his Sense was arraigned by one Part of his Neighbours, his Religion by a Second, and his Sincerity by a third" (I, 2).

However, it is certainly Mr. Allworthy's example which activates the pure love felt by Tom and Sophia. The purity of their alliance is emphasized by contrast with all the unhappy marital arrangements in the novel, matches which are marred by avarice, self-interest, and ill temper.

Thus, the marriage of hero and heroine cannot be read as ironic. Although the narrator affectionately mocks their ingenuousness and innocence, the two behave with tenderness and genuine feeling toward each other. If Tom has been prone to lust, as a by-product, in a sense, of his generosity, his heart has always belonged to Sophia. With his coming into his proper station in life, he repents of his former indiscretions and readies himself for a life of moral respectability. Fielding's language at the end of the novel, as he paints his truly happy ending, is straightforward and sincere: "To conclude, as there are not to be found a worthier Man and Woman, than this fond Couple, So neither can any be imagined more happy" (XVIII, 13).

However, it is important to note that in the highly contrived, intricately plotted world of *Tom Jones*, the characters are obviously fictional beings, created for the needs of the story. They have no existence outside the landscape of the novel, and, though the book ends happily, we feel that Tom and Sophia simply step out of the fictional universe and disappear offstage. The happy ending, though not ironic, is clearly a fictional contrivance, and the fate of the characters has been arranged primarily to satisfy the author's artistic scheme.

L.R.

SUGGESTED READINGS

Van Ghent, Dorothy, *The English Novel: Form and Function* (1961).
Watt, Ian, *The Rise of the Novel* (1957).

LAURENCE STERNE

C H R O N O L O G Y

1713	Born in Clonmel, Ireland. Son of Roger Sterne, an ensign in the army, and Agnes Nuttal Hebert Sterne. Spends the first ten years of his life living at a series of military posts with his parents; is lonely and unhappy.
1723	Is sent to school near Halifax in Yorkshire, having been given over to the care of his father's relatives.
1731	Death of Sterne's father, reportedly penniless, in Jamaica.
1733	Enters Jesus College, Cambridge University, to study for the priesthood; supported by his father's family, which had previous connections with Cambridge. Meets John Hall-Stevenson, a lifelong friend; later, Hall-Stevenson will be the owner of Skelton Castle, renamed "Crazy Castle," where he and Sterne will gather with a club of "Demoniacs" for wild antics.
1737	Receives B.A. from Cambridge; is ordained and appointed curate of the parish of St. Ives.
1738	Appointed to the living at Sutton-in-the-Forest, an obscure country parish.
1740	Receives M.A. from Cambridge.
1741	Marries Elizabeth Lumley, a clergyman's daughter; she is reputedly well-off, but the expected windfall does not materialize. The marriage is not a happy one; its troubles are exacerbated both by Sterne's flagrant infidelities and by the arrival from Ireland of Sterne's mother and her daughter, who expect to live off him; they settle nearby and vex him for years. Sterne does some

political writing for his uncle Jacques, a local Whig leader; is rewarded with the office of prebend for North Newbald. However, he refuses to continue this propaganda work, earning his uncle's lasting enmity as a result.

1744	Appointed to the living at Stillington.
1747	Sterne's sermon "The Case of Elijah" is published as a pamphlet, one of several to be printed during his preliterary years. They are notably lacking in serious doctrinal or devotional content.
1750	Sermon "The Abuses of Conscience" is published; it will later appear as a sermon of Yorick's in *Tristram Shandy*.
1751	Sterne's mother and sister enter a charity home in York, apparently by the connivance of Uncle Jacques, who hopes to blacken Sterne's name; a reputation as a man who neglected his mother will dog him thereafter.
1759	After being involved for several years in political controversies within the church, Sterne publishes the satire *The History of a Good Warm Watch-Coat*. It is scathing and controversial; at the request of friends, Sterne has most copies destroyed. However, the act of composing this work seems to have suggested literature as a serious endeavor to Sterne. Around this time, his wife appears to have suffered a mental breakdown; despite their many differences over the years, and his own sexual infidelities, Sterne is supposed to have treated her with sympathy and kindness during this period.
1760	Volumes I and II of *Tristram Shandy*, Sterne's greatest work, are published in London. The anonymity of the author, together with the book's unique humor, creates a sensation; the literary world clamors for information about the witty new author. Sterne then visits London, where he is lionized by the world of fashion; his charm and his bizarre sense of humor are much admired (though Dr. Johnson and other more serious moralizers consider his bawdy conversation scandalously inappropriate for a clergyman).
1761	Volumes III–VI of *Tristram Shandy* are published.
1762	Sterne's health, never robust, deteriorates; he travels to France for his health; is received as a literary hero in Paris, his fame having preceded him. After several months in France, he sends for his wife and daughter.
1762–1763	Sterne and his family live in the south of France. His health remains poor.
1764	Sterne composes two more volumes of *Tristram Shandy*, using details of his travels. Returns to England.
1765	Volumes VII and VIII of *Tristram Shandy* are published. Sterne returns to the Continent, staying in Italy and France until 1766.

1767   Volume IX of *Tristram Shandy* published. Sterne meets Eliza Draper, the 22-year-old wife of an East India Company official. He falls in love with her; she is the last and most serious of several extramarital attachments of Sterne's. (The relationship appears to have been a platonic one.) When Eliza leaves for India, Sterne begins to keep the *Journal to Eliza* for her sake.

1768   Sterne publishes A *Sentimental Journey*, an account of his second visit to Europe. Death of Sterne in London. He is buried in a London graveyard frequented at that period by grave robbers seeking corpses for use in medical studies; legend has it that Sterne's body was exhumed and ended up in the medical college at Cambridge, although no one has ever been able to identify his skull among those preserved there.

1904   The *Journal to Eliza* published in the edition of Sterne's works edited by Wilbur Cross.

ESSAY QUESTIONS WITH ANSWERS

35.1   *Tristram Shandy* contains a number of odd features, including blank, marbled, and black pages; a preface following the twentieth chapter; a one-sentence chapter; lines of type consisting of asterisks and arrows; and an unusually large number of parentheses and dashes. These devices break up the continuous flow of prose which generally characterizes a novel. What is the effect on the narrative of these departures from convention?

Answer   These idiosyncratic features of *Tristram Shandy* are designed to call into question the traditional methods of telling a story. They are intentionally comic, of course; but the philosophical implication they carry is that human life does not naturally make a story, and that experience is essentially discontinuous and nonlinear.

Tristram abandons his characters at the moment before his own birth to launch into his preface (III,xx meaning Volume III, Chapter xx), a parody of conventional prefaces. This interruption wittily undercuts the convention of straightforward narration. Likewise, the squiggles constituting VI,xl are a visual joke, illustrating Tristram's refusal (despite his professed intentions) "to go on with my uncle Toby's story, and my own, in a tolerable straight line."

The technique of interruption destroys not only narrative conventions in general but, more specifically, the "realistic" conventions of novel writing. The book is revealed as a material object composed of pages and ink. Instead of drawing the reader into a fictional universe, Sterne forces his audience to stand back from the work. The narrator becomes a jester exhibiting set pieces and playing a series of rhetorical games. In doing this, he deflates the reader's expectations of coherence and illusion and arrives at comedy. The discrepancy between the novelistic norm and Tristram's clownish sallies produces an absurd world, a topsy-turvy universe which is both entertaining and funny. What Sterne is offering the reader is an aspect of reality rarely seen in literature: its absurdity, discontinuity, and quirkiness. This aspect of reality requires a narrative method different from any of the traditional ones, and it is this deviation from the norm which shocks us and strikes us as funny.

The conclusion of the novel epitomizes both the refusal to tell a story and the comic deflation of reader expectation. In the final exchange between Tristram's mother and Parson Yorick, Sterne admits that his entire novel has been a shaggy-dog story, an absurdist ramble rather than a coherent tale:

L—d! said my mother, what is all this story about?—
A COCK and a BULL, said Yorick—And one of the best of its kind, I ever heard. (IX, xxxiii)

35.2 What is *Tristram Shandy* about?

Answer The title of the novel is *The Life and Opinions of Tristram Shandy, Gentleman*, which suggests a work modeled on the conventional *bildungsroman*, a fictional biography which traces the moral development of the hero from youth to maturity. However, the book belies its title, for by the end of the ninth volume the reader has learned almost nothing about the hero. We know that Tristram suffered unfortunate accidents to his nose and "nether parts," and that he took a grand tour of the Continent as tutor to Lord Noddy's son; but we know little else.

However, the novel goes beyond the personal history of Tristram to encompass the domestic life of the Shandy household. The members of the family, Walter and Toby especially, are shown actively engaged in private pursuits, constructing a life out of the pastimes of philosophical speculation or war games. In depicting these pastimes as obsessions, Sterne introduces the psychological motif of ruling passions. The characters fend off unpleasantness and retreat into private life by riding their "hobbyhorses." (In the eighteenth century, hobbyhorses not only were ridden by children but were something of a fad among gentlemen.) For example, Toby's mock-war, reenacting the siege of Namur (1695) on the bowling green of the Shandy estate, is his way of turning aggression into play and so healing (at least psychologically) his old war wound. Walter is certainly preoccupied with names, but most prominent is his position as the "learned wit" of the Shandy family. Of course Walter's extreme efforts at erudition end in theories and theorizing that only add to the comic incongruities of the novel.

Tristram has his own obsessions—with noses, window sashes, and the issue of his geniture. But as narrator he generally rises above fixed obsessions, his own and those of his father and uncle. The preoccupations of the characters become material for Tristram to play with, and his narrative is the larger game which incorporates all the others: Toby's, Walter's, Yorick's, the Widow Wadman's, and so on. In playing out this narrative game, he demonstrates the characteristic workings of the human mind, which, in Sterne's universe, is constantly engaged in meandering journeys triggered by free association, not in a rational search for meaning but in an attempt to deal with the pains and preoccupations of life. For his theories on the workings of the human mind, Sterne is certainly indebted to the philosopher John Locke. Locke's *Essay Concerning Human Understanding* (1690) provided the eighteenth century with its main basis for comprehending the learning process. Locke propounded the theory of the *tabula rasa*, that is, that man is born with a "blank slate"—the mind—onto which an experience felt and learned through the senses is reflected.

Thus, the story the narrator tells is neither chronological nor traditionally biographical. It is organized to illustrate the flow of thought and the human impulse toward play. Behind the novel is the image of *homo ludens*, man as playful creature. Furthermore, the novel suggests that man is also a creature of sentiment. The importance of "sentiment"—fellow feeling, sympathy, or sensitivity—is illustrated in the story of Le Fever, in the treatment of Bobby's death, and, in general, in Toby's unfailing kindness, exhibited not only to the Widow Wadman but even to an insignificant fly.

The novel, then, is about psychological processes. *Tristram Shandy* demonstrates a way of responding to the world at large, returning again and again to the two key tendencies Sterne sees in men: playful gamesmanship and emotional sympathy. What is charmingly odd about the book is the way it depicts a particularly real but limited segment of human responses which had rarely, if ever, been given literary form before.

35.3 *Tristram Shandy* contains running references to the subjects of noses, window sashes, and Toby's war wound. How are these subjects related? What do these subjects contribute to the novel as a whole?

Answer   The "nose" in the novel, appearing in scenes ranging from Tristram's accident at birth to "Slawkenbergius's Tale," is clearly a euphemism for the male sexual organs. The window-sash episode is similarly symbolic, referring obliquely to Tristram's accidental circumcision. Furthermore, the running allusion to Toby's war wound has the effect of a bawdy joke: the question "where was Toby wounded?" becomes a play on words, referring both to geography and to anatomy.

This concern with the male anatomy is reinforced by a multitude of anecdotes and references scattered throughout the novel, from the episode of Yorick's chestnut to Toby's very name (which was an eighteenth-century slang word for "posterior"). These sexual allusions supply a comic, deflationary view of man and at the same time a psychological portrait of impotence and anxiety. Both the theme of hobbyhorses and the discontinuous, seemingly chaotic form of the work point up this state of mind (and in some cases body), which afflicts the narrator as well as the major characters. The level of anxiety is reflected in the disjointed form of the book; it is as though the type of experience is too strange or perhaps extreme to be contained within the rational form of the traditional narrative.

Tristram's life, from its very beginning, disappoints Walter's elevated hopes and plans for his son. The slip of the forceps and the window sash are physical mishaps which deflate the philosopher's pronouncements about man's status. Furthermore, the accidents constitute a kind of literary joke: they undercut the very concept of a hero and express the classical concept of Nemesis in homely, comic terms.

The psychological implications of the sexual innuendos in the novel become most explicit in the story of Uncle Toby and the Widow Wadman. When Toby perceives that the widow's interest in where he was wounded involves not a map but his own personal "geography," he flees in alarm. The episode suggests Toby's actual impotence, an incapacity hinted at in Tristram's case as well.

Taken together, the allusions to private parts indicate a sexual anxiety, disguised by comic events and bawdy tales. It is the function of the jokes, misnomers, and euphemisms to turn the anxiety into a verbal and literary game, just as it is the function of the characters' hobbyhorses to distract them from their various psychological anxieties.

35.4 On hearing of his son Bobby's death, Walter delivers a long consolatory sermon which turns out to be a mock-elegy. Because of episodes like this, Sterne has been attacked as a cold, amoral, even sacrilegious writer, willing to sacrifice all positive human values for the sake of a joke. Is this assessment fair?

Answer   Walter's incorporation into his sermon of many classic commonplaces on death begins to assume a parodic aspect as the catalogue grows longer and longer. This oratorical response is in character, for throughout the novel, Walter typifies the eloquent man, ready to theorize and expostulate at the drop of a hat. (Trim exemplifies exactly the same tendency when he apostrophizes on the subject of mortality at the literal dropping of his hat, in the kitchen downstairs.)

Sterne is not just a brittle satirist in this scene, for Walter illustrates a psychological truth about man's response to grief: his impulse to seek escape from the pain of loss by resorting to traditional wisdom and to resounding speeches. Furthermore, the author provides another viewpoint on death in the person of Toby. Toby typifies the silent man, inarticulate but full of feeling. He is deeply moved by Bobby's death, as both his tears and his allusions to God indicate. Thus Walter and Toby represent the opposite ends of Sterne's human spectrum: the tendency toward play (in Walter's exhibition of learned wit) and the tendency toward sentiment (in Toby's sensitive reflections on death).

L.R.

SUGGESTED READINGS

Kittle, Arnold, "Richardson, Fielding, Sterne," in *An Introduction to the English Novel*, Vol. I (1951).

McKillop, Alan, *The Early Masters of English Fiction* (1956).

Traugtt, John, *Tristram Shandy's World* (1954).

Van Ghent, Dorothy, "On *Tristram Shandy*," in *The English Novel* (1953).

JANE AUSTEN

C H R O N O L O G Y

1775	Born at Steventon in Hampshire. Daughter of George Austen, vicar of the local parish, and Cassandra Austen. She is the seventh of eight children; her six brothers will be successful in various middle-class professions (commercial, military, religious). Jane and her sister Cassandra will be extremely close all their lives.
1782	Sent to Oxford and then to Southampton for a brief period of schooling, interrupted by illness which necessitates her returning home.
1783	Spends one year at the Abbey School at Reading. This completes her formal education. However, she is a voracious reader, and her family spends much time in group reading and in performing theatricals. By the age of 16, Jane will have filled three notebooks with stories, plays, and burlesques.
1793	Is at work on *Elinor and Marianne*, an epistolary novel later reworked into *Sense and Sensibility*.
1796	Begins work on *First Impressions*, an early version of *Pride and Prejudice*.
1797	George Austen writes to Cadell, a London publisher, offering *First Impressions* for publication; he receives no reply. Jane is at work on *Susan*, later to become *Northanger Abbey*.
1801	George Austen retires; the family moves to Bath, where they are forced to live a more frugal life.
1803	The London publisher Crosby buys the manuscript of *Susan* but fails to publish it.

465

1805   Death of George Austen. Jane begins work on *The Watsons*, a novel she is never to finish.

1806   Jane, Cassandra, and their mother move to Southampton.

1809   The Austens move to Chawton Cottage in Hampshire, a house made available by Jane's brother Edward, who had been adopted by a wealthy relative. Their way of life becomes fairly comfortable again; they live as middle-class, provincial country folk, much like those in Austen's novels.

1811   *Sense and Sensibility*, recast as a third-person narrative, is published by Austen at her own expense. Like all her works, it is published anonymously. The book is an unexpected success; by 1813, she reports that she has sold all copies of the work and netted £140. Austen begins work on *Mansfield Park*.

1813   *Pride and Prejudice* published. (Austen writes to her sister, "I want to tell you that I have got my own darling child from London; on Wednesday I received one copy sent down by Falkner. . . . I must confess that I think her [Elizabeth Bennet, the novel's heroine] as delightful a creature as ever appeared in print.") Austen's brother Henry reveals to friends Jane's secret authorship, but she remains retired from the literary world, living a quiet country spinster's life.

1814   Publication of *Mansfield Park*. Austen begins work on *Emma*.

1816   *Emma* is published; it is dedicated, by permission, to the prince regent, indicating the esteem with which Austen is held in literary circles. Austen's brother Henry buys the rights to *Susan* from Crosby; she begins work on revising it. Also at work on *Persuasion*. Austen's health failing.

1817   Begins the novel *Sanditon*; it is never completed. Death of Jane Austen; she is buried at Winchester Cathedral.

1818   Posthumous publication of *Northanger Abbey* (revised version of *Susan*) and *Persuasion*.

ESSAY QUESTIONS WITH ANSWERS

Pride and Prejudice

36. 1 Letters have played an important part in the history of the English novel, beginning with Richardson's *Pamela* and *Clarissa*; these epistolary novels consisted almost entirely of letters. In Jane Austen's *Pride and Prejudice*, letters survive as a literary device. Discuss the use of letters in the novel.

Answer One of the ways in which Jane Austen defines the small world of Hertfordshire, which constitutes the social context of the novel, is through the frequent exchange of letters. Austen includes some twenty letters in her narrative, suggesting the importance of correspondence in a closed circle of acquaintances with few amusements other than the exchange of news. Taken as a whole, the letters imply much about social convention in the English countryside in the early nineteenth century—the concern with polish, politeness, and place, as well as the preoccupation with the minute details of daily life.

Each letter also provides a glimpse into its writer's character. For example, Caroline Bingley betrays a hint of her essentially frivolous and catty nature in her first "friendly" overture to Jane:

> If you are not so compassionate as to dine to-day with Louisa and me, we shall be in danger of hating each other for the rest of our lives, for a whole day's tête-à-tête between two women can never end without a quarrel. (I, 7, meaning Volume I, Chapter 7)

The hyperbole and the archly sophisticated tone sketch a portrait of a flighty and somewhat snobbish young lady indulging in a whim.

Perhaps the most telling instance of characterization via letter is Mr. Collins's lengthy note of introduction to Mr. Bennet. The circumlocutions, the left-handed compliments, and the self-aggrandizing style all reveal the clergyman as a ridiculous popinjay who, as Mr. Bennet anticipates, will provide comic amusement for the company: "There is a mixture of servility and self-importance in his letter, which promises well. I am impatient to see him" (I, 13).

In a similar way, every other letter in the novel reveals something about the character of its writer. Jane's letters to Lizzie are loving, sweet, cheerful, and brave; Mr. Gardiner's letters to Mr. Bennet are sensible, businesslike, tactful, and generous; and Mrs. Gardiner's letters to Elizabeth are warm, solicitous, and encouraging. The letters of Mr. Darcy, the hero of the tale, tell us much about him. Both his reserve and his warmth, his pride and his compassion are underscored in the crucial letter explaining his motives in the Bingley and Wickham affairs. From the icily correct opening ("Be not alarmed, madam, on receiving this letter") to the closing, which betrays his affection ("I will only add, God bless you"), the epistle demonstrates the complexity and richness of his character.

Darcy's letter indicates a third function of the correspondence in *Pride and Prejudice*, that of propelling the plot forward by means of revelation and explanation. The small mysteries and misunderstandings which abound in the early part of the novel are dispelled by means of a series of important letters addressed to Elizabeth: Darcy's letter defending his conduct against her bitter charges; Jane's letter describing Wickham's elopement with Lydia; and Mrs. Gardiner's letter describing Darcy's benevolence in rescuing Lydia from disgrace. All three operate to establish Darcy's character in Elizabeth's eyes and to change her feelings toward him.

Darcy's letter is, in fact, the turning point of the entire novel, in that it forces Elizabeth to recognize the truth not only about others but about herself. Prejudiced by her own vanity, which had initially been both stung by Darcy's indifference and flattered by Wickham's attentions, she has seriously misjudged both men. On concluding her reading of Darcy's letter, Elizabeth comes to the realization that "Till this moment, I never knew myself" (II, 13).

Letters thus function on several levels in the novel. They are the vehicles for both comic caricature and profound characterization, both trivial gossip and important revelation. Most broadly, they define the social world of Hertfordshire as a minuet of gesture and response, of emotion controlled and channeled through language.

36.2   The novel as a genre has traditionally been a forum for the moral evaluation of human character. In *Pride and Prejudice*, much of the action revolves around the analysis of character, and the climax of the book occurs when Elizabeth finally arrives at a true judgment of the people who surround her. What techniques does Jane Austen use to convey moral judgments to the reader?

Answer The discussion of character in *Pride and Prejudice* occurs on two levels: in the fluid medium of the omniscient narration and in dialogue between the characters. The concern with evaluating behavior pervades the book, from the most trivial gossip exchanged between Mrs. Phillips and Mrs. Bennet to the subtle analysis of motives in which Elizabeth engages. As the title suggests, the novel focuses on the danger of misjudging the character of others through those most common of social failings, pride and prejudice.

The ironic viewpoint of the narrator establishes her omniscience, authority, and comic distance. The very first line of the novel, "It is a truth universally acknowledged, that a single man in possession of a good fortune, must be in want of a wife," suggests the self-interested judgments of the community at large and, more particularly, as we find out two sentences later, those of Mrs. Bennet with her five marriageable daughters. The ironic tone of the narrator invites us to detach ourselves from the attitudes of the characters and judge their comic foibles from a moral perspective. In addition to ironic evaluation, the narrator offers explicit judgments as well. Thus, in the opening of the book the narration directly characterizes the indolent charm of Mr. Bennet, the petty obsessions of Mrs. Bennet, and the idle vanity of Lydia and Catherine.

Further commentary is provided by the characters themselves. In a novel where very little occurs besides conversation, the dialogue becomes the chief "action." Thus it is through dialogue, and the related device of the letter, that characters reveal themselves and their attitudes toward each other. For example, Mr. Collins's first letter is a piece of character revelation through its style alone; furthermore, it elucidates the character of others by evoking a variety of responses, including Mrs. Bennet's approval, Elizabeth's skepticism, and Mr. Bennet's mockery. Another illustration is the discussion at Netherfield of Bingley's impetuous character, which evokes Bingley's own self-portrait, Darcy's astringent criticism, and Elizabeth's warm defense.

The crucial test of moral judgment in the novel revolves around the characters of Wickham and Darcy. The narrator is unusually silent in these two cases, leaving the reader to make his own evaluations on the basis of their actions as well as various reports and rumors about them. Thus, the bad impression made on Elizabeth by Darcy's initial coldness is reinforced by Wickham's fallacious account of him. The question of each man's true character remains unsettled until Darcy's letter adjusts the scale of moral judgment in his own favor.

Throughout the novel, gossip and news serve the function of both obscuring and elucidating the natures of the principal characters. It is Elizabeth's task to detach herself from the prejudices of her social group in order to arrive at something like the clear-eyed omniscience of the narrator. The theme of moral judgment, and of an integrity achieved through a trial of the emotions, is thus central to the novel as a whole.

36.3 Discuss the relationship among the following incidents in *Pride and Prejudice*: the marriage of Mr. and Mrs. Bennet; the marriage of Charlotte Lucas and Mr. Collins; the courtship of Wickham and Miss King; and Elizabeth's reaction to Pemberley.

Answer All these incidents relate to two of the major themes of *Pride and Prejudice*: money and marriage. Austen treats love and property as interdependent interests rather than conflicting claims. Though the novel emphasizes the importance of emotional integrity, it never minimizes the fact that in Austen's society marriage is an economic event.

Given this central proposition, the Bennet marriage must be viewed as a failure on two counts. Mr. Bennet has exhibited both a lack of emotional integrity in his youthful infatuation with a woman lacking in common sense and goodwill, and a lack of financial sense by spending his income in the prospect of a male heir. As a consequence, a real disaster befalls the Bennet household; Lydia's shameful escapade is the indirect result of her father's abdication of his responsibilities and of her mother's vanity.

The serious "moral" of this story is passed on by Mr. Bennet to his favorite daughter, Elizabeth: "My child, let me not have the grief of seeing *you* unable to respect your partner in life" (III, 17).

Another failed marriage is the alliance between Charlotte Lucas and Mr. Collins. Although suitable in terms of fortune and social position, it is a union without affection. Despite Mr. Collins's protestations of love for Charlotte, the easy transference of his ardor for Elizabeth, accomplished in a single day, exposes him as a shallow fool. His main aim in marriage, as in everything else, is to please his patron, Lady Catherine de Bourgh, while Charlotte's motives spring from her practical assessment of her chances in the marital marketplace:

> Without thinking highly either of men or of matrimony, marriage had always been her objective; it was the only honorable provision for well-educated young women of small fortune, and however uncertain of giving happiness, must be their pleasantest preservative from want. (I, 22)

Although Elizabeth finally accepts her friend's marriage as a reasonable accommodation to circumstances, it is clear that the couple can never achieve a real partnership of the kind which Elizabeth seeks for herself and which is obviously Austen's ideal.

Elizabeth also recognizes the practicality of Wickham's affection for the well-to-do Miss King. This affection, based entirely on Miss King's claim to £10,000, is at first received by Elizabeth as "wise and desirable for both." But in the end this attempt at marital union is revealed as worse than a failure: it is a fraudulent imposition designed only to satisfy the villainous Wickham.

Elizabeth's reaction to Pemberley, the Darcy family estate, might seem, at first, unrelated to the marriages and alliances discussed so far. However, her response sheds new light on her whole relationship with Darcy. Up until this time, Elizabeth has indicated not the slightest interest in money: she has refused both Collins, who would have ended the problematic entail on Mr. Bennet's estate, and Darcy, who would have made her mistress of £10,000 a year. However, as she admires the natural beauty of Pemberley, she becomes aware of the importance and splendor of such a great house: "to be mistress of Pemberley might be something!!" (III, 1). The eighteenth-century novelist and poet Sir Walter Scott went so far as to say that it is the sight of Pemberley that secures Elizabeth's love for Darcy. This is perhaps overstated, given that Elizabeth's heart has already been affected by Darcy's letter and will later be touched by his changed behavior toward her at Pemberley itself. Still, Austen gives Pemberley importance in the development of Elizabeth's feelings by according it a lengthy description and a significant place in the narrative. Elizabeth's regard for Pemberley indicates the growing maturity of her character, as affection becomes intertwined with other feelings, including prudence, respect, esteem, and gratitude.

In the union between Elizabeth and Darcy, Austen clearly demonstrates the proper congruence between love and social position. In this happiest of endings, the couple combines all the comfort and security that Pemberley offers with deep personal affection.

36.4 *Pride and Prejudice* is unmistakably a comic novel. Analyze the features of the book which contribute to its comic tone.

Answer On the broadest level, the novel conforms to a classic pattern of comedy: a rigidly ordered society is first disrupted by the forces of romantic illusion and misunderstanding, and finally reintegrated through the cohesive powers of marriage. The arrival of Bingley and Darcy at Netherfield Park creates in the neighborhood of Hertfordshire a turmoil which does not subside until the end of the book when both young men are properly matched. Jane Austen develops the theme of marriage by means of example, ranging from Mr. Collins's absurd courtship of Elizabeth and then of Charlotte Lucas to the mature love arrived at by Darcy and Elizabeth. In the disruptive effect of the scoundrel Wickham on the Bennet household, Austen explores the serious consequences of romantic illusion, with Lydia and Wickham forming a dark contrast to the happier matches. The pairing off of Jane with Bingley and Elizabeth with Darcy provides the happy ending required by the genre; furthermore, the double marriage, a common feature of romantic comedy, suggests the social dimension of romantic love, which extends beyond the individual's lot to comprehend a generation's future.

In addition to the generic and structural elements of comedy, *Pride and Prejudice* also possesses features of the comedy of manners. Central to the idea of comedy of manners is the sense of a game being played out according to the rules of social convention. In Austen's world, the rules can easily rigidify into comic obsessions. In Mr. Collins's pomposities and Mrs. Bennet's frivolous whims, Austen creates caricatured images of the human propensities to self-interest and self-importance. This is placed in contrast to the witty repartee of Darcy and Elizabeth, especially the latter. Although she is a participant in the game of social manners, she is at the same time a detached observer who can move freely outside the limits of the game. Her acerbic comments on the subjects of love, music, the accomplished gentlewoman, and the proper gentleman display a sympathy between her temperament and that of the ironic narrator. Thus, Austen uses comedy both to capture a particular society and to place it within the context of rational judgment.

Emma

36.5 Jane Austen wrote, on beginning to compose *Emma*, "I am going to take a heroine whom no one but myself will much like." Evaluate Emma's effect on the reader in the light of Austen's own judgment about her character.

Answer Austen sets forth her judgment of Emma's character very clearly in the first paragraphs of the novel. Though "handsome, clever, and rich," Emma has "the power of having rather too much her own way, and a disposition to think a little too well of herself." An extension of her pride and willfulness is found in her fantasy of omnipotence, which takes the form of endless matchmaking. These character flaws help to create the "unlikable" quality Austen predicted for her heroine.

Part of the unsympathetic quality of Emma derives from her contrast with her setting. Instead of blending into the quiet, even idyllic, milieu of Highbury, Emma stands somewhat apart, isolated by her intellect, irony, and independence. In part, her flaws are attractive, stemming from superiority of mind and a vivid imagination, but they remain flaws nonetheless.

If this initial portrait of Emma is complicated by Emma's personal flaws, our final picture of her is as a fully rounded human being. The novel is essentially about the development of her character, involving both self-recognition and reformation. Small moments of recognition occur throughout the novel, in each case where Emma has been guilty of misapprehension and self-indulgence. For example, in the Mr. Elton episode, she repents of her encouragement of Harriet's hopes and vows not to interfere again. When Jane Fairfax first arrives in Highbury, Emma, regretting her past dislike of Jane, makes a short-lived attempt at friendship. However, her self-awareness does not extend to the vanity at the heart of these enterprises. Only Mr. Knightley's gradually increasing influence with her is able to produce a lasting change in her behavior. She finally reveals that she has learned a lasting lesson that will affect all her future relationships when she says to Jane Fairfax: "Oh! If you knew how much I love everything that is decided and open!" (III, 16, meaning Volume III, Chapter 16). This process of growth helps to win the sympathy of the reader for Emma.

In addition, Jane Austen keeps the narrative focus almost entirely upon Emma's sensations and notions, thus guaranteeing our identification with her whimsical heroine. Throughout the book, even when Emma is treated ironically, as in the Elton episode, her wrongheadedness is more amusing than distasteful. Furthermore, the reader is with Emma during her recognition scenes and is provided with an inner glimpse of her essentially benevolent nature. This technique turns *Emma* almost into a tour de force. Though Austen insists that no one will much like her heroine, she produces almost the opposite effect.

36.6 Unlike *Pride and Prejudice*, which is structured around the pairing off of several couples, *Emma* uses the triangle or trio as a basic structural principle. Discuss some of the trios in the novel.

Answer The trios in the book contribute to its complicated seriocomic tone. Romantic love is naturally made up of duets, and the intrusion of a third party leads inevitably either to comic cross-purposes or to poignant disappointment. In *Emma*, the romantic triangles evoke tension, on the one hand moving the novel toward farce and on the other toward tragedy.

The incongruous aspect of threesomes is vividly embodied in the person of Mr. Woodhouse, whose "humorous" temperament creates a continuing strand of domestic farce throughout *Emma*. Preoccupied with his own health and comfort, he thinks of marriage as disruptive to his personal serenity, and thus he constantly inserts himself between romantic partners. When the novel opens, just such a disruption has occurred, with "poor" Miss Taylor's marriage to Mr. Weston. Mr. Woodhouse continually lays claim to Mrs. Weston's affections, just as he demands the attentions of his married daughter Isabella. Though the odd trios thus created are essentially comic, as Mr. Woodhouse steadfastly ignores the demands of love and marriage in favor of his own needs, the final trio has a somber tone. The decision of Emma and Mr. Knightley to live at Hartfield with her father suggests a poignant restriction, willingly undertaken, on the married couple's happiness. Mr. Woodhouse, himself fixed in his role as a fussy father, cannot permit others to change and develop.

The triangle involving Mr. Elton, Harriet Smith, and Emma is mainly farcical. Here the comic aspect resides in Emma's blind misreading of the state of everyone's affections. Having decided that Mr. Elton and Harriet were meant for each other, she refuses to see what is evident to everyone else, including the reader: that she herself is the object of Elton's passion. The ironic rendering of this story makes Emma's gestures and manipulations incongruous and comic. However, the heroine's energetic, wrongheaded maneuverings are not merely ridiculous, for they lead ultimately to a serious entanglement of intentions and feelings. Throughout the novel Harriet remains a victim, suffering from Elton's cruelty and Emma's further ideas of matchmaking, until finally she is so confused and self-deluded as to think that Mr. Knightley is in love with her. Only her timely marriage to the entirely appropriate Robert Martin saves her from a loveless future and relieves Emma of the burden of guilt.

The two central triangles of the book, Fairfax–Churchill–Emma and Churchill–Emma–Knightley, are more serious in tone. In the Fairfax–Churchill–Emma triangle, there is little comic irony, for the reader identifies with Emma's reading of the situation. Furthermore, the misunderstanding is the result not of Emma's comical fantasies but of willful deception. In some ways, Emma's embarrassment may be regarded as a farcical comeuppance, the proper conclusion to all her misguided matchmaking. However, the situation has tragic overtones in that both women have been mistreated in the cavalier game of courtship. In the final triangle, the happy ending of the book is in jeopardy because of Knightley's conviction that Emma loves Churchill. Though there is the effect of comic boomerang, the episode underscores the serious consequences of casual dalliance.

Part of the difference between *Pride and Prejudice* and *Emma* derives from the different "mathematics" of the two books. Though misunderstanding is crucial in *Pride and Prejudice*, the confusion arises from the cross-purposes of two characters—precisely, as Austen tells us, from Darcy's pride and Elizabeth Bennet's prejudice. In *Emma*, tension grows out of the unstable groupings of figures, so that misjudgments multiply and divide the characters.

36.7 Early in the novel (I, 9), Emma and Harriet collect a number of charades, enigmas, and riddles to copy down in a "thin quarto of hot pressed paper." To what extent does this parlor game encapsulize the social life of Highbury?

Answer The episode involving the charade book may be taken as a symbol of all the guessing games played in the novel. Emma, as Mr. Knightley wryly says, has a "genius for telling and guessing," and in the case of Mr. Elton's charade she cleverly arrives at the solution, the word "courtship." But characteristically she mistakes the riddle's central meaning, for she believes the closing salutation to be directed to Harriet Smith when it was meant for her.

Again and again in the closed society of Highbury, this kind of game occurs, with Emma presiding; and again and again, she guesses wrong. Attempts to guess the objects of affection of Elton, Frank Churchill, and Knightley occupy a great deal of Emma's time. She must further exercise her wits on the question of who gave Jane Fairfax the pianoforte, on Jane's relationship with Mr. Dixon, and on Harriet's infatuation with a nameless gentleman. She plays an alphabet game with Churchill, where the words "blunder" and "Dixon" appear prominently, and at Box Hill she demands amusing conundrums from each of the party. In every case, Emma's clever yet wrongheaded interference deepens rather than clarifies the mysteries.

The games range from trivial to serious. Charades, anagrams, and puns may be classed with whist playing and rubbers of bridge as social pastimes, suggesting the constant search for diversion of a lively mind like Emma's in a narrow provincial town. However, she tries to use these parlor games in her more serious pursuit of reading minds and characters; the little games serve the larger one of designing matches. The play at this point turns dangerous, for to treat love as a matter of playful manipulation is to violate feeling, commitment, and honor.

The impropriety of playing with human feelings is best demonstrated in the case of Frank Churchill. His secret innuendos to Jane, which try her modesty, and his amorous banter with Emma, which flatters her vanity, are cruel manipulations designed for his own amusement. Emma acknowledges a similarity between herself and Churchill. She says:

> I am sure it was a source of high entertainment to you, to feel that you were taking us all in. Perhaps I am the readier to suspect, because, to tell you the truth, I think it might have been some amusement to myself in the same situation. I think there is a little likeness between us. (III, 18)

It is true that a love of riddles is common to Frank and Emma. The difference is that Frank promotes mystery through conscious deception, while Emma's love of conundrums grows out of a lively and essentially benevolent imagination. Furthermore, when Emma finally outgrows the pastime of guessing games and discovers the mystery of her own heart, she recognizes the value of candor.

36.8 Discuss the standards of civility and morality implied in the novel.

Answer Jane Austen intended *Emma* to be very much an "English" novel. Standards of behavior and moral conduct are intimately tied to a concept of national temper, and Austen makes it clear that the moral system underlying *Emma* is one she considers distinctively English. The sense of the ultimate goodness of English life radiates even from the landscape: "It was a sweet view— sweet to the eye and the mind. English verdure, English culture, English comfort, seen under a sun bright without being oppressive" (III, 6). Implicit in this description are ideas of benevolence, kindliness, and moderation, the very features which distinguish Mr. Knightley as the best, and most English, of gentlemen.

In contrast stands Frank Churchill, whose attraction, lying solely in his superficial social graces, lacks moral substance. There is even the intimation that he is somehow a foreigner in the well-regulated, sociable world of Highbury. He is an alien in this world chiefly because his civility is separated from morality, rather than an expression of it. As Mr. Knightley says of him, "No, Emma; your amiable young man can be amiable only in French, not in English. He may be very very amiable, have very good manners and be very agreeable; but he can have no English delicacy toward the feelings of other people—nothing really amiable about him" (I, 18).

Part of Emma's development in the novel consists of her learning to wed her outward civility to precisely that "English delicacy toward the feelings of other people" to which Knightley refers. Her early tendency to observe the

letter but not the spirit of social decorum is exemplified in her sendin
on a duty call to the Martin family: "Fourteen minutes to be given
with whom she [Harriet] had thankfully passed six weeks not six mon
Emma could not but picture it all. . . . It was a bad business" (II, 5).

This kind of restricted civility also characterizes Emma's relationsh
the Bateses. She bypasses their house whenever she can and visits only
shortest permissible time, wishing to avoid the endless and inane chatter
poor Miss Bates. Finally, Emma is guilty of a genuine cruelty at the Bo:
outing, when she glibly makes an allusion to Miss Bates's incessant talk.
Mr. Knightley, the touchstone of English behavior, who points out the inju
to the spinster's feelings.

It is a measure of the extent of Emma's maturation that she not only recognizes the truth of this criticism but at last acts upon it. She not only visits
the Bateses but comes to genuinely understand their situation, including that
of Jane Fairfax.

The little gestures of kindness in the novel, such as Mr. Knightley's sending
apples to the Bateses and Mrs. Weston's unfailing concern for Mr. Woodhouse's
health, add up to a picture of a society founded not only on good sense but on
decency and consideration. In this attractive world, civility and morality come
together.

L.R.

SUGGESTED READINGS

Harding, D. W., "Regulated Hatred in Jane Austen," *Scrutiny*, VIII (March 1940).

Mudrick, M., *Jane Austen: Irony as Defense and Discovery* (1952).

Watt, Ian, ed., *Jane Austen: A Collection of Critical Essays* (1963).

INDEX

INDEX